*Fall in.* Frederick's grenadiers leaving their quarters, summoned by the beat of the drum to assemble around the colors in the village square. "When the battalion marches, it must leave all of its lodgings simultaneously. This is a good precaution against desertion." (A. Menzel, *Illustrationen zu die Werke Friedrichs des Grossen,* Berlin, 1886.)

*A break in the ranks.* "If the soldier should drink during a halt this could be fatal, and the officer must prevent it rigorously." Frederick's instructions were that the troops should drink nothing while on the march except water mixed with vinegar. (A. Menzel, *Illustrationen zu die Werke Friedrichs des Grossen*, Berlin, 1886.)

*Frederick the Great*

*on the Art of War*

Two young officers, exhausted from studying Frederick's military instructions and plans. (A. Menzel, *Illustration zu die Werke Friedrichs des Grossen*, Berlin, 1886.)

EDITED AND TRANSLATED BY
*JAY LUVAAS*

# *Frederick the Great*
# *on the*
# *Art of War*

**DA CAPO PRESS**
A Member of the Perseus Books Group

Library of Congress Cataloging-in-Publication Data

Frederick II, King of Prussia, 1712–1786.
  [Selections. English. 1998]
  Frederick the Great on the art of war  /  edited and translated by Jay Luvaas.
    p.    cm.
  Excerpts from Frederick II's military writings.
  Includes bibliographical references and index.
  ISBN 0-306-80908-7 (alk. paper)
    1. Frederick II, King of Prussia, 1712–1786—Military leadership. 2. Military art
  and science—Germany—Prussia—History—18th century. 3. Military educa-
  tion—Germany—Prussia—History—18th century. 4. Prussia (Germany)—His-
  tory, Military—18th century. 5. Strategy—History—18th century. I. Luvaas, Jay.
  II. Title.
  DD405.33.F7413    1999
  355.02—dc21                                                          98-16791
                                                                          CIP

First Da Capo Press edition 1999

This Da Capo Press paperback edition of *Frederick the Great on the
Art of War* is an unabridged republication of the edition first
published in New York in 1966. It is reprinted by arrangement
with The Free Press, a division of Simon & Schuster, Inc.

Published by Da Capo Press, Inc.
A Member of Perseus Books Group

Manufactured in the United States of America
10 9 8 7 6 5 4 3 2

*To my son RANDY*

# Preface

FREDERICK THE GREAT'S *Instructions for his Generals* has long held a deserved place among the military classics. As do the *Reveries* of Marshal Saxe and Guibert's *Essai général de tactique*, Frederick's *Instructions* constitutes a basic source for the study of warfare as it was practiced in the eighteenth century. Regarded as a precious legacy by German soldiers of a later generation, the book was published in various editions in France and England. As late as the eve of the American Civil War, General Joseph E. Johnston, testifying before a congressional commission investigating the course of instruction at West Point, declared that the time had arrived to set aside the study of the organization of the French army and return to the earlier studies of Frederick.

Yet Frederick's later writings are virtually unknown, except to those who have access to the collected *Oeuvres* published over a century ago in Germany and the subsequent German translation, the *Werke*, that appeared shortly before the First World War. It is in the essays written during and after the Seven Years' War that Frederick's mature thoughts on war are to be found. These are the observations of a general far wiser and more experienced than was the author of the more renowned *Instructions*, which, after all, was written during the first phase of a long and colorful military career.

With few exceptions, these later writings incorporating the experiences of the Seven Years' War are not available in English translation. Frederick's histories of the Silesian and the

Seven Years' War form a part of the *Posthumous Works* translated by Thomas Holcroft and published in England in 1789, along with his essays on the politics of Machiavelli, the generalship of Charles XII, and the condition of the Prussian army after the treaty of Hubertusburg, but for all practical purposes this set is available to only a few and, in any case, the translation needs to be updated. There is also a badly mutilated translation of Frederick's most significant military treatise, the *Eléments de castramétrie et de tactique*, published in 1811 in England under the misleading title *The Strategical Instructions of Frederick the Second*. This contains, however, only fragments of the original text and seems to be taken largely from the legends to the plates that appeared later in the collected *Oeuvres*, and it too has become a collector's item. With this trifling exception none of the later military writings, nor even the earlier instructions for the administration and tactical employment of the cavalry, infantry, and artillery, is currently available in English.

This book attempts to fill the gap by presenting a balanced selection of Frederick's complete and random thoughts on war. It has not been an easy book to prepare, for the Prussian King wrote in two languages—German, of which he had no command, and French, of which an earlier translator complained that Frederick "wrote with all the easy indifference of a king." Over half of the present volume is translated into English for the first time. In preparing these translations I have worked from the language in which the original was written, except in the case of the *Military Testaments* of 1752 and 1768, which could be located only in German translation. For the sake of a uniform style I have also reworked Holcroft's translations after comparing them with the original French. Some passages have been altered merely in punctuation and paragraph organization, or by rewording an occasional phrase; others have been practically rewritten to conform to the style of the text. The footnotes should indicate the nature and extent of my activities in this respect.

My job as editor is complicated by the fact that Frederick wrote for a variety of reasons—to amuse himself or to clarify his own thoughts, to teach his system to a subordinate or communicate to his successors the lessons taught by experience, or to issue fresh instructions to those entrusted with the training and discipline of his armies. Frederick's writings therefore contain many passages that are redundant or differ from each other only in details of expression, and his military writings considered as a whole are as disorganized as the French after their rout at Rossbach.

My first editorial chore was to select those passages from Frederick's military and military-political writings that seem most fully to represent his views or articulate his ideas. I then tried to fit the individual pieces into an organization that would embrace the essential military activities in the eighteenth century and at the same time do justice to Frederick's mature thoughts on war. A chapter based upon his historical works is included in order to illustrate how he applied his own maxims in the field and to provide a sampling of his writings in another area. I would have preferred to maintain the integrity of the individual essays, but I could do so only at the sacrifice of much that seemed important and interesting, and with a result more nearly resembling Frederick's shattered lines after Torgau than his orderly and systematic approach march to Leuthen. Whatever today's scholars might think of this organization, Frederick, I feel sure, would forgive me for exercising my *coup-d'oeil* on such difficult terrain.

To achieve a uniform style I have also resorted to the irregular and perhaps questionable device of combining fragments from different essays into the same chapter and, on occasion, into the same paragraph. I can assure the reader that none of the sentences thus transplanted is in an environment where the context has been changed, which obviously would lead to distortion. I have served notice every time a change occurs by having the first words from a different source printed in even small capitals; this new source then continues until the next even small capitals. This should make it relatively easy to distinguish one source from another. Occasionally, substantial portions of the original text have been deleted or stray paragraphs from the same source, inserted; in these cases the reader is alerted by a paragraph ornament at the beginning of the passage in question. Again, the new passage continues until the next ornament signals another shift. When only a few words have been omitted, this is indicated by the usual ellipsis marks. Most of the subheads are mine except in one or two chapters, but they have been enlisted to perform the same duties that they did for Frederick. Those borrowed from Frederick are in roman capitals; those supplied by me are in italic capitals. The source of each selection is indicated by the conventional footnote. In referring to the illustrations appearing here, I use my own system of numbering rather than Frederick's, and number the plates 1 through 32.

A book of this sort contains many technical terms that may not be familiar to the reader. Individuals and battles mentioned in the text are identified in footnotes, but to keep notes within reasonable limits a glossary of eighteenth-century military terms has been added as Appendix I, and the most important words defined there are designated with a star the first time they appear in the text.

Because Frederick never attempted to synthesize all his thoughts on war, this volume should be regarded as a record of the opinions he held at one time or another about a multitude of subjects relating to war and not as a final or complete treatise on war itself. In this respect it is an artificial (but hopefully not a superficial) work. However it does offer a number of intimate glimpses into military conditions in the eighteenth century and it should preserve something also of the spirit and personality of the greatest general of the age.

I am heavily indebted to Professor Herbert Rowen of Rutgers University who, as editor of the series in which this volume initially was scheduled to appear, conceived the project and overcame my well-founded reluctance to try my hand at translations. Offering guidance when requested and encouragement whenever needed, he, more than any other individual, is responsible for the completion of this book.

Foremost among my other creditors are Professors Maxwell Jacobs and Robert Crispen of the Allegheny department of modern languages. In checking my translations against the original French and German, these colleagues generously shared their time and their knowledge. To them I owe many a pleasant hour as well as numerous improvements in the text, and if any errors escaped their eyes I quickly accept the blame. Other friends helped along the way. Mrs. Harriet McLamb cheerfully stretched the interloan library facilities so that all the books were on hand when and for as long as they were needed. Professor Richard Brown of Allegheny College made available the facilities of his department for reproducing whole sections of Frederick's untranslated works and Mr. Wilbor Kraft and Mr. Raymond Baker, also of Allegheny College, read the manuscript and contributed helpful suggestions. I am indebted to my parents for invaluable assistance in reading proofs. Similarly I owe my thanks to Professor Frederic Hollyday of Duke University for his suggestions in bibliography and also for the gift of a number of military prints. Finally, I gratefully acknowledge the materials and advice offered by Dr. Richard Pearse of Durham, North Carolina, and Professor Theodore Ropp of Duke University. Viewing Frederick from different angles, each—the one a friend who has much to teach and the other my teacher as well as my friend—could detect some significant aspect of Frederick's writings that I had missed. The introductory chapter has benefited as a result.

I gratefully acknowledge permission of Penguin Books Limited to reprint a selection from John Butt's engaging translation of Voltaire's *Candide*, and of the Verlag von Reimar Hobbing GmbH., Essen (previously Berlin), for the right to reproduce the excellent maps of Torgau and Bunzelwitz from volume IV, *Die Werke Friedrichs des Grossen*.

Jay Luvaas

*Allegheny College*
*Meadville, Pennsylvania*

# Contents

# ILLUSTRATIONS

**PLATES**

*Frederick the Great*

*on the Art of War*

I

# Frederick and the Art of War

REFLECTING UPON the art of war during his exile at St. Helena, Napoleon often cited the campaigns of Alexander, Hannibal, Caesar, Gustavus Adolphus, Turenne, Prince Eugene, and Frederick the Great. The history of their campaigns, he contended, "would be a complete treatise on the art of war." Tactics, drill evolutions, the science of engineering and artillery —these techniques could be learned from textbooks "much in the same way as geometry," but in Napoleon's estimation no rational man could expect to learn from a grammar how to write the *Iliad* or one of Corneille's tragedies. Nor, by the same token, did he believe that it was possible to master the higher branches of the art of war except through experience and a knowledge of the campaigns of the Great Captains.[1]

Only three of Napoleon's Great Captains wrote of their experiences, and of these, Frederick was far and away the most prolific and analytical. Caesar's *Gallic Wars* was written in haste and with the intention of deluding a credulous public.[2] Turenne's *Memoirs* do not cover his last campaigns and, because of the dull style and the natural reserve of the author, often fail to reveal the reasons underlying his military decisions.[3] If both works were instructive to later generations (during Frederick's lifetime eight editions of Turenne's *Memoirs* were published) neither was written specifically to instruct an army or its leaders. But in Frederick's skilled hands even history had a didactic function, and when he wrote sometimes for his own amusement—which surely was the case with "his best piece in verse,"[4] *The Art of War*—Frederick's purpose was still in part pedagogical.

> You, who one day by right of birth will possess
> The Sceptre of our kings, their sword, their scales,
> You, the blood of heroes, the hope of the state;
> Harken, young prince, to the lessons of a soldier
> Who, educated in the camps, sustained in alarms,
> Now summons you to glory, and instructs you in the
> profession of arms.[5]

Because he wrote on nearly every aspect of military activity, Frederick's thoughts on the subject deserve a hearing. Educated in the classics, familiar with the military works of the previous generation, well informed on military developments elsewhere on the Continent, and the seasoned veteran of a dozen campaigns, no one is better qualified than he to comment upon the art of war in the eighteenth century. As a young and impressionable prince, Frederick had accompanied Prince Eugene during the Rhine campaign of 1734 and had heard daily lectures from that celebrated general on "those great rules and maxims" of war.[6] Years later, as the old and cynical Fritz, he angrily told a young, ambitious officer named Blücher, who was to achieve lasting fame at Waterloo, to go to the Devil. In the eventful years that separated these symbolic encounters Frederick had thoroughly learned his trade, developing the art of war to the maximum limits within the framework of existing social and political institutions and in the process establishing a tradition that would be a long time dying in Prussia.

### FREDERICK'S CAMPAIGNS

To the reader with a bent for military history Frederick probably stands out as a field commander, the last of the Great Captains before the French Revolution and Napoleon revolutionized warfare. For this reason, and also because his recorded observations contain many references to his own campaigns, a brief outline of the part he played during the two Silesian Wars and the Seven Years' War might be helpful.

Twenty-eight years of age when he ascended the Prussian throne in 1740, Frederick promptly initiated enough liberal reforms in law, economics, and religion "to make a philosopher swoon with delight."[7] But friends and well-wishers like Voltaire, who had looked to the day of the philosopher king, soon realized that Frederick had another side to his make-up. His arduous training had included a course in military studies, and whatever else can be said about the harsh treatment Frederick William I had prescribed for his son, he had, at the very least, imparted a stern sense of duty. Before the year was out Frederick decided to take advantage of the death of the Emperor Charles VI, to whose Hapsburg possessions the young Maria Theresa now fell heir, and to stake his own inheritance—a full treasury, an efficient bureaucracy, and a disproportionately large and well-trained army—on a power play for Silesia.

On December 16, 1740, Frederick began his invasion of Silesia. Within seven weeks his army had overcome bad roads and wretched weather to occupy all of the contested territory except for three fortresses, and one of these was taken by assault after the main Prussian forces had entered winter quarters. In late March Frederick again took the field, with the stronghold of Neisse as his immediate objective. A surprise counterstroke by the Austrians, however, compelled him to fall back in haste when his supply magazine at Ohlau was threatened. On April 10, 1741, the two armies clashed on the snow-covered fields near Mollwitz.

Advancing in four columns, the Prussians deployed into the customary two lines, 300 paces apart, two miles in length, cavalry massed on the wings, and sixty heavy guns along the front. When the Prussian cavalry on the right wing was unable to hold its ground against the assaults of the superior Austrian horse, and the battle seemed lost, Frederick followed the advice of Marshal von Schwerin and rode from the field to avoid capture. "I could not allow myself to be taken," he explained later. "What a humiliation for the first step I had taken on the path to glory."[8] He had ridden nearly fifty miles before he learned the outcome. The years of training and drill under his father had paid off: the Prussian infantry with their superior discipline and firepower had survived repeated cavalry charges before advancing "with the greatest steadiness, arrow-straight, and their front like a line" to victory.[9]

Mollwitz greatly enhanced Frederick's confidence and prestige although, like many of the battles that followed, its main benefits were political rather than military. It encouraged France to intervene in the war in support of a rival claimant to the Imperial throne, and this in turn led to conciliatory negotiations with Maria Theresa, whose concern for Silesia became secondary to the need to defend Vienna against an invading army of French and Bavarians. Frederick used this interlude to improve his cavalry both in training and doctrine, and in February, 1742, he resumed active operations by invading Moravia as part of a cooperative effort against Vienna. But the country was too destitute and his allies too dilatory to provide the necessary assistance, and in April Frederick abandoned his expedition and withdrew into Bohemia. "Winter campaigns," he had discovered, "are the most condemnable of all expeditions" and as such they should be avoided. "The best army in the world cannot bear up under them for long."[10]

Frederick's second battle was fought May 17, 1742, at Chotusitz, where he met an Austrian counterthrust. This time the cavalry won its spurs, Frederick won his own victory, and in June of that year a new peace treaty was negotiated giving Prussia all of Silesia and the county of Glatz.

Frederick jumped into the war again in August, 1744, when he invaded Bohemia. In September he besieged and captured Prague. Then, leaving the Elbe, which served as a vital artery for his fleet of nearly five hundred supply vessels, Frederick pushed into central Bohemia in hopes of catching the Austrians, who were falling back from the Rhine, between his army and a pursuing French force. But again the French failed to appear and it was Frederick who nearly was caught. Supplies grew scarce, Prussian convoys fought for their lives against swarms of pandours, as the Austrian light troops were called, and Frederick was unable to maneuver the Austrians into battle. (His opponent on this occasion was Marshal Traun, whose campaign in Frederick's judgment constituted "a perfect model which every general who delights in his profession ought to study.")[11] When his supply lines were threatened Frederick withdrew in haste to Silesia and took up winter quarters.

The campaign of 1745 commenced with the invasion of Silesia by a joint force of Austrians and Saxons. On the theory that "if you want to catch a mouse, leave the trap open,"[12] Frederick permitted his enemies to cross the mountains before he sprang the trap at Hohenfriedberg. Here, on June 4, a great battle was fought. Spurred on by the King's general order to take no prisoners, the Prussian cavalry came of age when it routed the cavalry of the Austrian right wing. Meanwhile, in what amounted to practically a separate action, the Prussian infantry of the right flank overran the Saxons. The result was Frederick's greatest tactical success thus far: within three hours the invaders, suffering disproportionately heavy losses, were in full retreat into Bohemia, followed rather than pursued (in military parlance there is a significant difference) by the victorious Prussians. For the next two months the armies glared at each other from behind their respective intrenched camps along the Elbe as detachments waged "petty war" upon enemy supply convoys and outposts. At length Frederick, short of supplies and in danger of being cut off from Silesia, was forced to fall back. At Sohr, on September 30, he found his way blocked by a superior force of Austrians, but by changing his front under fire—an extremely hazardous and unorthodox maneuver—and then throwing the weight of his line against the Austrian left flank, he managed to transform certain defeat into another brilliant victory. In November he blocked an

Austrian attempt to drive a wedge between Silesia and Berlin when he rapped the vanguard of the approaching enemy at Hennersdorf, and this opened the way for his own invasion of Saxony. While his army was investing Meissen, another Prussian force commanded by Prince Leopold of Anhalt-Dessau, better known as the "Old Dessauer," decisively defeated the Saxons at Kesselsdorf (December 15),[13] and on Christmas Day the second Silesian war officially came to an end. With his hold on the new province of Silesia confirmed and five impressive victories to his credit, Frederick had become "the Great."

In 1756 Prussia was again at war. Convinced that if he did not strike first, a coalition of Austria, Russia and France eventually would compel Prussia to wage war under less favorable circumstances, Frederick swooped down upon Saxony in late August, pinned the Saxon army to its fortified camp at Pirna, and then successfully warded off an Austrian attempt to relieve Pirna in the hard-fought but indecisive battle of Lobositz (October 1). In less than two months the initial campaign was over: the 14,000 Saxons who surrendered at Pirna were "forced to volunteer" in the Prussian army[14] and the stage had been set for the second act.

Frederick's campaign in 1757, the details of which are related in chapter VII, began with his invasion of Bohemia. Advancing in four columns, Frederick's forces united before Prague where, on May 6, in "one of the furious battles of the world,"[15] he managed at heavy cost to drive the Austrians into the city's fortifications. Because he lacked sufficient strength to invest the city and at the same time drive away the relieving army under Marshal Daun, Frederick failed to accomplish his strategical objectives, and a sharp defeat at Kolin (June 18) forced him to divide his army and evacuate Bohemia. After a series of marches and countermarches, during which his Hanoverian allies were defeated by the French in the west, the Swedes invaded Pomerania to the north, the Russians were victorious in the battle of Gross-Jägerndorf in East Prussia, and an Austrian raiding column had actually entered Berlin, Frederick encountered a mixed French and Imperial force at Rossbach. There, on November 5, he won the cheapest victory of his career. This victory increased England's commitment to military operations on the Continent, making it possible for the army under Prince Ferdinand of Brunswick, one of Frederick's most capable lieutenants, to keep the French off the King's back while he turned to face the Russians and Austrians.

Frederick next marched to Silesia to retrieve his slipping fortunes there. Instilling new spirit into the remnants of the army that recently had suffered defeat at Schweidnitz and Breslau, Frederick won a brilliant victory at Leuthen where, with vastly inferior forces, he attacked and threw back upon the center, the Austrian left wing. No other army and probably no other general of that day could have done it. Even this battle, which put an entire Austrian army out of working order until the next spring, failed to produce victory. "Tis a plaster on my wounds," was Frederick's diagnosis, "but it is far enough from healing them."[16]

The year 1758 constitutes a watershed in the course of the Seven Years' War. Perhaps at no other time were conditions so favorable for a decisive blow against Austria, the heart and spirit of the enemy coalition. After recapturing Schweidnitz in mid-April, Frederick carried the war into Moravia, where he besieged Olmütz preparatory to a possible thrust against Vienna. But his main problem was one for the commissariat rather than the military engineer, for Frederick's siege lines at Olmütz were 120 miles from his nearest magazines, and when an indispensable convoy of some 3,000 wagons was destroyed en route by an Austrian detachment, Frederick had no choice but to raise the siege and withdraw to the north. Later in the summer he left Silesia to meet a Russian threat to his dominions east of the Oder. Determined "to triumph or die,"[17] Frederick assaulted the Russians at Zorndorf. This battle, fought on August 25, was probably the bloodiest of the war. Tactically a draw, Zorndorf destroyed the fighting spirit of the Russians, who subsequently retired and remained inactive for the rest of the campaign, leaving Frederick free to deal with the Austrians in Saxony. By a series of incredible marches that averaged nineteen miles a day, Frederick managed to save Dresden, but Daun, the Austrian commander, avoided a pitched battle until he was able to surprise Frederick in his camp at Hochkirch (October 14). This battle, in which Frederick lost one-third of his effectives and one hundred guns, virtually ended the campaign of 1758. By "the indolence in their movements and the sluggishness in the execution of their plans," the allies had permitted Frederick to exploit the advantage of interior lines.[18] But as Frederick himself sadly recognized,

> our campaign is over, and there has nothing come of it, on one side or the other, but the loss of a great many worthy people, the misery of a great many poor soldiers crippled forever, the ruin of some provinces, the ravage, pillage and conflagration of some flourishing towns. Exploits these which make humanity shudder. . . .[19]

Never again would Frederick command the resources for offensive war. Henceforth he would wage a war of attrition, maneuvering desperately and often brilliantly to keep his enemies off balance and separated until winter should freeze military operations and provide a chance to refit and recruit.

Frederick's strategy for 1759 reveals that he could play the part of Fabius as well as that of Hannibal. He explained to his young companion de Catt:

> Our campaign will not begin so early, because this time I shall not be the aggressor, unless a favourable opportunity presents itself; then, I shall certainly seize it. The Austrian gentlemen who think that I love nothing but fighting will be mistaken this time, and I will show them in this campaign that if the great Fabius has a pound of lead in his breeches, I have two on each buttock.[20]

Before the campaign ended Frederick almost had a fatal dose of lead in another part of his anatomy, for at Kunersdorf

(August 12, 1759), where he had rushed to strike the Russians after maneuvering against Daun in defense of Silesia, Frederick attempted to storm a formidable position and suffered disaster. Of the 43,000 troops he had led into battle, hardly 3,000 existed as an organized force by nightfall. Nearly half of the Prussian army lay dead or wounded on the field and Frederick, failing even to meet a hero's death at the head of his valiant soldiers, seriously contemplated suicide. But the Russians did not exploit their victory, Frederick's spirits as well as his army quickly recovered, and despite the surrender of Dresden and the loss of an important detachment at Maxen in November, Frederick somehow survived the critical campaign of 1759. For this "miracle of the House of Brandenburg," Frederick owed much to the efforts of his brother, Prince Henry, whose extraordinary marches enabled Prussia to retain Breslau.

The campaign of 1760, which began with the loss at Landshut of another Prussian corps, illustrates Frederick's resourcefulness and vitality in maneuver. "A perfect masterpiece of strategic skill," according to Clausewitz,[21] this campaign found Frederick avoiding disaster in Silesia by successfully fighting off two Austrian armies in the battle of Liegnitz (August 15). After a march that forced the Russians to evacuate Berlin, Frederick again turned his attention to Saxony, where he won another battle at Torgau on November 3.[22] Although this victory was in no sense decisive it did succeed in eroding his opponents' will to win, and in a war of attrition the psychological factor becomes increasingly significant.

Perhaps the best that can be said for the campaign of 1760 is that it enabled Frederick to survive and to take the field the next spring for his sixth campaign. By means of his intrenched camp at Bunzelwitz, described by a contemporary as "a masterpiece of judgment in ground and . . . a model of sound, true and consummate field engineering,"[23] Frederick once again was able to stave off disaster by preventing the Russian and Austrian armies from combining to overwhelm him. Later, however, the Austrians seized the great fortress of Schweidnitz, which in effect gave them control of a large slice of Silesia and, according to Carlyle, "is judged to have been the hardest stroke Frederick had in the course of this war."[24]

Unexpected relief came early in 1762, when the Empress Elizabeth died and was succeeded by Peter III, an admirer of Frederick. Russia thereupon switched sides, the Swedes as a consequence were encouraged to seek a separate peace, and for the first time since the opening campaign Frederick was now free to concentrate his attention upon the Austrians. When a palace revolution subsequently removed Peter from the scene —and Russia from the war altogether—Frederick persuaded the commander of the Russian contingent serving with him to remain long enough to tie down a portion of the Austrian army while he ousted the rest from the heights of Burkersdorf. According to Carlyle, whose political opinions and vigorous and heroic prose sometimes conceal the fact that he had a sure grasp of the military factors involved,[25] Frederick's conduct of this, his last battle (July 17, 1762), is "reckoned by all judges a beautiful plan, beautifully executed, and once more a wonderful achieving of what seemed the impossible, when it had become the indispensable."[26] The Prussians recaptured Schweidnitz in October (it exchanged hands four times during the war), Prince Henry won a great victory at Freiberg in the final battle of the Seven Years' War (October 29), and in February, 1763, a peace treaty was signed at Hubertusburg. By this treaty Prussia retained all of her gains from the first two Silesian Wars.

Frederick's last campaign was against the Austrians in the War of the Bavarian succession of 1778. By this time, however, the Prussian army, by virtue of the fact that it was accompanied by more artillery, had lost much of its former mobility, and it is also evident that Frederick himself had lost his appetite for the offensive. The Austrians remained safely beyond reach in their formidable intrenchments, and eventually mounting supply difficulties caused this "insipid" campaign, as Frederick called it,[27] to degenerate into what the troops labeled contemptuously a "potato war." By autumn the two Prussian armies under the King and Prince Henry had withdrawn respectively to Silesia and Saxony, and Frederick returned from the peace negotiations the following spring, not as a conquering hero, but rather "as a defendant who had just won a suit."[28]

## FREDERICK THE GENERAL

In exploring the secrets of Frederick's generalship one finds several explanations for his successes in the Silesian wars and his survival in the titanic struggle with the great powers of Europe. No small share of the credit should go to his opponents, "superannuated generals," many of them,[29] limited in their actions—which Frederick was not—by their respective heads of state. At no time did all of Prussia's enemies show any interest in coordinating their operations against him. It is Napoleon's sober judgment that "everything tends to prove that he could not have resisted France, Austria and Russia for one campaign, if these powers had acted in earnest; and that he could not have sustained two campaigns against Austria and Russia, if the Cabinet of St. Petersburg had allowed its army to winter on the theatre of operations."[30] Napoleon's verdict, at least insofar as the general conduct of the war is concerned, must be allowed to stand. What saved Frederick in the final analysis was the lack of any real cooperation or determination on the part of his enemies—and his own indomitable spirit. "It is all very well to say that the King of Prussia is ruined, his troops are not what they were and he has no generals. All this may be true, but his spirit is still the same and it is that which brings all to life." Such was the opinion of another Frenchman, in 1760;[31] two centuries later this would appear to be also the verdict of history.

Frederick was fortunate too in the army he led. Under Frederick William I the Prussian army had become the fourth largest in Europe and second to none in quality, with the sound beginnings of a common doctrine after 1714,[32] meticulously drilled under the sharp eye of the Old Dessauer, and bound together by rigorous discipline. A reliable replacement system was assured with the introduction of the Canton system in 1733, giving each regiment a recruiting district to draw upon whenever quotas were not filled by voluntary enlistment.

Frederick contributed to the Prussian army very little that was new, except for the creation in 1758 of the first horse artillery. He was not a great military organizer or reformer like his father, but he knew how to take care of the good sword he had inherited. Frederick continually increased the size of the army. After Mollwitz he overhauled the cavalry and doubled the size of his field artillery, both of which he continued to strengthen because the Austrians excelled in these areas. Between the wars he became a dedicated student of his profession, watching developments in other armies, experimenting with new formations in his annual reviews, refining old regulations and providing new ones, and striving in every way to educate his officers and adjust the balance among the three arms. Often he could be seen on the drill ground, stop watch in hand, calculating the number of shots fired per minute. On annual maneuvers he was so demanding, we are told, that families used to pray that their loved ones would commit no mistakes during those "fearful three days." When he did spot a deficiency Frederick made his displeasure known. In 1754, for example, he sentenced the famous Bayreuth dragoons to three months' extra drill for their sloppiness in a review.[33] By the variety and precision of its movements and the rapidity of its fire, the Prussian army soon came to enjoy a reputation comparable to that enjoyed by the Italians in music, or the English empiricists in philosophy.[34]

Major General Henry Lloyd, who had served for a time with the Austrians, described the Prussian army as "a vast and regular machine. . . . They have a facility in manoeuvring beyond any other troops . . . and their victories must be ascribed to this chiefly for all the genius of the leader can do nothing without it, and almost everything with it."[35] While this minimizes the role of Frederick, it does point up the fact that the basic tactical problem in all eighteenth-century armies was to achieve superior firepower, and this depended upon the ability of the troops to deploy from columns of march into lines of battle and on their speed in reloading and firing. The army that excelled in both could usually win battles, provided it was not heavily outnumbered, and Frederick once went so far as to claim that "the speed with which the Prussian could reload trebled the firepower and made him the equal of three adversaries."[36]

Frederick generally tried to exploit the superior mobility, discipline, and firepower of his army by throwing the weight of his force against a portion—usually a wing—of the enemy line of battle. Improvisation in battle had demonstrated to Frederick what could be accomplished with a single wing against the extremity of the enemy's line, and in the years following the Silesian wars he did not forget the lesson learned at Hohenfriedberg and Sohr. Frederick tried at Prague and again at Kolin to strike his opponent's right flank, but in both instances his battle plan was frustrated by the precipitous action of a subordinate and he was forced to make a frontal attack instead. At Rossbach, however, the cavalry of the left wing and a mere seven battalions of infantry were enough to put the French to rout, and at Leuthen the Prussian right wing advanced in battalion echelons, with each battalion waiting for the unit on its right to proceed fifty paces before marching off to attack the Austrians. When it worked, as it did at Leuthen, Frederick's famed oblique order could enable a small army to overrun a force half again its size, but much depended upon the terrain, the agility of the troops, and the energy of the opposing commander. "None but Prussian troops," explained a veteran of Liegnitz and Torgau years later, could execute this particular maneuver

> with the precision and velocity indispensable to it. . . . Forming itself in this way, a mass of troops takes-up in proportion very little ground; and it shows in the distance, by reason of the

mixed uniforms and standards, a totally chaotic mass of men heaped on one another. . . . But it needs only that the commander lift his finger; instantly this living coil of knotted intricacies develops itself in perfect order, and with a speed like that of mountain rivers when the ice breaks.[37]

Paradoxically the very instrument that enabled Frederick to outmarch, outmaneuver, and usually to outfight his enemies also imposed rigid limitations upon his generalship. Like every other army in Europe except that of Russia, the Prussian standing army was based upon recruitment rather than conscription, although a career in the ranks was such that only the dregs of society and drifting mercenaries were willing to volunteer. Force and deception therefore were indispensable in obtaining recruits, and iron discipline was essential if the men were to be kept in the ranks. The experience of Voltaire's Candide, who fell in with a couple of Prussian recruiting agents,[38] was rather more than less typical of thousands each year. The story is always worth telling.

Having survived one disaster, poor Candide:

> . . . perished with cold and hunger, and without a penny in his pocket . . . dragged his weary limbs to a neighboring town called Waldberghoff-trarbk-dikdorff, where he stopped at an inn and cast a pathetic glance towards the door.
> Two men in blue noticed him.
> "There's a well-made young fellow, chum," said one to the other, "and just the height we want."
> They went up to Candide and politely asked him to dine with them.
> "Gentlemen," said Candide modestly, "I deeply appreciate the honour, but I haven't enough money to pay my share."
> "People of your appearance and merit, Sir, never pay anything," said one of the men in blue; "aren't you five feet five inches tall?"
> "Yes, gentlemen, that is my height," said Candide, with a bow.
> "Very well, Sir, sit down; we'll pay your share, and what's more we shall not allow a man like you to go short of money. That's what men are for, to help each other."

"You are quite right," said Candide. . . . His new companions then asked him to accept a few shillings. Candide took them gratefully, and wanted to give a receipt; but his offer was brushed aside, and they all sat down to table.

"Are you not a devoted admirer . . . of the King of the Bulgars?"

"Good Heavens, no!" said Candide; "I've never seen him."

"Oh, but he is the most amiable of kings and we must drink his health."

"By all means, gentlemen," replied Candide, and emptied his glass.

"That's enough," they cried. "You are now his support and defender, and a . . . hero into the bargain. Your fortune is made. Go where glory waits you."

"And with that," Voltaire concludes, "they clapped him into irons and hauled him off to the barracks."[39]

Candide escaped his dilemma in the usual way—by deserting at the first opportunity. Desertion, in fact, was such a widespread problem in the eighteenth century that it directly influenced tactics and logistics. Because he could not trust his troops, for example, Frederick rarely pushed his patrols more than a couple of hundred yards in front of the main body during the campaign of 1745, which naturally reduced his intelligence of enemy movements.[40] In battle there was constant need to keep the men under strict supervision, which discouraged the employment of skirmishers in loose formations. The precautions that Frederick had to take to avoid desertion augmented the difficulties of pursuing a beaten enemy after dark,[41] greatly reduced the number of night marches, were an important factor in determining the order of march and the security of camps, and increased the dangers involved in foraging.

Frederick could appeal to the ambition and love of glory in his officers with some success, but the rank and file could not be similarly motivated. Nor was it possible, before the awakening of a national spirit in response to the wars of Napoleon, to appeal to the soldiers' sense of duty, although pride of fatherland and a common religion—as manifested whenever the army sang a powerful Lutheran chorale going into battle, as at Leuthen—did constitute a unifying force of sorts. The main difficulty was that native-born Prussians in Frederick's armies generally were in the minority, although the proportion of *Landeskinder* to *Auslandern* changed after 1763 in favor of the former.[42] With Saxons swept into his army in wholesale lots and innumerable lads like Candide impressed against their will or better judgment, Frederick had to keep his troops in line—figuratively as well as in battle—by iron discipline and fear. Prussian soldiers, he insisted, should be taught to dread their own officers more than the enemy. "Good will can never induce the common soldier to stand up to such dangers; he will only do so through fear."[43] By these methods Frederick usually managed to retain complete control over his troops in battle, but often at the expense of his own freedom of action.

On the strategic level the restrictions were imposed more by the transport and supply systems of the eighteenth century. "It is not I who commands the army," he once complained, "but flour and forage [who] are the masters."[44] Tied to a chain of supply depots and magazines, forever hampered by the lack of good roads (and lacking, incidentally, Napoleon's manpower to build better ones), his army burdened by impedimenta light by comparison with the practice in other armies of his day but far in excess of that carried by Napoleon's troops,[45] Frederick's strategy often was dictated by the need to cover important provinces or to protect lines of supply. Even though he was able to stretch his supply lines farther than most contemporaries,[46] there were practical limits in time and distance beyond which even Frederick could ill afford to venture from his magazines. It has always been true that an army travels on its stomach, but in Frederick's day the length of time that it might spend in a given area often was determined by the need for men, money, and provisions. More than once he took up a position primarily "to eat all there is to eat, so that the enemy may not be able to maintain in this neighborhood any large body of troops during the winter."[47]

Under these conditions important strategical objectives often could be attained by the capture of a major fortress or by threatening enemy supplies and communications. Frederick was more eager to accept battle than most of his contemporaries. However even Frederick had to resort to the intricate, indecisive maneuvers that the next generation of soldiers tried to elevate into a geometric system and that later strategists, steeped in the theories of Clausewitz and the campaigns of Napoleon, were at a loss to understand. To them, the strategy of the eighteenth century seemed to display the spirit, delicacy, and mathematical harmony characteristic of baroque art and music, and in the words of one eminent theorist of the late nineteenth century, "a real strategist of that period believed that he could lead no more than three men over the gutter without a logarithm table."[48]

Frederick never stooped to such artificialities, but he, too, was limited in human and material resources to a degree that later generations, profoundly influenced by two revolutions, the French and the Industrial, often failed to appreciate. For the nature of his army and the structure of linear tactics (which deprived generals of adequate reserves in battle) combined to make a vigorous pursuit after a victorious battle possible only to the next defile. If this was a handicap, it must also be considered a blessing, for otherwise Frederick might never have survived Kolin, Hochkirch, or Kunersdorf to fight another day. The conventional attitude of Frederick's contemporaries on this matter supposedly was expressed in the previous century by Turenne, after one of his victories, when the famous French general proceeded to "give thanks to God, bury the dead, announce our victory" and finally "to profit from the victory by pursuing the enemy."[49] The first would never have occurred to Frederick, deist that he was, and probably he would have disagreed with Turenne's order of priority, but even in his eyes battle was but one of several means to an end, that being "to force the enemy to consent to an advantageous peace as soon as possible."[50]

## FREDERICK THE MILITARY WRITER

There remains Frederick the military writer, for even on campaign his pen was scarcely less active than his sword. In his personal correspondence, his confidential instructions to his generals, and in his numerous regulations for infantry, cavalry, and artillery, Frederick tried to assimilate—and disseminate—the lessons he learned from experience and the study of military history.

Frederick was a pragmatist. He thought always in terms of the present and the concrete rather than the theoretical or the abstract. "Our reason only works upon matters upon which our experience throws light."[51] When Captain Guichard, whose book on the warfare of the ancients made him a welcome member of Frederick's military retinue (and an indispensable source for Gibbon's *Decline and Fall*),[52] once contended that the Roman soldier was more heavily laden than the Prussian infantry of their own day, Frederick promptly stripped a grenadier of a saber, sixty cartridges, a knapsack, and a gun. Then, handing Guichard the equipment, he forced the poor captain to stand at attention for the better part of an hour to prove his point. He subsequently remarked to de Catt:

> You will agree that you can only judge of certain things by comparison. Our friends, the authors, decide things in their study, and it is well to correct their ideas by practice. . . . Our captain will no longer pass judgment, if he ever writes again, so lightly as he did, after the experience he has been put through, which seemed . . . to sadden him somewhat.[53]

Frederick applied his common sense and experience to every military question of the day. When his friend Voltaire praised Charles XII of Sweden "to the skies" although Voltaire possessed "not a shred" of military knowledge,[54] Frederick drew upon his own experiences in adjusting Charles' reputation a little.

Frederick apparently taught himself by organizing his

thoughts in writing. Frequently he made extracts from the writings of others; always he memorized whatever seemed important or interesting. "Do as I do," he urged young de Catt: "learn something by heart every day. . . . If you do not train your memory it will rust, and there is no knowledge without it." Even in intellectual exercises Frederick remained something of a drill sergeant, for in his own writings intended for the education of his officers, he always reiterated his main points in the conviction that "it is by repetition that we acquire clear ideas, that we understand things properly and imprint them strongly on our minds."[55]

But repetition cannot long command the attention of most readers today, and so it has been necessary in the present volume to compress and realign (to use a good military term) Frederick's encyclopaedic thoughts on war. It is only fair to caution the reader, however, that he must not expect to find here an original treatise on the art of war with maxims as useful in the atomic age as they were in the day of Rossbach and Leuthen. This was not Frederick's purpose in writing, nor was it the way he was apt to approach the subject.

On the contrary, these selections teach us essentially what they were supposed to teach Frederick's own officers: how best to tackle a military situation with the army Frederick had at his disposal, with the enemy he was likely to face, and under the conditions that governed military operations at the time. *The Art of War* thus conveys an intimate picture of men in arms during one of the most colorful periods in military history, and at the same time it provides fresh insight into Frederick's own methods and the thoughts behind his actions.

There is much in these writings that is significant. Certainly Frederick's sketch of the evolution of the Prussian army to 1740, the manner in which it was organized, trained, and employed in his own day, and the terrible price it paid during the Seven Years' War constitutes a vital chapter in the history of the German army and explains the origin of some attitudes —particularly among the officer caste—that have lasted into the present century. His account of the battles of Kolin, Rossbach, Leuthen, Torgau, and the famous intrenched camp at Bunzelwitz gives some idea of Frederick's abilities as historian and offers a taste of the military operations of the Seven Years' War. Frederick's version of these great battles enables the reader to view him as he saw himself—"the reasons behind my actions, the mistakes I made, which I do not disguise and excuse . . . and the means I used to repair them."[56] His treatment of what was involved whenever the army marched indicates the scope of the logistical problem and the reasons underlying many of his strategic decisions. The analysis of the generalship of Charles XII reveals as much about Frederick as it does about that incredible Swede and is useful both as an antidote to the biography by Voltaire and as a summary of what Frederick himself practiced and believed.

The following selections also reveal that what was said of the Prussian military leaders in the wars for German unification in the next century—that their successes "were not so much owing to the manifestation of any great military genius . . . as to the vast capacity for taking trouble . . . in anticipation of war"[57]—was in large measure true of Frederick as well. How water should be administered to the troops on the march, the position of each officer in the dispositions for battle, ways in which military intelligence can be extracted from the civilian population and inferred from the cooking habits of the Austrians; the type of artillery to take along on a winter campaign; when to use ricochet fire, the most suitable type of horse for hussars and cuirassiers, ways to safeguard convoys and foraging parties, tricks to look for at muster days—in these and a hundred kindred matters there was no detail too small to escape the notice of the King. History has produced commanders who have been more brilliant or successful, but few have matched Frederick's intimate knowledge of the art of war at every level.

In time of peace Frederick experimented with new tactical forms and maneuvers: the passage of a defile in pursuit of a defeated army (1749), the attack in battalion echelons (1751), crossing a water course on prepared bridges under enemy fire (1753), the retreat of a corps of infantry before enemy cavalry on level terrain and through a defile (1755).[58] Unfortunately the published works of Frederick the Great do not contain his observations on these occasions, but the chapters in this volume dealing with tactics at least embody the results of his exercises.

It follows that Frederick's own military thought progressed as he conducted his maneuvers, scrutinized reports from other armies (he even sent an observer to report upon the operations of his French allies in 1746),[59] tightened his grasp on military literature, and pondered the meaning of his own campaigns. The reader can detect a marked change in Frederick from the time he wrote his *Military Instructions* in 1747 until he produced what in many respects stands as his most significant contribution to military literature, the essay on the *Elements of Castrametation and Tactics* (1770). Originally, for example, he contended that it was the bayonet that won ground, and the ground gained that decided the battle. But after the Seven Years' War he was more conscious of terrain as an active element in both tactics and strategy and he stressed firepower and the need for artillery preparation in the attack. In his earlier writings Frederick devoted comparatively little attention to strategy (the 1753 edition of the *Military Instructions* even omitted the short section "Projets de campagne" found in the original),[60] possibly because he was fighting a single enemy and kept his army, for the most part, concentrated under his own leadership. But those who spend their lives trying to understand something of war often move from the particular to the general, from tactics to strategy, and Frederick was no exception. During the Seven Years' War he had to conduct operations on three or four fronts simultaneously and it became increasingly necessary, particularly since so many of his trusted subordinates were killed in the early campaigns,[61] to instruct his independent commanders in the principles of strategy.

Perhaps the most revealing portion of the book is Frederick's analysis in 1758 of the changing Austrian method of waging war. No other document better illustrates the new role of artillery and the growing importance of intrenched camps. "This little *moorsel*," as Frederick described it,[62] contains practical suggestions on the choice of camps, the precautions to be observed on the march, and the dispositions to be made on the day of battle. But more important still is the fact that it also documents the turning point in Frederick's strategy in the Seven Years' War. Lacking the strength to carry the offensive into a fourth campaign, Frederick's impulse now was to play for time and be prepared to exploit any opportunity that was offered. Hereafter he would maneuver for time, position, and the opportunity to catch and overwhelm isolated enemy detachments. Enough small victories added together could reduce the enemy to the defensive and undermine his will to fight, and to Frederick it made little difference "what means are used, as long as one wins superiority."[63]

To later generations, however, the difference was often significant. Saturated with the concept of absolute war as developed by Clausewitz, mindful of the decisive results of Sadowa and Sedan, and aware of Germany's need to avoid involvement in a protracted war of attrition on two fronts, German military writers in the 1880s tried to link Frederick and Napoleon by claiming that each in his way had pursued a strategy geared primarily to producing the decisive battle. Theodor von Bernhardi was the most representative of this school of strategy, and according to Bernhardi, Frederick alone among his contemporaries looked to the destruction of his enemy's forces as the one decisive thing in war. But there were others, notably the military historian Hans Delbrück, who were not involved in the attempt to provide historical justification for current military doctrine and who therefore argued that Frederick never really rose above the eighteenth-century point of view that maneuvering was just as important as battle.[64] The debate between advocates of the *Vernichtungsstrategie*, who aimed at the annihilation of the enemy's armed forces, and adherents to the

*Ermattungsstrategie*, who claimed that Frederick actually had followed a strategy of exhaustion in which battle "was merely one of several equally effective means of attaining the political ends of the war," lasted for a generation. Each side could point to enough examples from Frederick's campaigns to present a convincing case, depending upon whether one chose to emphasize Frederick's operations before or after the pivotal campaign of 1758. Frederick's own comments likewise seem to support either side, according to his mood at the time. One day he would stress the need for "a great battle to decide our fate," yet on another occasion he would write that "if we hold out well through this campaign the enemy, weary, worn out, and exhausted by the war, will be the first to want peace."[65] Did Frederick belong to the school of Hannibal or Fabius, of Marshal Traun or Napoleon? One is reminded of Bronsart von Schellendorf's cynical observation: "It is well known that military history, when superficially studied, will furnish arguments in support of any theory or opinion."[66]

Perhaps the answer is to be found in Frederick's writings. His *Reflections on Some Changes in the Method of Waging War* proves that he was not doctrinaire nor was he glued to any particular system. Obviously his preference and all of his instincts were for offensive action in strategy as well as tactics, "but in war, as in everything else, a man does what he can and seldom what he desires."[67] The powerful new artillery and greater significance of intrenched camps caused Frederick to turn away from the tactical lessons of Prince Eugene and Turenne and to develop new ideas, in his treatise on castrametation and tactics. To the extent that circumstances and his dwindling manpower forced Frederick to resort to a strategy of maneuver calculated to exhaust rather than to defeat his enemies, the exponents of *Vernichtungsstrategie* were correct in their appraisal.

This does not mean, however, that given a choice, Frederick would have anticipated Napoleon's strategy of manipulating masses for the purpose of destroying the enemy in battle. First, unlike Napoleon, Frederick waged no war of conquest after his initial invasion of Silesia in 1740, and then his objective was limited to the acquisition of a province. Throughout the Seven Years' War his objective remained "to bring Silesia into the safe harbor of a well-guaranteed peace." Clausewitz, the first military theorist to comprehend the forces unleashed in modern war, particularly admired Frederick for his ability, "while pursuing a great object with very limited means," to undertake

> nothing beyond his powers, and *just enough* to gain his object. . . . We find, therefore, in the whole of his conduct of war, a restrained power, always well balanced, and never wanting in vigor, which at the critical moment rises to astonishing deeds, and at the next moment swings quietly on, accomodating itself to the play of the most subtle political influences.[68]

The advocates of *Vernichtungsstrategie*, moreover, might find it difficult to explain why Frederick in his later writings never committed himself to their concept of strategy. In the Seven Years' War he lacked the necessary manpower to expect to win by the decisive act of battle after 1758, and those who saw Frederick as cast from the same mold as Napoleon could explain the basic differences between the two by pointing to the restrictive conditions of eighteenth-century warfare. But Frederick not only lived in the eighteenth century; he was a typical product of the age of Bach and Voltaire, and it is significant to note that in his *Reflections on Projects of Campaign* (1775), in which he allowed himself a comfortable margin of superiority in numbers in his hypothetical campaigns against France in one case, and Austria in the other, it was not by decisive battle so much as by penetrating into France or Austria and threatening the capital that Frederick expected to persuade the enemy to come to terms. "Figure that the entire French army would quickly abandon Flanders after the beginning *of the second campaign* to cover Paris and that, by acting vigorously against this army, the French minister would hasten to conclude peace. . . . The embarrassment of the Austrians would become extreme, and I believe that, placed in a position where they risked losing Vienna, they would go along with any peace proposals."[69] Neither his subsequent conduct of the war in 1778 nor the *Reflections on the Measures to Take in Case of a New War with the Austrians* that he wrote a year later[70] refute this position, and a glance at his suggested plan of campaign in 1779 shows Frederick invading Bohemia and in a second campaign striking for Vienna. Always willing to accept battle under promising circumstances, neither in this document nor in his earlier essay on projects of campaign does Frederick convey the impression that decisive battle was the sole or even the primary objective of maneuver. For the concept of total victory did not march in step with Frederick's faith in the balance of power, and in evaluating his writings as well as his actions, we must remember that the general always subordinated his strategy to the policies of the king.

The suggestion of balance is present also in Frederick's treatment of tactics, for he repeatedly stresses the advantages of what, for want of a better term, we may call "limited liability" in the attack. Frederick is willing to commit only a portion of his forces until a certain point in the battle is reached and it becomes apparent that his attack will succeed. The wing of his battle line that he holds back thus acts as a reserve during the early stages of battle, and in case of defeat it provides a covering force while the rest of the army falls back in safety.

While Frederick's thoughts were never presented as a unified system he nevertheless believed that there were certain basic principles common to both tactics and strategy, and these he explained by frequent use of the siege analogy. Ever since the days of Vauban and his regulated sieges during the wars of Louis XIV, the rules of siegecraft had been more or less fixed and complete. First, the besieging army gathered men and supplies beyond range of the guns of the fort to be attacked. Next, a trench would be dug in the direction of the fort and a siege line, called the first parallel, running at right angles to the line of advance, would be established to harbor men and siege artillery. Then, usually at night, zig-zag lines called saps would be pushed forward until a second parallel was constructed; more saps, a third parallel, and so on until the attacking force had been brought in relative safety almost to the foot of the glacis,* the protective slope leading to the outer walls of the fort. "A highly formalized and leisurely procedure,"[71] this method of attack spared men and minimized the element of luck, which is why Frederick applied the same principles in the conduct of battles and campaigns. Indeed, he even may be said to have extended the concept of linear tactics to the realm of strategy, so opposed was he to the idea of a deep strategical penetration into enemy territory. Each campaign served as a parallel, bringing the army ever closer to the heart of the enemy's power, and just as any commander of a besieged work could be expected to surrender once a breach in the walls had been achieved and an attack was imminent, so it was reasonable to assume that the enemy might willingly discuss terms once his capital was in jeopardy.

Frederick was not especially original as an organizer, tactician, or strategist; neither do his writings on war reflect much originality. Because his overriding concern was to prepare his army to meet problems facing Prussia at the moment, his collected writings in no sense form a balanced or complete treatise on the art of war. The organization of the present volume, and therefore the emphasis, has been the work of the editor and not Frederick. If there should appear to be gaps in the material presented, either of us might be to blame. An editor is always vulnerable in what he selects, and Frederick himself ignored the important factor of sea power and paid little attention to the history of military operations beyond what the classics contained or what had occurred in central Europe since the emergence of Brandenburg-Prussia in the previous century. He was interested in Eugene, not Marlborough; and his concern was for the backwoods of Silesia rather than Pennsylvania, although in the Seven Years' War the military operations in one had some connection with events in the other.

These limitations in time and space do not detract from the historical interest of the book, nor need they deprive it of all its instructional value. Many of our basic institutions, like Frederick's military writings, grew out of the need to meet a crisis or solve some problem, but this does not necessarily mean that either the institution or all of the concepts embodied in this volume grows obsolete as conditions change. The Magna Carta is important today, but not for the same reasons that motivated the barons who presented their demands to the king.

In a sense this is true also of *The Art of War*. Prussian training and drill, which most armies were quick to imitate in the expectation that herein lay the secret of Frederick's victories,[72] soon outlived their usefulness even though they persisted in some armies, notably the British, until the time of the Crimean war. But British officers still might have profited in the nineteenth century from the observations of Frederick, who had also often waged war in areas where the roads were poor, supplies were scarce, and the cost of replacing the individual soldier was abnormally high. In these circumstances Frederick had more to teach than Napoleon, which perhaps is one reason that Sir Charles Napier could write to his brother, the famed historian of the Peninsular war, in the midst of his campaign in Scinde:

> I have found Frederick of Prussia's instructions very useful. I cannot tell how, except that they are practical, and bring many things before me as I work; and they are in one little volume, whereas I have to hunt through your six volumes, and through Napoleon's nine, which are therefore useless to me; for I cannot carry them, and would not have time to hunt out passages. Even Frederick's little book might be much less, and thus be better. Jomini is too voluminous; the Archduke Charles is better, but not altogether what I want and mean; Fred is the man.[73]

Moltke, who was every bit as pragmatic in his thought as Frederick, drew upon other lessons from Frederick's experiences during the Seven Years' War, and it is no coincidence that the German General Staff began to produce its monumental history of Frederick's wars at about the same time that it had become apparent that the next war would involve Germany simultaneously on two fronts. In view of the current revival of interest in the first World War, one is tempted to remark that the generals on both sides could have learned a few fundamental lessons from Old Fritz. In contrast to Frederick, who always was willing to abandon conquered territory in order to keep his army intact and free to act, the German High Command in 1914-16 had stubbornly insisted that not a foot of terrain should be surrendered voluntarily.[74] The allied leaders could similarly have spared countless lives in 1915 and 1916 had they been as quick as Frederick to sense the presence and full implications of siege warfare, or as receptive as he to the need for change.

Later Frederick served the Nazi propagandists as a source of inspiration in an uncertain hour. An anthology of Frederick's thoughts on war and politics that appeared in 1939 opened with his address to the generals on the eve of the first campaign for Silesia. "Gentlemen, I undertake a war for which I have no other allies than your bravery and good will. My cause is just and I trust in my fortune."[75] And a collection of Frederick's portraits was published with an introduction by none other than Reichsmarschall Hermann Göring.[76]

Does Frederick have a message for our times as well? Having grown accustomed to the idea of absolute war and total victory, we tend to become impatient and frustrated in the conduct of the Cold War. By one of the great paradoxes of history, just at the moment that technology and science have given endless dimensions to warfare, we find our actions limited by our mutual fears. In struggling to educate his own officers, it is possible that Frederick might also help to enlighten us as we undergo that mental retooling essential to our understanding of wars which of necessity, and for our very survival, must remain limited.

# NOTES: CHAPTER I

1. *Memoirs of the History of France during the Reign of Napoleon, dictated by the Emperor at Saint Helena to the Generals who shared his Captivity* (London, 1823), II, 12, 54, 187-89.

2. Guglielmo Ferrero, *The Life of Caesar* (New York, 1962), pp. 364-66.

3. Eugene Carrias, *La Pensée militaire française* (Paris, n.d.), p. 128; General Max Weygand, *Turenne, Marshall of France* (Boston, 1930), pp. 149-50.

4. Thomas Carlyle, *History of Friedrich II of Prussia, called Frederick the Great* (London, 1886), IV, 222.

"L'Art de la guerre," in *Recueil des oeuvres du philosophe de Sans-Souci* (n.p., 1762), p. 249.

6. *Frederick the Great: the Memoirs of his Reader Henri de Catt* (*1758-1760*), Translated by F. S. Flint with an Introduction by Lord Rosebery (Boston, 1917), I, 73-74.

7. Pierre Gaxotte, *Frederick the Great*, translated by R. A. Bell (London, 1941), p. 192.

8. De Catt, *Memoirs*, II, 139.

9. As quoted in Carlyle, *Frederick the Great*, III, 201.

10. *Instruction militaire du Roi de Prusse pour ses généraux* (n.p., 1761), pp. 195-96.

11. Frederick, *The History of My Own Times*, translated by Thomas Holcroft (London, 1789), II, 130.

12. As quoted in Theodore Ayrault Dodge, *Great Captains: Showing the Influence on the Art of War of the Campaigns of Alexander, Hannibal, Caesar, Gustavus Adolphus, Frederick and Napoleon* (Boston, 1889), pp. 147-48.

13. This was the last battle fought by the Saxons as a nation. Ludwig Reiners, *Frederick the Great: a Biography*, Translated and adapted from the German by Lawrence P. R. Wilson (New York, 1960), p. 121.

14. Carlyle, *Frederick the Great*, IV, 456.

15. *Ibid.*, p. 495.

16. As quoted in *ibid.*, V, 144.

17. Reinhold Koser, *König Friedrich der Grosse* (Stuttgart, 1903), II, 178.

18. See below, p. 275.

19. As quoted in Carlyle, *Frederick the Great*, V, 234.

20. As quoted in de Catt, *Memoirs*, II, 109. Frederick's detailed

analysis of the military situation at this period of the war is found below in chapter VIII.

21. Karl von Clausewitz, *On War*, Translated from the German by O. J. Matthijs Jolles, with a Foreword by Colonel Joseph I. Greene and a Preface by Richard McKeon (Washington, 1950), p. 119.

22. The battle of Torgau is described below, chapter VII.

23. Captain J. G. Tielcke as quoted in Carlyle, *Frederick the Great*, VI, 68-69.

24. *Ibid.*, p. 89.

25. The strategic pedagogue of the British army in the nineteenth century, Major General Sir E. B. Hamley, had a high regard for Carlyle as a military historian. "A man who can in a science so eminently practical, and which has for the most part been so pedantically treated as the science of war, discard the pedantry, arrive at common-sense conclusions, and describe military operations with unusual spirit and lucidity, must possess faculties of whose existence there was little evidence in his former works." (Hamley), "Carlyle's Frederick the Great," *Blackwood's Edinburgh Magazine*, XCVIII (July, 1865), 39. A more recent scholar has examined Carlyle's use of his sources to conclude: "Carlyle quits himself like a historian. His sources were as large as the resources of his day permitted, his search for facts was dogged, his handling of inevitably differing sources was judicious, and his treatment of his facts within his own narrative was with two exceptions fair." Richard Albert Edward Brooks, "Introduction," in Thomas Carlyle, *Journey to Germany Autumn 1858* (New Haven, 1940), p. xxxiv.

26. Carlyle, *Frederick the Great*, VI, 142.

27. Koser, *König Friedrich der Grosse*, II, 533.

28. Gaxotte, *Frederick the Great*, p. 420.

29. Reiners, *Frederick the Great*, p. 268.

30. Napoleon, *Memoirs*, III, 317-18.

31. As quoted in Reiners, *Frederick the Great*, p. 210.

32. Frederick William I introduced comprehensive infantry regulations in 1714, roughly twenty years before similar ordinances appeared in France (1732) and Austria (1737). Robert Ergang, *The Potsdam Führer: Frederick William I, Father of Prussian Militarism* (New York, 1941), p. 66.

33. Major General John Mitchell, *Biographies of Eminent Soldiers of the last Four Centuries* (Edinburgh, 1865), p. 302; Koser, *König Friedrich der Grosse*, I, 535; Herman von Petersdorff, *Fridericus Rex: Ein Heldenleben* (Berlin, 1925), p. 181.

34. Commandant Colin, *L'Infanterie au XVIIIè Siècle* (Paris, 1907), p. 135.

35. Major General Henry Lloyd, *History of the Late War in Germany* (London, 1766-81), II, xxxvii.

36. Frederick claimed that "the speed with which the Prussian could reload trebled the firepower and made him the equal of three adversaries." A more recent estimate is that the Prussian infantry could fire three or four rounds per minute as against one or two in the other armies. Oliver Lyman Spaulding, Hoffman Nickerson and John Womack Wright, *Warfare: A Study of Military Methods From the Earliest Times* (Washington, 1937), p. 559. Lloyd gives the rate of fire as four rounds a minute for the Prussian armies, two or three rounds a minute for all other armies. Even this conservative estimate gives the Prussians a significant edge over their opponents. See E. M. Lloyd, *A Review of the History of Infantry* (London, 1908), pp. 154-55.

37. As quoted in Carlyle, *Frederick the Great*, V, 127-28.

38. This is inferred from the fact that they were dressed in blue, the traditional color of Prussian uniforms, and were concerned that Candide be at least five feet five inches tall, the average height of Frederick's new regiments. *Candide* was written in 1758, at a time when Frederick and Voltaire were each trying to get the best of each other in their mercurial correspondence, and the butt of Voltaire's ridicule was the philosopher Leibnitz, for whom Frederick had a healthy respect.

39. Voltaire, *Candide or Optimism*, translated by John Butt (Penguin Books, 1962), pp. 22-23.

40. Gerhard Ritter, *Friedrich der Grosse: Ein historisches Profil* (Heidelberg, 1954), p. 164. Ritter's chapter "Vom Wesen friderizanischer Kriegführung" contains an excellent description of eighteenth-century warfare.

41. *Beiträge zur militär- und Kriegsgeschichte. I. Rückzug und Verfolgung Zwei Kampfarten 1757-1944* (Stuttgart, 1960), p. 58.

42. Under Frederick William I, two-thirds of the army were Prussian subjects, and as late as the battle of Kesselsdorf (1745) this proportion prevailed, (Carlyle, *Frederick the Great*, IV, 156). Frederick reversed this ratio in the period between the wars, so that of his 132,000 men in 1751, probably no more than 50,000 were native-born. During the Seven Years' War he got soldiers wherever he could find them. In February, 1763, his army contained 37,000 foreigners and 103,000 natives, and at the time of his death in 1786, the Prussian army comprised 110,000 native-born as against 80,000 foreigners, See below, chapter III; Erwin Dette, *Friedrich der Grosse und sein Heer* (Göttingen, 1914), pp. 16-17; Ritter, *Friedrich der Grosse*, p. 163.

43. See below, p. 78.

44. As quoted in Bernhard Schwertfeger, *Kriegsgeschichte und*

*Wehrpolitik; Vorträge und Aufsätze aus drei Jahrzehnten* (Potsdam, 1938), p. 34.

45. Napoleon's soldiers, for example, camped under the open sky when they could find no quarters, whereas Frederick, to keep his army in good health and to prevent it from melting away, generally used tents. These tents required an additional 60 pack animals for every infantry regiment. Ritter, *Friedrich der Grosse*, p. 168.

46. According to one biographer, Frederick did not rest until he had found a way that would permit him to march twenty-two days from his magazines, while most eighteenth-century generals dared venture only five days from the nearest magazine or fifteen miles from a navigable river. Petersdorff, *Fridericus Rex*, p. 184.

47. As quoted in de Catt, *Memoirs*, II, 223.

48. Freiherr von der Goltz, *Von Rossbach bis Jena und Auerstadt: Ein Beitrag zur Geschichte des preussischen Heeres* (Berlin, 1906), p. 361.

49. As quoted in Schwertfeger, *Kriegsgeschichte und Wehrpolitik*, p. 19n.

50. See below, p. 310.

51. As quoted in Gaxotte, *Frederick the Great*, p. 291.

52. See Carlyle, *Frederick the Great*, V, 260-61.

53. As quoted in de Catt, *Memoirs*, I, 46.

54. *Ibid.*, I, 154. See below, chapter IX.

55. As quoted in *ibid.*, I, 95, 118.

56. As quoted in *ibid.*, II, 84-85.

57. *Journal of the Royal United Service Institution*, XIX (1867), 398.

58. The Historical Section of the German General Staff has studied the peacetime maneuvers conducted by Frederick during the decade preceding the Seven Years' War. See "Die taktische Schulung der Preussischen Armee durch König Friedrich den Grossen wahrend der Friedenzeit 1745 bis 1756," in Grossen Generalstabe, Abtheilung für Kriegsgeschichte, *Kriegsgeschichtliche Einzelschriften*, XXVII-XXX (Berlin, 1900-1902), 389-708.

59. Grossen Generalstabe, Abtheilung für Kriegsgeschichte, "Friedrich des Grossen Anschauungen vom Kriege in ihrer Entwickelung von 1745 bis 1756," *ibid.*, XXVII (Berlin, 1899), 232.

60. The 1747 edition is contained in Major Thomas R. Phillips, ed., *Roots of Strategy* (Harrisburg, Pa., 1940), pp. 311-400. All selections from the *Military Instructions* in the present work have been translated by the editor from the 1753 edition, which was captured by the Austrians in 1760 and subsequently published in France and England.

61. Thirty-three Prussian generals died in the first four years of the

Seven Years' War. Chester V. Easum, *Prince Henry of Prussia, Brother of Frederick the Great* (Madison, Wisconsin, 1942), p. 6on.

62. De Catt, *Memoirs*, II, 85-86.

63. See below, p. 273.

64. Spenser Wilkinson, "Recent German Military Literature," *United Service Magazine*, V (1892), 96-99; Gordon A. Craig, "Delbrück: the Military Historian," in Edward Mead Earle, ed., *Makers of Modern Strategy: Military Thought From Machiavelli to Hitler* (Princeton, 1942), pp. 272-75. The detailed arguments of Bernhardi and Delbrück are found in Theodor von Bernhardi, *Friedrich der Grosse als Feldherr* (2 vols., Berlin, 1881); and Hans Delbrück, *Friedrich, Napoleon, Moltke* (Berlin, 1892); *Geschichte der Kriegskunst im Rahmen der politischen Geschichte* (Berlin, 1920), IV, 439-44.

65. As quoted in Carlyle, *Frederick the Great*, V, 486; and Easum, *Prince Henry of Prussia*, p. 79.

66. As quoted in Prince Kraft zu Hohenlohe-Ingelfingen, *Letters on Artillery* (London, 2d ed., 1890), p. 108.

67. As quoted in de Catt, *Memoirs*, I, 132.

68. Clausewitz, *On War*, pp. 119-20.

69. See below, chapter IX. In his *Réflexions sur les mesures à prendre au cas d'une guerre nouvelle avec les Autrichiens* (1779), Frederick reiterated his plans to force Austria to make a "reasonable peace" by threatening Vienna.

70. Not included in the text because the plans are too detailed and basically do not differ from the plan of campaign suggested in his *Réflexions sur les projets de campagne*, which forms the basis of chapter VIII.

71. Henry Guerlac, "Vauban: The Impact of Science on War," in Earle, ed., *Makers of Modern Strategy*, p. 39.

72. "Old Frederick," Napoleon claimed, "laughed in his sleeve at the parades of Potsdam, when he perceived young officers, French, English and Austrian, so infatuated with the maneouvre of the oblique order, which was fit for nothing but to gain a few adjutant-majors a reputation." Napoleon, *Memoirs*, VII, 327. Frederick's influence upon the French army is manifest in the writings of Guibert and Baron de Pirch, onetime page of the Prussian king. (Carlyle, *Frederick the Great*, VI, 155-56; Robert S. Quimby, *The Background of Napoleonic Warfare: The Theory of Military Tactics in Eighteenth-Century France* [New York, 1957], pp. 200 ff.) In modified form his general principles also formed the basis of the organization and tactics introduced into the youthful United States army by Baron von Steuben, one of Frederick's staff officers during the Seven Years' War. (Oliver Lyman Spaulding, *The United States Army in War and Peace* [New York, 1937], p. 87.)

Prussian drill was first introduced in the British army in 1792 by Sir David Dundas, whose regulations remained in use almost unchanged until after the Crimean War. (Lieutenant Colonel C. Cooper King, *The Story of the British Army* [London, 1897], pp. 239-40.) According to one critic, the regulations of Dundas were translated literally from "the ill-digested and confused treatise" of von Saldern, who utterly misrepresented the tactics of Frederick. ("W," "Cavalry and Infantry Tactics," *United Service Magazine*, 1832, No. 3, 11-16.)

73. Quoted in Lieutenant-General Sir William Napier, *The Life and Opinions of General Sir Charles James Napier* (London, 1857), III, 365-66.

74. Colonel Friedrich von Boetticher, "Friedrich der Grosse," in Major General von Cochenhausen, *Führertum: 25 Lebensbilder von Feldherren aller Zeiten* (Berlin, 1930), p. 224.

75. Ernst Ludwig Werther, *Das Eherne Herz: Friedrich der Grosse im Siebenjährigen Krieg. Briefe, Berichte, Aufzeichnungen* (Munich, 1939), p. 5.

76. *Das Bildnis Friedrichs des Grossen. Zeitgenössische Darstellungen* (Berlin, 1942), p. 5. Frederick is also treated as a living legacy in Franz Riedweg, *Friedrich der Grosse: Soldat, Staatsmann, Denker* (Berlin, 1942). "Heute haben sie wieder ein friderizisches Deutschland vor sich" ("Today you again have Frederick's Germany before you")—Hitler.

## II

# The Sovereign and the Study of War

Frederick's thoughts on war stem from his conviction that the successful king must understand the use—and abuse —of military force as an instrument of policy. The king must also, for reasons suggested below, know how to organize and train his armed services, even to the point of acting in time of war as his own commander-in-chief. Before the advent in the following century of the famed Prussian General Staff, which formulated doctrine, provided meticulous peacetime planning, and guided the actions of those members of the royal family whom tradition had placed in positions of high command, the military fortunes of the kingdom rested squarely on the shoulders of the sovereign. Frederick's critique of the political views of Machiavelli indicate that he understood this even before he became King; as he grew older he showed increasing concern that the military education of his successor should not be neglected.

The first selection comes from the *Anti-Machiavel*, which was published anonymously on the eve of the first Silesian war in 1740. Frederick's later views are taken primarily from the *Political Testaments* of 1752 and 1768, which were published *in full* for the first time soon after the first World War, and from the various histories that he wrote so his successor might derive some benefit from his own rich experience.

## THE DUTY OF SOVEREIGNS

SINCE MACHIAVELLI wrote his political *Prince*, the face of Europe has changed so much that it can no longer be recognized. If some great general in the age of Louis XII were to come back into the world he would find himself much at a loss. He would see war now carried on by bodies of men so numerous that they can hardly be subsisted in the field, yet are .kept up in peace as well as war, whereas in his age, to execute great enterprises and strike decisive blows a handful of men sufficed, and these were disbanded as soon as the war was over. Instead of coats of mail, lances, and harquebusses with matches, he would find the army furnished with uniforms, firelocks, and bayonets. He would see new methods of encamping, besieging, and giving battle, and find the art of subsisting the troops as necessary now as that of conquering was before.

But what would Machiavelli himself say upon seeing this new political face of Europe, and so many princes who were scarcely known in his day now being ranked with the greatest monarchs? What would he say upon seeing the power and authority of sovereigns firmly established, the present manner of negotiating, and that balance settled in Europe by the alliance of many princes and states against the over-powerful and ambitious, a balance solely designed for securing the peace and tranquility of mankind?

All of these things have produced such universal change that Machiavelli's maxims cannot be applied to modern politics. . . . He assumes that a prince who has a large territory, a numerous army, and a full treasury may defend himself against his enemies without foreign supplies. I venture to contradict. . . . Let a sovereign be ever so formidable, he cannot defend himself against powerful enemies without the assistance of allies. If the most formidable prince in Europe, Louis XIV, was reduced to the greatest distress and was nearly ruined by the war of the Spanish Succession, if for want of foreign assistance he was unable to defend himself against the alliance of so many kings and princes, how should a sovereign who is less powerful be able to resist the joint attacks of his neighbors, to which he may often be exposed, without allies?

It is often said—and often repeated without much reflection —that treaties are useless because they are never observed in all points, and that the present age is no more scrupulous in keeping faith than any other. I answer that although many examples may be produced, ancient, modern, and some very recent of princes who have not fulfilled all their engagements, yet it is always prudent and necessary to make alliances. For your allies otherwise will be so many enemies; and if they refuse to send you supplies when you need them, you may at least expect them to observe an exact neutrality.[1]

IT IS A KNOWN TRUTH in politics that the most natural and consequently the best allies are those who have common interests and who are not such close neighbors as to be involved in any dispute over frontiers. Sometimes it happens that strange accidents give birth to extraordinary alliances. In our own time we have seen nations that had always been rivals and even enemies united under the same banners. But these are events that rarely occur and that never can serve as examples, for such connections can only be momentary, whereas the other kind, which are contracted from a unity of interests, alone are capable of execution. In the present situation in Europe, when all her princes are armed and preponderating powers rise up capable of crushing the feeble, prudence requires that alliances should be formed with other powers, as much to secure aid in case of attack as to repress the dangerous plans of enemies, and to sustain all just pretensions by the help of such allies. . . .

Nor is this sufficient. We must have eyes and ears among our neighbors, especially among our enemies, which shall be open to receive and faithfully report what they have seen and

heard. Men are wicked. Care must be taken especially not to
suffer surprise, because surprises intimidate and terrify. This
never happens when preparations are made, however vexatious
the event anticipated. European politics are so fallacious that
the wisest men may become dupes if they are not always alert
and on their guard.[2]

ALLIANCES may be broken in the following cases: (1) When
the ally fails to fulfill his obligations; (2) when the ally medi-
tates deceit and there is no other course except to deceive first;
(3) when a superior force oppresses and makes it necessary
to break a treaty; and finally, (4) when one lacks the means
for continuing the war. That despicable thing called money,
by I know not what fatality, influences all affairs. . . .

To me it appears evident that a private individual ought to
keep his promise scrupulously even though he should have
made it thoughtlessly. If injured, he can always resort to the
protection of the laws, and whatever the outcome, it is an
individual alone who suffers. But where is the tribunal that
can redress a monarch's wrongs, should another monarch forfeit his engagement? The word of an individual can only involve an individual in misfortune, while that of a sovereign may
draw down calamities on nations. The question then will be
reduced to this: Must the people perish, or must the prince
violate a treaty?[3]

MACHIAVELLI speaks . . . of the *principini*, those diminutive
sovereigns who, having only small dominions, cannot send an
army into the field. He advises them chiefly to fortify their
capitals in order to secure themselves and their troops in time
of war. Those Italian princes discussed by Machiavelli are
really a breed of mongrels, half sovereign and half subjects.
They only appear as sovereigns by the number of their do-
mestics. The best advice that one can give them would be . . .
to lessen a little the opinion they entertain of their own grandeur, the extreme veneration they have for their ancient and
illustrious pedigree, and their inviolable zeal for the scutcheons.
Men of sense claim that they had better assume no rank in the

world other than what is due a noblemen of easy fortunes; that they ought to climb down from the scaffold of their pride and maintain at most no more troops than would be necessary to guard their palaces against robbers, if indeed any robbers could be reduced to the starving condition of seeking a subsistence in those palaces; that they ought to raze and demolish their ramparts and walls and everything that gives their place of residence the appearance of strength. The reasons are these: most of those petty princes, especially in Germany, ruin themselves by spending excessive sums to maintain that grandeur with which they are intoxicated, and to support the honor of their family they reduce themselves to beggary and want. There is hardly a second son of a younger brother who does not believe himself to be something like Louis XIV. He builds his Versailles, keeps his mistresses, and maintains his armies. . . .

The reason these little monarchs do not need to fortify their capitals is very plain: they can hardly be besieged at any time by their equals, for their larger neighbors would presently intervene and offer to mediate, an offer they are not at liberty to refuse. Thus instead of bloodshed, two or three dashes of a pen are enough to terminate their quarrels.

What can be the use of their fortified towns? If they were strong enough to endure a siege as long as that of Troy against their equals, they would not be able to hold out as long as Jericho against a powerful prince. Besides, if they lie between two mighty neighbors who are at war, they have no choice but to observe neutrality unless they would be totally ruined. And if they join with either belligerent, their capitals become the frontier towns of that Prince's dominions. . . .

In short, to make war, give battle, and attack and defend fortified places* is the business only of powerful sovereigns, and those who effect to imitate them are no wiser than the man who counterfeited the noise of thunder and believed himself to be Jupiter.[4]

THE MILITARY SYSTEM ought . . . to rest on good principles that experience has shown to be valid. The genius of the nation ought to be understood—what it is capable of, and how far its safety may be risked by leading it against the enemy. . . .

There are states which, from their situation and constitution, must be maritime powers: such are England, Holland, France, Spain, and Denmark. They are surrounded by the sea, and their distant colonies force them to keep a navy and to maintain communication and trade between the mother country and these detached members. There are other states such as Austria, Poland, Prussia, and even Russia, some of which may well do without shipping and others that would commit an unpardonable error in politics if they were to . . . employ a part of their troops at sea when they stand indispensably in need of their services on land.

The number of troops maintained by a state ought to be in proportion to the troops maintained by its enemies. Their forces should be equal, or the weakest is in danger of being oppressed. Perhaps it may be argued that a king ought to depend on the aid of his allies. This reasoning would be good if allies were what they ought to be, but their zeal is only lukewarm, and he who shall depend upon another as upon himself will most certainly be deceived. If frontiers can be defended by fortresses, there must be no neglect in building nor any expense spared in bringing them to perfection. France has provided an example of this, and she has realized its advantages on different occasions.

But neither politics nor the army can prosper if the finances are not kept in the greatest order and if the prince himself be not a prudent economist. Money is like the magician's wand, for by its aid miracles are performed. Great political views, the maintenance of the military, and the best conceived plans for the well-being of the people will all remain lethargic if not animated by money. The economy of the sovereign is useful to the public good because, if he does not have sufficient funds in reserve either to supply the expenses of war without burdening his people with extraordinary taxes or to give relief to citizens in times' of public calamity, all these burdens will fall on the subject, who will be without the means he needs most in such unhappy times.[5]

IT IS IMPORTANT for the King of Prussia to rule independently. If a political system does not emanate from a single head it can no more be established and maintained than Newton could have been able to discover the law of gravitation working in concert with Leibnitz and Descartes. . . . The prince must design his system and put it into operation himself. Because his own thoughts lie closer to his heart than do the ideas of others, he naturally will pursue his plans with the zeal necessary for their success. Thus, his self-esteem, which chains him to his work, will also redound to the needs of the fatherland.

All branches of the state administration are intimately tied together in one bundle: finances, politics, and military affairs are inseparable. Not one, but all of these departments must be uniformly well administered. They must be steered in a straight line, head to head, as the team of horses in the Olympic contest which, pulling with equal weight and speed, covered the course and brought victory to their driver. A prince who rules independently and has fashioned his political system himself will not find himself in difficulty when he must make a quick decision, for he directs everything toward his established goal.

Above all, he must have acquired the greatest knowledge conceivable in the details of military affairs. One produces poor campaign plans at the round table, and where do the best plans lead if they are wrecked through the ignorance of those entrusted with their execution? A King may be the most able man, the best economist, the most subtle statesman—he will still fail as commander in chief if he neither knows the needs of an army nor cares about the countless details of its maintenance, if he is unaware how an army is mobilized, remains ignorant of the rules of war, or understands nothing of training troops in the garrison and leading them in the field. . . . The King of Prussia must make war his particular study and encourage the zeal of those who have chosen the noble and dangerous profession of arms.

Prussia is surrounded by powerful neighbors. . . . You must therefore be prepared for frequent wars. Hence it follows that the military in Prussia must be given the foremost positions, just as they were with the Romans, conquerors of the world, in the period of their ascendancy, and as in Sweden when Gustavus Adolphus, Charles X, and Charles XII filled the world with their fame, and the glory of Swedish names penetrated to the most distant lands. Offices, honors, and rewards bestowed alternately spur and encourage talent. To shower praise upon merit arouses high-minded rivalry in the heart of the nobleman, drives him to enter the army and acquire knowledge, and provides him with fortune and distinction. It makes no sense to despise officers and at the same time to ask them to serve with honor. To encourage a profession that constitutes the power of the kingdom, to respect the pillars of the state (if I may call the army that), to prefer army officers to the breed of soft and insipid men good only for decorating an ante-chamber— that is to say, not to bestow favor too highly nor to act capriciously, but to give honor where honor is due—is really a small enough offering of incense on the altar to officers who stand ready at any moment to shed their blood for the fatherland.

I myself have waged war and observed that colonels sometimes have decided the fate of the state. War cannot be conducted without encountering decisive battles that determine the fate of the kingdom. To win a battle gives the victor gay courage; to lose one strikes the vanquished to the ground. As a result of the battle of Ramillies [1706] France lost all of Flanders. Höchstädt [1704] cost the Elector of Bavaria his Electorate and all of Swabia. The battle of Turin [1706] ejected the French from Lombardy, and Villaviciosa [1710] placed Philip V on the Spanish throne and forced Charles VI to renounce Spain. It is for this reason that Henry IV said "a battle has a long tail."

On important and decisive days such as these one learns to treasure the value of good officers and to love them, if he sees with what proud defiance of death, what indestructible endurance they put the enemy to flight and remain master of the victory and the battlefield. It is not enough, however, to pay them respect only when they are needed and their deeds win your applause. In peacetime they must also enjoy the respect that they have so rightly earned for themselves. Esteem and distinctions rightfully belong to those who have shed their blood for the honor and preservation of the state.

In monarchies everyone looks to the ruler. The public follows his inclinations and seems ready to follow every stimulus that he gives. It is for this reason that the Roman prelates were luxurious and fond of show under Leo X and apathetic and indifferent under Sixtus V; that England was inclined to cruelty under Cromwell and devoted to the gay life under Charles II; that the Netherlands, although a republic, became a warlike nation under the animated example of the Prince of Orange; that the Roman Empire under Titus and the Antonines was still heathen and under Constantine, who was the first to accept the new cult, was converted to Christianity.

So in Prussia the ruler must do that which is most useful for the good of the state and therefore he must place himself at the head of the army. In this way he gives esteem to the military profession and preserves our excellent discipline and the order introduced among the troops. . . . If he possesses no expert knowledge, how will the king judge order and discipline among the different regiments and units? How can he improve what he himself does not understand? How can he blame the colonels for their mistakes and indicate to them at once the way in which they have been wrong and instruct them how to put their regiments in good order? If the king himself understands nothing of regimental and company economy, of troop leading and the art of maneuver, will he be so imprudent as to interfere? In this event he would expose himself to ridicule just as much as he would through ordering false troop movements. All this knowledge demands constant exercise, which one can only acquire if he is a soldier and applies himself to military service with unbroken diligence.

Finally, I venture the assertion that only the ruler can introduce and maintain this admirable discipline in the army. For often he must summon his authority, strongly censure the individual without regard for person and rank, reward others generously, have the troops mustered whenever possible, and not overlook the slightest negligence. The king of Prussia therefore must of necessity be a soldier and commander in chief. This office, which is courted in all republics and monarchies with diligence and ambition, nevertheless is held in low regard by the kings of Europe, who believe that they lose some of their dignity if they lead their armies themselves. But the throne turns out to be a disgrace if effeminate and lazy princes abandon the leadership of their troops to generals, and thus implicitly avow their own cowardice or incapacity.

In Prussia it is certainly honorable to work with the flower of the nobility and the elite of the nation in strengthening discipline. For it is discipline that preserves the fame of the fatherland, gives it respect in peace, and produces victory in war. One would have to be a completely pitiful human being, bogged down in inertia and unnerved by high living, if he wished to shrink from the trouble and work that the maintenance of discipline in the army demands. But in exchange for his efforts, the king certainly would find his reward in victories and fame, which is even more valuable than the highest peak of grandeur or the pinnacle of power.[6]

THE ART OF WAR is just like any other art: used correctly it can be profitable; abused it is fatal. A prince who wages war from unrest, frivolity, or wanton ambition deserves to be punished just as much as a judge who murders an innocent man with the sword of justice. That war is virtuous which is waged in order to maintain the authority of the state, preserve its security, aid allies, or check an ambitious prince who plots conquests contrary to your interests. . . . There is no finer and more useful art than the art of war when practiced by decent men. Under the protection of the noble defenders of the fatherland the peasant tills his fields, courts uphold the law, commerce thrives, and all business is pursued peacefully.[7]

THE AMBITIOUS ought never to forget that arms and military discipline are much the same throughout Europe, and that alliances have the general effect of producing equality between the forces of belligerents. In these times, therefore, all that princes may hope from the greatest advantages is to acquire, after accumulated success, some small frontier town or some suburb, neither of which will pay interest on the debts incurred by war or contain nearly as many people as the number who have perished in the field.

Since the art of war has been so well understood in Europe, and policy has established a certain balance of power between sovereigns, great enterprises but rarely produce such effects as might be expected. An equality of forces, alternate loss and success, cause the opponents to find themselves much in the same state of reciprocal strength at the end of the most desperate war as at the beginning. Exhausted treasuries at length are productive of peace, which ought to be the work of humanity, not of necessity.[8]

AS FOR THE MANNER in which a prince ought to make war, I agree entirely with Machiavelli. Indeed, a great king ought always to assume command of his troops and to regard the camp as his place of residence. This is what his interest, duty, and glory require. As he is the chief magistrate in distributing justice to his people in times of peace, so he ought to be their chief protector and defender in war. When a prince is his own general and present in the field, his orders are more easily suited to all sudden emergencies and are executed with greater dispatch. His presence prevents that misunderstanding among the generals which is so often prejudicial to the interests of the sovereign and fatal to the army. More care is taken of the magazines, ammunition, and provisions, without which Caesar himself at the head of 100,000 men would never be able to accomplish anything. As it is the prince himself who gives orders for the battle, it seems to be his province to direct the execution of these orders, and by his presence and example to inspire his troops with valor and confidence.

But it may be objected that every man is not born to be a
soldier and that many princes have not the talents, experience,
or courage necessary for commanding an army. This objection
may be easily removed: a prince will always find generals
skilful enough to advise him, and it is sufficient for him in this
case to be directed by their advice. Besides, no war can be
carried on with great success if the general is under the direction of a ministry which is not present in the camp and consequently is unable to judge of sudden occurrences and to give
orders accordingly.[9]

## THE STUDY OF WAR

There are two ways, according to Frederick, to learn the
art of war. The best teacher obviously is experience, and
after his first battle in 1741 Frederick "made profound
reflections on all the faults he had committed and endeavored to correct himself in the future." Mollwitz, he
later wrote, "was the school of the King," and Marshal
Traun's campaign against the Prussians in 1744 "is a perfect model, which every general who delights in his profession ought to study and, if he has the abilities, to
imitate." Like the French following the Seven Years'
War, the Prussians after their defeat at Jena in 1806, the
British after the war in the Crimea (1854-56) and in
South Africa (1899-1902), and the Germans in the years
following World War I, Frederick learned to snatch useful lessons from the jaws of defeat. "Good fortune," he
observed, "is often more fatal to princes than adversity:
during the former they are intoxicated with presumption;
the second renders them circumspect and modest."[10]

WHOEVER WISHES to master the art of war must study it
continuously. By no means do I believe that I have exhausted
it, but am rather of the opinion that one lifetime is not enough
to attain this goal. For experience from one campaign to another has taught me new principles, and still there remain innumerable things that fate has given me no opportunity to

experience. Yet I have seen enough to produce general rules that are of special application in Prussia.[11]

WHAT IS THE USE of life if one merely vegetates? What is the point of seeing if one only crams facts into his memory? In brief, what good is experience if it is not directed by reflection. Vegetius[12] stated that war must be a study and peace an exercise, and he is right.

Experience deserves to be investigated, for it is only after repeated examination of what one has done that the artists succeed in understanding principles and in moments of leisure, in times of rest, that new material is prepared for experiment. Such investigations are the products of an applied mind, but this diligence is rare and, on the contrary, it is common to see men who have used all of their limbs without once in their lives having utilized their minds. Thought, the faculty of combining ideas, is what distinguishes man from a beast of burden. A mule who has carried a pack for ten campaigns under Prince Eugene will be no better a tactician for it, and it must be confessed, to the disgrace of humanity, that many men grow old in an otherwise respectable profession without making any greater progress than this mule.

To follow the routine of the service, to become occupied with the care of its fodder and lodging, to march when the army marches, camp when it camps, fight when it fights—for the great majority of officers this is what is meant by having served, campaigned, grown gray in the harness. For this reason one sees so many soldiers occupied with trifling matters and rusted by gross ignorance. Instead of soaring audaciously among the clouds, such men know only how to crawl methodically in the mire. They are never perplexed and will never know the causes of their triumphs or defeats.[13]

## THE LESSONS OF MILITARY HISTORY

"History," Frederick once declared, "is the school of princes; it is their duty to inform themselves of the errors

of past ages in order to avoid them, to learn how essential
it is for them to form a system and pursue it step by step.
. . ."[14] Although professing to believe that "most of our
historians are compilers of falsehood interspersed occasionally with truth," Frederick was an historian in his
own right, "the only modern sovereign to have written
detailed accounts of all his campaigns." The following
introduction to his *History of the Seven Years War* reveals his philosophy of history; the prefaces he wrote to
special editions of the major works of the Chevalier Folard
and General Antoine de Feuquières, for the benefit of his
officers, illustrates his view that history is the proper basis
for military theory.[15]

I HAVE PREVIOUSLY WRITTEN a narrative of the two wars
that Prussia waged in Silesia and Bohemia. This narrative was
the work of a young man and the product of that frenzy for
writing which in Europe has become a kind of epidemic dis-
ease. After the peace of 1746 I renounced history, because
political intrigues when they are unproductive do not merit
more consideration than the cabals of private society, and the
interior administration of a state does not furnish sufficient
materials for history.

The war that broke out in 1756 caused me to change my
opinion. It has been preceded by so much artifice, and the
number of our enemies was so superior to the forces of Prussia,
that a history of subjects of such importance appeared to me
not unworthy of being transmitted to posterity. For this purpose I wrote at the conclusion of each campaign memoirs on
the events it had produced while the memory of them was
fresh. . . . In this work I have had two principal objects in
view. The first was to demonstrate to posterity that avoiding
this war did not depend upon me, and that the honor and the
welfare of the state prevented my consenting to peace under
conditions other than those stipulated when peace was concluded. My second purpose was to relate all military operations
as clearly and with as much precision as possible, that I might

leave an authentic record of the advantageous situations as they occurred in the provinces and kingdoms where war was made for the instruction of the house of Brandenburg, whenever it may again have to contend with the house of Austria.[16] FOR PRUSSIANS are under the necessity of thinking about war because they have a restless and turbulent neighbor. . . . It is necessary to prepare for such an eventuality, which is more than probable, if not certain. Whoever does not reflect now on what he can best do in such a situation will not have time to think maturely when he must begin operations.[17]

IF WAR, as it is probable, is carried to these lands, then you have the advantage of operating in well-known territory. Read my *Memoirs*: there I mention all the camps in addition to everything that is to be considered in connection with them. Study the maps: you will find them noted there. It is a greater advantage to take the field thus prepared. All positions, all camps, all marches are known and made. It is only a question of using them correctly and playing everything to its advantage.[18]

IT IS NOT PROBABLE that any similar chain of causes should, in a short time, produce the same circumstances as those during the Seven Years' War. . . . In similar cases the judgment ought to dictate the part that should be taken. One ought particularly to be guarded against servile imitation, which is wrong. And why? Because generals never are placed in situations that are exactly the same. There may be something relative in their positions, I allow, but examine them well and infinite varieties will be found because nature, in every sense fruitful, neither creates the same appearances nor repeats the same incidents. It would therefore be bad reasoning to say "Marshal Luxemburg was in exactly the same situation as I am, he acted in such a manner, I will act the same." Past facts are good to store away in the imagination and the memory: they furnish a repository of ideas whence a supply of materials may be obtained, but one which ought to be purified by passing through the strainer of the judgment.

I therefore repeat, the details of the last war ought only to be employed as an augmentation of the magazine of military ideas and to prove the value of some principal positions, which will remain determinate so long as the country shall not change its face and nature shall not be overwhelmed. Let these examples serve also to inform the politician of vast projects that the human mind can never penetrate, however extensive it may be, because their minute combinations must be developed in order to foresee or regulate events that depend on future contingencies. We can explain past incidents clearly, for their causes are now discovered, but we always deceive ourselves about the future, which is concealed by secondary causes from our rash and prying inspection. That the expectations of politicians should be disappointed is not a phenomenon peculiar to the present age. It has been the same during all the ages in which human ambition gave birth to grand projects.[19]

I GO ON CITING to you Prince Eugene as the greatest warrior of this century. Follow him in Hungary and watch him undertake the siege of Belgrade. See his army, surrounded by the Turks, wait patiently for a Turkish detachment to be sent across a small stream that separated them, and then march against the enemy and win a decisive victory that forced the Sultan to make peace. . . . Whoever reads the campaigns of Prince Eugene must not limit himself to memorizing his military exploits. He must work hard mainly to examine thoroughly his over-all views and particularly to learn how to think in the same way.[20]

IT IS THEREFORE NECESSARY for those who believe themselves worthy to benefit from the campaigns of someone like Prince Eugene by inquiring why this march was made or this battle fought? What was the disposition on a given occasion? Why was this wing refused and the other used to attack? The would-be general must examine the camps, judge the terrain, and visit the advance posts to give himself a picture of the total disposition. He must exercise judgment in these matters and make himself capable of commanding detachments, for it is by this road that he will attain the command of armies.[21]

## THE CONTRIBUTIONS OF MILITARY THEORY

In 1748 Frederick, wishing to experiment with the new tactical system of the Chevalier de Folard (1669-1752), invited the celebrated theorist to visit him at Berlin. Because the Chevalier's advanced age prevented the trip, Frederick subsequently had an extract prepared from Folard's most noted work, *Histoire de Polybe traduite du grec, avec une commentaire* (6 volumes, Amsterdam, 1729), which he published for the benefit of his own officers. The following is his introduction to the *Extrait tiré des commentaires du Chevalier Folard.*[22]

THE WORK that we present to you might be called *The Mind of M. de Folard.* The visions and ravings of this illustrious soldier contain treasures. We have recovered the diamonds buried in a dung hill, and, instead of six large quarto volumes, we present to the devotee a fourth of only one. The system of columns has been removed, and only the military maneuvers of which he gives an exact description, his wise critique on the conduct of a few French generals, reliable tactical rules, individual and ingenious examples of defenses, and some plans providing material for reflection more useful than even the plans themselves have been saved.

We need not censure the Chevalier de Folard because he has devised a particular system of war. Rather, we ought to applaud what his work has been able to contribute to an extract as useful as the one that has just been made. Of the vast number of books that are written, precious few are solid gold, and there are even fewer from which as much good material can be drawn as from the *Commentary of Polybius.* It would further human knowledge if instead of writing new books, we would apply ourselves to making decent extracts from those that are already in existence. Then one would hope to avoid wasting his time by reading. We hope that soldiers will be grateful, in presenting them with the essence of Folard's work, for having been spared reading the entire six volumes.

The art of war, which certainly deserves to be studied and investigated as much as any of the other arts, still lacks classics. We have few. Ceasar in his *Commentaries* scarcely teaches us anything other than what we see in the war of pandours.* His expedition to Britain is nothing different, and a general in our day could learn only from the disposition of Caesar's cavalry at the battle of Pharsalus. Nothing is to be learned from all of the wars that occurred during the later Empire.[23]

We see the military art reborn during the revolt of the Netherlands. It was there that Turenne, the pupil of Prince Maurice of Orange, learned this art that had been neglected for so many centuries. The *Memoirs of the Last Two Campaigns of Turenne in Germany*[24] ranks among our best military classics, followed by Feuquières, the severe critic of generals of his day. One can add here Santa Cruz, *Military and Political Reflections*, and de Quincy, *Military History of the Reign of Louis XIV*, which becomes important for the study of campaign plans not because they serve as models, but because one sees by their success wherein he has failed to take appropriate measures. The mistakes of others enable us to acquire experience at their expense.

Following these works one might include the abridged and condensed edition of Folard. Those who have taken pains to publish this edition have in mind only the greatest glory of the service by trying to make it easy for officers to study their art and a profession that leads to immortality.[25]

THAT HARSH CRITIC, the judicious Feuquières, has related minutely all the mistakes that generals committed in his day. He has, in a manner of speaking, developed the anatomy of campaigns that he witnessed by showing the causes of success and the reasons for failure. He has indicated the road that must be followed if one desires to instruct himself, and by which researches the first truths, which are the basis of the art, are discovered.[26]

## THE CASE FOR MILITARY EDUCATION

De Quincy's *Histoire militaire du règne de Louis XIV* was an important signpost on this road to knowledge. Frederick had portions of this work extracted and translated into German, and sent them in 1772 to the regiments for study by the officers. Frederick himself contributed the following introduction.

THE NUMBER of the nobility who devote themselves to the profession of arms is considerable in every country, but the motives that induce them to choose such an illustrious profession are not the same. Some, destitute of the good things of this world, regard the service as a last resource that provides them with an honest living. Indifferent, they in their indolence depend upon time to advance them in their turn; they believe that to have served long and to have served well are one and the same thing, and as long as they cannot be reproached for some serious breach of duty, they remain content.

There are others who are addicted to the frivolities so common to our age. They surrender to pleasure and dissipations and are anything but soldiers, which, after all, is their profession. And finally there are those—but always the smallest number—who, fired with noble ambition, are determined to make their own way in the world by their courage, capacity, and wisdom; men who, thirsting to be taught, desire only the opportunity of being enlightened and of increasing the sphere of their knowledge. It is precisely for this type of officer that this extract of sieges . . . toward the end of the last century and the beginning of the present one has been prepared. We have been careful to select those which have been the most famous in the period covered, in order to show to the inquisitive person the resources that the art and the mind found for the attack and defense of fortified places.

Whoever wishes to pass for a skillful officer must combine an endless amount of knowledge and talent. He must know how to drill his soldiers to make them capable of executing the required evolutions. He must, no matter how little he thinks about promotion, have a complete knowledge of tactics, of the art of maneuvers, of attacks, defenses, retreats, marches, passages of rivers, convoys,* forages, and all of the dispositions that war in the field requires. He must have full knowledge of the country in which he must wage war; he must be a master at castrametation,* of the use and advantage that can be derived from terrain, and of the way of distributing the troops and having them fight with superiority.

But, in addition to all this knowledge, an infantry officer cannot ignore without shame matters concerning the attack and defense of fortresses. This service depends solely on the infantry, and there are few campaigns where there has not been some town besieged or defended. This provides occasions for the officer to distinguish himself. An officer who ignores the art will not know how to benefit from it because his ignorance gets in the way, whereas the officer who has devoted some of his leisure hours to study this aspect of war properly finds a hundred occasions to display his merit, which necessarily must send him on to his fortune.

It is to facilitate such learning and to make it palatable that this book has been translated and brought to light in the present form. It is hoped that those who really love their profession will be very glad to find a new way to instruct themselves, and the translator will be well satisfied for his troubles if, by means of the knowledge distributed in this book, he can contribute to the fame and fortune of those who will read and know how to profit from it.

Every art has its rules and maxims. One must study them: theory facilitates practice. The lifetime of one man is not long enough to enable him to acquire perfect knowledge and experience. Theory helps to supplement it, it provides a youth with premature experience and makes him skillful also through the mistakes of others. In the profession of war the rules of the art never are violated without drawing punishment from the enemy, who is delighted to find us at fault. An officer can spare himself many mistakes by improving himself. We even venture to say that he must do it, because the mistakes that he commits through ignorance cover him with shame, and even in praising his courage one cannot refrain from blaming his stupidity. What an incentive to work hard! What reasons to travel the thorny road to glory! And what loftier and nobler compensation is there than to have one's name immortalized for his pains, and by his work.[27]

## NOTES: CHAPTER II

1. Frederick, *Anti-Machiavel: or, an Examination of Machiavel's Prince. With Notes Historical and Political* (London, 1741), pp. 106ff. Minor liberties have been taken with this translation for the sake of uniform spelling and style.

2. Frederick, "An Essay on Forms of Government and on the Duties of Sovereigns," *Posthumous Works of Frederick II, King of Prussia*, trans. Thomas Holcroft (London, 1789), V, 17-18 [*Duties of Sovereigns*]. In this and in the subsequent Holcroft translations I have changed spelling, punctuation, and a few awkward sentences for the sake of a uniform style.

3. Frederick, *The History of My Own Times*, trans. Thomas Holcroft (London, 1789), I, xvi-xix.

4. Frederick, *Anti-Machiavel*, pp. 110-15.

5. Frederick, *Duties of Sovereigns*, pp. 19-21.

6. Frederick, "Das politische Testament von 1752," *Die Werke Friedrichs des Grossen* (Berlin, 1912), VII, 164-67 [*Testament von 1752*]. The Political Testaments of 1752 and 1768 had not been made public by the Hohenzollern family at the time the original edition of the *Oeuvres de Frédéric le Grand* (30 vols., Berlin, 1846-56) was published and hence are available only in German.

7. Frederick, "Das Militärische Testament von 1768," *Werke*, VI, 246 [*Testament von 1768*].

8. Frederick, *History of my own Times*, I, xxiv-xxv; II, 300-301.

9. Frederick, *Anti-Machiavel*, pp. 123-39.

10. Frederick, *History of my Own Times*, I, 129; II, 130.

11. Frederick, *Testament von 1768*, p. 246.

12. Flavius Vegetius Renatus, a prominent Roman writer of the fourth century, is the author of *De Re Militari*, one of the most influential military treatises in the Western world from Roman times until the time of Frederick.

13. Frederick, "Réflexions sur la tactique et sur quelques parties de la

guerre, ou Réflexions sur quelques changements dans la facon de faire la guerre," *Oeuvres*, XXVIII, 153-54 [*Réflexions sur la tactique*].

14. Frederick, *History of my own Times*, I, xxvi-xxvii.

15. *Ibid.*, I, xi. Frederick's historical writings are discussed in G. P. Gooch, *Frederick the Great: the Ruler, the Writer, the Man* (London, 1947), pp. 298-327.

16. Frederick, *The History of the Seven Years War*, trans. Thomas Holcroft (London, 1789), I, vii-viii [*Seven Years War*].

17. Frederick, "Réflexions sur les mesures à prendre au cas d'une guerre nouvelle avec les Autrichiens, en supposant qu'ils suivent la même méthode d'une défensive rigide comme dans la dernière campagne de 1778," *Oeuvres*, XXIX, 144.

18. Frederick, *Testament von 1768*, pp. 260-61.

19. Frederick, *Seven Years War*, I, viii-ix; II 369.

20. Frederick, "Réflexions sur les projets de campagne," *Oeuvres*, XXIX, 79-80 [*Projets de campagne*].

21. Frederick, "Règles de ce qu'on exige d'un bon commandeur de bataillon en temps de guerre," *Oeuvres*, XXIX, 63.

22. Folard's system comprising the column and mixed order of battle and emphasizing shock tactics is analyzed in Robert S. Quimby, *The Background of Napoleonic Warfare: The Theory of Military Tactics in Eighteenth-Century France* (New York, 1957), pp. 26-41.

23. This does not represent Frederick's view, accurately, for in his military instructions to his generals he suggested that they might do well to imitate Caesar's passage of the Rhine, and in his advice to his successor he drew attention to Sertorius, whose skillful campaign against Pompey in 76-72 B.C. made him "the master of defensive warfare." See Frederick, *Instruction militaire du Roi de Prusse pour ses généraux* (Frankfort, 1761), p. 116; and *Testament von 1768*, p. 254.

24. (M. Deschamps), *Mémoires des deux dernières campagnes de Monsieur de Turenne en Allemagne et de ce qui s'est passé depuis sa mort . . .* (2 vols., Paris, 1678). It would appear that Frederick was in error in attributing authorship of this work to Turenne. See Frederick, "Avant-propos de l'extrait tiré des commentaires du Chevalier Folard sur l'histoire de Polybe," *Oeuvres*, XXVIII, 100.

25. *Ibid.*, pp. 99-101. The works referred to are Feuquières, *Mémoires de M. le Marquis de Feuquières, contenant ses maximes sur la guerre, et l'application des exemples aux maximes* (Amsterdam, 1731); *Réflexions militaires et politiques, traduites de l'espagnol de M. le marquis de Santa Cruz de Marzenado, par M. de Vergy* (8 vols., Paris, 1738), and Charles Sevin, Marquis de Quincy, *Histoire militaire du règne de Louis XIV* (4 vols., Paris, 1726).

26. Frederick, "Réflexions sur la tactique," p. 154.

27. Frederick, "Avant-propos," *Oeuvres*, XXIX, 51-53.

# III

# *The Military Instrument*

## THE PRUSSIAN ARMY FROM ITS ORIGINS
## TO THE REIGN OF FREDERICK THE GREAT

Frederick's successes as a general were due in large measure to the quality of his army. For this reason, and also because his tactical exercises were tailored specifically to the capabilities of this military instrument, the following selections are included. The history of the Prussian army to 1740 is taken from Frederick's first venture into history, *Mémoires pour servir à l'histoire de la Maison de Brandebourg*, and is reproduced virtually intact except for the occasional deletion of the names and numbers of effectives of the individual regiments.

*THE FIRST ELECTORS* of the house of Brandenburg maintained no regular army. They had only a mounted guard of one hundred men and some companies of Landsknechts* distributed among the chateaux or fortified places, the number of which was increased or diminished according to the need. When they feared war the Electors and the estates convoked the general levy; that is to say, the general arming of the entire country. The nobles were obliged to form the cavalry and their vassals, organized into regiments, had to comprise the infantry. This way of raising troops and forming armies was the general practice in Europe at the time: the Gauls, Germans, and Bretons had always made similar use of it, and the practice has endured to the present day in Poland, where the arming of the entire nation is called the *Pospolite Ruszenie*. Like the Poles, the Turks have stuck with this custom, for with the exception of a regular body of 30,000 Janissaries that they maintain, they have never waged war without arming the peoples of Asia Minor, Egypt, Arabia, and Greece, all of whom are under their domination.

To return to the history of Brandenburg: when John Sigismond[1] thought that he was on the verge of acquiring the succession of Jülich and Berg he anticipated that he would have to uphold his rights by force of arms. He therefore decreed a general arming of 787 knights, who put in an appearance at the place of assembly. From this number he selected 400 of the most adroit. The noblemen furnished, in addition, 1,000 foot soldiers, not counting the pikemen, who were placed under the command of Colonel (Hillebrandt von) Kracht. The towns sent an additional 2,600 men into the field. These troops were maintained at the expense of the estates and as a rule they were paid only for three months, after which time each would return home. The Elector would name his officers, and as soon as the need for these levies ceased, the troops would be disbanded altogether.

The stormy regency[2] of George William [1619-40] provides some examples of this kind of arming. In 1620, on the occasion of the Thirty Years' War, the estates raised troops by allowing them to collect money throughout the country to provide for their subsistence. The peasants were ordered to donate a penny each time they were asked, but at the same time the peasants also were given the right to hit the soldiers if the latter were not content with this amount. What was the success of this ridiculous arrangement? Instead of acquiring soldiers, the prince only established a corps of beggars.

In 1623 the court issued an edict directing all subjects except priests and municipal magistrates to report with arms and baggage to a designated place where some commissioners had them pass in review. From this number, 3,900 were chosen and distributed into twenty-five companies of infantry and ten squadrons of cavalry. After the Peace of Prague [1635] Count von Schwartzenberg[3] persuaded George William to augment his troops and maintain them by means of subsidies that the Spaniards and the Empire would make available. According to this minister's plan, the number of troops was to be increased to 25,000.

The levies were made and these troops took the oath to the Emperor and to George William. When they passed in review at Neustadt-Eberswalde . . . they comprised a total of 8,000 foot and 2,900 horse. Klitzing, who commanded this army, is the first general mentioned in the history of Brandenburg. These troops were augmented or reduced according to the times, the needs and the occasions, but never did they exceed 11,000. Upon his death George William bequeathed an army of 3,600 foot and 2,500 horse to his son.[4]

Frederick William [1640-88] attained the regency in a time of distress. To ease the burden on his provinces, which were drained of money and men, he reduced the number of troops. The cavalry, upon refusing to take the ordinary oath, was disbanded, and in order to appear meritorious in the eyes of the Emperor, the Elector transferred 2,000 horse to the Imperial army, retaining only 200 horse and 2,000 foot. . . .

Frederick William was the first Elector who maintained in his service a *corps d'armée*\* that was regularly trained. The infantry battalions comprised four companies of 150 men each; one-third of the battalion was armed with pikes and the rest had muskets. The infantry wore uniforms and cloaks. The cavalry provided their own arms and horses, carried half-armor,[5] fought by squadrons, and often took their cannon with them.

In 1653 the Elector and the Count Palatine of Neubourg disagreed over the succession of Cleves. On this occasion the Elector increased the size of his army, raising fifty-two companies of cavalry and eighty-two companies of infantry, and the Count of Wittgenstein entered his service with . . . three

regiments of each. After the Elector had resolved his differences
with the Count Palatine, he disbanded the greatest number of
these troops.

The war that broke out soon after between Charles Gustavus and the republic of Poland led to a new increase. The
Elector, supported by Swedish subsidies, made the utmost
effort to put the army in a condition of readiness. According
to the archives, his cavalry was increased to 14,400—a number
that would seem to have been much exaggerated were it not
for the fact that the names of the commanders and units have
been preserved. . . . And since it was the intention of the
Elector to attack the Poles, whose main force consisted of
cavalry, it is possible that he wanted to oppose them with the
same arm, and in a proper condition to command their respect.
His infantry increased to 10,666. . . . During the entire course
of the war waged by the Prince and the Swedes in Poland,
Waldeck,[6] in the capacity of lieutenant general, commanded
the troops from Brandenburg. Part of this army followed the
Elector in Poland; the rest of the troops were distributed in
the provinces.

After Frederick William had made peace with the Poles he
marched to the aid of the Danish king, whom Charles Gustavus
besieged at Copenhagen. He entered Holstein at the head of
4,000 infantry and 12,000 cavalry, half of which were composed of the Emperor's cuirassiers.* Following the Peace of
Oliva [1660], the Elector again reduced the number of his
troops, but not by a considerable amount: at least he afterwards
maintained a number of generals, which surely proves that he
must have had a proportionate number of soldiers. Marshal
Sparr[7] is the first to have held the rank of marshal in the service
of Brandenburg. . . .

When the war of 1672 began, the Elector maintained 23,-
562 soldiers. The army that he led in Alsace to assist the Emperor was 18,000 strong. Later increased to 26,000, this army
participated in the glorious campaign in Pomerania, which the
Elector conquered, and in Prussia, where he expelled the Swedes.

Upon Frederick William's accession to the regency, the troops were poorly paid and maintained, a condition that lasted until the year 1676, when Grumkow,[8] the minister of finance, introduced the excise tax in the towns. This fixed and assured revenue was earmarked for the war chest. The pay of a foot soldier was one and one-half crowns per month; that of the officers was little enough. During the Polish War and the war of 1672 Frederick William maintained his troops sometimes by Swedish subsidies, sometimes by the subsidies of the Austrians, Spaniards, and French. But after 1676 the increased revenue provided by the excise tax, the acquisition of the Duchy of Magdeburg, and the improvement of his provinces, which gradually recovered from the distress they had suffered in the Thirty Years' War—all these resources, carefully administered, provided Frederick William with the means to maintain independently a considerable body of troops.

At the death of the Great Elector his field army contained . . . 36 infantry battalions, each comprising 4 companies 150 men strong, 40 cavalry squadrons, 120 troopers to the squadron, and 18 companies of garrison troops, making a grand total of 21,000 infantry, 2,700 garrison troops, and 4,800 cavalry—28,500 in all.

In those days the infantry fought in ranks five or six deep. Pikemen made up one-third of a battalion; the rest were armed with German muskets. Although poorly clothed, the infantry had in addition to its uniform, long cloaks rolled up and folded on the shoulders, in much the same fashion as the antique busts of the Roman consuls. When the Elector made his celebrated expedition to Prussia during the winter, he had half-boots distributed to all of the foot soldiers.

His cavalry still wore entirely the old armor and could scarcely be disciplined because each trooper provided his own horse, clothes, and weapons, which gave the entire aggregation a motley appearance. It would appear that Frederick William preferred his cavalry to his infantry, for he fought at the head of the mounted arm in the battles of Warsaw [1656] and

Fehrbellin [1675]. So much confidence did he place in the
cavalry, that one frequently reads that it was accompanied by
artillery. Manifestly this preference was not without foundation: considering the nature of his estates, which for the most
part are plains, and the troops of his neighbors, nearly all of
whom were mounted, the Elector preferred his cavalry to the
infantry since they offered possibilities for more general employment.

No magazines at all were formed in Frederick William's
day. The country in which war was waged provided for the
troops with regard to pay as well as provisions. One encamped
only when the enemy approached and he could or wanted to
bring on a battle. For these reasons a country once depleted
was abandoned: vagabond armies desolated one province after
another, and wars lasted even longer when the armies were
small, self-sufficient, inexpensive, and when the generals who
led them found means of enriching themselves by prolonging
the hostilities.

Old Derflinger and Prince George of Anhalt enjoyed the
greatest reputation among the Elector's generals.[9] Had the
advice of the latter been followed in 1673, the Elector would
have attacked Turenne and perhaps defeated him. The Prince
of Anhalt was considered a sage: Derflinger was the adven-
turous one. Derflinger served his master well in the surprise
attack upon Rathenow [1675], in the pursuit of the Swedes
after the battle of Fehrbellin, and in urging the extraordinary
diligence of the troops in the Prussian expedition. After Derflinger, the most esteemed of the generals was Görschen, who
surprised the Swedes in Prussia near Splitter, and Treffenfeldt,
who expelled them entirely from this duchy.

The art of fortifying places, as well as that of attack and
defense, was completely unknown. The Elector did not have
even a mediocre engineer in his service. He busied himself for
six months before Stettin, although the works were wretched
in the extreme, and he took Stralsund only by setting it afire
with his bombs.* The works that he built to surround the walls

of Berlin were poorly constructed, having long curtains* and bastions with flat faces* so that no work was flanked. War is the same as the other arts: it is not perfected in a day, and it is enough that in the realm of tactics the Elector has left some examples that will serve for all time as lessons to the most skillful captains.

The reign of Frederick, first King of Prussia, is filled with frequent reductions and increases in the size of the army, with foreign subsidies, as he received them, serving to determine whether the number rose or fell. After the death of Frederick William the number of troops had been increased: battalions were set at five companies each, and seven new battalions were raised. . . . The next year, in 1689, ten battalions and six squadrons from Brandenburg joined the Dutch service. After the Peace of Ryswick [1697] the number of companies per battalion was reduced to four, and the strength of the company to eighty men, which meant that eighty companies both of infantry and cavalry were discharged. In 1699, the fifth company was restored in each battalion. In 1702 . . . [five] regiments were given twelve companies each and turned over to the service of Holland, where they remained throughout the War of the Spanish Succession. In 1704 and 1705, the King organized all of the cuirassier regiments with three squadrons in each and the dragoon regiments with four. At his death [1713] his army . . . numbered 30,000 combatants.

At the beginning of the eighteenth century the use of the pikes was abolished, with *chevaux de frise** being substituted. Pikes were useful only in defending foot soldiers against cavalry: in sieges, intrenchments, and on a hundred other similar occasions the pikemen served no practical function. The old officers hated to part with this weapon, for the habit of many years had made them prejudiced in its favor, but war continually improves upon itself, and even the matchlocks[10] were forsaken because rain often extinguished the matches. They were replaced by fusils.*

During the reign of Frederick I, discipline was established

in the troops, who became inured to the hardships of war both in Flanders and in Italy. The officers who served in Flanders learned their profession with the Dutch, who were then our tutors: the English troops provided an example of great neatness that we also imitated.

The Margrave Philip, great master of the artillery, was the first who endeavored to obtain tall men: the grenadier* companies of his regiment were of more than ordinary height, an example imitated by both the Prince of Anhalt and the Royal Prince. Since that time officers began to be particular about the kind of men that they employed as soldiers, taking only large, strong, and robust individuals.

All of the troops had uniforms. It is true that those who wished to serve in the cavalry paid for the privilege, but they were armed and clothed at the expense of the Crown. The foot soldiers were extravagantly burdened in the field. Besides their arms and cloaks they carried their tent, haversack, and [stakes for] the *chevaux de frise*. They still fought in four ranks.

The Prince of Anhalt,[11] who had campaigned with Prince Eugene in the Empire as well as in Italy and Flanders, had made a profound study of the military profession. He frequently commanded the Prussian auxiliary troops . . . and he forced them to adhere to a rigorous discipline. A strict observer of discipline, he advanced it to that high point of obedience where it constitutes the greatest strength of an army, but since his attentions were limited to infantry the cavalry was much neglected.

So many officers who had made war in Flanders, the land of fortified places where one had only to besiege and defend cities, finally enriched us in the art of fortification, and many acquired enough understanding to command the attacks and in the trenches, or to defend a besieged fortress. Frederick I had Magdeburg and Wesel fortified after the method of Vauban and Coehorn. He had in his service General Schöning, commandant of Magdeburg, who well understood this phase of war, and Bodt, who was accused however of being a more skillful mason than engineer.[12]

The wars in Flanders, along the Rhine and in Italy had molded many officers of good repute in Prussia. The Margrave Charles, who died in Italy, covered himself with glory in the battle of Neerwinden [1693]. General Lottum, who commanded some detachments of the army of Flanders . . . was highly regarded, and Count Finck gave evidence of his capacity at Malplaquet [1709], where he carried the French entrenchments and there stood his ground although the Imperial cavalry was driven back from the position three times.[13] And at the battle of Oudenarde [1708] General Natzmer, at the head of the *gendarmes*,* broke through three lines of French cavalry and there displayed prodigious valor.

Towering above them all was the Prince of Anhalt. He it was who performed the most brilliant actions, who enjoyed the general confidence of the troops, who saved Styrum's army at Höchstädt [1703] by a masterly retreat, . . . and who contributed much to the victory at the second battle of Höchstädt [Blenheim], so fatal to the French. Prince Eugene acknowledged him as the main author of the victory of Turin [1706]. In him great prudence was combined with rare valor, but for all his great qualities he scarcely had any that were good ones.

This about describes the army and the generals who commanded it when Frederick William, the second king of Prussia, mounted the throne. This prince augmented the soldiers' pay, which he established at two crowns a month in addition to an allowance of six *groschen*[14] for jackets, leggings, shoes, and so forth.

In 1714 the infantry companies were fixed at 120 men. In 1717 the King created the Leopold regiment, which he formed from prisoners taken in the war against Charles XII. Three years later he established five squadrons as the standard for all cavalry regiments, two companies to the squadron and sixty men to each company. In 1718 he created the Schulenbourg dragoons, five squadrons of them, and he swapped a dozen

Japanese vases for a dragoon regiment that the King of Poland wanted to disband. . . . Henceforth this regiment was known as the Porcelain Regiment. In 1726 the mounted grenadiers of Schulenbourg, Wense, and Platen were doubled in size, each one consisting then of ten squadrons.

From 1726 to 1734 he augmented the infantry by one officer per company; he raised . . . four regiments and two battalions, afterward adding to each battalion a company of one hundred grenadiers. The artillery was organized into two battalions, one for service in the field and the other for garrison duty. He created a militia corps of 5,000 men, the officers and noncommissioned officers of which received half pay. This militia was assembled every year for fifteen years for the purpose of drill. After all these increases the Prussian army now stood at 72,000 —sixty-seven infantry battalions, 111 cavalry squadrons, and five battalions of garrison troops. . . .

The entire army, infantry as well as cavalry, was quartered in the towns, where discipline could be introduced and maintained. The King published a military Regulation instructing each officer in his duty; and he himself saw that it was done. At the head of every corps was an officer respectable from the standpoint of age and service, and these strengthened subordination by their example and severity. Every year the King reviewed the troops and had them go through some evolutions, and since he was his own inspector he was not in the least deceived.

When these new exercises were first introduced the officers were unaware of the easy method that later was found to teach them, and they were rhetoricians only at cudgeling, which rendered this work long and difficult. In each regiment the officer corps was purged of those men whose conduct or birth fell short of the standards of the profession that they must create. After that time the refinement of the officers permitted among their companions only men beyond reproach.

The battalions were arrayed in four ranks but they fired only in three. The battalions contained four divisions,* with two platoons in each division aside from the grenadier company. The Prince of Anhalt, who had studied war as a profession, had noticed that the fusils had not been used to the fullest possible advantage; he invented some iron ramrods and found the way to instruct soldiers to load with incredible speed. After 1733 the front rank loaded with fixed bayonets.

Drill was performed at that time in the following manner: first the manual exercise was performed, followed by the loading of muskets by platoons and by divisions. Then the troops advanced, firing in the same way. Retreats were conducted along similar lines, after which two squares, impracticable for use against the enemy, were formed. The drill was finished by a very useful *feu de haie.*\* All of these evolutions, however, were always made with so much precision that the movements of a battalion resembled the workings of the springs in the finest watch.

The King abolished the cloaks and shortened the dress of the infantry. To lighten the burden on the march he designated two pack horses per company to carry the soldiers' tents and blankets in the field. He also had the foresight to institute supply magazines in all of his provinces, which served to assist the people in times of want and provided him with ready-made magazines for the army in times of war.

Toward the year 1730 the rage for large men reached such a point that posterity will find it difficult to believe. The common remuneration for a man five feet ten inches tall . . . was seven hundred crowns; a man six feet tall received 1,000 crowns, and if he was larger the amount increased still more. There were several regiments that contained nobody under five feet eight inches. The smallest man in the army measured a good five feet six inches.

To introduce order in these enlistments, which were made throughout the country with confusion and led to a thousand lawsuits between regiments, the King in 1733 divided all of the provinces into cantons. These cantons were allotted to the regiments, which could draw upon them for thirty men annually during peace and up to one hundred in time of war. This system made the army immortal by providing it with a secure recruiting ground by which it has unceasingly regenerated ever since.

The cavalry, just like the infantry, was composed of very large men mounted on enormous horses. They were giants on elephants who knew neither how to maneuver nor fight. There was never a review without some trooper falling to the ground from sheer awkwardness. They were not masters of their horses, and their officers had no idea of cavalry service or of war, no knowledge of terrain or of the theory or practice of cavalry evolutions in battle. These good officers were like farmers who looked upon their companies as farms from which they could glean as much as possible.

Moreover, the long peace had corrupted the service. At the beginning of Frederick William's reign the order and discipline of the regiments had been refined, but since there was nothing left to accomplish in this respect, attention became focused only on the sort of thing that caught the eye. The soldier polished his fusil and equipment; the trooper, his bridle, saddle, and even his boots. The horses' manes were plaited with ribbons, and at length neatness, which in itself serves a useful purpose, degenerated by ridiculous abuse. If the peace had lasted beyond 1740, I am satisfied that today we would be decked out in rouge and beauty spots. But more deplorable still, the higher art of war was completely neglected, and our mind grew narrower from day to day as we concentrated on trivia.

Despite all this abuse the infantry was good: severe discipline and full order reigned. But the cavalry was neglected completely. The King personally had seen the Imperial cavalry repulsed three times at the battle of Malplaquet, and in the sieges of Menin, Tournai, and Stralsund, where he also was present, there had been no chance for cavalry to shine. The Prince of Anhalt was nearly as prejudiced as the King: he could not forgive Styrum's cavalry for the defeat in the first battle of Höchstädt, and he surmised that the mounted arm was too fickle to be depended upon. These unfortunate prejudices were so fatal to our cavalry that they remained without discipline, and consequently they were of no use afterwards.

The infantry officers applied themselves a great deal to their profession: those of the cavalry, nearly all of whom were distributed in the small villages, had less ability and acuteness than the others. There were more brave than wise men among the generals: of the whole lot the Prince of Anhalt was the only one capable of commanding an army. He knew it, and by his superiority he turned everything he could to his advantage in order to be courted and to excel.

During the reign of the King, the fortifications of Magdeburg and Wesel were completed, and that of Stettin was commenced under the command of Colonel Walrave, but directed by the Prince of Anhalt. The King created a corps of thirty engineers, which was formed in these different works. He filled his arsenal with artillery trains for the field and for sieges; he had first-rate artillery officers, and the cadets, this nursery of officers, filled all of the vacancies caused by death. What contributed even more to their success was that these young men came from a military school with all the knowledge that an officer must have.

Such was the progress of the Prussian army until the death of the late King. One could apply to this army what Vegetius said of the Roman forces: "Their discipline enabled them to triumph over the cunning of the Greeks, the strength of the Germans, the size of the Gauls, and over all of the nations on earth."[15]

## EIGHTEENTH-CENTURY WARFARE

In *The History of My Own Times* Frederick gives a broader picture of the rise of national armies and the changing conditions of war.

THE EMPEROR FERDINAND I kept an army of scarcely 30,000 men. Charles VI in the war of 1733 paid 170,000 without oppressing his people. Louis XIII maintained 60,000; Louis XIV 220,000 and even as many as 360,000 during the War of the Spanish Succession. Since this time every prince, even the most petty, has augmented his military forces in imitation. In the war of 1683, Louis XIV raised as many men as he could in order to have a decided superiority over his enemies. He disbanded none after the peace, which forced the Emperor and the German princes to keep as large an army on hand as they could afford. Once established, this custom was perpetuated.

War became increasingly expensive. The provisions for the magazines swallowed up enormous sums, since large numbers of cavalry had to be maintained and assembled in their cantonments before the opening of the campaign and the season for forage.

The infantry of standing armies underwent an almost total change as a result of tacticians' efforts to bring it to perfection. Before the War of the Spanish Succession half of the men in each battalion carried pikes and the other matchlocks, and they fought armed six deep. The pikes were used against cavalry, their muskets kept up a weak fire, and their matches often made them misfire or flash in the pan. These inconveniences brought about a change in weapons: pikes and matchlocks were discarded and replaced by fusils and bayonets, combining the formidable effect of fire and sword. With this increase in firepower the battalions step by step diminished their depth, which gave them a more extensive front. That military mechanic, the Prince of Anhalt, introduced iron ramrods and placed the ranks three deep.

The late king, by his infinite assiduity, introduced a wonderful order and discipline among his troops and a precision hitherto unknown in Europe in their movements and maneuvers. The Prussian battalion became a walking battery: the speed with which the Prussian could reload trebled the firepower and made him the equal of three adversaries. Other nations afterwards imitated the Prussians, but with less success.

Charles XII had introduced the custom of adding two cannon to each battalion. In Berlin cannon were cast of three, six, twelve, and twenty-four pounds—light enough to be worked by hand and advanced in battle with the battalion to which each belonged. All these new inventions transformed an army into a moving fortress, against which every approach was formidable and murderous.

The French in 1672 invented transportable copper pontoons. This easy way of constructing bridges rendered rivers useless as barriers. To the French also is due the art of attack and defense of fortresses—Vauban especially approached perfection in the art of fortification. . . .

This age has seen the revival of light-armed troops: the Austrian pandours, the French legions, the Prussian free battalion, and the hussars, originally from Hungary but imitated in all other armies, have replaced the Numidian and Parthian cavalry so famous in the Roman wars. Any uniform was unknown to the ancient military; and it is not a century since this practice was generally adopted.[16]

## THE COMPOSITION OF ARMIES

EXPERIENCE HAS SHOWN that the national troops of a state are always the most serviceable. . . . I agree with Machiavelli that a state is generally but ill served by mercenary troops, because they can never act with as much fidelity and courage as men who fight for their possessions and families. It is particularly dangerous for a prince to allow the people to languish in a state of inactivity and to grow soft and effeminate at a time when the fatigues of war harden and discipline their neighbors.

It has often been observed that a nation that recently emerged from a Civil War is far superior in valor to its neighbors, for in a Civil War all the people are soldiers. There is more room for merit and less for favor, and every man has more frequent opportunities to discover and improve his military talents.

There are some particular cases, however, that must be excepted from Machiavelli's general rule. If a country does not produce a sufficient number of men for raising a complete army and replacing the losses in war, mercenary troops are absolutely necessary for supplying the needs of the state. In this case, several expedients are found for removing the difficulties and dangers to which a state is exposed by employing mercenaries. The mercenaries are mixed with the native troops so as not to make a separate and independent body. Both are subject to the same discipline in order to make them equally faithful, and particular care is taken that the number of foreign troops does not exceed that of the national ones. . . .

Most European armies consist of national and mercenary troops. Those who inhabit cities or who till the soil are exempted from military service upon paying a certain tax for maintaining the soldiers who defend them. For this reason our armies for the most part are composed of the dregs of society —sluggards, rakes, debauchees, rioters, undutiful sons, and the like, who have as little attachment to their masters or concern about them as do foreigners. How different are these armies from those of the Romans, who conquered the world. Desertions, which are now so frequent in all armies, were unknown among the Romans. Those who fought for their families, their household gods, their fellow-citizens, and everything that was dear to them never betrayed so many interests by their cowardice and desertion. It is the security of the sovereign princes of Europe at present that their troops are so much alike that in this respect they have no advantage over one another. Only the Swedes are citizens, peasants, and soldiers at the same time but, on the other hand, when the Swedes march off to war there are too few inhabitants left at home to till the soil. Therefore their power is by no means formidable. They can execute nothing without ruining themselves in the long run, as well as their enemies.

¶ A King ought not to make war solely with foreign troops. If possible he should depend upon none but his own, and he should export rather than import auxiliaries. Prudence will teach him that he must put himself in a condition of fearing neither his enemies nor his friends. . . . Such powers as have no need of mixed or auxiliary troops ought certainly not to employ them, but as few European princes are in such a situation, I believe that they are in no danger from their auxiliaries as long as these do not outnumber their own troops. . . . As for the Swiss troops in the service of France . . . it is certain the French have owed many victories to their valor and conduct and reaped signal advantages from their service—so much so, in fact, that if the Swiss and Germans employed in the French infantry were to be dismissed, their army would be much less formidable than it is at present.[17]

OUR REGIMENTS are composed half of our own people and half of foreigners who have been enrolled for money. The latter have no particular attachment to our service and wait only for the first opportunity to desert. The question therefore is to prevent desertion.

The composition of my troops requires infinite attention on the part of those who command them. It is necessary always to make them observe the most exact discipline and to take great care for their welfare. It is also necessary that Prussian soldiers be better fed than nearly any other troops in Europe.

Some of our generals contend that a man is only a man, and that if the loss of one is made good the particular individual involved does not effect the whole. This may apply to other armies but it is not true of ours. If a well-trained soldier deserts and is replaced by another who is equally well-trained, then it is a matter of no consequence. But if a soldier who has been trained in the use of arms for two years in order to give him a certain degree of proficiency should desert and be replaced by a bad subject, or not be replaced at all, eventually the consequences will be injurious.

We have seen that through the negligence of officers in this particular, regiments have lost their reputation and have found themselves diminished by desertion. Such a loss weakens the army at a time when it is essential for it to be at full strength. You will lose your best forces if you do not give this matter the greatest attention, and you will not be in a position to make good your losses. Although Prussia is well populated, it is doubtful whether you will find many men with the stature of my soldiers, and even assuming that you could, does it follow that they could be drilled overnight?

An army is composed for the most part of idle and inactive men. Unless the general keeps a constant eye over them and forces them to perform their duty this machine, which is artificial and cannot be made perfect, soon will disintegrate, and in the final analysis only the concept of a disciplined army will remain.

It is therefore necessary to accustom the troops to work without letup. The experience of those who have not been deficient in this respect offers convincing proof that it is very necessary to keep the soldiers busy and that every day there are abuses to be corrected which pass unobserved by those who make no attempt to discover them.

This constant and painful attention may appear harsh to a general, but its consequences will bear good dividends. What advantage will he not gain with troops so brave, so smart, and so well disciplined? A general who would pass for a foolhardy person would only be acting by established rules with us. He can run any risk and undertake any enterprise that man is capable of executing. Besides, the soldiers will not allow a man to remain amongst them who is capable of any weakness; one would certainly not notice this in the other armies.

I have seen officers and common soldiers dangerously wounded who nevertheless would refuse to abandon their posts or fall to the rear to have their wounds dressed. With troops such as these one could conquer the entire world if the victories were not as fatal to oneself as to the enemies. For you can undertake anything with them provided you do not let them lack provisions. On the march you will outstrip the enemy by speed; if you attack the enemy in a wood you will force him from it; if you make your men climb a mountain you will disperse anyone who offers resistance and then the battle becomes only a massacre. If you send your cavalry into action they will charge through and demolish the enemy at sword's point.

But since it is not enough merely to have good troops, and since a general through ignorance, loses all of his advantages, I will speak [later] of the qualities of a general and give rules which in part I have experimented with at my own expense, and in part the great generals have given me.[18]

## THE CANTON SYSTEM

THE NUMBER OF INHABITANTS in the Prussian provinces does not exceed 4,500,000 souls. Deduct from this number 2,250,000 women, together with minors and old folks, and there remain 1,000,000 men capable of bearing arms. If we should want to form an army comprising native Prussians only, then we would have to draw 160,000 men from this million. That however would exceed every expectation, for as things stand at present all of the Prussian provinces together furnish only 70,000 soldiers, and even this is a high number to endure. It is much more difficult for the same cantons in wartime to be able to raise 25,000 additional men for the regiments and the powerful artillery train which has become necessary.

The formation of cantons originated with my father in 1733. This useful measure is wisely contrived. The sixty native Prussians in each company are disbanded for ten months out of the year and the funds thus saved can be used for recruiting, for the war chest [*Die Wartenbergsche Kasse*], and for the captains. These sixty Prussians come from the same region; many, in fact, know or are related to one another. Integrated with foreigners, they make an excellent unit. The cantons spur on competition and bravery, and relatives or friends are not apt to abandon each other in battle. Resident farmers and their future heirs are exempt from military service. Only the younger sons and servants must serve. The subprefects attend the draft and release everybody whose loss would be disadvantageous for the state.

¶ The cantons make the regiments immortal, since they perpetually replace their losses. They are the lifeblood of the state. If the rural population did not make the arid soil productive through their labor, then society and government would be ruined. One must guard these useful, hard-working people as his favorites, and in time of war one should draw recruits from his own land only if forced by dire necessity.

¶ How can one spare the cantons? Where are the necessary recruits to be found? In Saxony, which will always constitute a theater of war whenever we fight the Austrians, all able-bodied men will be drafted. The inspectors will hold reviews over their inspectorates so that accurate lists of those missing are at hand. The captains who let off one of the Saxons to be recruited in return for money will be severely punished. The enemy deserters will be enlisted and distributed in small groups so that there are never too many in the same regiment. Trained men will be taken from the garrison regiments and replaced by conscripted Saxons and deserters.

With strict compliance to all of these measures the entire army needs no more than four to five thousand recruits annually. This number is high, to be sure, but the fields still will not be depopulated. Also, recruiting officers can be sent to those German countries where recruiting is not forbidden. If worst comes to worst, then our cantons are our last resource.[19]

## THE PRUSSIAN INFANTRY

IT USED TO BE OUR CUSTOM to form regiments from the largest men possible. This was done for a reason, for in the early wars it was men and not cannon that decided the victory, and battalions of tall men advancing with the bayonet scattered the poorly assembled enemy troops—which could not compare in bodily height with ours—with the first attack. Now artillery has changed everything. A cannon ball knocks down a man six feet tall just as easily as one who is only five feet seven. Artillery decides everything, and infantry no longer do battle with naked steel.

Nevertheless one must be careful not to go from one extreme to the other. If a man of gigantic proportions no longer is of use to us, a man of average height still is, and I should like to see the old regiments maintain an average height of five feet six[20] and the new ones, five feet five. The first king had men seven and one-half feet tall and did not get excited about a soldier six feet eleven inches in height. But neither do I want men who are too small, for our soldiers have to drag with them a knapsack and sixty cartridges, a pretty considerable load, and if they are too small and weak they succumb to fatigue, the number of stragglers increases, and it no longer is possible to make a forced march. We have not yet attained the ideal height but we will soon if peace lasts, for then the population of the cantons will increase and there will be more recruits to choose from.

It is numbers that make the army awe-inspiring. At present [1768] I am increasing the infantry, and I would prefer many men five feet four inches in height rather than a smaller number five feet six inches tall. For if it is a question of occupying a position, it depends not so much upon the size as upon the number of men.

Even if the number is attained, however, the men still are worth nothing if they are undisciplined. An army, if one wishes to accomplish anything with it, must obey and be in good discipline, which in turn rests upon obedience and punctuality. Discipline begins with the generals and works down to the drummer boys. Its foundation is subordination: no subordinate has the right to contradict orders. If the commander orders, the others must obey. If the officers do not do their duty, then still less can the common soldier be expected to perform his: it is a chain in which no link can be missing.

Many soldiers can be governed only with sternness and occasionally with severity. If discipline fails to keep them in check they are apt to commit the crudest excesses. Since they greatly outnumber their superiors, they can be held in check only through fear. For this reason any contradiction will be severely punished and no quarter will be given those who raise their hand against noncommissioned officers, especially company officers. Theft, desertion, every violation of subordination, negligence on post, throwing away cartridges to avoid firing during musketry exercises, absence when ordered to report for duty—in brief, everything that works against sound practice, the service, and subordination is an offense to be punished severely.

The officers must not succumb to gambling or to the dissolute life, but must possess good manners and ambition, conduct themselves as honorable men, and be punctual in every assigned task. Above all they should not be satisfied with their present position in the army but should strive to advance themselves and to prepare for higher positions.

Everything that one can make of the soldiers consists in giving them an *esprit de corps*, or, in other words, in teaching them to place their regiment higher than all of the troops in the world. Since officers must necessarily lead them into the greatest dangers, the soldiers (since they cannot be influenced by ambition) should fear their officers more than all the dangers to which they are exposed. Otherwise nobody will be in a position to lead them to the attack against three hundred guns that are thundering against them. Good will can never induce the common soldier to stand up to such dangers: he will only do so through fear.

More than discipline and *esprit de corps*, however, is needed to make a good army. The army must also be quick, skilled, mobile, and able to execute the orders of the generals. Otherwise, even the commander's ability will be undermined by the ignorance of the troops and he will not be able to develop his art and resourcefulness. One must instruct the generals and staff officers, subalterns, and soldiers.

The instruction of the soldiers includes musketry, advances, and evolutions. Battles will be won through superior firepower. With the exception of attacks against fortifications, the infantry that can load the fastest will always defeat those who are slower to reload, as Rossbach, Liegnitz, and Torgau,[21] to mention only a few battles, clearly demonstrate. It is for this reason that I have been so insistent since the [Seven Years'] war that the infantry load quickly and the soldier become as skilled as possible. We are making steady progress, but we cannot slacken. The daily parades, both small and large, keep the soldier in practice. He learns to march forward without vacillating and breaking up the line. The fundamentals of drill are established daily during the *Wachtparade*, when the officers learn to select their objective point [*nehmen der Richtpunkte*], march in alignment, execute all of the important movements that can be done with troops, and to break off and advance— in a word, the officers learn here to do everything in detail that the army performs on a large scale. If these maneuvers are all accurately observed and practiced every day then the army will remain virtually undefeatable and always awe-inspiring, as long as it has a capable commander.

Inasmuch as one individual cannot supervise all of these details of regimental service I have appointed an inspector to look after each unit. These officers are responsible for the execution of instructions issued to the troops. They also are the instrument whereby equality of discipline is attained, so that one man is treated as another without undue mildness or severity. The inspectors report to me regarding the conduct of the officers, bring those to my attention who through bad behavior, negligence, and stupidity are courting dismissal, and recommend those who have earned distinction through their industry or talent. They inspect the regiments frequently, have them drill, improve their shortcomings, and hold the reviews if governmental duties prevent my traveling in the province myself. And finally, they preside over muster days [*Enrollierungen*] and see to it that the cantons will not be deceived by the captains, which in former days happened only too often.

Every year I review the regiments which are assembled in Potsdam, Berlin, Stargard, Magdeburg, and Silesia, whose troops constitute the core of the army, for it is a true proverb that states: "The master's eye makes the horse fat." The officer will be motivated by ambition, and nothing feeds ambition more than the sight of the ruler and all the princes setting good examples. If these regiments were not assembled and drilled under the scrutiny of their King so often, everyone would be apt to grow careless. They are accustomed to seeing their King at the head, and this custom should be maintained. Besides, all reprimands and punishments, all distinctions that the war leader bestows in front of the assembled troops constitute a spur for ambition and emulation. One man will act out of fear of punishment; the other is driven by the desire to earn reward.

Above all, you must bear in mind that the Prussian state is split up, that Brandenburg has no natural boundaries, and that we can maintain ourselves only so long as we have a good army. Then you will perceive that everything concerning the army must be an affair of honor with us, and that we dare not spare either worry or effort, but must lead the army by our good example in order to keep it at a high pitch of military efficiency.

Since the reviews occur in the spring, if the ground is in condition, one must limit himself to executing on a large scale what occurs on the parade ground in detail. Since the officers cannot possibly be trained at reviews and can learn only on terrain simulating war conditions, I assemble larger bodies of troops in the fall, after the harvest, for the benefit of the generals and officers only, rather than for the rank and file. There the officers learn to execute orders punctually and to exploit the terrain thoroughly. The generals learn to maneuver their brigades skillfully, the officers, to lead their battalions well. They are required to execute all kinds of attacks and retreats on all types of terrain and under varied warlike conditions.

If they are not instructed in this manner, the officers can commit the greatest mistakes without even knowing it. Through the ignorance of the officers and generals more than one battle already has been lost, more than one undertaking wrecked. One cannot emphasize strongly enough the need to impress upon the officers the rules of the art of war and to insist that these rules be followed. The art of war is so important for the state that it is astonishing how often it is neglected. And why? You cannot become a shoemaker without having apprenticed a long time and without having made shoes, but in other countries generals and colonels are promoted who have smelled powder only on the hunt! The general who has waged war only on the map will be greatly embarrassed when he must oppose the enemy. The only possible way to train those who have never participated in war is to have them lead troops on different kinds of terrain. Then they can sharpen their eye for ground and learn how to exploit its advantages and shortcomings, they are exercised in tactics and the different formations, they attain knowledge of all the advantages that can be drawn from the terrain and grow accustomed to use these in every situation as soon as they have to maneuver against the enemy.

## THE PRUSSIAN CAVALRY

My father left me poor cavalry. Almost no officer understood his trade. The riders were afraid of their horses, they almost never mounted them, and they could drill only on foot much like infantry. The heavy troopers and large horses made the cavalry so awkward that during the first Silesian war it was necessary to reorganize this arm completely.

We want no large men for the cavalry: five feet five inches to five feet seven is large enough for the cuirassiers and dragoons, and five feet two to five feet five will do for the hussars, provided that the men are strong and powerful and not sickly, too young, and too weak.

Large horses are completely useless. The cavalry horse must be between five feet one inch and five feet three inches tall—no Frisian horses, which are too heavy, but rather horses from Holstein and also the New Mark and East Prussia. Our dragoons have smaller horses still—five feet two inches. All dragoon

regiments form their third rank from Tartar horses and a few
are mounted completely with this breed, since they can be
used every day and hence, because they often encounter the
enemy, they become more accustomed to war. The hussar
horses come from the same land and are almost as good, for
nimble horses give a unit a great advantage over one mounted
on heavier horses. The rider can place more trust in his horse,
and the better mounted he is, the bolder he becomes.

What I have said of infantry discipline pertains also to the
cavalry and so I need not repeat it. But the instruction of the
two arms is basically different. Infantry drill covers weapons
and limbs; that of the cavalry is concerned with horsemanship
and the obedience of the horse. Both require unending pains.
In order for each man to ride like a stall-master the squadron
must receive the same instruction, man for man, horse for horse,
that is given throughout the army. If the machine is to run like
clockwork it becomes all the more necessary for the individual
parts to be made with the same care. How could even mounted
men defeat the enemy if they ride fainthearted and uneasy in
the saddle?

Once the individual horsemen are trained they are then
placed in rank and file and learn how to move in unison. They
must execute all evolutions briskly and above all attack with
impetuosity, without wavering and breaking formations and
directly against the point where the leader indicates. Horses
have four legs and therefore must possess the advantage of
swifter movement. For with the cavalry attack it is not the size
of the horse but the impetuosity of the charge that turns the
scale.

All that can be accomplished in the spring is to train horse
and rider and the entire regiment in the great attacks and the
different formations and maneuvers with the advanced- and
rear-guards designed to cover the army and the retreats, and
to make sure that each drill becomes purely mechanical except
for those men schooled in patrol rides, where independent
thinking becomes indispensable. Flankers and patrol riders therefore will also be especially selected and trained.

I have instituted cavalry inspectors on the same basis as those with the infantry in order to supervise the uniform training of regiments, inspect the troops often, and see to it that my instructions are carried out. There are, to be sure, capable generals and regimental commanders who are brave and possess other good qualities but who are at the same time unable to uphold order, and it is just as difficult to find four severe inspectors as it is to find as many good commanders.

In many instances the dragoons must dismount and fight on foot if the infantry is not in position. Therefore they learn to attack on foot just like the infantry. Since this is required of them only in an emergency, however, one must not insist upon great perfection in the movements and the attack. Their main service is always on horseback. The hussars have carbines which in many cases have accomplished good service where it was a matter of driving enemy hussars away from woods or villages where they had established themselves.

I have always reviewed the cavalry myself and drilled them so that they realize that the exercises they must perform emanate from me. In this way I hope also to inspire and encourage those motivated by ambition, men who perform their work only as day laborers. First I have them perform evolutions, movements, and attack formations that constitute the foundation for all war maneuvers. Then I have them execute a few formations or dispositions that are encountered every day in the field and comprise, so to speak, the bread-and-butter tactics in the presence of the enemy.

The Silesian regiments have the advantage of moving into maneuvers after planting time. Those regiments about Potsdam and Magdeburg that are assembled in the fall have the additional advantage that each company represents a squadron. Therefore, the officers, even before they are given a larger command, learn their trade and prepare themselves for future advancement. Here they learn how to judge the terrain and to keep track of all enemy movements in order to capitalize upon their mistakes. Our hussar officers excel in all these matters: they have an eye for terrain, they are self-confident, and they are eminently experienced. Our dragoon officers have performed creditably in recent campaigns, largely because they have met the enemy in battle more often than the rest of the cavalry. The cuirassier officers are still comparatively immobile, for with their heavy horses I cannot use them in detachments and cannot utilize them for every type of duty.

## THE PRUSSIAN ARTILLERY

Since it has become the fashion to fill the field camps with guns and to make lavish use of artillery, we too cannot refrain from keeping this arm strong. My father had only a single battalion of field artillery. I doubled it in 1742, when the army was enlarged, and at that time I believed that I had enough. In the last war the artillery was increased to six battalions and even that still is not too much, although we have, in addition, two garrison battalions for the fortresses.

To keep up the artillery, however, would be entirely pointless if one did not at the same time carefully drill and strictly supervise it. This is why I have located it at Berlin, where it is drilled each spring in firing and in all duties connected with the service. These exercises are divided into two categories: service in the field and siege warfare. In the open field the artillerymen are required to move the guns themselves when the army advances, to keep the battalion distance, to aim as accurately as possible, and to fire rapidly. In defensive positions the gunners must measure the field of fire so that they know the distance they must shoot in an arc, straight ahead, or with case shot.*

In sieges the main task of the gunners is to overcome the fortress artillery. Experience has taught us that this is more quickly and reliably accomplished if three guns concentrate their fire against the same embrasure. The training of bombardiers* also depends upon knowing the distances that can be reached with the minimum or maximum powder charges, but it is based especially on the laying out of mortar batteries.

These must be so placed that they bring the same point under bombardment with a crossfire. Despite all the trouble that is taken to perfect the art of firing, however, complete accuracy will never be attained: too much depends upon atmospheric conditions and wind direction. Still, for all that, well-trained gunners always have an advantage over those who are poorly drilled.

Since the last war the artillery has become a real drain on the national economy. Counting the last 300,000 talers that I paid in June,[22] we have spent a total of 1,450,000 on this arm. The amount seems enormous, but it must be remembered that I have one hundred cannon of different caliber in reserve for the field army, that I have armed Silberberg,[23] that I have organized an entire new siege train, and that the fortresses are supplied with spare carriages, planks, and all necessary equipment for a siege. Add to this the thousands of bombs and cannon balls that have been consumed in war and must be replaced.

No matter how large these expenditures, it is still necessary to add a new expense no less essential, namely the molding of seventy ten-pounder howitzers according to a new invention that will fire grenades 4,000 feet. These guns will play a prominent role in attacking defensive positions or mountain heights where ordinary cannon can accomplish nothing.

The general of artillery also supervises the management of the powder mills. Heretofore we have produced only 4,000 hundredweight of powder annually. In 1769 this number will increase to 5,000, since I have added 20,000 talers to the previous budget of 60,000. We need 6,000 hundredweight, which we can deliver in 1770 if I further increase the state of powder mills by 19,000 talers. I do not mention here the provisions in the armories, since all the details will be found in my strongbox and because these provisions must accumulate from year to year. For the instruction of my successor, however, I must remark that we have consumed during the recent wars 12,000 hundredweight of powder in each campaign. . . .

## THE PRUSSIAN QUARTERMASTERS AND ENGINEERS

Tactics becomes a useless art if it is not adapted to the terrain. A correct knowledge of the terrain gives one amazing resources in time of adversity. On this foundation rests true success, and most of the generals who lunge to a misfortune must attribute this solely to the neglect of a rule or even to their ignorance. The land is to the soldier what a chessboard is to a chess player who wants to make moves with his pawns, castles, and so forth.

The Greeks gave the young citizens who dedicated themselves to the trade of weapons instruction in tactics, geometry, and military geography. I have perceived how useful such an arrangement is in Prussia and have imitated it. I have young, talented officers do work under my supervision on everything relating to castrametation, fortification, and the dispositions for war operations. . . . But the young men, with their great frivolity and inclination for leading a dissolute life, make no great progress. They must become employed with the different armies for camp and march and be assigned to the detachment commanders in order to seek out positions and determine the march of their columns. Here they learn all possible dispositions and work always on a large scale. In time, distinguished generals must emerge from this group if they do not fall by the wayside through their unfortunate inclination for dissolution.

Engineer officers can become employed in two ways. A few have talent for the art of field fortifications, and these can be distributed among the army. Others are limited to the attack and defense of fortified places: these must be allotted and drawn near to the fortresses when a siege is intended.

A great fault of our infantry officers is their slight interest in fortification and their grossest ignorance of terrain and how to take advantage of it. They drill their men well, to be sure, and that also is very necessary and essential, but they neglect that knowledge that officers such as they cannot spare. Thanks to the fortification schools that I have established in all the provinces,[24] our young officers will become superior to their predecessors. When they have reached the highest positions, the effects of much better training will be noticed.

## FORTRESSES

Most of my fortresses are in Silesia. I have had them strengthened now without regard to cost, for it is better to have no fortresses at all than to have poor ones. My system places the defense of works in the covered way* and in the depth of the ditches, dry as well as wet, and I take every possible precaution to make a surprise attack impossible. The defense of the covered ways depends essentially on mines and a few advanced works that keep the enemy at a distance and force him to besiege the fort before he can approach the glacis.

Schweidnitz will be ready next year [1769]. Kosel is finished already. Work will be done next year on Silberberg, Neisse, and also Breslau: I hope to have all three fortresses ready by 1770. Meanwhile a number of casemates are still necessary, which I will have erected if I am still alive. As soon as Silberberg is constructed the old castle of Glatz must be improved. The old, delapidated buildings must be torn down, good casemates laid out, and the plan of Lieutenant Pinto[25] must be partially put into effect. Then there remains only the ditches of Glogau to cover and deepen and the Galgenfort to be made higher.

With these fortresses completely built the occupation of Silesia is assured. Then it is merely a question of a good choice of officers to whom one can entrust their defense, but that is more difficult than one thinks.

The fortress of Silberberg has been laid out in order to have a free entry into the duchy of Glatz and to be able to relieve the Glatz fortress in the event the enemy besieges it. Silberberg also protects and covers the left flank of the Landshut camps, one of the most important for the protection of

Lower Silesia. The campaigns of the Austrians in the years 1757[26] and 1760 have shown the importance of the fortification of Breslau. The city must, at the very least, be sufficiently fortified to hold off the enemy for two months, which is enough to enable you to dispatch help.

I have two fortresses in Pomerania and one, just as important, in Neumark. When the Russians fought us only Kolberg retarded their advance very long. Equally good is Kustrin. This fortress is protected through its swamps. But Kolberg must be improved: I have had the plan drawn up, along with the harbor fortifications, and, God willing, the work will be finished in 1770.

Also Stettin, the capital of Pomerania, requires some precautions. The most important works are: deepening the ditches and drawing together all outlying works, as well as the mine galleries in the glacis, which still are entirely lacking. The fortification of Damm, which serves as a bridgehead for the right bank of the Oder, is good. To be sure it is only an earthenwork, but the surrounding swamp makes it unapproachable.

Of Spandau only a word. It is in truth merely a hole and appears more as a fortified war magazine than a fortress. If war and enemy invasions are to be feared, then a good fortress must be planned where the ordnance works are situated.

The most important of all our fortresses is Magdeburg, the place of refuge of the royal family and the last prop of the state. Although the city is rather strongly fortified, two different steps still seem to me to be desirable: connecting the city fortifications with Fort Bergen, and placing mine galleries in the glacis. The fortification of Sudenburg is of value only until an enemy should open communication trenches. I would not advise placing troops there in case the enemy seriously besieges the place. Meanwhile, the forces that undertake such a difficult siege must bear two things in mind—the vast extension of lines of circumvallation that Magdeburg demands, and the completely flat and open environs that would give us an almost certain victory when our army advances to its relief.[27]

## THE PRICE OF SURVIVAL: THE PRUSSIAN ARMY
## AFTER THE SEVEN YEARS' WAR

SEVEN CAMPAIGNS, during which seventeen pitched battles
and almost as many minor but no less bloody combats had been
fought, three sieges undertaken by the army and five sustained,
(without enumerating attacks on the enemy winter quarters
and other military expeditions of a similar nature) had so far
ruined the army that a great part of the best officers and veteran
soldiers had perished in the field. To give some idea of this we
need only recollect that winning the battle of Prague alone
cost 20,000 men. Let us add to the calculation that we had
40,000 Austrian prisoners and that Austria had nearly as many
of our own, among whom more than three hundred officers
must be enumerated; that the hospitals were full of the wounded,
and that seldom could more than one hundred men be found
in the foot regiments who had served at the start of the war.

Above 1,500 officers had fallen in the different actions, which
greatly diminished the number of nobility; and those of that
class who remained in the country were either old men or
children incapable of serving. The lack of gentlemen and the
numerous vacancies left in all the regiments forced us to appoint
officers who were not of noble birth. There were some battalions in which no more than eight officers remained, the others
being dead, prisoners, or wounded. It may easily be concluded
that under such afflicting circumstances, the old corps themselves were destitute of order, discipline, and exactitude and
consequently were destitute of energy.

Such was the condition of the army when it returned to its
former quarters after the Peace of Hubertusburg [1763]. At
that time the regiments contained more natives than foreigners.
The companies were each 162 strong, forty of whom were
dismissed so that they could be used in the cultivation of the
earth. The free battalions served to complete the garrison regiments from which native soldiers were discharged in like num-

ber when they obtained more than the complement of recruits. One hundred and fifty men were dismissed from each cavalry regiment, four hundred from each hussar regiment, and thus the provinces gained by the reform 30,780 farmers of whom they stood in need. Nor was this all. The number of natives in the regiments formerly had been discretionary: now it was fixed at 720 men for each regiment, with the remainder to complete the companies being raised abroad.

The soldiers from the cantons had permission to marry without the consent of their captains. Few of them remained in a state of celibacy; the majority were better pleased to contribute to the increase of population. The results of these good regulations corresponded to the expectations of the government, and in the year 1773 the number of men enrolled considerably surpassed that in the year 1756.

In former times the captains had recruited their companies themselves with the money they drew from the six months' pay, a method that had given rise to great abuses. The officers enlisted men by force in order to save the money; everybody complained about the practice, and no prince would allow such violence to be committed upon his territories. The mode of this economy therefore was changed, and only General Wartenberg was allowed to receive the six months' pay, from which thirty crowns per month were deducted for the use of the captains, exclusive of their pay. The surplus was used as enlisting money, which annually produced from 7,000 to 8,000 soldiers raised in foreign states who, accompanied by their wives and children, formed a military colony of about 10,000 people.

¶ Nothing could have been more difficult than the reestablishment of order and discipline in the infantry, which had been so exceedingly degraded. Severity was necessary to render the soldier obedient, exercise to make him active, and long habit to teach him to load and fire his piece four times per minute, to march in line without fluctuation, and in fine, to be able to perform all the maneuvers that might be required of him in the various operations of war.

Yet when the soldier had accomplished all this it was still more difficult to train the young officers and to impart that degree of understanding necessary for their profession. In order to give them practice in the different troop movements one had them maneuver in the vicinity of their garrisons. They had to practice the different deployments, attacks on the plain, attacks against fortified positions and towns, the movements with the advance and rear guard, the formation of squares, so that they learned to attack as well as to defend themselves. In this manner they spent the entire summer, each day repeating a part of their lesson. In order to make these drills uniform, the troops were assembled twice a year, once in the spring and again in the fall, at which times they conducted only exercises similar to what they would encounter in the field—attacking and defending fortified positions, foraging, making war marches of all kinds, and waging mock battles. . . .

It must not be imagined, however, that the maneuvers immediately after the peace were of the best kind. Time must be allowed for practical tactics to become habitual and easily executed by the troops. That desired precision did not begin to emerge until 1770, from which time the army, assuming a new face, might have been led by the commander with great confidence. . . .

To acquire such a degree of perfection, in which the welfare of the state was so much interested, the officer corps was weeded of all persons of low birth. This class of people was placed in garrison regiments, where they at least equalled their predecessors who, being too infirm for service, had been placed on the pension list. And because Prussia did not furnish a sufficient number of gentlemen to supply the needs of the army, foreigners were engaged from Saxony, Mecklenburg, or the Empire, among whom some good officers were obtained. It is more necessary than one might think to pay such attention to the choice of officers, because as a general rule the nobility possess honor. Of course it must be conceded that sometimes merit and ability are encountered in persons of low birth, although such incidents are rare, and when men of this description are found they ought to be cherished. In general, however, the nobility have no means of obtaining distinction save by the sword. If they lose their honor they can not find refuge, not even in their paternal mansions. However, a man of mean birth, after having been guilty of base actions, returns to his father's occupation without blushing or regarding himself dishonored. . . .

¶ The attention which was paid to bring the field regiments of infantry to perfection did not prevent similar care being given to the troops destined to serve in garrison. Men who defend towns may render service as essential as those who win victories. These regiments were purged of all suspicious persons among the officers as well as the soldiers; they were disciplined in the same manner as the field regiments, and whenever the King reviewed his troops in the provinces the garrison regiments participated with equal distinction. The men in the garrison were inferior in height to the field infantry, but there was none among them who stood less than five feet three. Although they did not load with the same speed as the regular infantry, there was not a general in the year 1773 who would not gladly have had them in his brigade.

The cavalry had by no means sustained the same proportionate losses as the infantry, for the horse had been victorious on all occasions, so that the veteran soldier and the veteran officers were nearly alike preserved. Whenever war drags on, it is always the infantry that suffers, and on the contrary, the cavalry by the same process acquires perfection. Particular care was taken to supply this respectable corps with the best horses that could be obtained.

However, reproaches were due to some of the Prussian cavalry generals who, while leading detachments, had caused the infantry to maneuver clumsily. Similar errors might also be imputed to some of the infantry officers who employed their cavalry with an equal lack of discernment. That such gross mistakes might be prevented in the future, the King wrote a work on tactics and castrametation that contained general rules both for offensive and defensive warfare. . . .[28] This methodical work, full of self-evident precepts that had been confirmed by the experience of all past wars, was issued to the inspectors who in turn gave it to be read by the generals, as well as by the commanders of infantry battalions and cavalry regiments. With the exception of these copies, however, the greatest attention was paid to prevent it from becoming a matter of public knowledge. The treatise bore better fruit than might have been expected; it enlarged the understanding of the officers concerning maneuvers, the meaning of which they did not previously comprehend. Their intelligence made very visible progress, and as success in war principally depends on the dispositions that are executed, and as the greater number of able generals in an army assures the greater success, there was reason to believe that, after so much trouble had been taken to instruct the officers, orders would be exactly followed and generals would not commit faults great enough to cause the loss of a battle.

According to the custom established during the last war, the artillery has become a principal part of the army. The number of field pieces had been so prodigiously augmented that the practice had degenerated into abuse. Yet, in order to avoid any disadvantage, it was necessary to possess as many guns as the enemy, and for this purpose the field pieces began to be restored to a proper state. . . . The fortresses were provided with timber and stakes for the use of batteries, and as it was determined to have an artillery reserve for the army, 868 additional field pieces were cast. All of these various articles, with an increase of 60,000 hundredweight of powder, were sent to the arsenals about the end of 1777. The disbursements for the artillery and the repair of its carriages and train amounted to 1,960,000 crowns. The sum was great, but the expense was necessary. At the commencement of the war in 1756, Prussia had only two battalions for its artillery train. This number, being very inferior to that of the foe, was increased to six battalions, each of 900 men, besides the companies that were detached and distributed through the various fortresses. After the peace the corps remained on its former establishment and large barracks were constructed at Berlin so that the artillery might always be assembled and therefore might be better and more uniformly disciplined.

¶ The army had made many campaigns, but the general headquarters had often been in need of good quartermasters. The king desired to form such a corps and he selected twelve officers who already possessed some knowledge of fortification, in order to instruct them himself. They were taught to lay down plans, make out situations for the corps, fortify villages, intrench heights . . . indicate the marches of columns and especially to examine and sound the depths of marshes and streams in person. This insured that no error of negligence might be committed and that no fordable stream nor a marsh which the infantry could cross without wetting its ankles would be selected to anchor the flank of an army. Errors like these are of great consequence, for if it had not been for such the French would not have lost the battle of Malplaquet nor the Austrians that of Leuthen.

The education of young men of quality who devote themselves to arms is a subject that merits the utmost attention. They may be trained from their youth to the exercise of their destined profession, and by good instruction their abilities may be quickened, like the ripening of fruit which is but the better for being premature. During the last war the education of the cadet corps had been so degenerate that the youth who were sent from this corps could scarcely read and write. In order to chop out the root of this evil the King placed General Buddenbrock at the head of this institution; he was beyond doubt the most capable man in the kingdom for this office. Good teachers were selected at the same time, and their number was increased proportionally as the number of students grew.

· In order that the young nobility of Pomerania might no longer be in want of education when their parents were too poor to afford the fees themselves, the King instituted an academy in the town of Stolpe, where fifty-six boys of condition were maintained, clothed, and taught at his expense. After having acquired the first elements of knowledge and having finished their philological and grammatical studies, they were entered among the corps of cadets, where their education was completed. They were instructed principally in history, geography, logic, mathematics, and the art of fortification—all subjects with which an officer ought to be acquainted.

At the same time an academy was formed for the higher education of the most promising cadets. The king regulated the forms of this academy himself, and wrote the *Instruction for the Academy of Nobles in Berlin* [1765], which presented the course of studies and the education of those who attended. The most able professors in Europe were recruited, and fifteen young gentlemen were educated there under the tutoring of five governors. Their whole education tended to development of their judgment. The academy prospered and since has furnished useful subjects who have been placed in the army.

¶ General Wartenberg, who directed the military economy, was as active in his department as the other officers were in theirs. He took advantage of peace to prepare for war. In 1777, 140,000 new muskets had been fabricated at Spandau; a complete set of swords for the cavalry had been made, as well as bandoleers,* saddles, bridles, girdles, kettles, pickaxes, hatchets, and a supply of tents for the whole army. These immense stores were deposited in the two large buildings called the army wardrobes, except for the muskets, which were arranged in the arsenal.

In addition to all this, the sum of three millions had been set apart to remount the cavalry in time of war and to replace the uniforms that might be lost in battle. Another sum was destined to meet the expenses for an increase of twenty-two battalions. . . . Two military magazines were formed, one at Magdeburg and the other in the fortresses of Silesia, each containing 840,000 bushels of grain to maintain two armies of 70,000 men for the space of a year. The first was destined for troops that might act toward Bohemia or Moravia, and the second for those operating on the side of Saxony or Bohemia. The value of these magazines was estimated at 1,700,000 crowns. They were in part depleted during the three years of dearth . . . but in 1775 they were again completed and restored to their former state. . . .

But the magazines of General Wartenberg and the great subsistence depots at Magdeburg and in Silesia were not enough to enable the army to enter the field with the necessary promptness. One of the most difficult tasks was to find and collect enough horses to put such a vast machine in motion. The proliferation of artillery required an immense number of horses to transport the guns; still more were necessary for the baggage, tents, officers, and provisions. The total was estimated at 60,000.

After the peace the army had been placed on an establishment of 151,000 men. The troubles that arose in Poland, arousing fear of a new war,[29] persuaded the King in 1768 to add forty men to each company in twelve infantry regiments. To house these levies it was necessary to build barracks. . . . The hussars and troops of Bosnia, formerly amounting to only 1,100 men, were increased to 1,400; a battalion of one thousand men was levied . . . for the defense of Silberberg. These different increases brought the peace establishment of the army up to 161,000, where it has remained.

Such efforts were necessary. Circumstances made it a duty to prepare for all eventualities. During the course of the year 1771, while negotiations were carried on with the greatest warmth . . .[30] it was resolved that all cavalry should be remounted and that the number should be augmented. Eight thousand horses were purchased at one time, causing rumors to spread soon after throughout Europe, which persuaded the court of Vienna that the Prussian King was determined to support his ally, the Empress of Russia, with his whole power.

The agreement of the three courts caused the partition of Poland. . . .[31] Considered from a military point of view this acquisition was of great importance, for it joined Pomerania to Prussia Royal. That the King was forced to abandon all the provinces that were separated or too distant from the bulk of his domains may have been observed in reading the history of the last war. These were the provinces on the Lower Rhine, those of Westphalia, and especially Prussia Royal. The last was found not only separated but cut off from Pomerania and the New Mark by a deep and very wide river. In order to support Prussia Royal, or East Prussia, it was essential to be master of the Vistula, and after the dismemberment of Poland the King was able to build fortresses on the banks of that river and to secure crossings as he thought proper. Thus he not only could defend the kingdom against its enemies but, should misfortune strike, he could use the Vistula and the Netze as good barriers to prevent the enemy from penetrating either into Silesia, Pomerania, or the New Mark.

Considered from another point of view, this acquisition provided the means of augmenting the army considerably. The peace establishment was increased to 186,000 men, and it was determined that by adding free battalions and other similar corps that its number in wartime should be 218,000. . . . In 1773 the army consisted of 141 infantry battalions, 63 cuirassier squadrons, 70 dragoon squadrons, 100 hussar squadrons, not counting the field artillery, which comprised 9,600 gunners and bombardiers, 1,200 fortress artillerymen, and 36 garrison battalions.

¶ The extraordinary expenses of the army for the duration of a campaign were calculated and, to avoid error, an estimate was made based on the most expensive campaign of the last war, during which the most bloody battles had been fought— the campaign of 1757. It is better in this kind of evaluation to increase rather than to diminish the amount, because there is no evil in a surplus but great risk in deficiency.[32]

NOTES: CHAPTER III

1. Elector of Brandenburg, 1608-19. The editor is indebted to those who compiled *Die Werke Friedrichs des Grossen* for identifying many of the names that appear in Frederick's history of the Prussian army.

2. Frederick uses the word *régence* instead of *règne*, or reign, for this was the term for the municipal or local administration in Germany. Properly speaking, none of the Electors of Brandenburg could reign before Emperor Leopold I recognized the Elector Frederick III of Brandenburg as Frederick I, King *in* Prussia, in January 1701. France recognized the kingdom of Prussia in the Treaty of Utrecht in 1713, which made it possible for Frederick's successors to claim the title "King *of* Prussia," and hence to rule.

3. Count Adam von Schwartzenberg, chief minister of the Elector of Brandenburg and commander of the army. His government has been likened to the military dictatorship of Wallenstein during the Thirty Years' War. See Hajo Holborn, *A History of Modern Germany 1648-1840* (New York, 1964), pp. 53-54.

4. The names and numbers of effectives for the various regiments in the Prussian service have been deleted: only the total for each arm is given.

5. In contrast to full armor, which has a closed helmet and a complete suit of mail, half-armor consists of an open-crested helmet, breast- and back-piece. *Die Werke Friedrichs des Grossen* (Berlin, 1913), I, 176n.

6. Count George Frederick von Waldeck.

7. Field Marshal Otto Christof Sparr (1605-68) commanded the Prussian army in the absence of the King during the war of 1655-60, and acted as chief of staff when Frederick William took the field himself. Holborn, *History of Modern Germany*, p. 65.

8. Joachim Ernest von Grumkow became commissary general for war in December, 1679.

9. George Derflinger, a Protestant and an Austrian by birth, was lured from the Swedish to the Prussian service by the Great Elector and elevated to the supreme command when Field Marshal Sparr died in 1668. John George, Prince of Anhalt, was an influential figure at court as well as a successful soldier: he was Frederick William's brother-in-law.

10. Frederick uses the term *musket,* which is probably an abridgement of "match-jusket" (*Lunten-Muskete*). See Hans Delbrück, *Ges-*

*chichte der Kriegskunst im Rahmen der politischen Geschichte* (Berlin, 1920), IV, 305. The fusil was also known as the "firelock."

11. Prince Leopold I of Anhalt-Dessau, (1676-1747) known to many as "the Old Dessauer," fought at Höchstädt (1703, 1704), Blenheim (1704), Cassano (1705), Turin (1706), and Malplaquet (1709). He also played a conspicuous part in the war against Charles XII in 1715.

12. Sébastien le Prestre, Marquis de Vauban (1633-1707), Louis XIV's great military engineer, had devised systems of fortification and siegecraft that still dominated the field in Frederick the Great's day. His great Dutch counterpart, Baron Menno van Coehorn (1641-1704), is probably best remembered for his invention of the trench-mortar that bears his name. Major General Lüdecke-Ernest von Schöning entered the service of the Elector of Saxony after the Rhine campaign of 1692. Jean de Bodt, a Frenchman, joined the Prussian army in 1700.

13. Lieutenant General Count Albert Konrad Finck von Finckenstein was one of two military men later selected to direct the education of the young Frederick, then age six. See Robert Ergang, *The Potsdam Führer: Frederick William I, Father of Prussian Militarism* (New York, 1941), p. 216.

14. *Groschen:* a small silver coin worth slightly more than a penny.

15. Frederick, "Du militaire depuis son institution jusqu'à la fin du règne de Frédéric-Guillaume," *Oeuvres de Frédéric le grand* (Berlin, 1846-56), I, 176-95. This portion of the History of Brandenburg is not included in the original edition of *Mémoires pour servir à l'histoire de la Maison de Brandebourg*, published in 1751.

16. Frederick, *The History of My Own Times*, trans. Thomas Holcroft (London, 1789), I, 70-74.

17. Frederick, *Anti-Machiavel: or, an Examination of Machiavel's Prince. With Notes Historical and Political* (London, 1741), pp. 140-51.

18. Frederick, *Instruction militaire du Roi de Prusse pour ses généraux.* Traduite de l'Allemand par Monsieur Faesch, Lieutenant-Colonel dans les Troupes Saxonnes ([Frankfurt], 1761), pp. 1-3, 6-9 [*Instruction militaire*].

19. Frederick, "Das militärische Testament von 1768," *Die Werke Friedrichs des Grossen* (Berlin, 1913), VI, 225-27.

20. "Five feet six" is assumed, since the only unit of measurement that Frederick mentions specifically is inch (*zoll*). Quite possibly the omission can be attributed to whoever translated the Military Testament from the original French into German.

21. For Frederick's account of the battles of Rossbach and Torgau, see below, chapter VI.

22. This was written in November, 1768.

23. See below, p. 87.

24. Courses of instruction in fortification and geography were offered to officers during the four winter months at the places of inspection, beginning in 1763. *Werke*, VI, 242n.

25. Count Ignaz Pinto, major and quartermaster. *Ibid.*, p. 243n.

26. See below, chapter VI.

27. *Testament von 1768*, pp. 225-36, 237-40, 242-44.

28. Most of this treatise on castrametation is reprinted below, chapter VII.

29. In October, 1763, the King of Poland died, and Catherine the Great of Russia sought Frederick's support in manipulating the election of Stanislaus Poniatowski as his successor. This action blocked the election of an Austrian prince and provoked a local war between Russia and the Greek Orthodox Catholics, on the one hand, and the Confederates, a Roman Catholic, anti-Russian association backed by France and Austria, on the other. When the Turks jumped in against Russia in support of Polish "liberties" (the Russians, be it noted, claimed to be fighting on behalf of "religious toleration"), the civil war threatened to expand into a renewal of the European war.

30. These were the negotiations among Austria, Russia, and Prussia leading to the first partition of Poland.

31. The first partition of Poland (1772) Prussia acquired West Prussia, about 16,000 square miles, except for Danzig and Thorn, which remained Polish.

32. Frederick, "Memoirs after the Peace: Chapter III: Of the Military," *Posthumous Works of Frederick II, King of Prussia*, trans. Thomas Holcroft (London, 1789), IV, 145-67.

# IV

# The Army on Campaign

No understanding of eighteenth-century warfare is possible without some knowledge of the problems involved in feeding and moving armies. Frederick wrote a special treatise on the subject, "Des marches d'armée, et de ce qu'il faut observer à cet égard," the most important sections of which are reproduced below, along with observations from his other military writings to illustrate how the army lived in camp and in the field.

*THE WARS* I have conducted have provided the opportunity for deep reflection about the principles of the great art that has raised or destroyed so many kingdoms. . . . I have therefore considered it necessary to pass along my observations to you. After me, you have the greatest interest in the command; to you, by this time, an indication of my thoughts must suffice; finally, you in my absence have to act according to my principles.

In this work I have blended my own observations with those I found in the writings of the greatest generals, and the resulting synthesis I have used for the training of our troops.

I write only for my officers. I speak only of that which is applicable for the Prussian service, and I have no other enemy in mind than our neighbors [the Austrians]—the two words unfortunately have come to mean the same thing. I hope that my generals will become more convinced through reading this work than through anything that I could say to them orally, and that they recognize that the discipline of our army is the foundation for the fame and maintenance of our state. If they have this point of view, then they will be more diligent about maintaining on every occasion the regulations among the troops, in full force and vigor, so that it cannot be said of us that we let the weapon of our fame become blunt in our hands. . . .

With all of the following observations I am assuming that my rules for the army are virtually the catechism of my officers, and in this work I treat only that which concerns the army commander and is the greatest and most difficult in the art of war.[1]

## WHAT MUST BE OBSERVED FOR THE MARCHES OF AN ARMY

YOU WISH TO KNOW what principles must be followed to regulate properly the marches of armies. This is an extensive subject and one that consequently requires knowledge of an infinite number of details, depending upon the objective of the march, the nature of the country where war is waged, the relative position of the two armies, and the season when the operations are undertaken. There are marches by cantonments,* marches by columns, night marches, day marches, movements of the entire army, or movements of detached corps. Each situation requires different considerations.

The essential thing for the proper regulation of marches is to have as extensive and accurate knowledge of the country as possible, because the clever man, the skillful warrior, makes his dispositions according to the terrain. He must adapt his dispositions to the locale, because the terrain will never be bent to any dispositions unsuited to it. This knowledge therefore is the basis of everything that one can undertake in war: without it, chance decides everything. . . .

### MARCHES BY CANTONMENTS

After war is declared between belligerent powers each assembles its troops into armies, and this union is made by marches of cantonments. Troops that move after a long rest are ruined if required to make too difficult marches at first. In the initial days they must cover at most only about fifteen miles.[2] Form the columns from troops of the different provinces and have them march on as broad a front as possible so that each battalion or regiment can have its own village or small town in which to bed down for the night. You must know the size of the villages in order to billet the troops according to the individual houses. If these marches occur in the spring or before the harvest, the soldiers can be billeted in barns, in which case a modest size village can contain a battalion without any difficulty. After three days on the march one day of rest must be taken.

As soon as you enter enemy country you must form an advance guard that camps and precedes the army by a day's march, in order to send back news about everything and, in the event the enemy is assembled, to give you time to reunite your forces. If you are far from the enemy, you can continue to be cantoned, but you must draw the troops closer together and canton them by lines and in order of battle. When you are within three days' march from the enemy you must camp according to the rules and march in the accustomed order.

You take too great a risk in separating your forces. The enemy could capitalize on this negligence, fall on your troops, seize your quarters, and perhaps, if he acts energetically, defeat you in detail and from the beginning of the campaign force you to take flight ignominiously. Thus you would lose your affairs entirely.

## WHAT MUST BE OBSERVED IN MARCHES MADE IN ADVANCE OF THE ARMY

The general must have a fixed plan of his operations. He will therefore pick an advantageous spot where he wishes to advance to make his camp. It is necessary then to know all the roads in order to regulate the columns. The number of columns should never exceed the number of roads leading to the new camp, because you create confusion and scarcely save time whenever one column is forced to leave a road and crowd the tail of another.

Avoid especially marching through villages; no column should pass there unless marshes absolutely prevent you from taking other roads, or unless the bridges that you must cross are to be found there. If it is level country the army will be able to march in eight columns, two of cavalry on the wings and six of infantry in the center.

The army must always be preceded by a considerable advance guard, which is stronger in cavalry if the terrain is smooth, and comprised predominantly of infantry if the ground is rugged. This advance guard must precede the army by a mile or two so that it can notify it of everything that goes on, and investigate and clear the terrain through which the columns must pass.

The baggage must be distributed equally behind the six infantry columns, covered by the rear guard following the cavalry columns and by a body of troops left behind to follow the equipment.

Such are the ordinary rules that are generally followed in the great movements of armies.

Marches made in the vicinity of the enemy are the most difficult and demand the most precaution because, in assuming that an active opponent should wish to take advantage of your decampment,* it is necessary to foresee everything so as not to be beaten on the march. . . .

### FLANK MARCHES

Before undertaking a march by either enemy flank you must send officers of the quartermaster's corps with small patrols to reconnoiter the places and roads as well as the camp that you wish to occupy. This will help to determine the number of columns you will use and especially the posts that you will have occupied on the march, assuming that the enemy moves to attack your army. It is on these elements, very accurately detailed, that the disposition must be made.

You will send the heavy baggage to the rear, ten miles behind the camp that you will want to take. This baggage must march in as many columns as the terrain will permit. Let us assume, now, that you should want to occupy a position toward the enemy's right.

On the evening before the march, just as soon as it is dark, you must send detachments to occupy the most important places —posts that could be taken on the march in the event you are attacked. These detachments must be formed there according to the rules, and the places should be abandoned only when the army has passed by. They will therefore all be placed upon the right, between the enemy and the columns for which they constitute the rear guard, if everything occurs peacefully.

No matter how many roads there are, the army will march in two lines only, by the left. All other roads lying to the left will be for the light baggage and the pack horses, which are placed on the side in order to get rid of this encumbrance, which could lead to confusion if the army should be forced to fight.

If the enemy wishes to engage in battle, the first line [i.e. the right-hand column] moves at first sight to occupy the post held by the covering detachments and is followed by the second line. The entire army is formed, with the cavalry on the wings where you can either leave them or have them form a third line, according to events. The detached corps form the reserves or are placed on the flanks of the army or behind the second line on either side, wherever you judge that you will need them. As soon as you are in this position you have nothing to fear from the enemy and you might possibly even win a victory over him. If nothing interrupts the march, these detached corps then form the rear guard, the troops enter their camp, and the heavy baggage is brought up in safety. Manifestly the same procedure must be observed if you march to the left of the enemy.

## RETREATS IN THE PRESENCE OF THE ENEMY

If you want to withdraw before the enemy this is what you must observe. Get rid of all the heavy baggage beforehand by sending it to the rear, in the camp that you want to take. This must be done at an early hour in order to clear the road for the columns so that the troops find no obstacles in their march. If you fear that the enemy wishes to engage in a rear-guard action, you must make as many columns as possible so that the army leaves its camp *en masse* and by its swiftness prevents the enemy from catching up. Even when two columns should be forced to reunite at some point during the course of the march you should not worry, for the main thing is to get away quickly to avoid any engagement.

The army will form a large rear guard which will be so located that it can cover the march of the columns. You can even decamp before daybreak, so that at dawn even the rear guard is already far from camp. Some battalions and squadrons of the tail end of the columns must be designated to form behind defiles, on heights, or near woods to protect the rear guard and safeguard its retreat. These precautions slow up the march considerably, but they do guarantee safety. If the Prince of Orange had followed this method when he retreated from Seneffe [1674], he would not have been beaten by the Prince de Condé. This teaches us never to deviate from the rules and to follow them rigorously on all occasions, to be sure not to be taken unawares.

If the enemy makes a vigorous attack upon the rear guard the army must halt and if necessary even take a position to support and pull back this rear guard, if the latter finds itself in need of such assistance. If nothing troubles it, the army pursues its way and goes into camp at the indicated place.

### MARCHES TO ATTACK AN ENEMY

The first thing you must reflect upon is the enemy position. The disposition of the attack must have been made after having reconnoitered the location of the enemy's camp and his defensive arrangements. The order of the march must be based upon the plan that you have to form your attacks, and upon the wing with which you propose to act and that which you wish to refuse. The heavy baggage must have been sent to to the rear beforehand in order to get rid of this encumbrance, and the light baggage must follow the army covered by a light escort if it is not practical to leave it in camp, which would be preferable.

If the enemy camp is so situated that to attack it requires a flank march, your army must form three columns only, one comprising the first line, another, the second, and the third, the reserve. The pack horses form the fourth and fifth columns.

If you must advance straight ahead against the spot you desire to attack, you should have a strong advance guard that precedes the army by a mile or two. You will form yourself into as many columns as there are roads leading to the places where you wish to form your line of battle. The adjutants, having laid out the distances, could take up the positions themselves according to the disposition that the general will have given for the attack.

If you defeat the enemy you do not need prepared roads for the pursuit: you have only to follow by the roads that his flight indicates. If you are repulsed, having attacked with only one wing, you must cover the retreat with the other wing, which is still intact and thus serves as a rear guard, and you can return to your former camp by the same routes that you came.[3]

## GENERAL INSTRUCTIONS FOR THE MARCH

IN . . . CANTONMENTS a noncommissioned officer or at least a lance-corporal must be placed in charge of each house where soldiers are billeted, and the following day, when the battalion marches, it must leave all of its lodgings simultaneously. This is a good precaution against desertion.

On the march, the battalion commander will take care to go neither too fast nor too slow with the head of the column, so that the battalion is always together and in good order. . . . When the army encamps he will continually look after the punctuality of the guards and sentinels, . . . the cleanliness of the camp, and the cuisine of the soldier so that nothing is lacking. . . .

He must never leave his troops when the army is marching, and if the heat on the road is excessive, he can mix a little vinegar with water to give to the soldier, which will do him no harm as long as he stays on the move. But if the soldier should drink during a halt this could be fatal, and the officer must prevent it rigorously.[4]

THE . . . COLUMNS WILL BE LED by the chasseurs who have reconnoitered the roads. A detachment of carpenters with wagons laden with beams, joists, and planks will march at the head of each column to throw bridges over the small rivers.

The heads of the columns must take care not to outstrip each other during the march, and the generals should make sure that the battalions march closed up and without leaving any intervals. Officers commanding the divisions will carefully preserve their distances.

When passing through a defile[5] the heads of the columns will march slowly, or will halt to give the column time to get back to the proper distances. . . . When you cross defiles, woods, or mountains, you should divide your columns, with infantry at the head of each, and cavalry to bring up the rear.

If there is a plain in the middle of your line of march, then assign the center to the cavalry, and the infantry forming the two outside columns will cross through the woods. But this applies only to a march that is not made too near the enemy. If the enemy is near at hand you will be content to place some grenadier battalions at the head of each cavalry column so as not to break up your battle order.[6]

ARTILLERY GIVES the most trouble on the march. When you are near the enemy you have no choice but to drag the heavy guns along with their assigned brigades. If you march at a distance from the enemy, then you must detach some battalions to protect the artillery, especially in the event of a forced march. For nothing tires the infantry as much as having to make continuous halts in order to extricate guns stuck fast in in the deep ruts or to raise up a gun carriage that had tipped over.

We have followed the practice of using servants attached to the train, incapable men who cannot be relied upon, to look after the horses. In the last war these men were placed under inspectors. Old officers no longer capable of further service in the field led the brigades and they had old noncommissioned officers as subalterns. This measure is absolutely necessary if the machine is to run, for if the horses die through the negligence of the train servants, then it is good-by artillery.[7]

## SUPPLIES AND PROVISIONS

IN ADDITION to the regimental wagons that carry an eight-day supply of bread, the commissariat has wagons fixed to carry provisions enough for a month. . . . The wagons should be drawn by horses. We have also made use of oxen, but to our disadvantage. The wagon masters must take very good care of their horses and it is up to the general of the army to keep the situation well in hand, because through the loss of these horses the number of wagons will be diminished, and with that the quantity of provisions. Moreover, unless these horses are properly nourished they do not have strength enough to bear up under the necessary fatigue.

¶ In addition to the provision wagons, the army always carries iron ovens, the number of which, being insufficient, has been increased. At each stop those must be set up to bake bread; on all expeditions you must be provided with enough bread or biscuit to last ten days. The latter is very good, but our soldiers like biscuits only in soup and do not know how to use them to best advantage.

When you march in enemy territory, make a depot of flour in an occupied town near the army. During the campaign of 1745 our depot originally was at Neustadt, then at Jaromircz, and finally at Trautenau. Had we advanced further we could not have found a safe depot beyond Pardubitz.

I have had hand mills made for each company, which will find them exceedingly useful. You will use soldiers for these mills who will carry the grain to the depot and receive bread in return. With this meal you will be able not only to save your magazines but also to subsist for a long time in camps which otherwise you would be forced to leave. Moreover, you will not find it necessary to make as many convoys, and fewer escorts will be needed.

I must enlarge a little on the subject of convoys. The strength of escorts depends upon the fear that you have of the enemy. Infantry detachments are sent into the towns through which the convoys pass in order to give them a *point d'appui.*★ Often large detachments to cover the convoys are sent out, as was the case in Bohemia. In all treacherous countries you must use infantry to escort the convoys and have these joined by a few hussars to reconnoiter the march and provide information of places where the enemy could be lying in ambush. Even on the plain I prefer infantry to cavalry as escorts and I have been well satisfied with them. For the minutiae of escort duty I refer you to my military regulations. An army commander can never take too many precautions to safeguard his convoys. One good rule for covering convoys is to send troops in front to occupy the defiles through which the convoy will pass and to push the escort a league[8] in front, on the side of the enemy. This maneuver will secure the convoy and mask it.

### OF SUTLERS,★ BEER, AND BRANDY

If you contemplate some enterprise against the enemy, the commissary must scrape together all of the beer and brandy that can be found *en route* so that the army does not lack either, at least during the first days. As soon as the army enters enemy territory all of the brewers and distillers, especially of brandy, must be seized so that the soldier does not lack a drink, which he cannot do without. As for the sutlers, these must be protected, especially in a country where the inhabitants have fled and abandoned their houses so that articles of food can not be had even for payment. At such times one is justified in not treating the peasants with too much kindness.

Sutlers and the soldiers' wives must be sent in search of cattle and all kinds of vegetables. But at the same time you must be sure that the provisions are sold at a reasonable price so that the soldier is in a position to pay for them and the sutler makes an honest profit. I should add here that the soldier is issued two pounds of bread daily and two pounds of meat per week gratis while he is on campaign. This is an indulgence which the poor fellow richly deserves, especially in Bohemia, where one wages war in a desert. When you have convoys brought to the army, have them followed by several herds of cattle reserved for the nourishment of the troops.[9]

IN WAR THE MAGAZINES last only for the first year. As soon as hostilities commence one must think of additional supplies. Then it is up to the commissariat to make arrangements for laying out provisions. In Silesia we draw grain partly from Poland, and the Elbe army is supplied from Saxony. The managers of the field war-commissariats must keep a strong hold on their subordinates, for they are the greatest swindlers around. Even with the eyes of Argus one cannot discover their tricks. They have a hundred ways to conceal their thefts. . . . They must therefore be watched over by spies, soldiers, and civil officials.[10]

### DRY AND GREEN FORAGE

BY DRY FORAGE we mean oats, barley, hay, chopped straw, and the like. Have it transported to the magazine. The oats must be neither musty nor mouldy, otherwise the horses will develop mange and farcy and become so weakened that they are not serviceable even at the start of the campaign. Chopped straw, which is given to the horses because it is the custom, only fills the belly—it provides no nourishment.

The primary reason for having forage collected and carried to the magazine is to get the jump on the enemy at the start of the campaign or when you wish to make some distant enterprise. But rarely can an army venture far from its magazines while it is forced to give dry forage to its horses, because the transport is too cumbersome. An entire province often cannot furnish the requisite number of vehicles, and generally such vehicles are not used in an offensive war unless there are no rivers that one can utilize in transporting forage. During the Silesian campaign all of my cavalry lived on dry forage, but then we only marched from Strehla to Schweidnitz, where there was a magazine, and thence to Grottkau, where we were in the vicinity of the Brier and the Oder.

When you have worked out a plan for a winter campaign, have enough hay to last five days tied in bundles for the cavalry to carry on their horses. If you wish to wage war in Bohemia or Moravia you must wait until spring, otherwise you will ruin all of your cavalry. Forage in the fields for grass and wheat, and when the harvest is in you can forage in the villages.

When you are encamped where you plan to remain for some time, have a reconnaissance made of the forage and after evaluating the amount, make the distribution for the number of days you wish to remain.

Large foraging parties are always escorted by a body of cavalry, the size of which is determined by the proximity and the potential threat of the enemy. Forages are made by the entire army or by the wings.

Foragers are always assembled on the road you want to take, sometimes on the flanks and occasionally at the head or rear of the army. Hussars form the advance guard. If the country is flat the foragers are followed by cavalry; if it is uneven the infantry marches first. The advance guard will precede the march of a fourth of the foragers, followed by a detachment of the escort which is always part infantry and part cavalry, then another segment of foragers, after which comes a detachment of troops, and then the others in the same order. An hussar troop will close the march of the rear guard and bring up the rear of the entire column. In all escorts the infantry will be accompanied by its artillery and the foragers will always be armed with their carbines and swords.

When you arrive at the place for forage, form a chain and

place the infantry near the villages, behind the hedges and sunken roads [*les chemins creux*]. You will mix cavalry and infantry to form a reserve, which you will place in the center to give help wherever the enemy should attempt to penetrate. The hussars will skirmish with the enemy to keep them occupied and away from the forage. When the encircling chain of troops is placed, divide the field among the foragers by regiments. Great care must be taken by the commanding officers that the trusses be made large and be well bound together.

When the horses are laden, the foragers are to return to camp by troops protected by small escorts, and when they have all departed, the troops of the chain are to assemble and form the rear guard, followed by the hussars.

The rules for foraging in villages are nearly the same except for the single difference that the infantry will be placed around the village and the cavalry, to the rear on ground suitable for mounted action. Forage only in one village at a time, and then another, so that the troops forming the chain are not over-extended. . . .

When you occupy a camp near the enemy where you wish to remain for some time, attempt to seize the forage lying between your camp and that of the enemy. Then forage for five miles around the camp, beginning with the most distant fields and saving the nearest for the last. But if it is a temporary camp, forage in the camp and the immediate vicinity.

### CAMPS

In order to know if you have made a good selection for your camp, see whether a slight movement on your part will force the enemy to make a more extensive one or if, after one march, he will find it necessary to make still more. Those which will involve the fewest movements will be the better camps. An army commander must choose his camp himself, since the success of his enterprises depends upon it and often it must become his battlefield.

Since there is much to be observed about this aspect of war,

I shall go into the subject in detail without saying how the troops ought to be placed in their camp, which I have already covered in previous military regulations. I will confine my remarks here to great measures and matters concerning the general himself.

All camps are designed to answer two purposes—the defensive and the offensive. Camps where an army assembles belong to the first category; here you are concerned only with the accommodations for the troops. They must be encamped in small bodies near the magazine but so situated that they can form a line of battle quickly. And since this kind of camp ordinarily is far from the enemy you have nothing to fear on that score. . . .

The first rule that must be observed in all camps . . . is to select ground where the troops are near woods and water. We Prussians intrench our camps as the Romans did earlier to avoid not only the enterprises of the enemy light troops, which are very numerous, but also to prevent desertion. For I have always observed that when our redans* are linked together by lines all around the camp there is less desertion than when this precaution is neglected. No matter how ridiculous this fact may appear, it is nonetheless true. One expects to find grass in a rest camp, which is designed to watch the enemy who has not yet made his movements so that you can be guided by his maneuvers. Since you seek only rest in such a camp, you pitch it so that the front is covered either by a river or a marsh, or any other means that renders the front of the camp unapproachable. The camp of Strehla was of this type. If the rivers and streams in front of the camp do not contain enough water, make dams in order to deepen them.

The army commander must never remain idle in such a camp where he has little to fear from the enemy. He can and must devote all of his attention to the soldiers and take advantage of this rest to re-establish discipline with vigor. He will make sure that the duty is performed strictly and according to the book, that the officers on guard are vigilant and sufficiently instructed in the duties of their post, and that the cavalry and infantry guards are placed according to the rules that I have issued.

The infantry in rest camps will perform their drills three times a week and the recruits, every day. On some occasions the entire corps will go through its maneuvers. The cavalry also must perform its evolutions if not engaged in foraging. The general will see to it that the young horses and new recruits are well trained. He must know the complete condition of each unit and he must also visit the horses, commending those officers who have taken care of them and severely rebuking those who have been negligent. For it is not to be believed that a large army runs itself. It contains many people who are indolent, idle, and slothful, and it is the business of the general to get them moving and force them to do their duty.

If this kind of rest camp is employed in the manner that I have indicated it will be of very great utility. Once order and uniformity have been re-established in the service with the aid of these camps, they will be retained throughout the entire campaign.

Camps are formed wherever you forage, no matter how near or far away the enemy. . . . Forage camps must be difficult of access when located in the vicinity of the enemy because foragers are regarded only as detachments that one sends against the enemy. Sometimes one-sixth of the army goes on forage; sometimes as much as one half. This gives the enemy a beautiful opportunity to attack you at your disadvantage, provided the favorable situation of your camp does not prevent him.

But even assuming that your post is excellent and that you obviously have nothing to fear from the enemy, there are other precautions that you must never neglect. You must carefully conceal the time and place you want to forage and not give the general who will command the foraging party his orders until very late on the preceding evening. You must send out as many detachments as possible, to be informed of any movements that the enemy may make, and unless very important considerations prevent you, you must forage on the same day as the enemy because then you risk less. But you must not depend too much upon this, for the enemy, observing that you send foraging parties out at the same time as his own army, might well order a forage and then have his foragers recalled to fall upon you with his entire army.

¶ Intrench your camp when you want to besiege a fortress, defend a difficult passage, and compensate for weaknesses in the terrain with fortifications. . . . The rules that a general must follow in the construction of all intrenchments are to choose a position carefully and to take advantage of all swamps and rivers, inundations and abatis★ by which you can render the extent of the intrenchments difficult. It would be better to make them too small rather than too large, for it is not intrenchments that stop the enemy, but the troops defending them. I would avoid making intrenchments if I could not line them with a chain of battalions and have an infantry reserve to move to any point needed. Abatis are good only while they are defended by infantry.

If you besiege a fortress and sit down behind the lines you must be abundantly provided with provisions. . . . But to cover a siege I would always prefer an army of observation to an intrenched camp, the reason being that experience has taught us that the old method of intrenchment is subject to caution. . . .

Bohemia is a country where a number of these camps are found. Often one is forced to occupy one against his will, because this kingdom by its very nature is a land of treachery.

I will repeat again that a general must guard against making any irreparable mistakes by the poor selection of his posts either by letting himself get trapped in a *cul-de-sac* or by occupying terrain that he can evacuate only by passing through a defile. For if his enemy is skillful he will be surrounded there, and since he will not be in condition to fight because of the nature of the ground, he will submit to the greatest indignity for a soldier—he will lay down arms without being able to defend himself.

In camps that are intended to protect a country, make your selection not on the strength of the place itself, but to strengthen vulnerable points where the enemy might break through. You need not occupy all the openings through which the enemy can come upon you, but only those that lead to his objective, where you can maintain your position without having to fear him, and where perhaps you might cause him to grow uneasy. In brief, you must occupy the post that forces the enemy to make a lengthy detour and that places you in a position to defeat all his plans by small movements.

¶ The front and flanks of an offensive camp must be closed, for you can hope for nothing on the part of the troops if you do not take the precaution of covering the flanks, which constitute the weakest part of an army. Our camp at Czaslau before the battle of [Chotusitz in] 1742 had this fault. We always occupy the villages on our wings or in front of our camp with troops we can withdraw on the day of the battle. Since the houses in our villages and those of our neighbors are of wood and are poorly constructed, the troops would be lost if the enemy set fire to them. An exception to this rule occurs when there are stone houses in these villages or cemeteries which do not touch the wooden structures. But since it is our principle always to attack and not to hold ourselves on the defensive, you must never occupy such posts unless they are at the head or in front of the wings of your army, in which case they protect the attack of your troops and cause the enemy much annoyance during the battle.

It is still essential to have the small rivers and the marshes in front or on the flanks of your camp sounded for depth so that you do not take a false *point d'appui* in case the rivers are fordable and the marshes accessible. Villars was beaten at Malplaquet because he believed that the marsh on his right was impassable, and it proved to be only a dry meadow that our troops crossed to take him in flank. You must examine everything with your own eyes. . . .

## HOW TO SAFEGUARD YOUR CAMP[11]

The infantry regiments will guard the front of the first line. If there is a river the pickets must be placed on the bank. The pickets of the second line will guard the rear of the camp.

Pickets will be protected by redans which are joined to light intrenchments, by means of which your camp will be intrenched in the manner of the Romans. You will occupy the villages on the wings or those that defend other passages within a mile or two from there.

The cavalry guards will be posted according to regulations. Of eighty squadrons we usually have had only three hundred on watch except when we have been near the enemy, as before the battle of Hohenfriedberg, when we marched to Schweidnitz, and again when we marched into Lusatia on the way to Naumbourg.

These advance guards must be a mixed force of all kinds of soldiers—2,000 hussars, 1,500 dragoons, and 2,000 grenadiers, for example. Every time you send such a body forward, the general who commands it must be a resourceful man, and since he is detached not to fight but rather to inform, he must know how to select his camps carefully . . . and send out frequent patrols to obtain intelligence, so that he is informed at every moment of what is going on in the enemy camp. Meanwhile, the hussars that you have retained will make patrols in the rear and on the wings of the camp. Finally, you will take every precaution that can guard you against enemy enterprises. Should a considerable body of troops slip between you and your rear guard you must go to its support, for it means that the enemy has formed a plan against it.

To include everything that there is to say on this subject I would add that generals in cantonments will occupy only those villages which lie between the [first and second?] lines: then they have nothing to fear.

## DETACHMENTS

It is an old rule of war, which I only repeat here, that he who divides his forces will be beaten in detail. If you desire to give battle, try to concentrate all of your forces—you can never make better use of them. This rule is so well founded that every general who has neglected it nearly always finds himself in trouble. I deserved to have been defeated at Sohr, if the skill of my generals and the valor of my troops had not rescued me from this misfortune. You will ask, then, if detachments ought never to be made, to which I will reply: sometimes it is necessary, but always it is a very touchy maneuver which you must risk only for very important considerations. Detachments must be proportionate to the circumstances.

Never make detachments when you are acting offensively. If you are in open country and master of some fortified cities, make only those detachments necessary for the protection of your convoys. Whenever you wage war in Bohemia or Moravia you will be absolutely compelled to detach a corps to insure the arrival of provisions. The mountain chain that the convoys have to cross requires you to send troops that will remain encamped on the spot until you have provisions enough to last several months and have made yourself master of a fort in enemy territory, where you can establish your depot.

While these troops are detached you will occupy advantageous camps where you can await their return. I do not consider the advance guard in any sense a detachment, because it must be within range of the army and never venture too near the enemy.

When you are forced to adhere to the defensive you often find yourself reduced to the necessity of making detachments. Those which I had in Upper Silesia were safe enough there, since they kept themselves in the vicinity of fortified strongholds.

¶ Officers commanding detachments must be steady, fearless, and prudent. The commander gives them general instructions but it is for them to decide whether to advance on the enemy or to retire before him, as circumstances dictate. They must always fall back before superior forces, but they must also know how to take advantage of numbers when superiority is on their side. Sometimes they will withdraw at night upon the approach of the enemy, and when the latter believes that they have taken flight they will return briskly to the charge and repulse them. They must have absolute contempt for light troops.

An officer commanding a detachment must think first for

his own safety and then, if he is able, he can make plans against the enemy. If he wishes to sleep in peace he must never allow his enemy to sleep, but must always form enterprises against him. Then if he succeeds two or three times he will force the enemy to remain on the defensive. . . .

Defensive warfare naturally leads us to make detachments. Generals with little experience wish to save everything: those who are wise consider only the principal point, seeking to ward off large blows and patiently suffering minor misfortunes in order to avoid large ones. He who attempts to defend too much defends nothing.

The enemy's army is the most essential object to keep in view. You must divine its plans and oppose it with all of your forces. We abandoned Upper Silesia to the pillage of the Hungarians in 1745 in order to be able to resist more vigorously the plans of Prince Charles of Lorraine, and we made detachments only after we had defeated his army. Then General Nassau chased the Hungarians out of the whole of Upper Silesia in fifteen days.

There are generals who detach troops when they are about to attack the enemy in order to take him in the rear when the battle is in progress, but this is a very dangerous movement since these detachments ordinarily lose their way and arrive either too early or too late. The detachment made by Charles XII on the eve of the battle of Pultawa lost its way and his army was defeated.[12] Prince Eugene failed in his stroke when he wished to surprise Crémone: the Prince de Vaudement's detachment, which was designed to attack the gate of the Po, arrived too late.

You must never make detachments on the day of battle unless you are in a situation comparable to that of Turenne near Colmar, where he presented his first line to the army of the Elector Frederick William while waiting for his second to move through defiles to attack and rout the Prince's flanks. . . . You must detach troops only after a victory to protect your convoys, and even then the detachments must remain within a mile or two of the army.

I will end this subject by stating that detachments that weaken the army by as much as one-third or one-half are very dangerous and therefore to be condemned.

¶ One of the most essential duties of generals commanding armies or detachments is to prevent desertion. This is how it is done:

1. By not encamping too near a wood or forest unless military considerations require it.
2. By calling the roll several times daily.
3. By sending out frequent hussar patrols to scour the country around the camp.
4. By placing chasseurs in the wheat fields during the night and doubling the cavalry posts at dusk to strengthen the chain.
5. By not allowing the soldiers to wander about and taking care that the officers conduct their troops to water and forage in formation.
6. By punishing marauding severely, since this is the source of all disorders.
7. By not drawing in the guards placed in the villages on marching days until the troops are under arms.
8. By forbidding, under rigorous punishment, the soldier to leave his rank or division on days of march.
9. By avoiding night marches unless there is absolute necessity for them.
10. By sending hussar patrols forward on both flanks while the infantry pass through a woods.
11. By placing officers at both ends of a defile to force the soldiers to return to the ranks.
12. By concealing from the soldier any retrograde marches you are forced to make, or by making use of some specious pretext that would flatter him.
13. By always seeing to it that the necessary subsistence is not lacking, and taking care that the troops are supplied with bread, meat, brandy, beer, and the like.
14. By examining desertion as soon as it creeps into a regiment or company. Inquire whether the soldier has had his bounty, if he has been given the other customary indulgences, and if the captain is guilty of any misconduct. On no account,

however, should there be any relaxation of strict discipline. Perhaps you will say that the colonel will give it his attention, but this is not enough. In an army everything must lead to perfection, to make it appear that all that is done is the work of a single man.

## MILITARY INTELLIGENCE

If you know the enemy's plans beforehand you will always be more than a match for him, even with inferior numbers. All generals who command armies try to procure this advantage, but there are few who succeed in it.

There are several kinds of spies: (1) ordinary people who become involved in this profession; (2) double spies; (3) spies of consequence; and (4) those whom you force into this unpleasant business.

Ordinary people like peasants, townsmen, and so forth, whom you send into the enemy camp can only be employed to discover the whereabouts of the enemy. Most of their reports are so incongruous and obscure that they only add to the uncertainties. . . . The statement of deserters for the most part is no better. The soldier has a good knowledge of what is happening in his regiment and where it is located, but nothing further. Hussars, being absent from the army most of the time and often detached in front, do not know on which side the army is encamped. In spite of these shortcomings you should have their reports written down: this is the only way to derive any advantage from them.

Double spies are used to convey false information to the enemy. There was an Italian at Schmiedeberg who spied for the Austrians. When we led him to believe that we would retreat to Breslau upon the approach of the enemy, he passed the word on to Prince Charles of Lorraine, who was taken in by it. For a long time Prince Eugene had the postmaster at Versailles in his pay. This wretch opened the letters and orders that the Court despatched to the generals and sent copies to Prince Eugene, who usually received them sooner than the French commanders. And Luxembourg won over a secretary of the English King who informed him of everything that was going on. The King discovered him and turned the delicate affair to his advantage by forcing the traitor to write Luxembourg and let him know that the allied army would make a large forage the following day. The French were nearly caught by surprise at Steinkirke [1692] and would have been entirely defeated if they had not fought with extraordinary valor.

It would be very difficult to find such spies in a war against the Austrians, not that they are less susceptible to bribery than any other people, but because their light troops, covering the army like a cloud, let nobody pass without being searched. This has given me the idea that it would be necessary to win over some of their hussar officers, who could be contacted during those moments of informal truce which have become customary with hussars who have skirmished with each other.

When you want to send misleading information to the enemy, or want to obtain intelligence about him, send a trustworthy soldier into his camp and have him report what you wish the enemy to believe. You can also have him carry handbills encouraging the enemy soldiers to desert. Then the emissary returns to your camp by a roundabout route.

If you can find no other way to obtain intelligence in enemy territory, there is another expedient, albeit harsh and cruel. Select some rich citizen with a large estate, wife, and children, and assign him an individual disguised as a domestic servant who knows the local language. Then force the citizen to go to the enemy's camp taking this man with him as his valet or coachman, under the pretext of having to complain of injuries committed against him. Threaten him at the same time very severely that if he fails to return with his "valet" after remaining a long while in camp, his wife and children will be hacked to pieces and his houses burned. I was forced to resort to this method when we were encamped at Chlum, and it worked.

I will add further that you must be generous and even lavish in the payment of spies. A man who risks his neck for your service deserves to be well rewarded.

The best way to discover the enemy's intentions before the

opening of a campaign is to discover where he has established his provision depot. If the Austrians, for example, made their magazines at Olmütz you could be sure that they planned to attack Upper Silesia, and if they established a magazine at Königgrätz, the Schweidnitz area would be threatened. When the Saxons wanted to invade the Elector Mark their magazines would indicate the road that they would take because their depots were at Zittau, Görlitz, and Guben, which are on the way to Krossen. The first thing that you must learn, therefore, is on what side and in what places the enemy will establish his magazines. The French made a double line of magazines, some on the Meuse and others on the Escaut, to prevent the enemy from discovering their intentions.[13]

When the Austrians are encamped you will be able to predict the days that they plan to march because it is their custom to have the soldiers cook on marching days. So if you notice much smoke between five and eight o'clock in the morning, you can safely assume that they will make a movement that day. Whenever the Austrians intend to fight they recall all large detachments of light troops to the camp. When this comes to your attention you should be on your guard. If you attack a post of their Hungarian troops and they stand unshaken, you can be sure that their main army is within supporting distance.

It must be added that if your opponent is always the same general, you can learn his mannerisms and penetrate his intentions by the way he acts. . . .[14]

## PLANNING THE MARCH

THE GENERAL'S PLAN must determine the dispositions to be used. When you are in your own country you have every possible assistance—detailed maps as well as inhabitants who can give you all of the necessary information. Then the task becomes easy. You have your order of battle. If you march by cantonments you merely follow this order and place each brigade as near as it is possible to assemble, and each line in its order. If you are far from the enemy each regiment should have the route that it should take and the brigade commander should be given not only the route of his regiments but even the list of villages where he must be cantoned.

In enemy country this becomes more difficult. You do not always have sufficiently detailed maps of the country and your knowledge of the villages is imperfect. Thus to compensate for these shortcomings the advance guard must assemble the inhabitants of the towns, boroughs, and hamlets and send them to the quartermaster general, so that he rectifies by means of the information they provide the rough draft of the march dispositions that he has drawn up from a simple scanning of the map. If the army encamps, you must have a reconnaissance made of all roads leading to the camp as soon as you have entered it. If you remain there you must send quartermasters and draftsmen, with the aid of patrols, to sketch the roads and the situations, so that you never act blindly and can procure in advance all of the facts you will need. In this way you can even have the camps reconnoitered in advance and . . . with the help of these sketches, draw up in advance the position that you desire to take. . . . It is true that when the armies are close to each other reconnaissance becomes more difficult, for the enemy likewise has detachments and light troops in the field, which prevent you from moving to the places you wish to reconnoiter.

Often you must conceal your plan, which makes these small expeditions more difficult still. Then you have no choice but to put pressure on the enemy simultaneously at different points and even to have places indicated where you have no desire to go, in order to hide your plan. Since you chase the enemy from different posts, you must employ the best quartermasters at the place where you seriously intend to act, for the wise man will never leave to chance what he can carry off with prudence. Above all, a general must never move his army without being instructed about the place where he leads it and without knowing how he will safely get it to the ground where he wants to execute his plans.

## PRECAUTIONS TO TAKE IN ENEMY COUNTRY
## IN PROCURING GUIDES

We had need of guides in 1760, while crossing Lusatia to march on Silesia. We sought them in the Wendish villages and when they were brought before us they let on that they could not speak German, which greatly distressed us. But on being informed that they would be beaten they spoke German like parrots. You must therefore always be on your guard with respect to guides taken in enemy country. Far from trusting them, you must bind those who lead the troops, promising them payment if they take you by the best and shortest road to the place you wish to go but assuring them also that you will hang them without pardon should they lead you astray. Only with severity and force can you compel the Moravians and Bohemians to fulfill this kind of duty. In these provinces you find inhabitants in the towns, but the villages are deserted because the peasants escape with their cattle and best effects into the forests or mountain valleys and leave their houses empty.

Their desertion causes considerable difficulty, because where does one obtain guides if not from one village to another? You must then resort to the towns, attempt to find some messengers or, lacking these, some itinerant butchers who know the roads. You must, moreover, force the burgomasters to furnish guides under penalty of burning the towns if they do not acquit themselves well. You can even resort to gamekeepers who are in the service of the nobles, and who know the environs. But whoever serve as guides, you must bridle them by fear and threaten them with the most severe treatment if they perform their commission poorly.

There is still a surer way of procuring this kind of knowledge, and that is to engage during peacetime some of the inhabitants who have a complete knowledge of the country. Such agents are trustworthy and through them, when you enter this province, you can win over others who will assist you and lighten the labor by providing knowledge of the details of the locality. As a rule maps are accurate enough for level ground, although it is often noted that they omit some village or hamlet. But the knowledge that matters most is that concerning woods, defiles, mountains, fordable streams or marshes, and river fords. It is of these, as well as the regions where there are only meadows or marshes, that one must have the best knowledge. In this connection it is necessary further to keep in mind the seasons of the year, which change the nature of the terrain through drought or rainfall, for it is often highly important for a general not to misinterpret his information.

The quartermasters must be cautioned, moreover, against evidence provided by common people. Sometimes even when they act in good faith they deceive you through ignorance, because they can only judge roads and places by the use they make of them and, lacking all knowledge of military affairs, they ignore the use that a soldier can make of terrain. In 1745, when the Prussian army wanted to withdraw into Silesia after the battle of Sohr, I had the people of Trautenau and Schatzlar brought before me for interrogation about the roads where I wanted to send my columns. They told me candidly that the roads were admirable and that they had no difficulty at all traveling there with their carts, and that many wagoners likewise used them. A few days later the army made this march. I was forced to make my dispositions for the retreat in these places. Our rear guard was vigorously attacked, but thanks to the precautions that I took, we lost nobody. These roads, from a military point of view, were very poor, but those who had given me the information understood nothing about it and . . . acted in good faith and without intention to deceive. You must therefore not rely upon the reports of ignorant civilians but, map in hand, consult them as to each type of terrain, note down what they say, and see from that if there is a way to sketch something on paper that gives a more accurate idea of the road than what is indicated on the map.[15]

## HOW TO CONDUCT YOURSELF
## WITH THE CIVIL POPULATION

WAR IS WAGED in three kinds of countries—your own, that of neutral powers, and enemy territory.

If my sole object were glory, I would never wage war anywhere except in my own country because of all of the advantages I would find there. For every man is a spy and the enemy cannot stir a foot without being betrayed. You can send out large detachments boldly and have them play all the tricks of which war is capable. If the enemy has just been defeated, each peasant becomes a soldier and proceeds to harass him. Frederick William the Elector had this experience after the battle of Fehrbellin, when the peasants killed more Swedes than had been lost in battle. For my part, I have seen the Silesian mountaineers bring us many Austrian fugitives after the battle of Hohenfriedberg.

When you wage war in a neutral country neither belligerent seems to have an advantage, and it then becomes a question of seeing which side will be able to win over the friendship and confidence of the inhabitants. To succeed in this you will observe the strictest discipline, prohibit marauding and all kinds of pillage, and punish such crimes with severity. Accuse the enemy of having pernicious plans against the country.

If the country is Protestant, like Saxony, play the role of protector of the Lutheran religion and seek to inspire fanaticism in the hearts of the lower classes, whose simplicity makes them easy prey. If the country is Catholic, speak only of tolerance, preach moderation, and blame the priests for all the causes of animosity between the Christian sects which, despite their arguments, are in basic agreement on the principal articles of faith.

As for the detachments you may wish to make, these must be based upon the support of the inhabitants. In our country you may run any risk, but in a neutral country you must be more circumspect—at least until you are assured of the inclination of all the peasants, or of the majority. In enemy country such as Bohemia and Moravia you must play it safe and for the reasons mentioned above, never risk making detachments. You must keep your eyes open. Most of the light troops will then be employed to escort convoys, for you must never expect to gain the affection of these people. In the Circle of König-grätz the Hussites are the only people who can be of any use to you. The lords there are traitors, although they would have it appear that they are kindly disposed toward us, and the same is true of the priests and magistrates. Their interest is tied to that of the house of Austria, and since this interest does not coincide with ours, you cannot, nor should you ever trust them.

The only subject left to discuss is fanaticism, that is, when you can arouse a nation on behalf of religious freedom and adroitly give the people the notion that they are oppressed by priests and lords. This may be said to be moving heaven and earth in your own interests.

Since the time these comments have been written the Empress Queen has considerably augmented the taxes in Bohemia and Moravia. You should take advantage of this fact to win over the affection of the subjects, especially if you lead them to believe that they will be treated with greater kindness if you were to conquer the country.[16]

## MARCHES DURING THE SPRING AND FALL

TWO CONDITIONS force an army to shorten its marches during these seasons—bad roads rutted and filled with mud and fewer hours of daylight. An army can travel only fifteen miles a day. Dragging the artillery and baggage through the mire absorbs considerable time, and you would fatigue too many men and horses if you wanted to make larger stages. If you find that the best roads take you a little out of the way, you must choose them in preference to the direct route and distribute the artillery behind the column that traverses the firmest ground. If you should send out detachments at any distance from the army . . . have the foresight not to give them twelve-pounder guns: six-pounders will be sufficient, and even so they will have plenty of trouble dragging them along with their ammunition and all the essential gear.

## WINTER QUARTERS

When the season is so far advanced that you can no longer continue the campaign, you must think of giving rest to the troops in winter quarters. Begin by setting up the cordon that must cover these quarters, where you place the number of troops designated for this function.[17]

THE CHAINS ARE FORMED in three ways, either behind a river, or by means of posts defending mountains, or under the protection of some fortified cities. In the winter of 1741-42, my troops, who were in winter quarters in Bohemia, took up their position behind the Elbe; the outpost line that covered them began on the right at Brandeis and extended through Nimburg, Kolin, Podiebrad, and Pardubitz to Königgrätz. I should add here that you must never depend upon rivers, since they can be crossed at any point when frozen over. . . . Nor should you place your trust in mountains: remember always the proverb: "Wherever a goat can cross, so can a soldier." As for the chains of quarters supported by fortresses, I would refer you to Marshal Saxe's winter quarters. They are the best. But you do not have the freedom of choice: you must make the chain according to the terrain that you occupy.

I will lay it down as a maxim that you must never cling stubbornly to any particular town or post in winter quarters if the enemy actively opposes you at that point, for you must devote all of your attention to making winter quarters tranquil. You should take care to place hussars at every link in the chain to observe all enemy movements.

For a second maxim, I would add that the best method to distribute the regiments in their winter quarters is by brigade, so that they are always under the attention of the generals. Our service requires also that the regiments be placed with their own generals, if it is possible. But there are exceptions to this rule, which will be made at the discretion of the commanding general.

Here now are the rules for the maintenance of the troops in winter quarters.[18]

WHEN THE ARMY moves into winter quarters, the first thought of the commander—if the campaign has lasted until the end of autumn—is to have all of his corps successively cleansed upon entering the quarters. Next he must have it bled, not all at once, but by companies, and as the surgeon general finds it necessary for the constitution of each soldier.

During the first days that the troops leave the tents and live indoors the commander will see to it that the windows are open so that the change between the raw air and the heat of the furnaces is not too abrupt. Without this precaution inflammatory maladies occur, and it is necessary to protect the veteran soldier as much as possible because it requires three years to produce a trained infantryman.

Those who constitute the chain of the winter quarters must above all take precautions against surprises, because that is what they have to fear most. If their battalions are in villages the commander must first build a closed palisade and erect some *flèches*★ in front of the entrances. This is why the King recommends so highly that his infantry officers study fortifications, because they cannot do without it during the course of a campaign.

If you occupy mountains you should construct redoubts★ there at different points, according to the terrain, with blockhouses inside them. These redoubts must be surrounded with palisades, the stakes alternated with long shafts . . . [as on plate 1], so that it would be impossible for the enemy to climb over them. . . . If you are behind a river, you must break the ice in the winter to prevent the enemy from crossing. I do not speak of cavalry patrols, which you must have in the field day and night to furnish news of the slightest enemy movement, nor of spies, of which you must have a number so that if one fails you the other can give news.

If the chain is not too uneasy and the service is not too

*Note.*

Ces sortes de redoutes peuvent se faire de deux façons; Ou vous placés les palissades sur le chemin couvert, ou vous les placés au rempart capital. Cette sorte de redoutes est bonne sur les hauteurs et les montagnes où le canon ne saurait endomager les palissades, mais elles ne feront pas le même effet dans la plaine où les palissades seraient ruinées bien vite.

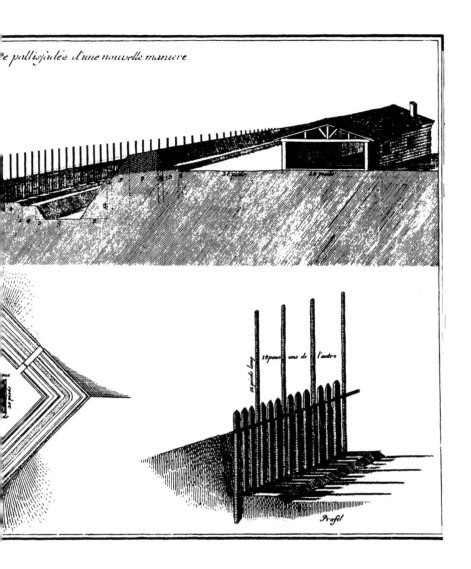

PLATE 1. Plan of a palisaded redoubt. This type of construction was designed particularly for heights and mountains, where enemy artillery could not easily destroy the palisades, or pointed stakes, located on the covered way. (*Atlas* to the *Oeuvres de Frédéric le Grand*, Plan 9.)

harsh the commander must drill his troops as much as circumstances permit. His glory is tied to the quality of his soldiers, and the sounder he keeps them, the better assured is his reputation.[19]

IF CIRCUMSTANCES absolutely require you to take up winter quarters in your own country, then the captains and subordinate officers should receive a gratuity in proportion to the ordinary allowance that they are given in winter quarters. The soldier will receive bread and meat gratis. But if winter quarters are in enemy territory, the general commanding the troops will receive 15,000 florins, the generals commanding the cavalry and infantry 10,000 each, lieutenant generals 7,000, and major generals 5,000. Cavalry captains each will receive 2,000, infantry captains 1,800, and the subalterns 100 ducates or 400-500 florins. The soldier will receive free issues of bread, meat, and beer furnished by the country, but he is not to be given money, since this encourages desertion. The commanding general will see to it that this is done in an orderly fashion and will permit no pillage. But he will not take issue with the officer over some petty profit that the latter is able to make.

If the army is in winter quarters in enemy territory the general of the army must take care that the necessary recruits are provided. He will distribute the districts so that, for example, three regiments are assigned to one and four to another. Each district will be subdivided into regiments as is done in the Prussian military cantons. If the states of the country wish to provide the recruits themselves, so much the better; otherwise you will use force. The recruits must arrive early enough for the officer to drill them and get them in condition to perform duty the next spring, but this should not prevent the captains from sending out recruiting officers.

Since the general in chief must become involved in all of this management, he should take care that the artillery horses and provisions that are obtained in the country as tribute are either furnished in kind or equalled in hard cash. Nor will he fail to be sure that the contributions are paid to the army treasury to the last florin. The enemy country also has to bear the expense of repairing all the baggage wagons and everything required for the outfitting of an army.

The general will give all his attention to see to it that the cavalry officers have the saddles, bridles, stirrups, and boots repaired and that the infantry officers provide their men with shoes, stockings, shirts, and gaiters for the coming campaign. They must, moreover, have the soldiers' blankets and tents mended, the cavalry swords filed, the infantry arms placed in good condition, and must have the artillery personnel prepare the necessary quantity of cartridges for the infantry. It still remains for the general to take care that the troops forming the chain are sufficiently provided with powder and ball and that nothing is lacking in the entire army.

Time permitting, it would not be a bad idea for the general to visit some of these quarters to examine the state of the troops and to be assured that the officers drill them and perform this duty uniformly, for he must have not only the recruits but also the old soldiers drilled to keep them in practice.

At the beginning of the campaign you will change the quarters of cantonments, distributing them according to the order of battle with the cavalry on the wings and the infantry in the center. These cantonments ordinarily have a frontage of twenty to twenty-five miles and are ten miles in depth. When the time comes for you to encamp, you contract them a little. I find that it is very convenient to distribute the troops in the cantonments under the command of the six senior generals. For example, one commands all the cavalry of the right wing and another, that of the left wing in the first line, and two others command that of the second; in this way the orders will be expedited most promptly and the troops will be most easily formed into columns to enter the camp.[20]

## WINTER MARCHES AND CAMPAIGNS

THIS KIND of expedition must be executed with a great deal of prudence; otherwise you risk seeing your army destroyed almost without a fight. Winter campaigns are made either to take possession of a country where the enemy does not have many troops or else to fall upon his quarters. Our campaigns in 1740-41 in Silesia and Moravia belong to the first category. We marched into Silesia in two columns, one skirting the mountains and the other extending along the Oder to clear the country and blockade those fortresses that it was not possible to take. . . . The fortresses remained blockaded until spring. Glogau was surprised, Breslau soon shared the same fate, Brieg was taken after the battle of Mollwitz, and Neisse fell at the end of the campaign. We entered Moravia in one column in 1741, capturing Olmütz. We were content to blockade Brünn, which the Saxons had to besiege in the spring of 1742. But this campaign was upset by the retreat of the Saxons and the inactivity of our French allies. We evacuated Moravia after having penetrated into Austria as far as Stockerau and after having seized a body of insurgents in Hungary which the court [of Vienna] wished to employ against our rear.

Such expeditions require a general to exercise all possible vigilance to avoid being surprised. For this reason we had a detachment constantly in front of the troops, another on the right, and a third on the· left, whose patrols informed us of all enemy movements. With that the cantonments were contracted: two or three battalions of necessity had to be content with a single village and their baggage was parked outside, defended by a redoubt. Thus no accident happened to us.

At the end of the year 1745 the Prince of Lorraine undertook a similar expedition. In the month of December he decided to invade Brandenburg from Bohemia by crossing Lusatia. Here are the mistakes he committed:

1. He marched without an advance guard and without cavalry which would skirt Silesia to give him news of the Prussians.
2. He saddled himself with too much baggage.
3. His cantonments occupied a frontage of fifteen miles and a depth of the same distance because his troops were not sufficiently concentrated. He would have been better off thinking of their security than their comfort.

4. Being near our frontiers, he formed neither columns nor order of march. We took advantage of his mistake, of course, and crossing the Queis we fell upon his quarters at Catholisch-Hennersdorff and captured 4,000 men. Our army camped on the place and Prince Charles who risked being taken in the rear, was forced to retire into Bohemia at a pace resembling flight rather than a retreat, losing his baggage and about twenty cannon.

Marshal Saxe's expedition on Brussels was made in the month of March. He fell on the allied quarters, dispersed them, and undertook the siege of Brussels, which he captured. He had most of his troops encamp and did not neglect to place large detachments between him and the enemy in order to receive word of the slightest enemy movement in good time.

Thus it is true that every general who does not neglect foresight nor deviate from the maxims of prudence must nearly always succeed. Thoughtless enterprises can enjoy success only with the greatest chances, because as a rule the foolhardy man perishes where the wise man prospers.[21]

## NOTES: CHAPTER IV

1. Frederick, "Forward" to *Die Generalprinzipien des Krieges und ihre Anwendung auf die Taktik und Disziplin der preussischen Truppen*, in *Die Werke Friedrichs des Grossen* (Berlin, 1913), VI, 3-4. This forward is not contained in the French edition from which the other selections from this work have been translated [*Werke*].

2. Frederick here uses the German mile, which is the equivalent of about five American miles. Hereafter all distances will be reduced to American measurements, unless otherwise indicated.

3. Frederick, "Des marches d'armée, et de ce qu'il faut observer à cet égard," *Oeuvres de Frédéric le Grand* (Berlin, 1846-56), XXIX, 97-103 [*Marches d'armée*].

4. Frederick, "Règles de ce qu'on exige d'un bon commandeur de bataillon en temps de guerre," *ibid.*, pp. 57-58.

5. Evidently the "defiles" that Frederick mentions so frequently in his writings often "were something entirely different than what is meant by the word today: a narrow place of about one hundred meters width between two woods which forced a battalion advancing

in line to break up and subsequently to deploy again passed for a defile, not so much because of the danger of passing through, but because it necessitated an unwelcome change in the formation. "Friedrich des Grossen Anschauungen vom Kriege in ihrer Entwickelung von 1745 bis 1756," in Prussia, Grossen Generalstabe, *Kriegsgeschichtliche Einzelschriften*, XXVII (Berlin, 1899), 248. See Plate 26.

6. Frederick, *Instruction militaire du Roi de Prusse pour ses généraux* (Frankfort, 1761), pp. 93-95 [*Instruction militaire*].

7. Frederick, "Das militärische Testament von 1768," *Werke*, VI, 229 [*Testament von 1768*].

8. About two and one half miles.

9. Frederick, *Instruction militaire*, pp. 15-20.

10. Frederick, *Testament von 1768*, pp. 223-24.

11. Further details on field fortifications and the defense of a camp are contained in Chapters V and VII.

12. See Chapter IX.

13. The reference is to the war of the Austrian Succession, in which France was opposed by Austria, England, and Holland and allied to Prussia. (1740-48).

14. Frederick, *Instruction militaire*, pp. 3-6, 20-26, 39-69, 77-86.

15. Frederick, *Marches d'armée*, pp. 113-15.

16. Frederick, *Instruction militaire*, pp. 86-90.

17. Frederick, *Marches d'armée*, p. 109.

18. Frederick, *Instruction militaire*, pp. 184-89.

19. Frederick, *Règles de ce qu'on exige d'un bon commandeur de bataillon en temps de guerre*, pp. 60-61. [*Règles d'un bon commandeur*].

20. Frederick, *Instruction militaire*, pp. 189-94.

21. Frederick, *Marches d'armée*, pp. 110-12.

# V

# The Anatomy of Battle

The attitude toward battle in the eighteenth century differed sharply from the conventional view, after the Napoleonic wars, that all planning and maneuvers were directed toward the climactic destruction of the enemy in a decisive engagement. In Frederick's day the battle was not necessarily the "payoff." Losses were difficult to make good, much time was required to produce an effective and disciplined soldier, and armies cost money. Maneuver therefore was often regarded as a desirable alternative to battle, and the difficulty in supplying armies further reduced the frequency of battles. The following passages are selected to show Frederick's concept of battle, which is more aggressive than the prevailing view among his contemporaries, and to illustrate the role and the limitations of the three arms (infantry, cavalry, and artillery) in a typical eighteenth-century action. Subsequent chapters reveal how Frederick's concept of the nature and mechanics of battle changed as a result of the Seven Years' War.

*BATTLES DECIDE* the fate of a nation. In war it is absolutely necessary to come to decisive actions either to get out of the distress of war or to place the enemy in that position, or even to settle a quarrel which otherwise perhaps would never be finished. A wise man will make no movement without good reason, and a general of an army will never give battle if it does not serve some important purpose. When he is forced by his enemy into a battle it is surely because he will have committed mistakes which force him to dance to the tune of his enemy.

It will be seen that on this occasion I am not writing my own panegyric, for out of five battles which my troops have fought with the enemy [in the Silesian wars] only three were premeditated, and I was forced into the others. At Mollwitz the Austrians had placed themselves between my army and Wohlau, where I had my artillery and provisions. At Sohr the enemy cut me off from the road to Trautenau so that I could not avoid battle without incurring the risk of losing my whole army. But let us examine the difference between forced battles and those that have been planned beforehand. How successful were the battles of Hohenfriedberg and Kesselsdorf, and the battle of Chotusitz brought us the peace!

In giving the rules for battles I would not maintain that I have not often erred through inadvertence, but my officers must profit by my mistakes. They must also rest assured that I shall try to correct them myself.

Sometimes both armies wish to engage in battle and then the affair is very soon settled.

The best battles are those that you force upon the enemy, for it is an established rule that you must compel the enemy to do that which is contrary to his wishes and best interests. There are several reasons for giving battle: to force the enemy to raise a siege, . . . to drive him from a province that he has seized, to invade his territory, to undertake a siege, to restrain his stubbornness when he refuses to make peace, or, finally, to punish him for a mistake. You will also force the enemy to fight when you fall upon his rear by a forced march and sever his communications, or when you threaten a city that it is in his interest to keep. But you will take good care in making this kind of maneuver not to place yourself at the same disadvantage or to take up a position that enables the enemy to cut you off from your magazines. The affairs where you run the least risk are those that you undertake against the enemy rear guard.

¶ To all these maxims I would add further that our wars must be short and lively, since a prolonged conflict is not in our interests. A long war gradually lessens our admirable discipline, depopulates our country, and exhausts our resources. For this reason, generals commanding Prussian armies should endeavor, however successful the affair may be, to terminate it promptly and prudently. They must not think, like Marshal de Luxembourg, who, when told by his son during the wars in Flanders: "Father, it appears to me that we could take still another town," replied: "Hold your tongue, you little fool! Would you have us go home to plant cabbages?" In a word, when it comes to battles we ought to be guided by the maxim of Sennerib of the Hebrews that it is better for one man to perish than an entire people.[1]

## THE IMPORTANCE OF TERRAIN

COMBATS ARE AFFAIRS in which small units are engaged or only a portion of the army is involved. Battles are general actions where all are engaged equally on both sides. In every occasion where it is a question of attacking the enemy, the way in which you must fight depends upon the terrain and the advantages that the enemy is skillful enough to procure for himself. . . . An enemy wishing to avoid combat seeks his advantages in terrain difficult to approach, cut up by ravines and sunken roads and limited by rivers or woods. He encamps on mountain tops or hills, he occupies villages, erects batteries, fortifies the ground to his own liking, places each arm where it is suitable, strengthens his infantry with the assistance of his cavalry and *vice versa*, and covers his front with *chevaux de frise*, redoubts, and intrenchments. These varied circumstances, adapted to different terrain, necessitate different dispositions on the part of the attacker. Terrain is the foremost oracle that one must consult, after which he can fathom the enemy dispositions by his own knowledge of the rules of war.[2]

## HOW TO UTILIZE TERRAIN

> Frederick therefore placed great emphasis upon what he called the *coup d'oeil*, or the ability to grasp the salient features and potential advantages of the terrain at a quick glance.

THE COUP D'OEIL, properly speaking, is reduced to two points. The first is to have the ability of judging how many troops a given position can contain, a trick that is acquired only through practice. After having laid out several camps, the eye at last will acquire such a precise dimension that you will make only minor mistakes in your calculations. The other and by far the most superior talent is to know how to distinguish at first sight all the advantages that can be drawn from the terrain. One can acquire and perfect this talent if he is in the least endowed with a fortunate bent for war. The foundation of this *coup d'oeil* without a doubt is fortification, which has rules that must be applied to the positions of an army. A skillful general will know how to take advantage of the slightest height, a defile, a sunken road, a marsh, and so forth. . . .

Knowledge and choice of terrain are both essential matters, but it is also necessary to know how to take advantage of them in order to distribute the troops in the proper places. Our cavalry, which is drilled to act with celerity, can fight only on level ground, whereas the infantry can be employed on every type of terrain. . . . Most of the orders of battle that exist today [1753] are outmoded, yet we persist in following former customs without being guided by the terrain, which causes one to make bad and erroneous use of the ground.

The entire army must be placed in an order of battle that is adapted to the configurations of the terrain. Level ground is chosen for the cavalry, but this does not suffice, for if the plain is only 1,000 paces in width and is bounded by a wood, where one can assume that the enemy has thrown some infantry to provide protective fire so their cavalry can rally, it will then become necessary to change the disposition and place infantry at the extremity of the wings to support your own cavalry. Sometimes all the cavalry is stationed on one of the wings; Sometimes it is placed in the second line; on still other occasions the cavalry wings are closed by one or two infantry brigades.

The most advantageous positions for an army are heights, cemeteries, sunken roads, and ditches. If you take advantage of these in arranging your troops you need never fear being attacked.

If you station your cavalry behind a swamp it will be of no use to you, and if you place it too near to a wood the enemy can have troops there that will fire upon your cavalry and throw it into disorder. . . . Your infantry can find itself in the same predicament if it is pushed too far forward on a plain without having its flanks protected, for the enemy certainly will capitalize upon such an error and attack the infantry on the side where it cannot defend itself.

The nature of the ground must always dictate our dispositions. In mountainous country I would place my cavalry in the second line, using them in the first line only in those places where they can properly act, with the exception of some squadrons to take the enemy infantry in flank should they come to attack me. It is a general rule that in every well-led army the reserve is formed of cavalry if the country is level, and infantry mixed with several squadrons of dragoons and hussars if the country is rugged and intersected with natural obstacles.

The art of distributing troops according to the terrain is to know how to place them so that they can act freely and be useful on all sides. Villeroi, who perhaps was ignorant of this rule, deprived himself of his entire left wing on the plain of Ramillies [1706] by placing it behind a marsh where it could neither maneuver nor assist his right wing.

## INFANTRY IN BATTLE

Infantry relies upon firepower for the defensive and the bayonet in the attack. . . . The entire strength of our troops resides in the attack, and we would be unwise to renounce the offensive without cause. . . . Always attack at the weakest point. On these occasions I would prohibit my infantry from firing, for it only retards their march, and it is the ground gained and not the number of enemy dead that gives you victory. The most certain way to insure victory is to march boldly and in order against the enemy, always endeavoring to win ground. An accepted practice is to give intervals of fifteen paces to squadrons in difficult and rugged terrain, whereas on level ground they are formed in one continuous line.

The infantry will keep only those intervals between battalions that are necessary for the cannon. Only when attacking intrenchments, batteries, and villages and also in the rear guard of a retreat should cavalry and infantry be arrayed checkerwise to give immediate support to the front line by having the second line move up through the intervals. This enables the troops to retire without disorder. It also allows them to provide mutual support for each other, which is a rule that must always be observed.

I will take this occasion to impart some principal rules that you will have to observe when you put your army in order of battle, irrespective of the nature of the terrain. The first is to give specific bearings [*des points de vue*]—a church steeple, for example—for each wing. . . . It is not always necessary to wait for the whole army to be in line of battle to begin the attack. Often the occasion presents you with advantages that must be exploited immediately or else they are wasted. A large part of the army ought to be in position, however, especially the first line. . . . If the regiments of this line are not all present, they should be replaced by others from the second line.[3]

THE OFFICERS of the regiments and battalions must take out the weapons the day before the battle and have them thoroughly cleaned, freshly loaded, and provided with sharp flints, and, in general, must have them in the best condition possible. The lads must each have sixty ball cartridges with them. . . .

If the army then will be deployed according to the prepared disposition, as soon as the soldiers are near the enemy, the command will be given to deploy* with half-battalions. The brigade and battalion commanders must take care to preserve the proper distance between the platoons and to be sure that the battalions are well attached to each other.

When ordered to deploy, that regiment standing on the cavalry wing must remain thirty paces from the neighboring squadron. The battalions must be formed closed; the generals and regimental commanders, however, must see to it that the battalions also are aligned. During the deployment the cannon carried by the battalions must advance in order to fire upon the enemy; as soon as the regiments are all deployed, then two cannon always move between the battalions. With the exception of these intervals, the battalions must stand otherwise entirely closed.

It is necessary throughout to impress upon the men that they are not to fire before ordered. The attacking wing must march upon the enemy in good order and well closed. Should some enemy cavalry be encountered which our own cavalry have not chased off, then it is well to observe the general rule that not all the fire be expended against the cavalry. Only that platoon which appears to be in imminent danger from the enemy cavalry must fire a volley at forty or at most fifty paces. The regiments meanwhile must continue to advance and the commander must take care that nobody stands still, let alone falls back. In any case, the regiments must always remain closed . . . thus leaving no gaps.

Should we encounter only enemy infantry when his cavalry is already in disorder, then a continuous strong advance must be maintained and those battalions of the attacking wing can open fire by platoons at two hundred paces. . . . The regimental commanders must see to it that such platoon firing is done in orderly fashion.

Since His Royal Highness is of the definite opinion that the enemy is not so much shattered as driven off by firepower, when His Majesty gives this command to the regimental commanders of the attacking wing, they themselves, insofar as it is possible, must press forward always in good order in real charges against the enemy. If, however, the enemy should display a capacity for resistance against all human expectations, then the battalions must attack when they are within twenty paces, or better still, within ten paces (at the commander's discretion), and give the enemy a strong volley in the face. Immediately thereafter they should plunge the bayonet into the enemy's ribs, at the same time shouting at him to throw away his weapon and surrender. (In all probability it will not occur to the Austrians to cross bayonets with us; rather it is to be assumed that when they see their cavalry defeated, the rest will soon follow.)

The second line, which must deploy three hundred paces behind the first, must observe its distance carefully while deploying. If enemy hussars or similar rabble are to slink around behind both lines, then the commanders must make an about-face and, wherever the commander deems it advisable, have one and then another platoon fire upon them. One cannon per regiment or one for each two battalions will be given to the second line. These must not be loaded with anything except case shot so that if it should become necessary to fire on hussars and their ilk with cannon, such equipment which shall have been parked behind the lines in a *wagenburg* will not be damaged.[4]

WE KNOW from experience that the valor of the troops consists solely in the valor of the officers—a brave colonel, a brave battalion. It has been seen in all our wars that when the commander has been brave the battalion has never been repulsed, unless, of course, the commander was previously wounded or killed.[5] THE MAJORS and regimental adjutants must remain behind the battalions during battle . . . because if they are out in front they get in the way. The majors, however, as well as the adjutants, must make every possible effort to fill gaps in the battalions from behind, to keep order, also to see to the proper alignment and encourage the men at every opportunity.

The oboists, drummers, and fifers, as soon as the battle begins should bring the wounded officers, noncommissioned officers, and enlisted men to the *wagenburg*. It should be impressed upon all of the men, however, that if any of them should be wounded and can get to the *wagenburg* under his own power, there he would find complete safety and would be properly cared for. The men must be told this so that they will not run away. One army surgeon per battalion must remain with the battle lines; the others, however, must stay with the regimental surgeons in the *wagenburg* so that they can tend to the wounded properly and therefore better.[6] HUMANITY AND GRATITUDE toward those who have staked their lives so often on behalf of the state bid you to care for them as a father. . . . There must be doctors and army surgeons in sufficient number. Above all, however, you must have a couple of old officers of proven honesty to be sure that each does his duty and that nobody steals victuals, soup, and whatever else the state furnishes for the care and healing of those who make this glorious sacrifice.[7]

THE BATTLE will begin with the cavalry attacking at full gallop. The infantry will march in long strides toward the enemy. Battalion commanders should take care that their troops pierce and break through the enemy and that they use their firearms only when the enemy has turned in flight. If the soldiers should commence firing without order they will be ordered to shoulder arms and advance without halting. When the enemy begins to give way, the infantry will fire by battalion. A battle conducted in this matter will very soon be decided.[8]

IF THE ARMY is attacked by the enemy while occupying a post, the commander must defend his position and hold it by firepower. In such cases rapid fire is the best. Since the soldier can exhaust his ammunition very quickly, it is necessary, before he has fired his last round, to send lance corporals from each platoon to the reserve ammunition cart to obtain cartridges and distribute them as quickly as possible.

¶ If you attack the enemy on the plain and find yourself with the wing and the units which attack, you must march them in good order against the enemy, begin the charge at three hundred paces, and at the slightest sign of confusion in the enemy ranks, march with lowered bayonets to bring about their defeat. If, on the other hand, you attack the enemy in a difficult position, the commander must prevent everybody from firing as much as he possibly can, because the shots fired uphill produce little or no effect. To win the battle you must win terrain, and the sooner you can get your men on the battle-field where the enemy is arrayed the more you spare them and the less murderous the battle will be.

But at the same time the commander must not indulge in too lively a pursuit unless his losses in the initial attack have been slight or all the participating units are joined together, or, especially, unless the brigade commander orders it expressly. If you have carried a height . . . you must remain content to chase the enemy from it and keep him under heavy fire as he descends the hill to escape. But this post must be protected. The infantry should not leave it to follow the fugitives: that is the business of the cavalry. The infantry must remain content to hold the post where it has won the victory.[9]

EXCELLENT USE could be made of light infantry troops, although those that we create will not be of high quality, as new levies, raised in haste, can never be. These troops, such as they may be, become useful when used wisely. Place them in the first line of attack. . . . They must go head down at the enemy to draw his fire and create confusion amongst his troops. This paves the way for the second assault line which, moving closed and in good order, will easily get the better of the enemy. When one desires to make an attack with the free battalions,[10] these must be followed by the heavy infantry in formation behind them so that the fear of the latter's bayonets compels them to attack briskly and with ardor.

On level ground the free battalions must be thrown at the extremity of the refused wings where they can protect the baggage, but they become really useful in rugged terrain where they can form a chain before the front and flanks of the army in villages and behind streams, or in occupying woods. Such as they are, they will protect you against any surprise because the enemy can attack you only after driving them away, which gives you time enough to arrange your line of battle.

If you encamp in wooded or mountainous terrain the free battalions ought to make patrols, and in such country you can use them for any undertaking aimed at surprising the enemy, as hussars are used on the plain. You must never entrust them with important posts that must be held, however, because they lack stability; and a person would be much mistaken indeed if he were so ill-advised as to employ them for duties for which they are not intended. . . .

## CAVALRY

I have sometimes had occasion to observe with pain and displeasure that our infantry generals take so little trouble to learn about cavalry that when they have mounted troops under their command they sometimes require them to do the impractical and often neglect to use them for tasks where they are especially competent. This compels me to give them a distinct idea of cavalry so that they recognize the principles and the characteristics of this arm and will have a good idea of how it is to be used.[11]

ALL MOVEMENTS of cavalry are swift. It can decide the fate of a battle in one instant. It must be used only at the right time.[12] FLAT COUNTRY is especially suitable for cavalry, since its movements must be rapid, its execution prompt, and its attacks decided in the twinkling of an eye. . . . For this reason you should never have cavalry act on marshy ground, where it becomes bogged down without being able to advance. You should never use it in large forests, where it cannot operate. You should never make it attack on terrain where the low ground is intersected by deep sunken roads, and it must not in any event approach woods where infantry will fire upon it. Above all, it must never pass through defiles in the presence of the enemy, where it is sure to be defeated unless the passage is supported by infantry and artillery fire. Cavalry cannot act on rocky ground or steep slopes. It attacks at the gallop; therefore the terrain must be smooth.[13]

GOOD CAVALRY makes you master of the land. Two or three sudden attacks which succeed, one after the other, suffice to intimidate the enemy to the point where he no longer has the courage to stand before you. I am personally convinced that our cavalry will show itself superior to any other cavalry on level ground if the disproportion in numbers is not too great.

There are as many different kinds of battles as there are types of terrain, so it would be impossible to state in advance what can happen in each battle.[14] IN INFANTRY BATTLES, by which I mean attacks on villages, mountains, and difficult positions, you should have the cavalry operate not by the wing but preferably through intervals [of infantry]. This is why the cavalry usually is arrayed in the third line and can operate only after the infantry has already made a gap at one place or another. Then one or two cavalry regiments can be used. In this case the brigade general must go quickly to the point where he must smash in and penetrate in column by squadrons to take advantage of the confusion amongst the enemy, as the *gardes du corps,* gendarmes, and Seydlitz regiments did at Rossbach, the wing of Seydlitz did at Zorndorf, and the gendarmes did at Hochkirch. Even if the troops march in disorder on such an occasion it makes no difference. The generals have to notice here that in case the enemy has posted cavalry in close order behind his infantry, the cavalry must not be too far away from their own infantry, because as our infantry pushes back the enemy infantry, pursues it, and puts it completely to rout, they are exposed if they follow it too far. There are a thousand things to notice, to know. If they should find infantry in formation beside infantry in flight, they can attack it without hesitation provided they can take it in the rear. This is always the most trustworthy attack for cavalry and it involves no risk. These movements must be performed with the greatest despatch so that the enemy does not have time to parry them.[15]

IN THE OPEN FIELD the cavalry must charge the enemy instantly and attack him: this is a fundamental rule and my most serious order. The ability to attack first certainly depends upon the army forming swiftly so that it is always ready before the enemy and cannot be surprised by him. If our cavalry is formed while the enemy is still deploying his, then our men have only half a job because they can attack the enemy in the process of moving.[16]

IF THE ENEMY is to be engaged in a main action, then the columns of cavalry, as soon as they arrive at the scene where they are to deploy, and provided there are no defiles ahead, must deploy with all squadrons. When ordered to deploy, the cavalry must march with the right wing immediately to the place where the army's flank is to be covered. The first squadrons of the regiments thus come to a halt in the first line, dress their line, pay careful attention to the distance between regiments, observe carefully the line upon their objective, and form themselves thus as quickly as possible. The head of the column marches slowly during the deployment; the first squadrons from the rear regiments, however, must ride forward at a brisk trot and then form.

¶ If there happens to be a hill in front of the cavalry deployment, then this should be occupied by the cavalry wing, since it is of the greatest advantage for cavalry to charge downhill whenever possible.

The intervals between the squadrons of the first line must be no more than ten paces. The second line remains three hundred paces to the rear and maintains intervals of sixty paces. The order of battle must be formed thus:

## ORDER OF BATTLE

The following order of battle was issued on July 25, 1744. Although the details of deployment and terrain would vary

from one battle to the next, it may be assumed that this
served as a model whenever conditions permitted.

Ziethen's hussar regiment in column on the right wing, two
squadrons in the front line, and five behind one another. The
first line keeps very narrow intervals; the second line, three
hundred paces to the rear, keeps wide intervals. Those squadrons from the second line standing next to the infantry, however, must move to within one hundred fifty paces of the first
line so that if the enemy wishes to approach the first line on
the flank they can come to its support and in turn attack the
enemy on his flank.

Three hundred paces behind the second line of dragoons
the Natzmer hussars fall in behind the left wing, and those of
Colonel Ruesch behind the right. The hussars on the flanks
cover the cuirassiers [in the front line]; the hussars behind the
second line cover them in the rear and thereby assure the
cavalry that they need be concerned about nothing except
the enemy standing before them. In the event that there is
room to spare on one wing, the general commanding the cavalry of that wing must be ordered to send as many squadrons
from the second line as may be necessary to fill the gaps, in
order to cover the flank. If, on the other hand, the area for the
cavalry wing is too confined, then the general commanding
the wing can form three instead of two lines, only he must always see to it that the intervals in the front line are only ten
paces, and preferably still less, and that the other two lines
maintain very wide intervals.

When the cavalry wing is thus formed and the enemy makes
no movements, then the general must ask the King if he should
attack. If, however, the enemy makes the slightest movements
at the time or the general perceives that he can attack with
advantage, then the generals are herewith authorized by the
King to do so without delay.

The King hereby forbids all cavalry officers, under penalty
of being cashiered, ever to allow themselves to be attacked by

the enemy in any action. Prussians must always attack the enemy.

When the general orders the attack, the line advances at a walk, quickens to a trot, and when two hundred paces from the enemy, the cavalry gives the horses free rein and gallops at full speed.[17]

IN THIS, and as a matter of prime importance in the attack, it must indeed be pointed out that the entire line fall upon the enemy's throat with its united power, not piecemeal or with one regiment after the other. To accomplish this the squadron commanders must trot up together and begin the gallop simultaneously, so that the entire line drives into the enemy all at once. When the great wall closes in this manner and simultaneously approaches the enemy with impetuosity, it is impossible to withstand it. If perchance a squadron in the first line is thrown into confusion because of a ditch or some similar obstacle, then the next squadron must move up from the second line immediately. And, by the same token, if the opposition at one place or another should prove difficult for the first line, then the second must support it at once without waiting for an order to that effect. When the first attack is over, each general with his brigade, indeed, even each *Rittmeister* with his squadron, must attack and drive off those of the enemy still standing before him. The squadrons as well as the regiments must give maximum aid and support to one another until they have put the enemy completely to flight.

When the enemy cavalry has been driven beyond the next defile, then the proper course of action for cavalry is two-fold: a portion must be detached to keep the enemy cavalry from returning to the battlefield while the rest proceeds to attack the enemy infantry in the rear in order to cut off its retreat. It is also very good if you can fall upon the enemy infantry in the flank and in the second line, but in this case an officer must be sent to apprise our own infantry so that they do not fire upon the enemy while the cavalry attack is in progress. Otherwise our cavalry will easily be thrown into confusion.

. . . I remind you only that the attack on the flanks of both enemy lines is the surest and shortest, because then the lines fall by heaps like a house of cards.[18]

WHEN THE BATTLE is fought on level ground and the cavalry is arrayed in battle order, each major general should place himself at the head of his brigade. I have prohibited the lieutenant generals from taking a position in front because it is their task to redress the disorder and see to it that the second line supports the attacks wherever it proves necessary. The essential thing in these attacks is to be sure that the flanks are well covered, that the second line carefully observes the first, that the regiments are always well closed, and that the nearer the cavalry approaches the enemy the more rapid the gallop. In this way there will be no confusion. When the enemy is repulsed the generals must look to the safety of their flanks, especially the second line. For the rest, the generals must take care to conserve the horses of their brigades and to keep good order among the officers and in all other things. If someone makes a mistake he should be arrested and severely punished. One ought not to put up with an officer capable of cowardice.[19]

IF THE BATTLE occurs in mountainous and difficult terrain, then it is not possible to make a great attack with all units simultaneously. Each general then must do the best he can with his brigade, for the ground in such places is quite varied and if the individual general does not know how to judge terrain and take advantage of the least opportunity that is presented to him, then he can do no good. . . . In affairs of this type the generals must look to the side as well as the front in order to support adjoining units, while at the same time attacking the enemy as vigorously and boldly as possible. If you attack strongly and in closed formations, then the squadrons cannot get intermingled and it may also be presumed that the enemy will be forced to retreat without offering great opposition. If, however, you do not attack him with the ranks properly closed, then the squadrons can become entangled and the individual man then decides the outcome. . . . The squadrons therefore must attack with closed ranks whenever possible, the first line remaining virtually without intervals so that no flank of any squadron is exposed to the enemy.[20]

THE SQUADRON COMMANDERS must be responsible for seeing to it that no cavalryman or dragoon uses either carbine or pistol during battle, but that they act only with sword in hand. Therefore cavalrymen and dragoons must be carefully impressed and instructed that so long as they have their carbines and pistols still loaded, these still remain of use to them.[21]

IN BATTLE we require our hussars to render the same services as the cuirassiers and dragoons.[22] They can be in the second line or else on the flank of the cavalry lines either to cover the latter or to outflank the enemy in the attack and fall upon his rear. If the enemy is defeated the hussars pursue them, with the heavy cavalry in support. When it is a question of attacking infantry I prefer the cuirassiers to the others because they have confidence in their breastplates.[23]

IT WILL BE SEEN from the foregoing that . . . the object of these maneuvers is to win time on every occasion and to decide the battle more promptly than hitherto has been the custom, and finally to destroy the enemy by the furious blows of our cavalry. The coward is swept away in the impetuosity of the charge in such a manner that he is forced to perform his duty as well as the brave man: no cavalryman is useless. Everything depends upon the vivacity of the attack.[24]

## CAVALRY IN COLUMN

For reasons to be explained later, changing tactical conditions during the Seven Years' War were no longer as favorable to cavalry, although this remained Frederick's favorite arm. In his later writings he hinted at a new cavalry formation.

Since everything in war has become an affair of posts and artillery combats, you must take the greatest care not to expose your cavalry needlessly to this terrible fire, which would destroy it unless it should have occasion to defend itself. You must therefore select low ground for protection against artillery fire and keep the cavalry entirely fresh until the moment its turn for action arrives. The right moment is when the enemy artillery begins to slacken its fire and the enemy infantry has already fired. Then, if your infantry has not decided the affair, and provided the slope leading to the enemy is not too rugged, have your cavalry charge the enemy infantry *in column,* as we have done at Zorndorf and Torgau, and you will obtain victory.[25]

FORTUNATELY NOBODY yet has cognizance of these column attacks of cavalry. Some cavalry generals will execute them as soon as it becomes necessary. The cavalry column is to be regarded as a state secret, just as the use of the ten-pounder howitzer. For as soon as these things are known they can be used against us and we lose the advantage of discovery. . . .

## ARTILLERY

What I have said about the development of artillery in time of peace covers in large measure what is required of it in the field. But because this does not exhaust the subject, I must add here a few more essentials.

We disperse the guns among the battalions and brigades. Each battalion of the first line receives 2 six-pounder howitzers and 1 seven-pounder, while every five battalions are assigned, in addition, a heavy battery of 10 twelve-pounders. The second line contains only long three-pounders, two per battalion,[26] and the brigades are given batteries of twelve-pounders just like the first line. The 40 ten-pounder howitzers are found in the reserve and will be placed by the army commander as he thinks best. Each free battalion has 2 small three-pounders.

We have conical twelve-pounders that are fit only for detachments in the bad time of the year, when rain has softened the roads. They do not carry as far as the others, but they have the advantage of light weight so that they can be transported also in the mountains and on poor roads.

In addition to this immense number of cannon we have the light [horse] artillery which, properly used, is of the greatest value. It consists of 20 six-pounders and four howitzers. Strong horses are required for teams to draw this artillery. The gunners are all mounted on Polish horses, led by a captain and two subalterns. The light artillery is as quick as the wind and can move to the place designated in less than a minute. If this invention were to be used every day then the enemy would imitate it and develop horse artillery of his own, but if it is kept secret and used only occasionally at the most important and decisive moments, as we did at Reichenbach, then no doubt we will derive the greatest advantage from it.[27]

In war one either attacks or is attacked, and if he himself is the attacker then he fights either in the open or else he assaults fortified positions. On the plain a prudent general will be sure to provide the attack wing with a great preponderance of artillery. If he attacks a fortified position and has a few hills in the vicinity, then surely he will place the heaviest batteries there, endeavoring to bring the enemy under a cross fire in order to blast a breech in that part of the enemy's camp under attack. If there are no heights near the enemy's position, then he can only use his howitzers, of which he must have a suitable number, to bombard the portion of the position under attack and pave the way for his troops to victory.[28]

I DISTINGUISH between the heavy guns and the field pieces attached to the battalions. The former should be planted on heights, and the smaller guns fifty paces in front of the battalions. In both cases the guns should be carefully aimed and fired. When within five hundred paces of the enemy, the field pieces will be drawn by the men and will remain to continue firing without letup during the advance. If the enemy begins to retreat, the heavy guns will move forward and fire a few rounds by way of wishing them *bon voyage*. Each piece in the first line must be served by six gunners and three carpenters from the regiments. I forgot to mention that artillery should commence firing case shot when the range is three hundred fifty paces.[29]

IT MUST BE IMPRESSED upon the artillery officers . . . that it is not enough merely to fire a great deal and rapidly. They must take good aim and direct their fire carefully to concentrate it on the side of the attack and to destroy, as much as they can, the enemy batteries firing upon our own troops. For the infantryman cannot fire while marching against the enemy, and he will be destroyed by the enemy's fire if our batteries do not help him.

But no matter how essential the services rendered by artillery in the attack of posts, it is more important still when it comes to defending them. A well-chosen position ought to deprive the assailant of his cavalry, his artillery, and even, as it were, of his infantry; for the cavalry could not bear up under the violent cannonade that it would have to endure if it approached you too closely; your high ground prevents the enemy from using his artillery, which cannot fire uphill; and the enemy infantry, which dares not fire while attacking, marches against you as if it were armed with a stick. To obtain all these advantages you must sweep the main avenues of approach with a cross fire from your guns; your gunners must aim carefully, know all of the distances, and avail themselves of grape shot when the time is right; your six-pounders must produce ricochet fire,★ and you must warn the gunners in time when you want to release the cavalry against the enemy.[30]

IF THE POSITION is well selected and there is no high ground in its front or on the flanks, then the first line is placed halfway up the hill and the second line, on the crest. The batteries of the first line will be so laid out that they fire obliquely and thus keep the entire front under a cross fire. The commanders of the heavy batteries similarly take their three distances—high angle fire, point blank fire, and case shot. If they fire their shells against the attacker the small howitzers are especially effective in such positions.

The guns of the second line do not come into action until a part of the first line is defeated and falls back upon them, in which case the artillery officers must take good care to direct their fire immediately upon the pursuing enemy. It is the task of the second line and its guns to drive back with well-directed shots those who think that victory is in their grasp. Above all you must pay the greatest attention to the flanks of the army and supply these with the largest number of guns possible in order to make them impregnable.[31]

IF IT IS A QUESTION of withdrawing, whenever you wish to abandon a position you must send away the large guns first: if the descent from the hill is steep you must also send away your field pieces, because if these should overturn in descending they run the risk of being lost to the enemy, which is a disgrace for the troops. If your army is defeated your first thought must be to save as many cannon as possible, at the same time taking pains to send some batteries forward quickly to the unit covering the retreat and to the first position where the troops are reassembled. In addition to this, the artillery officers must exert great vigilance to have reserve ammunition besides the ordinary ammunition for the cannon in all posts, and to have spare ammunition close to each brigade so that one is not defeated for lack of powder and ball. This could happen during a very obstinate battle.

I make no mention of the light artillery because the officers of this organization know the employment that is expected of them and they are fully in a position to execute anything practical that could be desired of them.[32]

## THE INCREASING IMPORTANCE OF ARTILLERY

The following "Instructions" written in 1782 represents Frederick's last words on the subject of artillery and shows how far his thought had progressed since the Silesian wars, when he had assigned artillery a relatively insignificant role. Although he had acquired new respect for it by 1756, it took the Seven Years' War to make him fully aware of its importance.

THE PREPARATIONS and different movements that precede a battle, regardless of whether one already is in the vicinity of the enemy and has him in view, often consume three to four hours, depending upon the ground where the enemy has taken his position and the obstacles that must be overcome before one can deploy. It is, however, always incorrect and dangerous if the artillery already opens fire as soon as it sees the enemy and believes him to be within range. Neither the defending nor the attacking party has anything to fear from artillery fire under these conditions, because it is almost without effect on either side. The defender expends his ammunition without advantage; the attacker, however, not only loses his powder, but performs his evolutions much more slowly. The enemy thus gains the time and the opportunity to place obstacles in the path of our attack, if not to render it completely fruitless.

I have perpetually called these errors of premature fire to the attention of my artillery. I know, to be sure, that the impassioned pleas of infantry officers and of the adjoining platoons often may induce the artillery to make this mistake, and your officers, to court favor with the infantry no less than to demonstrate their bravery, fire until they notice that half of their shots are expended. Then, for fear that they will exhaust their ammunition, they slacken their fire just at the moment when it should be the heaviest.

It also happens, however, that even the commanding general or one of the other generals will forget himself and order the artillery to open fire too soon in order only to deaden the senses of his troops [*um nur seine Truppen zu betäuben*] without taking into consideration the dangerous consequences it can have. Although the [artillery] officer has no choice but to obey, he must fire as slowly as he possibly can and aim the guns accurately so that all the shots do not go astray. The only time that such a premature fire is excused is if the general intends to draw the attention of the enemy to one side in order to mask other movements.

As soon as the guns are advanced to within six to seven hundred paces of the enemy you must make a continuous fire and keep it up for as long as you are very near to the enemy, for one shot with a cannon ball at such close range not only smashes through all the lines, but the noise of the projectile itself terrifies the enemy troops, and the whining noise overhead provokes far more fear than case shot at an excessive range.

An enemy seldom will endure such a well-directed fire at one hundred or eighty paces; if he holds his position in spite of you, then you must let him have it with case shot, and a few minutes will decide the affair.

You must, however, impress this fundamental point upon your officers:[33] never must they fire further than one hundred paces with canister* because the pellets will always become too scattered; a great many of them will strike the ground before they reach the enemy, many will fly over his head, and but few will do him any damage.

If the enemy cavalry attacks and tries to break into the flanks or elsewhere along the line, then the cannon must open fire on them with shot at a maximum range of eight to nine hundred paces, but it must be done with the greatest possible accuracy and rapidity. Generally the officers and batmen of the infantry, as soon as they become aware of the danger from cavalry, call out to the artillery to use case shot, and the artillery accommodates them. Your officers must not allow themselves to make this mistake, however: they must fire with solid shot for as long as they believe they still have enough time to switch to canister, and must deliver the first broadside at fifty to sixty paces.

You must instruct your gunners in advance that in such a situation they fire on command of the officers, not the entire battery simultaneously, but only half of the battery, so that a constant fire is maintained and the guns fire intermittently. Individual guns must not be fired, however, because single shots do not put enemy cavalry in disorder and delay his march so easily.

An officer who, with similar opportunities, does not allow himself to get disconcerted will never risk losing his guns, nor need he fear that the enemy cavalry will attain its goal. No cavalry will travel, at a gallop, more than two hundred paces in closed formation in a minute. Assuming that the cavalry will close up only for the last eight hundred paces, and assuming also that one cannon can fire four rounds per minute, then from a single battery of ten guns the cavalry receives 140-150 rounds of solid shot at the very least before it is fired upon with case shot. And because cavalry does not immediately attack at a gallop, but moves first at a trot, then at a canter, and finally at full speed, if your shots are well placed, then the enemy cavalry certainly will lose any desire to come within fifty paces of you to receive a round of case shot.

Above all I urge your officers at such occasions to keep their presence of mind. Then they will not risk abandoning their guns, nor will they find it necessary to withdraw prematurely for fear of losing them, thus leaving the infantry without support and forcing them to withdraw as well.

I must mention two other main mistakes common to all artillery: (1) it fires primarily against the opposing artillery and attempts to silence his guns; and (2) it seeks to site its guns on the highest ground found on the battlefield in order to stretch the range. Both are pernicious prejudices, and you must in fact do just the opposite.

In considering the first mistake, you must direct your entire attention and all of your fire on smashing the lines of enemy infantry, throwing them into disorder, delaying their advance, and preventing their orderly movements. When you have accomplished this, the enemy infantry will soon be defeated and his artillery, left alone, will be silent and will fall into your hands.

With regard to the second mistake, that of placing guns on hills so that they can shoot further, anyone can easily see that it is not only the range of the shot but also its effect that matters. If a shot fired from a hill actually strikes the enemy line, its effect will not be especially great because of its sloping angle, so the other lines have nothing to fear from it. If a shot should strike the ground in front of the enemy, however, in light soil it will remain stuck in the earth, and on solid ground, with a plunging fire, it will bounce over all the lines. However, if you should still find it necessary because of the terrain to locate your guns on heights, then these must never be elevated over twenty feet above the horizon, or you could place them also with a comparable elevation on the ridges of higher mountains.

If circumstances permit, you must never shoot over the heads of our own infantry. Always advance with your gun, for even if the advancing infantry suffers no damage from your fire, they will duck with each shot and consequently will make the advance more difficult.

Finally—and let this be your main rule—avoid all high angle fire as much as possible. When the terrain permits and you are not prevented by trenches, defiles, or small hills, fire nothing but ricochet shots. Such shots seldom fail and at close range smash through all enemy lines. Although I have confined my remarks to cannon, most of what I have said applies also to howitzers except that the latter can shoot somewhat farther with case shot because of the larger caliber of the bullets, and often will shoot from higher mountains toward intrenchments with high angle fire. In the plain, however, and primarily at not too great a range, you must likewise use ricochet fire.[34]

## THE THREE ARMS COMBINED

The following "Disposition" or general order of battle was written in camp at Schweidnitz in June, 1745, and was intended to be "invariably followed on all occasions." In light of later trends in cavalry and artillery some modifications undoubtedly were found to be necessary, but it does suggest the role of the three arms in battle as Frederick conceived it during the Silesian wars.

THE VANGUARD should not advance over two miles in front of the army, and should take all imaginable precautions continually to reconnoiter the enemy.

The army, marching in columns, should halt five miles from the enemy and form in order of battle.

When the army has advanced so far, the regiments should range themselves in the manner which His Royal Highness commands them.

The final line should march three deep in accordance with the regulations and must take care to keep in close order with the ranks straight and equal.

The brigade commanders should ride up and down their brigades and encourage their men to do their duty. Likewise must the regimental commanders, captains, and other subalterns commanding platoons exhort the soldiers to do their duty and make it appear to them as easy as possible.

The noncommissioned officers, standing two steps to the rear of the battalions, must not confuse the men with useless chatter, but should keep a watchful eye over them. If any soldier should attempt to run away during battle and should set as much as one foot out of his rank, the noncommissioned officer standing to his rear shall run him through with the short sword and kill him on the spot.

Having observed that at the late battle of Chotusitz the best soldiers were with the baggage, the King absolutely forbids such practice in the future, and the officers shall answer to it with honor and reputation, even with life and limb. Each regiment should employ only three captains at arms with the worst soldiers and the sick who are unfit for action to guard the baggage and the officers' equipment.

The regimental field pieces and such other artillery as the King may have along with him should be advanced approximately two hundred paces in front of the first line.

The grenadiers should be posted behind the first line on the right, left, and center. Three grenadier brigades of four hundred men each shall support the right wing of the cavalry, three others the left, and the rest shall be posted at the center behind the first line, to await His Majesty's orders. If the cavalry moved out for the attack are repulsed without having done their duty, as at Mollwitz, the grenadiers are to fire on them even if they have to shoot them down to the last man.

The majors and adjutants shall diligently see to it that their battalions do not fall into confusion and for that purpose shall ride continuously along the front to prevent all disorder in time.

The reserve corps, consisting of eighteen cavalry squadrons and six infantry battalions, shall be posted behind the first line on the right, left, and also in the center, and there await orders. The hussars shall file off the left wing and observe the enemy attacks, to act wherever it shall be necessary and proper.

If the fighting is heavy and many casualties occur, one regiment from the right and another from the left of the second line shall be sent behind the first to restore it wherever the general and brigade commanders deem it necessary. The second line shall be posted eight hundred paces behind the first, where it is to remain during the battle, with muskets shouldered; and the officers shall prevent, under pain of being broken, any soldier from leaving his rank.

Each officer commanding a platoon shall carefully inspect the soldiers' arms, and see to it that the pan holds the priming and that everything is in good order. . . . The soldiers should be exhorted to aim carefully and not fire too high so as not to waste powder and lead. . . .

As soon as His Majesty . . . shall cause the signal to be given by three cannon shot from the center, the artillery shall throw the enemy into confusion with a brisk fire and continue firing until the King sends orders by one of his adjutant generals to cease. The captains and lieutenants of artillery shall aim the guns themselves and not entrust it to the gunners.

When the bombardment has ceased, the signal for the attack shall be given by three cannon shot.

When the army, in close order, shall have come to within two hundred paces of the enemy, then, in order to accustom the soldiers to the fire and to blind them to danger, the infantry shall commence firing regularly by platoons. The first line, continuing the advance, shall take great care that no regiment breaks the line. The officers . . . must give the word of command loud and distinctly and take up position one pace before their platoons so that the men may hear the commands well and not wound each other by an irregular fire.

In the event the enemy's cavalry or hussars shall pierce the first line, then the regiment where they have broken through shall face about and charge against them.

If victory should fall to His Majesty and the enemy have been forced to yield, then the advance with continuous fire shall cease. The cavalry and hussars shall then move out and, together with those infantry regiments selected by the King or the commanding general, shall pursue the enemy. During the pursuit no soldier shall, under pain of death, leave his rank to plunder the dead or take booty. The officers shall answer for this.

The rest of the regiments not sent on the pursuit shall remain with muskets shouldered until they are commanded to order arms, but even then they must all remain standing in the ranks.[35]

## NOTES: CHAPTER V

1. Frederick, *Instruction militaire du Roi de Prusse pour ses généraux* (Frankfort, 1761), pp. 167-73 [*Instruction militaire*].

2. Frederick, "Pensées et règles générales pour la guerre," *Oeuvres de Frédéric le grand* (Berlin, 1846-56), XXVIII, 109-10.

3. Frederick, *Instruction militaire*, pp. 32-39, 151-54.

4. Frederick, "Disposition für die Sämmtlichen Regimenter Infanterie, wie solche sich bei dem vorfallenden Marsche gegen den Feind und der derauf folgenden Bataille zu verhalten haben," *Oeuvres*, XXX, 74-77 [*Disposition für infanterie*].

5. Frederick, "Règles de ce qu'on exige d'un bon commandeur de bataillon en temps de guerre," *Oeuvres*, XIX, 58 [*Commandeur de bataillon*].

6. Frederick, *Disposition für infanterie*, pp. 76-77.

7. Frederick, "Das Militärische Testament von 1768," *Die Werke Friedrichs Des Grossen* (Berlin, 1913), VI, 237 [*Testament von 1768*].

8. Frederick, *Instruction militaire*, p. 156.

9. Frederick, *Commandeur de bataillon*, pp. 58-59.

10. Free battalions were light infantry units raised by Frederick in the early stages of the Seven Years' War. Previously he had attempted to combat Austrian hussars and Pandours with light cavalry (i.e. dragoons and hussars), as indicated in his *Instruction militaire* (p. 109) and *Pensées et règles générales pour la guerre* (pp. 132-34). But soon after war broke out in 1756 he encouraged several officers to raise their own free battalions, which they would then command. Most of the recruits were deserters, especially from the French army, and even convicts were enrolled. Frederick complained that the officers themselves frequently joined the free battalions primarily for plunder. Because Frederick increased the number of free battalions from four in 1756 to twenty-six at the end of the war, it may be assumed that they performed useful services, although he seems never fully to have understood their capabilities. Austrian light infantry were used only for guerrilla warfare; Frederick frequently squandered his in attacks in pitched battles, and he used them in the first line of the attack not because they were an elite corps but for precisely the opposite reason—they were inferior troops and hence were expendable. He looked with scorn upon the experience of British regulars in America, and it was only after the war of the American Revolution that he formed free regiments and issued instructions for their employment. His "Instruction für die Frei-Regimenter oder leichten Infanterie-Regimenter," issued in December, 1783 (*Werke*, VI, 295-300), indicates that even at this late date Frederick had failed to grasp the unique characteristics and potential of light infantry, which in his view was never more than an inferior species of infantry of the line. Erwin Dette, *Friedrich der Grosse und sein Heer* (Göttingen, 1914), pp. 76-81.

11. Frederick, "Eléments de castramétrie et de tactique," *Oeuvres*, XXIX, 37, 40-41 [*Castramétrie*].

12. Frederick, *Testament von 1768*, p. 241.

13. Frederick, *Castramétrie*, p. 38.

14. Frederick, *Testament von 1768*, p. 240.

15. Frederick, "Instruction pour les generaux-majors de Cavalerie," *Oeuvres*, XXVIII, 171-72 [*Instruction pour cavalerie*].

16. Frederick, "Aus der Instruction für die Generalmajors von der Cavallerie," *Werke*, VI, 306. This particular item was written in August, 1748, and is not to be confused with the *Instruction pour les généraux-majors de cavalerie*, which appeared in 1759.

17. Frederick, "Disposition, wie sich die Officiere von der Cavallerie in einem Treffen gegen den Feind zu verhalten haben," *Werke*, VI, pp. 301-303.

18. Frederick, *Aus der Instruction für die Generalmajors von der Cavallerie*, pp. 307-308.

19. Frederick, *Instruction pour les généraux-majors de cavalerie*, p. 172.

20. Frederick, *Aus der Instruction für die Generalmajors von der Cavallerie*, pp. 307-308.

21. Frederick, "Instruction für die Cavallerie für den fall einer Bataille," *Oeuvres*, XXX, 57.

22. Cuirassiers were the heavy cavalry mounted on the largest horses and protected by the cuirass or breast-plate. Hussars were mounted on smaller horses averaging under fifteen hands in height, and carried no armor: both cuirassiers and hussars were armed with sword, two pistols, and a carbine. Dragoons were also mounted on smaller horses and carried, in addition to the sword, pistols, and carbine, a bayonet for use when fighting dismounted. The basic unit for all cavalry, although the number per regiment would vary with the type of cavalry, was the squadron comprising six officers, twelve noncommissioned officers, and about 130 troopers. The squadron was divided into four troops and in formation these lined up in three ranks, with the largest men and horses in front. Frederick's ideal was "that Cuirassiers and Dragoons should be as adroit as the Hussars," and that the latter "should be able to charge with as much cohesion as the heavy cavalry." Major W. H. Greenly, "The Cavalry of Frederick the Great: Its training, leading, and employment in War," *Journal of the Royal United Service Institution*, LIII (October, 1909), 1300-1326.

23. Frederick, *Castramétrie*, p. 39.

24. Frederick, *Instruction militaire*, p. 182.

25. Frederick, *Castramétrie*, pp. 38-39. Italics mine. The column attack of cavalry was first executed by Seydlitz against the Russians at Zorndorf in 1758.

26. Notice that here Frederick allots more artillery to the second line than he did during the Silesian wars, reflecting the general increase in the size and use of the arm that had occurred between the Silesian and the Seven Years' Wars.

27. The term used by Frederick is Light Artillery, but obviously he is referring here to the first battery of Horse Artillery that he created in the spring of 1759 to support cavalry in detached operations. This marks one of the few original contributions Frederick made to warfare. See Matti Lauerma, *L'artillerië de campagne française pendant les guerres de la révolution: évolution de l'organisation et de la tactique* (Helsinki, 1956), p. 55.

28. Frederick, *Testament von 1768*, pp. 229-30, 249.

29. Frederick, *Instruction militaire*, pp. 160-61.

30. Frederick, *Castramétrie*, pp. 42, 43.

31. Frederick, *Testament von 1768*, pp. 230-31.

32. Frederick, *Castramérie*, p. 43.

33. This document was intended for Frederick's chief of artillery.

34. Frederick, "Instruction für meine Artillerie," *Werke*, VI, 337-40.

35. Frederick, "Disposition, wie es bei vorgehender bataille bei seiner Königlichen Majestät in Preussen armee unveränderlich soll gehalten werden, wornach sich auch sowohl die generalität, als andere commandirende officiere stricte zu achten und solches zu observiren haben," *Oeuvres*, XXX, 145-50. A slightly different version in translation is contained in Thomas Simes, *The Military Guide for Young Officers* (London, 1774) I, 109-11.

# First Lessons in Tactics

Because Frederick's main purpose in writing was to instruct his subordinate generals in the art of war, he stressed only those rules or maxims that could be deduced from recent campaigns and refrained from advancing any speculative theories of his own. Using these proven principles as a foundation, he then constructed a number of hypothetical situations to show how the different rules might be applied. The following selections come primarily from Frederick's writings before the Seven Years' War—in other words, before he had experienced defeat and was forced to curb his actions because of dwindling resources and in the presence of an enemy who likewise had learned from the late campaigns for Silesia.

## GENERAL RULES TO BE OBSERVED
## WHEN APPROACHING AN ENEMY POSITION

*IF YOU MARCH* in closed columns, have them deployed at 1,500 paces from the enemy, never nearer for fear of the havoc of artillery.

If you form the oblique order[1] be sure to outflank the enemy with the attacking wing, otherwise when you advance the kind of quarter turn you have to execute in maneuvering toward him makes you fall on the second or third squadron—in case you are attacking cavalry—or the second or third battalion, if the enemy opposite consists of infantry, instead of outflanking them or at least hitting the extremity of the line.

Always outflank the enemy with your attacks . . . and never lead troops at random and in such a way that will cause you to become outflanked.

Always lead your infantry intact and in such a way that if a breach is made in your line, it is not toward the attacking wing.

If you are forced to shift some regiments from the flanks or the second line toward either wing, notify the other wing to restore a like number in the second line so that these, rejoining the attacking wing, can cover and fortify it.

In every case when you send a detachment in front of the army to assault a village, battery, and so forth, the battle line must, in marching, remain no more than one hundred paces behind the attacking unit in order to give it support and protection.

If you attack with the infantry in *échelon*, so arrange the brigades that they always provide mutual cover for the flanks. Do the same with cavalry. It cannot be repeated often enough that flanks constitute the Achilles' heel of the troops and as such they must always be protected and fortified.

Fire as little as possible with the infantry in battle: charge with the bayonet.

Never employ my column when the enemy has his cavalry in battle array behind his infantry. My column is effective only when the infantry commence firing, regardless how many troops one has in a line. Then, and provided no cavalry is found behind the enemy line, you can form a column from a battalion of the second line, with four cavalry squadrons to support it, and break through the enemy position.

Whenever you attack villages, have the first unit that enters take up its station there and use the units that follow for mop-up operations.

Always have cavalry in the second line as well as in the reserve. It need not remain too near and it must be kept out of range of enemy fire until the moment arrives for it to go into action.

Always station a platoon from the second line behind the artillery of the first.

Your flanks, three battalions strong, must have two grenadier companies in reserve.

Always keep three or four squadrons as a reserve behind the cavalry line in order to outflank the enemy, should the occasion present itself.

When attacking a strong, natural position, do not rush forward. March with the advance guard, reconnoiter the enemy position, make your dispositions accordingly, and, if possible, never seize the bull by the horns. If, on the other hand, the enemy's line is broken, attack him as brusquely as possible, without the slightest hesitation.

When desiring to attack troops in position, always take ten mortars with you. Formed in two batteries behind the line, these will enable you to bombard enemy batteries with a cross fire while the infantry advances to the attack.

Never bombard a village if the wind blows against you, but if the wind is in your favor, bombard it and reduce it to cinders.[2]

With these maxims as guidelines, Frederick proceeded to indoctrinate his generals by presenting his suggested solutions to a series of tactical problems similar to what they might expect to encounter in another war. As an instructor in tactics he preferred the case method as a vehicle for communicating his thoughts, because he believed that "it is impossible for the word to make as strong an impression on the mind as a drawing, which describes everything at a glance that one must comprehend and at the same time eliminates much useless and tiresome verbiage."

In the following examples, which for the most part are based upon Frederick's experiences and observations during the Silesian wars, Frederick assumes the strength of his army to be fifty-five infantry battalions and one hundred ten squadrons. He also assumes that his enemy will again be the Austrians. The accompanying "visual aids" are taken from his own works, principally the *Military Instructions* for his generals and the *Atlas* accompanying his published *Oeuvres*.

## PRELIMINARY MOVEMENTS [Plate 2]

IT IS EXTREMELY DIFFICULT to surprise the Austrians in their camp because of the number of light troops that surround it.

If two armies remain near one another the business will very soon be decided between them, unless one takes up an unassailable position secure from surprises, a circumstance that very rarely occurs between armies although it is nothing uncommon when detachments are opposed to each other.

To be able to surprise the enemy in his camp it is essential that the enemy never expect an attack and that he place unlimited confidence in the superiority of his troops, the strength of his position, the reports of his emissaries, or, finally, in the vigilance of his light troops.

Before formulating any plan you must first acquire complete knowledge of the terrain and the enemy position. Have the roads leading to the enemy camp examined and then make the general disposition of the army accordingly, being governed at

Avant garde.

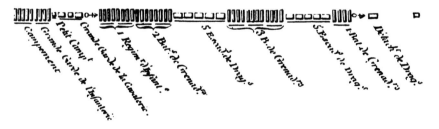

PLATE 2. An advance guard, comprising detachments of infantry and cavalry. (*Instruction militaire du Roi de Prusse pour ses généraux*, Plan 1.)

every point by the detailed knowledge of all the circumstances.

You should appoint chasseurs who are the most intelligent and the best acquainted with the roads to lead the columns. Be especially careful to conceal your plan, for secrecy is the soul of all these enterprises.

The light troops should take the lead on the march under several pretenses, but the real reason is to prevent any wretched deserter from betraying you. These hussars will also prevent the enemy patrols from approaching too closely and discovering your movements.

You must give the generals serving under you instructions to cover any conceivable eventuality, so that each of them knows how to act when the time arrives.

If the enemy's camp is located on level ground, an advance guard may be formed of dragoons which, joined by the hussars, will ride into the camp at full speed, throw it into confusion, and cut down everyone who appears before them. These dragoons must be supported by the whole army, with the infantry at the head of the army being employed particularly in attacking the enemy cavalry wings.

The advance guard should begin the attack half an hour before daybreak, but it is necessary that the army should not be more than eight hundred paces to the rear.

During the march [Plate 3] the most profound silence is to be observed and the soldiers must be prohibited from smoking tobacco. When the attack has begun and daylight arrives the infantry, formed into four or six columns, must march straight for the camp in order to support the advance guard. No firing will be allowed in the dark, since one runs the risk of killing his own men; but as soon as it is daylight you should open fire against all areas where the advance guard has not penetrated and especially against the cavalry on the wings, in order to force the enemy troopers who have no time to accouter their horses to abandon them and flee.

The enemy are to be followed even out of their camp, and all the cavalry should be sent after them to take advantage of the disorder and confusion. If the enemy have abandoned their

arms, a strong detachment should be left to guard the camp
while the rest of the army, without stopping to plunder, pursues the enemy as vigorously as possible. No efforts should be
spared to rout the enemy completely, especially since a similar
opportunity may not soon present itself, and by capitalizing
upon this occasion we may have a free hand during the entire
campaign.

Fortune intended to favor me with such an opportunity before the battle of Mollwitz, for we approached Marshal de
Neipperg's army, the troops of which were cantoned in three
villages, without meeting anyone. But at this time I had not

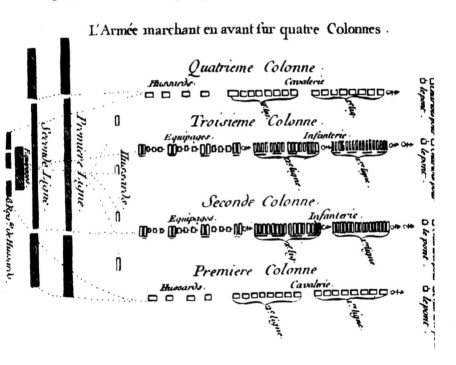

PLATE 3.  The approach to battle. Having encamped the night
before in line of battle, the army forms four columns of march
as it advances against the enemy. It will deploy again into line
of battle if a fight is imminent. (*Instruction militaire du Roi
de Prusse pour ses généraux*, Plan II.)

learned enough to be able to take advantage of the situation. I should have surrounded the village of Mollwitz with two columns and attacked it, at the same time detaching dragoons to the other two villages where the Austrian cavalry was stationed to throw these troops into confusion. The infantry following the dragoons would have prevented the Austrian cavalry from mounting. I am persuaded that their army would have been totally defeated.

¶ For my own part I shall never attack at night because the darkness causes so much disorder and most soldiers do their duty only when under the scrutiny of their officers and when they have punishment to fear.

## THE ATTACK

It is axiomatic that you must secure your own flanks and rear, and turn those of the enemy. This may be done in a variety of ways, although all are manifestations of the same principle.

¶ If a Prussian army is inferior to that of the enemy it need not despair of success: the general's dispositions will compensate for the lack of numbers. A weak army will always select difficult and mountainous country where the terrain is confined, so that the enemy finds his superior numbers useless and often an incumbrance to him when he cannot go beyond your flanks.

I should add here that flanks are supported better in country that is close and hilly than on level ground. We would never have won the battle of Sohr had the terrain not favored us, for despite the fact that the Austrians outnumbered our troops two to one, they were unable to outflank our wings and so the terrain rendered the two armies virtually equal.

The choice of ground is my first concern; the arrangement for the battle itself is second. Here my oblique order of battle can be employed to good advantage. By refusing or holding

back one wing to the enemy and reinforcing the attacking
wing, you can hit the enemy wing that you wish to take in
flank with the bulk of your forces.

An army of 100,000 that is outflanked will soon resign itself to the inevitable. As you can see . . . [Plate 4], the entire
effort is made by my right wing. A body of infantry rushes
unobserved into the woods to attack the enemy cavalry on

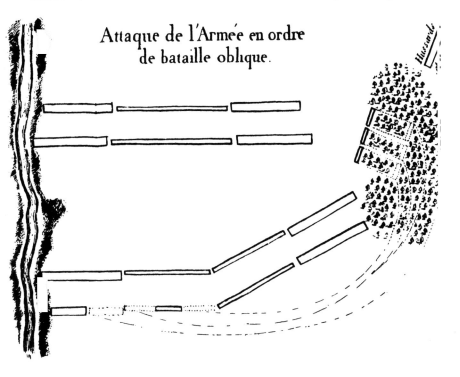

PLATE 4.   The oblique attack. Notice how Frederick would
anchor or "support" his left flank upon a river (or any other
natural obstacle), at the same time committing only a portion
of his army to the attack in the woods. Should this attack succeed, his entire army is in position to exploit the victory.
Should it fail, most of his troops are still fresh and thus can protect his retreat. (*Instruction militaire du Roi de Prusse pour
ses généraux*, Plan IX.)

the flanks and to protect our own cavalry attack. Some hussar regiments are ordered to take the enemy in the rear. Meanwhile, the army advances. When the enemy cavalry is put to flight, the infantry in the woods will hit the enemy infantry on the flank at the same time that the others attack it in front. My left wing will not advance until the enemy left is completely defeated.

By this disposition you will have the advantages of making contact with a small number of troops against a larger body and of attacking the enemy on one side where it will be decisive. Finally, if your right wing should by chance be defeated, only a portion of your army is injured: the remaining three-quarters of your army is still fresh and will cover your retreat.

If you wish to attack the enemy in a strong position, you must examine his strong and weak points before making your dispositions for the attack. Always choose that point where you expect to meet with the least resistance. Attacks against villages cost so many men that I have made it a rule to avoid them unless absolutely forced into it, because one runs the risk of losing the elite of his infantry.[3]

IN . . . [PLATE 5] the terrain on which I assume that the enemy has established himself constitutes a very strong natural position. My advice would be to avoid attacking him there if possible, but if it is absolutely necessary to attack, here is the way to go about it.

The entire battle must turn on the left, for the enemy's right is the least fortified. Here the cavalry, its left flank resting on the swamp, must make the effort with a great attack while the right wing remains beyond musket range to avoid any unnecessary casualties. The sunken road, which is very deep at this point, forms the boundary between the two armies. If the cavalry attack succeeds, you can march to the left with the infantry, turn the enemy's right, and take him in flank.

If you were to attack the enemy with your right wing you

would become involved in a murderous and uncertain affair, and one in which your losses would be frightful. Meanwhile I would place a mortar battery opposite the battery on the enemy right that flanks the cavalry in order to silence these guns, as indicated by the plan. Because I assume that the sunken road disappears toward the enemy right, I have even sent some battalions to my extreme left with a battery to fire upon the enemy cavalry in order to precipitate the flight and the rout.

In viewing the enemy position . . . [Plate 6], observe that his right is behind an abatis where he has a large battery flanking the village. Then comes a height occupied by infantry, next, the village, a small plain, woods filled with infantry, another small plain, and finally, on the left of the enemy line, the edge of a hill.

You must attack this terrain with the right wing in order

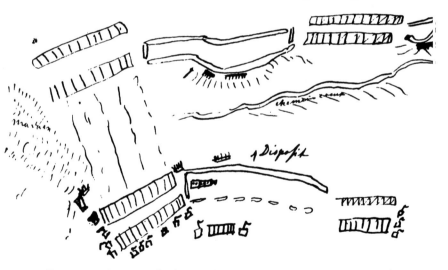

PLATE 5. Suggested plan against a strong position. The sunken road in front of Frederick's right wing prevents an attack against this part of the enemy position, but note how it also protects Frederick's right wing as the battle is decided on the left. (*Atlas* to the *Oeuvres de Frédéric le Grand*, Plan II.)

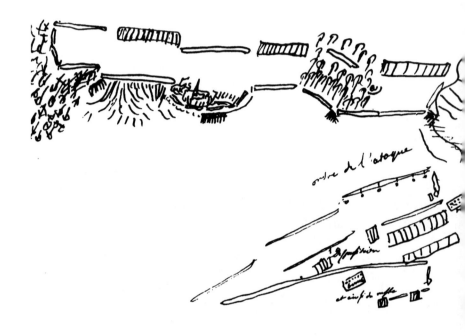

PLATE 6. An oblique attack against an enemy in position. The specific formation recommended on this occasion is indicated in the lower left. Each of the five infantry battalions comprising the attack forms a column once the enemy infantry has given way, enabling Fredèrick's cavalry to pass through the intervals to assault the enemy horse. (*Atlas* to the *Oeuvres de Frédéric le Grand*, Plan III.)

to avoid the abatis, the high ground, and the village, which would be deadly. I would favor an oblique order of battle. My mortar battery would be on the right and the cavalry in the second and third lines. Every effort should be made by the right. As soon as my infantry has smashed the enemy's left, a few battalions would penetrate the enemy's line to become master of the woods. In order to take the rest of the army in flank, the five battalions which have attacked the infantry, once they have overthrown them, will each form a column so that the cavalry can pass through the intervals and attack the enemy cavalry that might want to protect the retreat of the infantry [see Plate 6]. You must shove as much of the cavalry as possible through this gap so that they can hold out against the efforts of the rest of the enemy cavalry, which would come to the assistance of his defeated left wing. If your cavalry is repulsed you can always rally it under the protective fire of the five infantry columns.

[Plate 7] . . . contains a disposition so misleading that you cannot perceive the trap that the enemy holds for you. His first line covers his real position. His cavalry on the right is aligned with his second line in such a manner as to be guarded by the flank of his infantry, while the second line of this cavalry overlaps the first so that everything is covered. In front of the enemy line are some ravines, sunken roads, and ponds. The cavalry on the enemy's left is supported by an infantry square which in turn is protected by a swamp.

I would not attack the enemy's left because it is heavily fortified and the outlet from the pond restricts the front of my attack. I should decide therefore to attack with my left. My cavalry must attack by echelons, as you can see by the plan, with one squadron placed behind another on the right of the attacking cavalry wing to avoid the murderous infantry fire that it would receive in the flank. I must use the outlet from the pond to cover my right, and my infantry must attack on the left, as indicated.

The difficulty will come after we shall have overthrown

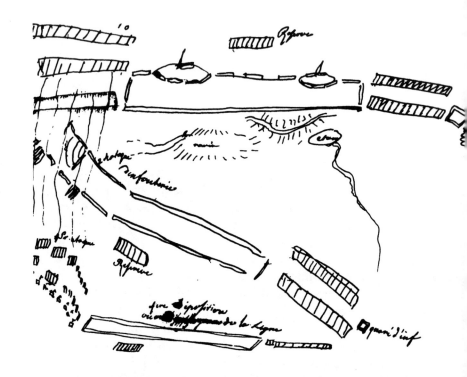

PLATE 7. Another attack against a strong position. Again Frederick takes advantage of a natural obstacle, in this case the outlet from the pond on his right, to protect the refused wing of his army while attacking *en échelon* with his left. His original disposition for the attack is indicated at bottom; final disposition shows the decisive attack against the enemy's right flank. Note how the enemy has strengthened his left flank with an infantry square. (*Atlas* to the *Oeuvres de Frédéric le Grand*, Plan v.)

the first line of infantry, for we then find a village full of infantry behind which the defeated enemy line can rally. Thus our victorious cavalry must turn at once after having pursued the enemy cavalry, in order to gain the rear of the village. Moreover, you must send your reserve there, and if it is necessary to attack the village this must be done with fresh troops from the second line. Once you have seized the village the battle is won, and there remains only the hot pursuit of the enemy.

By the disposition . . . [on Plate 8], notice that the enemy has covered the front of his cavalry and also three-quarters of his army with *chevaux de frise*, that he has one or two large batteries in his center, that he has thirty grenadier companies in the first line on his left supported by a second line comprising six ranks of Hungarians, sabers in hand, and that he covers his cavalry on the left wing with *chevaux de frise*. I am not discussing whether the enemy's disposition is good or bad: you have only to see mine and you can easily judge from that.

Notice that I mask my infantry columns behind the cavalry until they get to within six hundred paces of the enemy, at which point the infantry passes between the cavalry regiments, firing cannon while advancing on the enemy cavalry. If the latter remain where they are, with the *chevaux de frise* in front of them, my infantry then deploys and destroys them with artillery and small-arms fire. If the enemy cavalry grows impatient and removes the *chevaux de frise* in order to attack, my cavalry breaks into a gallop and ought to defeat them, always having the infantry columns in support to the rear. If the enemy cavalry is defeated, these infantry battalions deploy and take the enemy infantry in flank.

As for the enemy infantry, if the Austrian grenadiers have their Hungarians attack like the Turks, I would send two squadrons of cavalry from the front of my attacking force to the right and two others to the left to take the Hungarians in flank, and I would still have two squadrons in the second line to repulse those who might penetrate, not counting my large

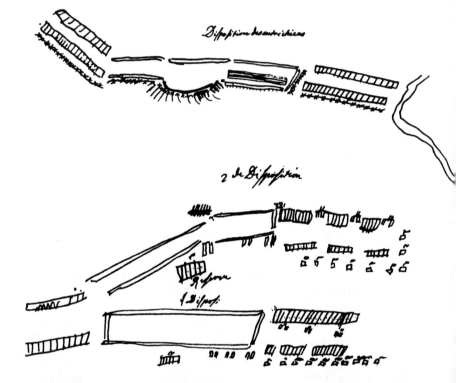

PLATE 8. Once again Frederick utilizes an obstacle, this time *chevaux de frise*, to immobilize his enemy. If opposing troops remain behind this eighteenth-century equivalent of barbed wire, Frederick will destroy them with his superior artillery and small-arms fire. If the enemy decides to remove the obstacles in order to launch cavalry against Frederick's attack, the Prussian cavalry is near enough to give support. The flow of the battle is indicated with the original line of battle as shown at the bottom and, above, the disposition of Frederick's army when it comes within range. (*Atlas* to the *Oeuvres de Frédéric le Grand*, Plan VI.)

guns that would do them great damage. Then the victorious cavalry has only to take the rear of the enemy's second line and I am convinced that he would be defeated without any difficulty.

The enemy's disposition . . . [on Plate 9] is more systematic and concealed and therefore is stronger than those described above. The front and flanks of the enemy's infantry are covered with *chevaux de frise;* his cavalry is placed in front of the infantry squares, which are surrounded by *chevaux de frise.* This cavalry must fall back if attacked by our cavalry so that when we are thrown into confusion by the fire of the enemy infantry and turn back, it can return to follow up our retreat. But since it is essential to consider and turn everything in the enemy's dispositions to good account, these *chevaux de frise* are of great advantage to us because his main line must have considerable trouble in advancing.

Here is how I propose to attack this army. Since the terrain itself in this instance does not strengthen any particular portion of the enemy line, the attack can be made either by the right or left—whichever appears to derive the greatest advantage from the ground. My inclination is to attack with the right. My infantry, at six hundred paces from the enemy, passes through the cavalry. I leave a column of two battalions with four guns on the flank and the eight other battalions, each deployed in two lines and provided with plenty of artillery, in front of the cavalry. The enemy cavalry will suffer so much from the fire of our artillery and the small arms of my infantry that it will have no choice but to attack my infantry or flee. If it attacks, that causes me no trouble—the fire of my infantry will defend itself on one side, and my cavalry is near enough to support it on the other. I have ten battalions of which that on the left of the second line could always cover the flank in case the enemy attacks it.

But it is much more likely to assume that since the enemy cavalry has received the order to retire behind the infantry squares it will do just that, in which case the square on the

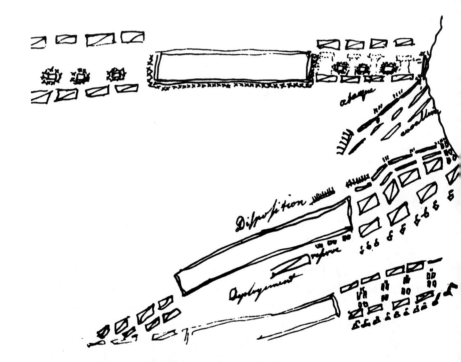

PLATE 9. Frederick, by moving his cavalry forward under the protective fire of his infantry and artillery, demonstrates the ideal cooperation of the three arms. If the enemy cavalry stationed in front of the infantry squares should attack, Frederick has enough artillery and infantry on hand to repel it. If the enemy cavalry withdraws behind its own infantry, then Frederick is free to move methodically against the infantry square, or human redoubt, on the enemy left. Either way he retains mobility. The bottom line illustrates Frederick's deployment; his disposition for the attack shows the advantages of the oblique order. (*Atlas* to the *Oeuvres de Frédéric le Grand*, Plan VII.)

extreme enemy left must be attacked first, and then the next square must be attacked. Meanwhile, have all the artillery of these detachments fire on these human redoubts as well as on the cavalry behind them. When the two squares on the left have been swept away, the cavalry may charge with fifteen squadrons, and the entire wing must follow it. Once the enemy cavalry is thrown back, our second line of cavalry must turn against the main battle line of the enemy and take it in reverse, and my right infantry wing must join the battalions that broke through the squares to turn the enemy infantry and take it in flank. The enemy can scarcely prevent me from making these movements since he is impeded by his own *chevaux de frise* and cannot execute a quarter-turn with an army in so brief a time. Also, the terrain can give us advantageous positions that we can use to thwart the enemy still more and force him to remain where he is.

The greatest care must be taken to impress upon the officers attacking this moving redoubt of the need to avoid excessive ardor. The troops must remain closed and in order because the enemy cavalry is always ready to take advantage of our slightest false movement. Above all, you must refrain from exposing the flank and firing by battalions: you should employ only the volley by platoons, and the attack of these redoubts should be carried out by means of a *coup de main* with fixed bayonets. You must be especially careful not to break ranks after the square has been shattered. Drive the enemy cavalry away with heavy artillery fire, and when you see that this is succeeding, form your first columns from battalions of the second line. Meanwhile the cavalry approaches the first line, which must form its columns only when the cavalry is immediately behind it. Then the cavalry must attack with fury. The left-hand regiments must take care not to be taken in flank by enemy regiments located nearest to the main battle line [*corps de bataille*].

This, I believe, is the best plan that can be devised. I do not deny that the job would be difficult, but I can think of nothing

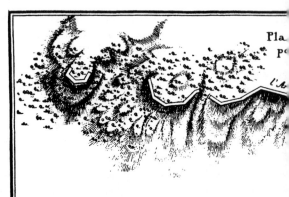

## Note.

C'est une regle generale qu'un Corps d'Infanterie traverse la plaine soit escortée de Cavalerie : mais dan... l'occasion où un Corps d'Infanterie marche pour appuyer l'armée, soit pour occuper un bois, un village, u... hauteur ; il est encore plus indispensable de le soutenir de la Cavalerie, car si l'ennemi attaquait ce Corps dans... marche avec sa Cavalerie, il l'arretterait tout le moin... ce qui lui donnerait le tems de jetter un gros Corps d'Infanterie à l'endroit que vous voudriés occuper... rendrait vain tout le projet d'attaque que vous aur... formé.

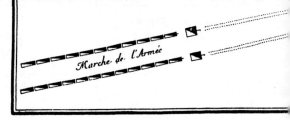

Marche de l'Armée

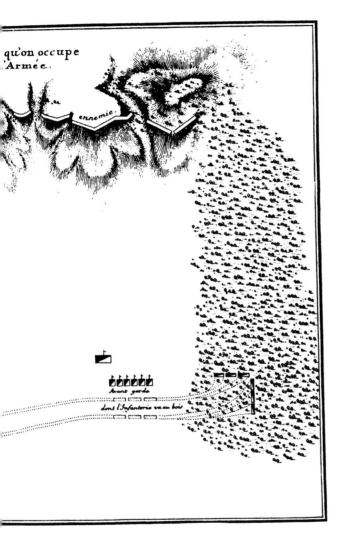

quon occupe
Armée.

ennemie

Avant garde

dont l'Infanterie va au bois

PLATE 10. Frederick's advance guard (see Plate 2) deploys for battle. The cavalry escorts the infantry across the open space, where the infantry takes its position in the woods to support the right flank of the army when it has deployed for battle. (*Atlas* to the *Oeuvres de Frédéric le Grand*, Plan 16.)

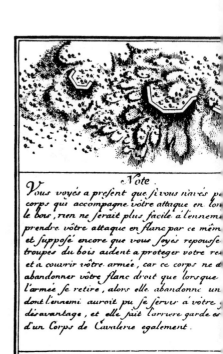

## Note.

Vous voyés a présent que, si vous n'avés p
corps qui accompagne votre attaque en lor
le bois, rien ne ferait plus facile à l'ennemi
prendre votre attaque en flanc par ce mêm
et supposé encore que vous soyés repousse
troupes du bois aident a proteger votre re
et a couvrir votre armée, car ce corps ne d
abandonner votre flanc droit que lorsque
l'armée se retire, alors elle abandonne un
dont l'ennemi auroit pu se servir à votre
désavantage, et elle fait l'arriere garde er
d'un Corps de Cavalerie egalement.

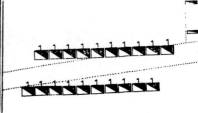

PLATE 11. The ideal formation, according to Frederick. The right flank rests on the woods. The attack is directed against the enemy's left flank and is supported by Frederick's main line of battle arrayed *en échelon*, with his cavalry guarding the exposed left flank. (*Atlas* to the *Oeuvres de Frédéric le Grand*, Plan 17.)

better or more certain than what I propose. I can break into an army arrayed in this manner only by attacking one of the flanks, employing my infantry always supported by cavalry, and utilizing as much artillery as the terrain and circumstances permit me to bring into action. Nor do I deny that the enemy, when he sees that I have decided to attack, will make efforts to extend his flank. However, to prevent the wing of his main battle line from bringing its artillery to bear against my attack, it is necessary to oppose his guns with a kind of battery that commands his respect, or at least keeps him from firing toward my attack.

In my opinion, the secret of the art of war is to upset enemy dispositions by diversions that force him to abandon his plans. Especially if one can compel him to change his dispositions, the battle is half-won, for his strength depends upon his stationary position, and if I make him move his troops the slightest movement breaks the integrity and destroys the strength of his battle line.[4]

YOU MUST ENDEAVOR as far as possible to protect the flank of the attacking wing by a wood, morass, or even a simple pit. This sometimes becomes impossible on level or in open country. If you find a wood on your right, where you propose to make the attack, and this wood extends to the enemy left flank, you must first send a body of infantry (escorted on the plain by cavalry) to occupy these woods and cover the flank of the army. . . . Moreover, this infantry in the woods must protect your attack when it advances against the enemy, or else you run the risk by your mistake that your attack will be taken in flank in the middle of its advance and will be routed shamefully. If the enemy has a long village, of which there are many in Silesia, on his flanks, you must first of all drive out the enemy and occupy the village in order to be able next to advance against his main army. I add here a plan of a wood which suffices for an understanding of this important precaution [see Plates 10 and 11].

[In Plate 12] I assume an attack on level ground; you will see how, according to my system, these attacks must be made. I place the right wing in motion while refusing the left (you could make this movement just as easily by attacking with the left and withholding the right) and order the cavalry of the right wing to attack if the enemy dispositions permit: if not, it must wait until its moment arrives.[5]

In a battle such as this, in open country, it is impossible to surround that part of the enemy army that you desire to attack. This plan, however, shows you how I outflank the enemy left. I draw back as much of my cavalry as I can from the right to protect it from enemy artillery, and you will notice that I have formed a square of four battalions [1] with cannon at the extreme right flank to fire on the enemy cavalry and at the same time protect the attack of our own. If even our own cavalry is repulsed, the fire from this square and from those troops protecting the flank of my infantry [2] give the cavalry protection behind which it may rally, and the hussars [3] are in range to fall on the enemy left flank if he wishes to pursue us.

The first line of the infantry attack formation [4] is 150 paces in front of the second line [5], which in turn precedes the battalion on the flank [6] by two hundred paces. The first brigade is one hundred paces farther to the front than the second [7], which is one hundred paces ahead of the third brigade [8], which is a like distance in front of the fourth brigade [9], so that when the first attack [4] is within three hundred paces of the enemy, the second is 450, the first brigade 650, the second 750, and so on. The second, third, and fourth brigades must not advance too rapidly so as not to risk everything simultaneously. If your attack can withstand the fire of case shot and bring confusion to the enemy, and especially if your victorious cavalry can hit the enemy in the rear, you will have risked only your attacks [4, 5] and will not lose half as many men as if you had engaged your entire line. Because of the destructive power of cannon firing case shot, the entire battle line could be completely destroyed if exposed to this fire. That is why

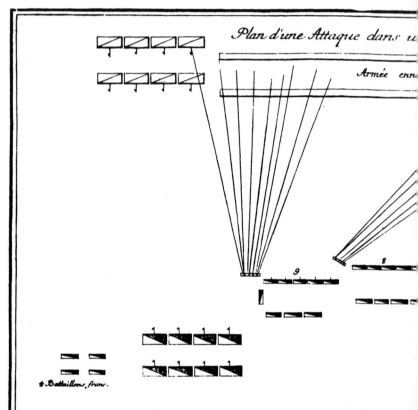

Plan d'une Attaque dans u...

Armée enn...

9

8

4 Bataillons, franc.

N°...

Dans une affaire de plaine, il est impossible d'embrasser la partie de l'armée e...
droite de l'ennemi ; Je recule autant que je peux ma Cavalerie de la droite pour...
Bataillons avec leur canon que jay formé la, pour tirer sur la Cavalerie ennemie, e...
2, et celuy du quarré la protègent suffisament, pour qu'elle se puisse rallier sel les ...
de l'Infanterie 4 est de 150 pas avant sa seconde ligne 5, et celle la de 200 avant l'ail...
100 pas de plus que la Brigade 8 ; celle la de 100 pas de plus que la Brigade 9 ; de sorte...
première brigade à 650, la seconde a 750, et il ne faut pas que la seconde, troisième et...
resiste au feu de cartouches et derange l'ennemi, surtout si votre Cavalerie victor...
mourir autant de monde, que si vous aviès engagé toute votre ligne, car le canon, e...
d'être détruit sans ressource ; c'est pourquoy il faut tacher de tenir le gros de l'armée...
l'artillerie qui se laisse attaquer, tire mieux et plus vite que l'artillerie qui attaque, de sort...
toute votre feu de canon comme cela est marqué dans le plan sur la partie de l'ar...
l'avantage que suppose que vos attaques soyent repoussées, votre aile droite se peut ...
en imposer à l'ennemi par la plus grande partie de vos troupes qui sont encore ...

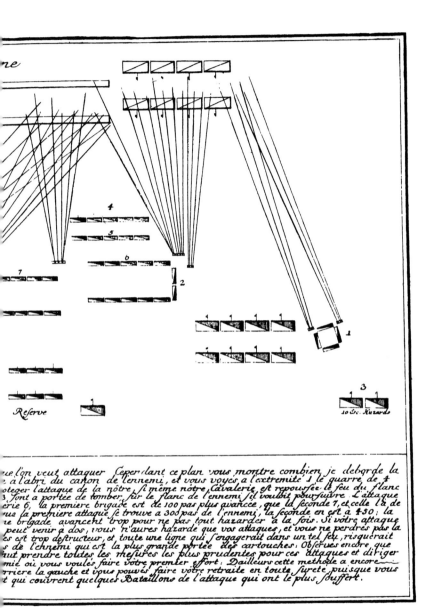

_ne_

4
5
6
7
2

Réserve

3
10 Esc. Huzards

que l'on veut attaquer. Cependant ce plan vous montre combien je deborde la
à l'abri du canon de l'ennemi, et vous voyes, a l'extremité 1 le quarré de 4
oteger l'attaque de la nôtre, fi même nôtre Cavalerie, eſt repouſſée, le feu du flanc
font a portée de tomber, fur le flanc de l'ennemi ſil vouloit pourſuivre. L'attaque
crie 6, la premiere brigade eſt de 100 pas plus avancée, que la ſeconde 7, et celle 1a, de
rue ſa premiere attaque ſe trouve a 300 pas de l'ennemi, la ſeconde en eſt a 450 ; la
ne brigade avancent trop pour ne pas tout hazarder a la fois. Si votre attaque
peut venir a dos, vous n'aures hazarde que vos attaques, et vous ne perdres pas la
es eſt trop deſtructeur, et toute une ligne qui s'engageroit dans un tel feu, riſqueroit
s de l'ennemi qui eſt la plus grande portée des cartouches, Obſerves encore, que
aut prendre toutes les meſures les plus prudentes pour ces attaques et diriger
mie où vous voules faire vôtre premier effort ; Dailleurs cette methode a encore
rriere la gauche et vous pouves faire vôtre retraite en toute ſurete, puisque vous
t qui couvrent quelques Bataillons de l'attaque qui ont le plus ſuffert.

PLATE 12. The attack _en échelon._ Details are contained in the
text, which is taken from the legend of the original map. (_Atlas_
to the _Oeuvres de Frédéric le Grand,_ Plan 18.)

you must try to keep the bulk of the army eight hundred paces from the enemy, since this is the maximum range for case shot.

Observe also that artillery on the defensive fires better and more rapidly than artillery advancing to the attack, so that you must take every precaution for these attacks and direct your entire artillery bombardment against that portion of the enemy line where you intend to make your first effort, as indicated on the map. This method, moreover, has the additional advantage that, assuming your attacks are repulsed, your right wing can fall back behind the left and you can make your retreat in complete safety, since you thus face the enemy with most of your troops still fresh and able to cover those battalions of the attack which have suffered the most.[6]

SOME GENERALS contend that the best place to attack a post is in the center. [Plate 13] will represent the situation of such a position, which I assume has two large towns and two villages on the flanks. The [enemy] wings will certainly be lost when you force the center, and by similar attacks you will win the most complete victories. Here I give the plan of it, and add that when you have penetrated the enemy line you should double the strength of your attack and roll back the enemy both to the right and to the left.

Nothing is so formidable in the attack of a position as batteries firing case shot, which does terrible slaughter among the infantry battalions. At Sohr and Kesselsdorf I witnessed the attack against batteries and made some reflections that I will pass on to you here.

Let us assume [Plate 14] that we wish to capture a battery of fifteen guns that could not be turned. I have commented that the fire of cannon and of infantry in support of the battery renders it unassailable. We can only seize the enemy batteries when they make a mistake. Our infantry attacking them, being half-destroyed, begin to give way; the enemy infantry, wishing to pursue, leave their post. By this movement their guns dare not fire and our troops, pressing hard at the heels of the enemy, reach the batteries almost at the same time as theirs and thus gain possession of them.

The experience of these two battles has given me the notion that in a similar case we should follow the example set by our troops by forming the attack in two lines, chessboard fashion [*en échiquier*], supported in the third line by some dragoon squadrons. The first line will be ordered to attack only weakly and then to withdraw through the intervals in the second line so that the enemy, deceived by this fake retreat, may abandon his post in order to pursue us. This movement will be the signal to advance and make a vigorous attack.[7]

[IN PLATE 15] it can be seen that the enemy position is excessively strong and that the only place he can be attacked is where he has placed his *chevaux de frise*. Let us assume that it is absolutely necessary to attack him. . . . Here is my plan.

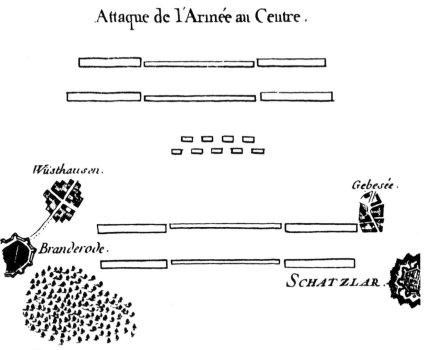

PLATE 13. Proposed attack against the center of the enemy line. Villages on either flank make the usual flank attack impracticable. (*Instruction militaire du Roi de Prusse pour ses généraux*, Plan x.)

Observe that I form my principal line of infantry and that
in front of it, opposite the point I wish to assault, I form two
lines of infantry. On each flank of the attack I detach two
battalions destined to attack or to mask the two redoubts threatening its flanks, while my two mortar batteries keep these under
incessant bombardment to facilitate the assault of the attacking

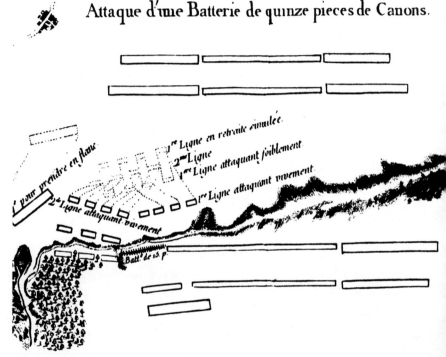

PLATE 14. A ploy to lure the enemy from a strong position.
Advancing in chessboard fashion, Frederick's first line attacks
weakly and then falls back through the intervals formed by the
second line. If the enemy swallows the bait and pursues, Frederick's infantry, aided by dragoons on the right, moves swiftly
to the attack. Maneuvers such as this would have been possible only with the training and discipline of the Prussian army.
(*Instruction militaire du Roi de Prusse pour ses généraux,*
Plan XI.)

units. The infantry must have many of its cannon fire while advancing toward the enemy line: it must march at a good pace and fire only when it reaches the enemy *chevaux de frise*. If it succeeds in dislodging the enemy infantry it must take over these *chevaux de frise* and maintain its position until the cavalry arrives. Then the infantry forms columns and allows the cavalry to pass through the intervals between them to attack the enemy. Such a gap made in the enemy position forces him to abandon his entire front, after which you can enter with your whole army and act as circumstances dictate. In my

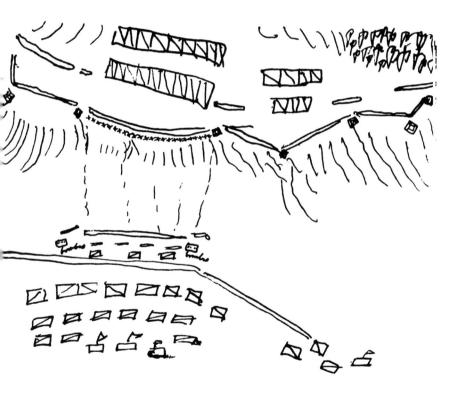

PLATE 15. Another type of frontal attack. Again, the key to Frederick's maneuver is the close cooperation of infantry and artillery. (*Atlas* to the *Oeuvres de Frédéric le Grand*, Plan VIII.)

opinion one can not inject enough vigor and spirit into these movements, when the enemy begins to crack, in order to put the finishing touch on his defeat.

You can see by all these different methods of attack how circumstances force a person to alter his dispositions, and that a hillock or a miry swamp must not be neglected for the little use that one can make of it. The main point is always to support one arm with another, strengthening cavalry with infantry and artillery and always having cavalry within supporting distance of the infantry. I must not neglect to point out that on all the occasions where combats involve only a portion of the line it is necessary to keep the reserve there, on either side, because in the event of a mishap this reserve can save the battle and give you victory.

Thus it can be clearly seen that the great art of a general consists in his knowing the terrain well, in profiting from every advantage, and in knowing how to make his disposition suitable for each occasion. In affairs of position the order of battle, to be any good, must be guided by that of the enemy and by the terrain where one intends to fight. I hope that these small sketches of terrain and of armies found posted there will give you at least some guidance, when seeing an army in battle array, of how to go about examining the terrain . . . anticipating the orders of combat that the enemy has given to his troops, and, on the basis of this knowledge, making your own dispositions for the attack.[8]

## ON THE ADVANTAGE OF MY METHOD
## OF ATTACK OVER THE OTHERS

DOUBTLESS YOU WILL HAVE NOTICED that the constant principle I follow in all my attacks is to refuse one wing or to engage only a detachment of the army with the enemy. My army serves as a base for the troops who attack and must become engaged only in succeeding stages, depending upon the outcome and the hopes that I have for success in my enterprise. This disposition gives me the advantage of risking only as many troops as may seem appropriate, and if I notice some physical or moral obstacle in my way I am free to abandon my plan, pull back the columns of my attack into my lines, and withdraw my army, placing it always under the protection of my artillery until beyond range of enemy fire. The wing that has been the nearest to the enemy then falls back behind my refused wing, enabling the latter to support and cover me when I am defeated. If then I defeat the enemy, this method enables me to achieve a more brilliant victory; if I am defeated, it reduces my losses considerably."

I DO NOT SPEAK [here] of different dispositions for river passages, retreats, and deceiving the enemy . . . but I recommend to all those charged with these duties that they think especially of protecting their flanks and strengthening infantry with cavalry, cavalry with infantry, and both by artillery; and that they unite these with the help of fortifications and mines, taking full advantage of the circumstances . . . and of the terrain in which they are placed.

## INTRENCHMENTS

It is not the custom of our neighbors to intrench themselves,[10] but if it should be found necessary to attack an intrenchment, it either must be decided upon the day that the enemy begins to work on his intrenchments or it must not be considered at all. For each moment lost is so much time gained for the enemy to make his works more formidable. The main thing to consider in matters concerning the attack itself is to utilize the terrain, ravines, or depressions to conceal the spot where you intend to make your greatest effort from the enemy, to prevent his sending troops there.[11]

MOST INTRENCHMENTS are taken because their flanks are not sufficiently protected. Turenne's intrenchment . . . was carried when the Prince of Anhalt found the necessary room to turn it, and that of Malplaquet was turned by the woods on Marshal Villars' left. Had the allies been aware of this circumstance at the beginning of the battle they would have saved their army 15,000 men.

If the flank of an intrenchment rests on a fordable river, the

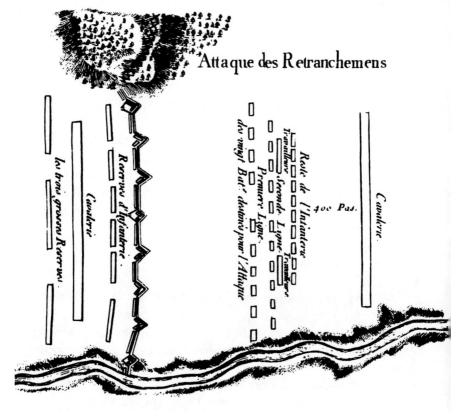

Attaque des Retranchemens

PLATE 16. Proposed frontal attack against enemy intrench-ments. Note Frederick's chessboard (*en échiquier*) formation, with the intervals between units in the front line covered by battalions in the second. (*Instruction militaire du Roi de Prusse pour ses généraux*, Plan VI.)

attack should be made on that side. The work at Stralsund constructed by the Swedes was carried because the attack was made
on the side of the sea where it was fordable. If the enemy intrenchments are too extensive and the troops occupying them
are compelled to cover more ground than they really can
defend, you should attack several points simultaneously. This
surely will give you possession of the works, provided your
intentions have been concealed from the enemy . . . and he
is unable to oppose you with sufficient forces.

[Plate 16] . . . will explain to you the following dispositions
of an attack against an intrenchment. I will form a line of
thirty battalions, with the left flank resting on the river. Twelve
battalions will constitute the attack on the left where I wish
to penetrate and eight other battalions will form the attack on
my right. The troops designated for the attack shall be arrayed
like a chessboard, with the battalions in the second line covering the intervals between the battalions of the first. The rest
of the infantry will be placed in the third line and behind them,
at a distance of four hundred paces, will be the cavalry. With
this disposition my infantry will keep the enemy in check and
stand ready to take advantage of his slightest false movement.

Care must be taken that each of these attacks is followed
by a number of pioneers with shovels, pick-axes, and fascines*
to fill up the ditch and make passages for the cavalry after the
intrenchment has been forced. The infantry comprising the
attack shall not commence firing until the intrenchment has
been carried and they are drawn up on the parapet in battle
order.

The cavalry will enter the work through the openings created by the pioneers and draw up in battle array to attack the
enemy as soon as they are in sufficient force. If repulsed, the
cavalry will proceed to rally under cover of the infantry fire
until the whole army has penetrated the enemy's works and
the foe is entirely routed.

I will repeat here . . . that I would never intrench my army

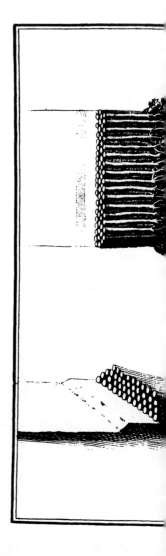

PLATE 17. Abatis, used in the eighteenth century to strengthen a position. (*Atlas* to the *Oeuvres de Frédéric le Grand*, Plan 10.)

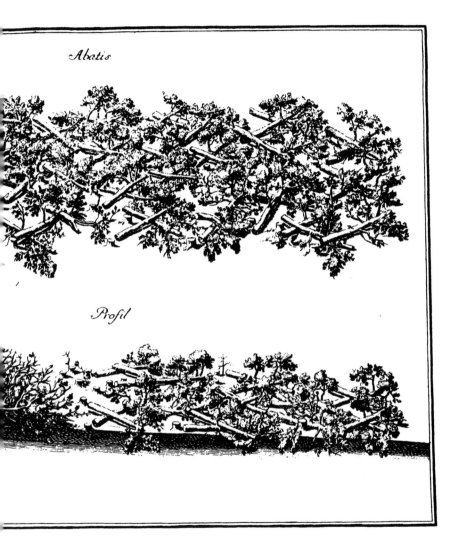

*Abatis*

*Profil*

Plan d'une red͏t

Profil
Façon dont le parapet doit
être construit pour que les
coups n'aillent ni trop haut
ni trop bas.

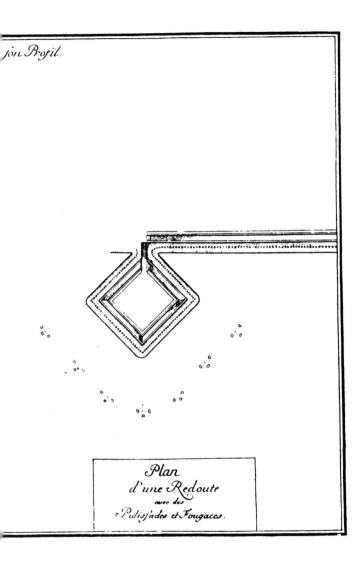

*son Profil.*

*Plan*
*d'une Redoute*
*avec des*
*Palisades et Fougaces.*

PLATE 18. Plan of an eighteenth-century redoubt, with profile. Note the palisade in the ditch, the *chevaux de frise* in front, and the mine, or *fougasse*, covering the approaches. (*Atlas* to the *Oeuvres de Frédéric le Grand*, Plan 8.)

except when it is my intention to undertake a siege, and I don't know if it would not be better even then to go out and meet the army marching to the relief of the fortress.

But assume for a moment that we should wish to intrench ourselves. In this case, this is my proposal for the most advantageous way to do it. You should save two or three large formations in reserve to be sent during the attack to those places where the enemy is making the greatest efforts. The parapet should be lined by battalions, with a reserve placed behind them close enough to be of assistance if needed. The cavalry will be drawn up in a line behind the reserves.

The intrenchment must be well protected at both flanks. If one flank rests on a river [as in Plate 16] the ditch should be extended far enough into the river that it cannot be turned. If the flank should rest on a wood, it must be closed at that end by a redoubt and a large abatis of trees should be made in the woods. You should make sure that the redoubts are well flanked [see Plates 17 and 18].

The ditch should be very large and deep and the intrenchments must be improved steadily from day to day by strengthening the parapet,* placing palisades* at the entrance of the barriers, digging pits, or even supplying the entire camp with *chevaux de frise*. The greatest advantage that you have is in the choice of the position and in certain rules of fortification that must be observed, namely to force the enemy to attack you on a narrow front and to make the attack only against the principal points of your intrenchment.

For a more precise idea of what I mean, see . . . [Plate 19]. The army that faces your intrenchment is hemmed in on one side by the river and you present a front to the attacker that outflanks him. He cannot attack your right flank because the batteries located at the extremity of this wing would take him in flank, while the redoubt in the center would take him in the rear. Therefore he could only attack the aforementioned redoubt in the center, which he will be forced to break into on the side of the abatis. And because you will anticipate this attack, you will strengthen the fortifications of this redoubt, giving it all the more attention since you have only this single work to fortify.

[Plate 20] . . . shows intrenchments of a different kind composed of salient and re-entrant redoubts that cover one another's flanks and are linked together with intrenchments. By this method of fortification the salient redoubts form the points of attack, and since there are only a few of these they require less time to be completed than if the entire front were to be

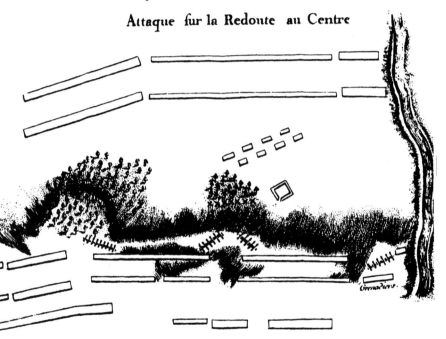

Attaque fur la Redoute au Centre

PLATE 19. A strong defensive position limiting the enemy's line of advance. Note how the batteries of artillery and the redoubt provide mutual support, thus fulfilling the same purpose as the bastions, redans, ravelins, and demi-lunes of a fortress. (*Instruction militaire du Roi de Prusse pour ses généraux*, Plan VII.)

PLATE 20. Intrenchments containing salient and re-entrant redoubts—a more formal application of the principle illustrated on
Plate 19. (*Atlas* to the *Oeuvres de Frédéric le Grand*, Plan 3.)

fortified uniformly. Because the musketry fire from each salient
redoubt must intersect with the fire from the redoubts on each
flank, the salient redoubts should never be more than six hundred paces apart.

Our infantry defends intrenchments by the fire of entire
battalions. Each soldier should be issued one hundred rounds,
but that will not prevent us from placing as many cannon as
we can between the battalions and in the salient redoubts. While
the enemy is at a distance our artillery should fire solid shot,
but when he has approached to within four hundred paces we
will begin to fire case shot. If the enemy, despite the strength

of your intrenchment and notwithstanding your stubborn fire, should pierce your works at one point, the infantry reserve will move up to repel him, and in the event this reserve should be forced to fall back, then your cavalry should make the last efforts to drive back the enemy.

Most intrenchments are carried because they have not been constructed according to the rules, or the defending troops are outflanked or become panic stricken: this stems from the fact that the assailant enjoys greater freedom and boldness in his movements. The . . . examples have shown that an intrenchment being forced, the entire army becomes discouraged and takes flight. I believe that our soldiers would have more resolution and would repel the enemy, but of what good are all these advantages if the intrenchments prevent you from benefitting from them. And since there are so many disadvantages to intrenchments, it naturally follows that lines* are even less useful. . . . I maintain that they are of no value whatever, since they cover more ground than there are troops to defend them. Several attacks can be mounted simultaneously against them and the enemy is tempted to force them. . . . My principle is never to place unlimited confidence in a post alone, unless it is physically proven to be safe from attack.[12]

# NOTES: CHAPTER VI

1. The oblique order refers simply to Frederick's practice of "placing his line within striking distance obliquely across the extremity of his adversary's line," either by extending one flank beyond that of the enemy or by advancing with his battalions in echelon to strike the enemy at or beyond his flank with the foremost. The idea did not originate with Frederick: Napoleon traced it back to Cyrus the Great at the battle of Thymbra in 548 B.C. and Epaminondas used it to defeat the Spartans at Leuctra in 371 B.C. Although the oblique order was actually executed without a hitch only once, at Leuthen (see Chapter VII), Frederick became its most successful practitioner in the eighteenth century, and the oblique order today is still automatically associated with his name.

2. Frederick, "Pensées et règles générales pour la guerre," *Oeuvres de Frédéric le Grand* (Berlin, 1846-56), XXVIII, 110-11 [*Règles générales*].

3. Frederick, *Instruction militaire du Roi de Prusse pour ses généraux* (Frankfort, 1761), pp. 126-33, 142-66 [*Instruction militaire*].

4. Frederick, *Règles générales*, pp. 111-17. A prime example of the futility of moving troops from a stationary position during battle is Leuthen, described in Chapter VII.

5. In this particular plan Frederick assumes that his army consists of sixty infantry battalions and one hundred cavalry squadrons, not counting the free battalions.

6. Frederick, "Eléments de castramétrie et de tactique," *Oeuvres*, XXIX, 20-21; *Atlas*, plate xviii [*Castramétrie*].

7. Frederick, *Instruction militaire*, pp. 146-49.

8. Frederick, *Règles générales*, pp. 117-18.

9. Frederick, *Castramétrie*, pp. 25-26.

10. But see below, Chapter VIII.

11. Frederick, *Règles générales*, pp. 122-23.

12. Frederick, *Instruction militaire*, pp. 133-42, 149.

# VII

# From the Pages of History

"To write history," Frederick once complained to a correspondent, "is to compile the follies of men and the blows of chance." Yet Frederick went to considerable trouble to prepare elaborate reports after each campaign, and even during the war he began to touch up the notebooks that he kept of his military activities, looking forward to the day when he could return to Potsdam and compile his memoirs.

Frederick wrote didactic history. His *History of the Seven Years War*, which he completed during the first year of peace, was intended "for him alone who will succeed me, for those of my family to whom it pleases him to show them, and for the few officers whom he may choose for special training." Writing, as he claimed "with that interesting impartiality which an historian should never lose sight of," Frederick hoped that this rather select circle of readers "will see the reasons behind my actions, the mistakes I made, which I do not disguise and excuse least of all, and the means I used to repair them."[1] The following accounts of Kolin, Rossbach, Leuthen, Torgau, and the intrenched camp at Bunzelwitz illustrate Frederick's basic principles of war: they include his best-fought battle, and his worst. Although Frederick appears to have been a better general than historian, the reader should bear in mind that this represents a serious effort to instruct his successor and the top-ranking generals so that they might benefit from his own experiences should Prussia again find herself at war in Saxony, Bohemia, or—God forbid—in Silesia. Like Caesar, Napoleon, and occasionally General de Gaulle, Frederick on such occasions referred to himself in the third person.

# THE BATTLE OF KOLIN

*18th June 1757*

SCALE OF MILES

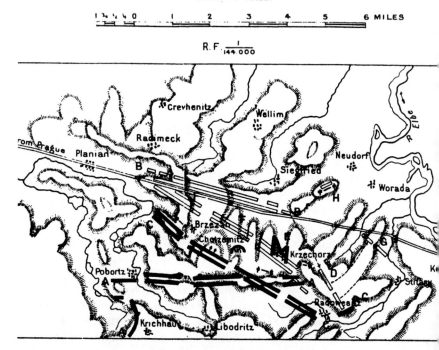

R.F. $\frac{1}{144,000}$

**A.** Austrian Army, 60,000 men, under Daun, with 180 guns—1st position.

**B.** Prussians under Frederic, 34,000 (18,000 Cavalry), 100 guns—1st position. Frederic decides turn Austrian right flank and heads towards Rodosowitz.

**C.** Daun's 2nd position.

**D.** Zeithen leading, gets isolated as Daun's Croat Skirmishers in village of Krzechorz and Chotzem annoy the flanks of Hulsen's and Manstein's battalions as they march across, and they wh to right and attack.

**E.** Hulsen carries the village, but is checked.

**F.** Manstein and right wing also checked.

**G.** Zeithen driven back. Prussian Army withdraws its 1st position. Prussian losses, 13,77 Austrian, 8000.

PLATE 21. Kolin. (Major Gerald Gilbert, *The Evolution of Tactics*, London, 1907.)

## KOLIN: THE CAMPAIGN [Plate 21]

When Frederick's army left winter quarters in the spring of 1757 to launch the second campaign of the Seven Years' War, it had to contend again with the powerful coalition of Austria, Russia, and France, to which recently had been added Sweden and the Empire. The allies could put about 400,000 men into the field; Frederick had but 150,000 not counting the 47,000 Hanoverians commanded by the Duke of Cumberland or the troops needed to garrison his fortresses. In the face of such odds Frederick's best, indeed his only chance for survival was to overwhelm one of his enemies before the others could unite against him.

The obvious target was Austria, the keystone of the alliance, whose armies were nearest and the most formidable. Convinced by the military situation and the impressions that Frederick had carefully cultivated that he had no choice but to remain on the defensive, the Austrian generals planned leisurely for an invasion of Saxony.

But Frederick struck first. Stripping Pomerania of troops in order to send a token detachment to the Duke of Cumberland's army of observation, which had to contend with a French force more than twice its size, and to give Field Marshal Lehwaldt enough troops (33,000) that he might hope to defend East Prussia against the Russians, Frederick assembled 112,500 troops for the campaign against Austria. On April 18, he invaded Bohemia: four Prussian columns poured out of the mountain passes before the startled Austrians could occupy unassailable positions blocking the way, and on May 2, Frederick's vanguard, following close on the heels of retreating Austrians, appeared before the walls of Prague. Four days later—the very day Frederick had anticipated in his original plan of campaign—the battle of Prague was fought. It was a bloody but barren victory that cost the Prussians 14,000 casualties and the life of Field Marshal Schwerin, one of the best Prussian generals, and succeeded only in driving the Austrian army into Prague. The Prussians then invested the city and erected batteries for siege artillery, hoping thereby that fire and hunger would complete its reduction.

Meanwhile, a second Austrian army, commanded by Field Marshal Daun, was marching to the relief of Prague and actually had approached to within ten miles at the time of the battle. With 30,000 enemy troops thus threatening his rear and 44,000 within the city fortifications, Frederick, on May 10, detached the Duke of Bevern with 17,800 troops to observe Daun. Although numerically superior, Daun was a cautious general, and so he fell back, constantly picking up reinforcements as he withdrew. Finally he received positive orders from Vienna to make every effort to relieve Prague. Now it was Bevern's turn to retreat and this, together with the realization that more time would be needed before he could expect to capture Prague, provoked Frederick into joining Bevern with 14,000 additional troops, in order to push Daun all the way back into Moravia.

On June 18, Frederick caught up with the Austrians in their camp on the heights south of the *Kaiser-strasse* from Prague to Vienna, near New Kolin. Frederick's army comprised 19,000 infantry, 14,000 cavalry, and 28 heavy guns besides the regimental or battalion artillery, about 33,000 men in all. The Austrians numbered 35,000 infantry, 19,000 cavalry and 60 heavy guns, making a total of 54,000. Despite the Austrian superiority, which was especially evident in cavalry and artillery, Frederick decided to attack.[2]


## KOLIN: THE BATTLE. JUNE 18, 1757

*THE KING'S SITUATION* became more . . . awkward day by day. His camp was confined, backed up against mountains; his front was unapproachable through the swamp and the stream that separated the two armies; but this was not the case on his right, which was poorly supported at Kaurzim and could have been turned by Marshal Daun whenever he wished . . . in which case the entire army would have been taken in flank and irretrievably defeated. The King was faced besides with a multitude of objectives so contrary that it was not possible to reconcile them at the same time, and he could neglect none without placing his affairs in considerable jeopardy. He had to cover the magazines of Brandeis and Nimburg, which provided the army of observation with its bread. He had to protect the blockade of Prague by preventing, with a weak corps, an army double the size of his from sending a detachment to Prague or moving there with the entire army. The more the inferiority of the Prussians was disclosed to the enemy, the more they had to fear sustaining considerable defeat in the long run. Even assuming that they could maintain their position in the camp, it still was not possible for them to prevent Marshal Daun from sending a large detachment which, skirting the banks of the Sazawa, would come to the rear of the Prussian corps in camp between Branik and Michle. This besieging army, attacked by the rear while the Prince of Lorraine would make a sortie from the city, would have found itself between two fires and consequently would have been totally defeated. If the King, taking another course, would have found it convenient to retire to Kosteletz or Teutsch-Brod [Böhmisch-Brod] he would find more advantageous camps there, but the inconveniences . . . would still exist, for by approaching the Elbe and covering the magazines, the road toward Prague would be left open; and by drawing more toward the Sazawa to protect the siege, the magazines would be left uncovered. This loss must be immediate—not to mention the fact that, by yielding ground in a country where there was forage, the army must retire into an area . . . where the provisions had already been consumed.

There were more forceful considerations still. Marshal Daun commanded an army of 60,000, which had been assembled by the Empress Queen at great expense. Was it to be presumed that, having so many troops in Bohemia, the court in Vienna would allow the Prussians to take Prince Charles of Lorraine and 40,000 men prisoner in Prague with impunity and in the presence of this army? It was known even that Marshal Daun had orders to risk everything to save the Prince. Thus it was really a question of determining whether the enemy should be left to attack the Prussians in their post, or whether it would be better to anticipate the Austrians by attacking first. Add to these considerations the facts that Marshal Daun had become so strong, it would have been impossible to take Prague without winning a second battle, and that it would have been disgraceful for the honor of the arms to raise the siege upon the approach of the enemy, since the worst that could happen would be to abandon this enterprise in the event of an enemy victory.

Besides what has been said, a more important reason forced the King to come to a decision: by winning another battle he would have a complete superiority over the Imperialists. The princes of the Empire, already uncertain and indecisive, would have implored him to grant them neutrality; the French would have found themselves upset and perhaps arrested in their operations in Germany; the Swedes would have become more pacific and circumspect. Even the court of St. Petersburg would have reflected differently, because the King soon would have been able to send help to his army in Prussia without running any risk and even to aid the army of the Duke of Cumberland. These were the important reasons that induced the King to attack Marshal Daun in his post. . . . [See Plate 21–A.]

The march began early on the morning of the eighteenth. Treschkow, with the advance guard, dislodged the enemy corps that had encamped the previous evening on the heights behind Planian, a necessary first step to clear the road to Kolin on which the army was to march in two columns. It filed off by the left in two lines opposite the enemy. Marshal Daun, discovering this movement, immediately changed his front and, marching by his right, extended along the top of the hills that ran toward Kolin [C]. Nadasti was placed before the King's army with 4,000 to 5,000 hussars, which a cavalry corps drove from one position to another, but they managed to retard the march of the columns. The Prussians continued to press these light troops until they had reached an eminence necessary to occupy in order to attack the enemy.

Since the troops did not arrive as promptly as might have been desired, the King profited by the interim to assemble his general officers and brief them on the disposition of the battle. From an inn found along the road of march, Marshal Daun's dispositions and the ground upon which it was necessary to act could distinctly be seen, and the following measures were taken.[3] It was resolved to attack the enemy's right flank because it was badly supported and the ground there was the most accessible. The Austrian front extended over rugged and steep crags at the foot of which were some villages strewn over the plain, filled with pandours. But the stronger they were on this side the less so were they on their right. Prussians already occupied the height where their left was to attack. In front of this, defended by Croats, was a lonely churchyard that had to be carried and then, by turning a little to the left, the Prussians could take Daun's army in flank and rear. It was necessary to feed this attack with all the Prussian infantry that was found in the army, for which reason the King proposed to refuse his right wing entirely to the enemy, and he severely forbade the officers who commanded it to pass beyond the highway to Kolin. This was all the more sensible because that part of the Austrian army posted opposite his right occupied unapproachable terrain. Had the position that the King prescribed for his troops been observed, he would have been able, during the action, to file off the battalions as he needed them to support the brigades making the first attack.

In addition, General Ziethen had orders to resist [the Austrian cavalry of the right wing under] Nadasti with forty squadrons so that it would not trouble the Prussian infantry in its operations. The rest of the cavalry was placed in reserve behind the lines. When everything was settled, General Hülsen[4] left at the head of seven battalions and fourteen pieces of artillery to begin the action. Of the twenty-one battalions that remained, six formed the second line and the remaining fifteen, the first.[5] Such was the disposition that would have rendered the Prussians victorious had it been followed.[6]

But instead, this is what happened. Ziethen attacked Nadasti's cavalry, routed it, and pursued it to Kolin so that it was separated from the Austrians and unable to impede the enterprises of the King during the battle. At one o'clock Hülsen attacked the cemetery and village on the height, where he met with no great resistance. He next mastered two batteries of twelve pieces each [E].[7]

Everything succeeded according to the wishes of the Prussians in this first attack, but then the errors that caused the loss of the battle occurred. Prince Maurice[8] commanded the left wing of the infantry, and instead of supporting it behind the village that Hülsen had just carried, he formed it 1,000 paces from this height. His line was in the air. The King noticed it and brought it near the foot of this hill. At the same time a lively fire from the right was heard indicating that that wing was engaged, and because he had to hurry and could not act otherwise, the King filled the gaps he found in his line with the battalions of the second line. Then he hurried to the right to determine what was happening there.

He found that Manstein, who had engaged his brigade so inopportunely at the battle of Prague, had committed a similar error. Observing some pandours in a village near the road that the column followed, Manstein made up his mind to dislodge them. He entered the village contrary to orders, drove out the enemy, pursued them, and found himself under the fire of case shot from the Austrian batteries. He in turn was attacked and the right wing of the infantry marched to his support [F]. By the time the King arrived on the spot the affair was so seriously engaged that there was no way of withdrawing the troops without being defeated. Soon the left wing likewise entered the contest, which the generals, however, could have prevented. Then the battle became general, and it was frustrating for the King to be only a spectator, not having a single remaining battalion at his disposal.

Marshal Daun profited from the Prussian mistakes like a great general. He had his reserve file off behind his front to attack Hülsen, who until that time had been victorious. Hülsen nevertheless held his ground, and if he could have been supplied with four fresh battalions, the battle would have been won. He even repulsed this Austrian reserve; the Normann dragoons then fell upon the enemy infantry, dispersed it, and took five colors. They next attacked the Saxon carabineers, whom they chased as far as Kolin.

Meanwhile the Prussian infantry of the center and right had gained some ground, without, however, having won any considerable advantage. These battalions, which had all suffered heavily from artillery and small arms fire, being diminished by one-half, left gaps between them three times as large as they should have been, and since there was neither a second line nor a reserve it was necessary to plug the holes with cuirassier regiments that had been placed some distance behind them. The Prince of Prussia cavalry regiment even attacked a body of enemy infantry and would have destroyed it had not a battery loaded with case shot fired opportunely upon it. Turning back in confusion, this regiment threw the regiments of Bevern and Prince Henry behind it into disorder. The enemy perceived this and immediately released his cavalry which, taking advantage of this moment, made the confusion universal. The King wanted to counterattack with the cuirassiers that were at hand, who might have, in part, retrieved the situation, but he found it impossible to put them in motion. He had recourse to two squadrons of the Meinicke dragoon regiment, which took the enemy cavalry in flank and drove it back to the foot of the hills. Of the line of infantry there remained only the first battalion of guards which still held its ground on the right. It had repulsed four infantry battalions and two cavalry regiments that had attempted to surround it, but a single battalion, however brave, cannot win a battle by itself.[9] Hülsen with his infantry and some cavalry that had been sent to him still maintained the ground from which he had driven the Austrians at the beginning of the battle. Here he remained until

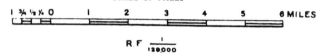

# THE BATTLE OF ROSBACH

### *5th November 1757*

#### SCALE OF MILES

| 1 ¾ ½ ¼ 0 | 1 | 2 | 3 | 4 | 5 | 6 MILES |

R.F. $\frac{1}{120,000}$

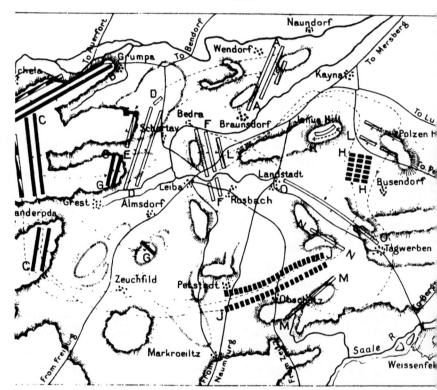

**A.** Prussian Army under Frederic, 23,000 (4000 Cavalry)—1st position, after crossing the Saale.
**B.** French and German Army, 55,000, under Soubise—1st position, after retreating from the Saale.
**C.** 2nd position taken up by Soubise.
**D.** Frederic moves to attack, but finds position of enemy too strong, and takes up a 2nd position F F between Bedra and Rosbach.
**G.** Detached force under St. Germain to observe the Prussians. Soubise makes flank march in full view of enemy.
**H.** His advanced guard of Cavalry.
**J.** His main body in column.
**K.** Frederic occupies Janus Hill and establishes battery of 18 guns.
**L.** Seidlitz moves round by Kayna and charges the French Cavalry, still in column, at the moment Prussian battery opens on it and destroys it.
**M.** Seidlitz rallies his squadrons in Tagwerben hollow and takes French main body in flank.
**N.** Prince Henry with 7 battalions attacks the head of it.
**O.** Prussian main body following in support completely routs the enemy.
Prussian losses—500. Allied losses—8000 killed, wounded and prisoners, and 70 guns.

## PLATE 22. Rossbach. (Major Gerald Gilbert, *The Evolution of Tactics*, London, 1907.)

nine o'clock in the evening, when he and the rest of the army were forced to withdraw. Prince Maurice led the troops to Nimburg, where he crossed the Elbe without being pursued by a single enemy hussar.

This action cost the King 8,000 of his best infantry. He lost sixteen guns which could not be carried away because the horses had been killed.[10] After the King had given his orders to the generals for the retreat of the troops, he hastened with all speed to his army at Prague, where he could not arrive before the next evening, and dispositions were made to raise the blockade of the city which the fatal day of Kolin no longer permitted him to continue.

A singular circumstance in the battle was that the Austrian infantry already had begun to retire and the cavalry was prepared to follow their example when one Colonel d'Ayasasa, on his own initiative, attacked the Prussian infantry with his dragoons at the moment when the Prince of Prussia cuirassiers had put them in confusion and when their success had caused his initial orders to be revoked.[11] No doubt the disorder in which the Austrians found themselves after such a stubborn battle prevented them from pursuing the Prussians. However, they were victorious. Had Marshal Daun shown more resolution and activity, his army, beyond any doubt, could have arrived before Prague on the twentieth, and the results of the battle of Kolin would have become more fatal to the Prussians than even their defeat.[12]

## ROSSBACH: THE CAMPAIGN [Plate 22]

Kolin, the first defeat Frederick had experienced, put an abrupt end to immediate plans for an offensive war in Bohemia. Two days after the battle he raised the siege of Prague and withdrew with part of his army to Leitmeritz, some thirty-five miles to the north, where he would be in position either to block an Austrian invasion of Saxony or to move against the Imperial and French armies threatening from the west. He kept 34,000 men under his own command: the rest, under his brother August William, Prince of Prussia, were located thirty miles to the east, where they could also watch Silesia.

The combined armies of Daun and Prince Charles, 93,000 strong, moved against the Prince of Prussia early in July. With only 34,000 men (including the survivors of Kolin) at his disposal, August William retreated northward, sacrificing several detachments and ultimately losing his magazines at Zittau, which was destroyed by an Austrian bombardment on July 22. Frederick broke camp that same day and rushed to join his brother at Bautzen. Here poor August William learned that Frederick would not tolerate incompetence even in a brother; he resigned and left the army in disgrace while Frederick waited for reinforcements and new supplies and then set out to maneuver the Austrians into a battle. "In this sad situation," he explained, "nothing is left for me but trying the last extremity. . . . and if we cannot conquer, we must all of us have ourselves killed."[18]

Frederick's despair mounted when he learned of the Duke of Cumberland's defeat on July 26, at the battle of Hastenbeck. Pursued by the victorious French, the Hanoverian "army of observation" retreated down the Elbe to Stade and capitulated. Meanwhile, a second French army under Marshal Soubise and the forces of the Empire commanded by the Prince of Hildburghausen had reached Eisenach and Erfurt respectively, and stood poised to invade Saxony. On August 11, the Russians invaded East Prussia; the Swedes were preparing to send an army of 17,000 into Pomerania.

This gave Frederick precious little time to lure the Austrians from their impregnable position near Zittau, and when his maneuvers failed to produce the desired battle, Frederick left Bevern, with 41,000 troops to contain the 105,000 Austrians under Prince Charles, while he hurried with a few battalions and squadrons to organize resistance against the combined French and Imperial armies in Thuringia. In mid-October, however, he was forced to suspend operations and strike out with the bulk of his army for

Berlin, which had been raided by a small Austrian column. It was then his intention to push on into Silesia, but when he learned that the allies had crossed the Saale and were moving on Leipzig, he turned back. Toward the end of October he assembled his forces at Leipzig, whereupon the allies fell back across the Saale.

Frederick followed, crossing the river on November 3, and encamping that night between Wernsdorf and Braunsdorf (A), several miles from the allied post (B). Although information obtained from prisoners brought in by hussar patrols made it clear that he was outnumbered (60,000 to 22,000) Frederick decided to attack. The left flank of the allies was exposed, and he was not one to let such an opportunity go begging.[14]

## ROSSBACH: THE BATTLE. NOVEMBER 5, 1757

The army left its camp before daybreak [November 4], with all of the cavalry forming the advance guard. Arriving at the place where the enemy position had been reconnoitered the previous evening, they could not find the enemy: no doubt Soubise, having considered the defect of his camp, had changed it the same night. He had extended his troops along a height in front of which was a ravine. [See Plate 22–C.] His right was supported by a wood, which he had fortified with an abatis and three redoubts furnished with artillery. His left was enclosed by a pond large enough that it could not be turned. The King's army was too weak in infantry to storm such a formidable post, for even had the defense been spiritless it still would have cost at least 20,000 casualties to carry the Austrian position.

Judging this enterprise to be beyond his strength, the King sent orders for the infantry to cross a marshy defile nearby to take the camp of Braunsdorf [D].[15] The cavalry followed him, forming the rear guard. As soon as the French observed that the Prussian troops were retreating they had their pickets advance with the artillery and keep up a warm cannonade, but without effect. All their musicians and trumpeters played fanfares; their drummers and fifers made cheers, as though they had won a victory. However vexatious this spectacle was for men who had never feared the enemy, it was necessary under the circumstances to gaze upon it with indifference and to place German phlegm opposite French giddiness and bluster.

That same night it was learned that the enemy was making a movement from his left to his right. The hussars were in the field at daybreak. They entered the camp that the French had just evacuated and learned from the peasants that the French had taken the road to Weissenfels. Soon afterwards a considerable body of troops was formed opposite the Prussian right, giving the appearance of a rear guard or troop which covered the march of an army. The Prussians paid little attention to these maneuvers because their camp was covered along the front as well as on both flanks by an impenetrable marsh, and there were only three narrow causeways by which they could be reached.

Only three intentions consequently could be attributed to the enemy: to retire by Freiberg into Upper Thuringia because they lacked subsistence; to take Weissenfels, although the bridges were destroyed; or to gain Merseburg before the King and cut off the passage of the Saale. But the Prussian army was much nearer to it than the French, and this maneuver was, moreover, less to be feared because it would lead to a battle having every hope of Prussian success, since it would not be necessary to attack a post.

The King sent many parties into the field and waited tranquilly until the enemy's intentions should be more clearly developed, for any ill-timed or precipitate movement would have spoiled everything. Intelligence, sometimes false, sometimes true, brought back by the scouts kept up this uncertainty until toward noon, when the head of the French columns were observed in the distance turning the Prussian left [J]. The Imperial troops also gradually disappeared from their old camp, so that the corps which was taken for a rear guard and was, in fact, the reserve of Saint-Germain,[16] remained alone opposite the

Prussians [G]. The King himself reconnoitered the march of Soubise and was convinced that it was directed against Merseburg. The French marched very slowly because they had formed different battalions in column, which arrested them each time the narrow roads forced them to break up.[17]

It was two o'clock when the Prussians struck their tents. They made a quarter-wheel to the left and began to march. The King kept pace with Soubise's army, his troops being covered by the marsh that begins at Braunsdorf and extends for more than a mile to a point within 2,000 paces of Rossbach. Seydlitz formed the King's vanguard with all the cavalry: his orders were to glide along by the hollows with which this country abounds, turn the French cavalry, and fall upon the heads of their infantry columns before they would have time to form. The King could only leave Prince Ferdinand,[18] who that day commanded the right wing of the army, the old guard of the cavalry, which he placed in one line to make a demonstration. This they could do very effectively because a part of the Braunsdorf marsh covered the right wing.

The two armies, marching on a parallel course, continually drew nearer to each other. The King's army carefully stuck to a small elevation that runs straight to Rossbach, but the French, apparently unacquainted with the terrain, marched along the bottom. The King had a battery [eighteen heavy guns] established on Janushügel, the fire of which was decisive in the action [K]. The French established a battery [eight guns] facing it on the low ground, and since it fired uphill it produced no effect.

While each side was making these arrangements, Seydlitz had turned the enemy's right without being noticed. He then pounced with impetuosity on the allied cavalry [L]. The two Austrian regiments formed to face him and sustained the shock, but finding themselves abandoned by the French, with the exception of Fitz-James' regiment, they were almost entirely destroyed.[19] The infantry of the two armies continued to march until their foremost ranks were within only five hundred paces of each other. The King would have wanted to gain the village of Reichardtswerben,[20] but since it was six hundred paces away and he expected the action to begin any moment, he detached Marshal Keith[21] there with five battalions, his entire second line. The King himself advanced at the same time to within two hundred paces of the two French lines [J], and he noticed that their order of battle consisted of battalions in columns alternately embraced in the deployed battalions, Soubise's wing was in the air, the Prussian cavalry was still occupied pursuing that of the enemy, so that only infantry could be used to out-flank the French right. For this purpose the King put two grenadier battalions in line, forming a hook with his left flank, with orders to make a half-wheel to the right the moment the French should advance. This would necessarily bring them on the enemy flank.

This disposition was punctually carried out: as the French came up they received the fire of the grenadiers in flank, and after having endured at most three volleys from the regiment of Brunswick[22] their columns were seen pressing to the left. Soon they had closed upon the deployed battalions that sep-arated them: the mass of this infantry became larger, heavier, and more confused by the moment. The more it threw itself on its left, the more it was outflanked by the Prussian front.

While the disorder increased in Soubise's army, the King was informed that a corps of enemy cavalry had appeared in his rear. He hastily assembled the first squadrons he could lay his hands on: scarcely had these been placed opposite those who were seen behind his front when the latter retreated in haste.[23] Then the *Gardes du Corps* and the *Gendarmes* were set against the French infantry [M], which were found in the greatest disorder. The cavalry attacked and easily dispersed the French infantry, capturing a considerable number of pris-oners. It was six o'clock in the evening when this charge was made. The weather was overcast and the darkness so great that it would have been imprudent to follow the enemy, in spite of the confusion that attended his rout. The King contented himself with sending different groups of cuirassiers, dragoons, and hussars after them, none of which exceeded thirty men.

During this battle ten battalions on the Prussian right had kept musket on shoulder without firing. Prince Ferdinand of Brunswick, who commanded them, had not left the marsh of Braunsdorf which covered a portion of his front. He had repulsed the Imperial troops opposite him with several artillery volleys which forced them to give ground. Only seven battalions of the King's army were under fire, and the entire battle lasted only an hour and one-half. . . .

The battle of Rossbach had cost the army of Soubise 10,000 troops; the Prussians took 7,000 prisoners and they captured sixty-three cannon, fifteen standards, seven colors, and one pair of kettle drums.[24] It is certain that in considering the conduct of the French generals one will have difficulty approving of it. Their intention manifestly was to drive the Prussians out of Saxony, but did not the interest of their allies demand rather that they should simply contain the King on their front, in order to give Marshal Daun and the Prince of Lorraine time to complete the conquest of Silesia? However little could they have delayed the King in Thuringia, the conquest of Silesia not only would have been made but the season would have become so rigorous and so far advanced that it would have been impossible for the Prussians to make the progress in Silesia of which we will immediately have occasion to speak. As for the battle they invited so inopportunely, it is certain that Soubise, through his instability and by his dispositions, made it possible for a handful of men to vanquish his army. But the manner in which the French court distinguished the merit of its generals is more surprising still: D'Estrées[25] was recalled for having won the battle of Hastenbeck while Soubise, having lost that of Rossbach, soon afterwards was made Marshal of France.

The battle of Rossbach, strictly speaking, was of value to the King only by enabling him to go and seek new dangers in Silesia. This victory became important only by the impression it made on the French and the remains of the Duke of Cumberland's army. On the one hand, Richelieu, as soon as he heard the news, left his camp at Halberstadt and retired into the Electorate of Hanover; on the other, the allied troops, ready to lay down their arms, received courage and revived their hopes.[26]

## LEUTHEN: THE CAMPAIGN [Plate 23]

Rossbach was Frederick's cheapest and in many respects his most important victory. In England the news of the battle caused rejoicing and restored public confidence in the unpopular Hanoverian war. The Duke of Cumberland's army, which had been disbanded according to the terms of the Convention of Klosterzevern in September, was resurrected, given vastly increased funds for the coming campaign, and placed in the capable hands of Prince Ferdinand of Brunswick, one of Frederick's most trusted lieutenants. Although the French continued to play an active part in the Continental war while fighting Britain overseas, Prince Ferdinand successfully parried French thrusts from the Rhine and the Main while Frederick gave the war against Russia and Austria his personal attention.

Rossbach also ended the myth of the invincibility of French arms that had followed the victories of Condé, Turenne, and Saxe. France had been humiliated to the point where even an international figure like Voltaire could complain that his friend Frederick "now has achieved everything that he has always set for himself: to please the French, make fun of them, and beat them. . . . Posterity will always be amazed that an Elector of Brandenburg after a great defeat at the hands of the Austrians, after the complete ruin of his allies, pursued in Prussia by 100,000 victorious Russians, hard pressed by two French armies which could fall upon him simultaneously, has succeeded in resisting everyone, holding his conquests, and winning one of the most memorable battles of this century. I guarantee that he will now let epigrams follow the lamentations. The present is not a good time for Frenchmen to be abroad. People laugh in our face, as though we had been the Prince de Soubise's adjutants."[27]

But Frederick found little time for epigrams. As the allies parted company and retreated to take up winter quarters, the Imperial army southward along the Main and its tributaries and the French to the west, near Richelieu's army in Hanover, Frederick returned to Leipzig. On November 13, he set off with about 12,000 troops for Silesia, entrusting Keith with a detachment to keep the Austrians occupied in Bohemia and leaving his brother Henry, an extremely talented general, in command of the troops left behind in Saxony.

Frederick's objective was to retrieve slipping fortunes in Silesia, where Bevern had marched in September followed by Prince Charles. On October 26, the Austrians had besieged the great fortress of Schweidnitz, Frederick's chief stronghold in Silesia, which, to everyone's surprise, fell only sixteen days after the first parallel was opened. Frederick then ordered Bevern to attack the main Austrian army at the first opportunity, but on November 22, Bevern's army was swamped by superior Austrian forces and the city of Breslau, along with impressive quantities of guns and supplies, was taken. Bevern's shattered army retreated down the Oder to Glogau, whence it moved southward under Ziethen, the cavalry commander, to join Frederick's army at Parchwitz on December 2.

Frederick's first task was to rebuild the morale of Ziethen's troops, who were "discouraged and overwhelmed by the memory of recent defeat." Through conversation, informal chats with the soldiers, extra rations, and even wine, Frederick managed to tune up his army. In the following address to his generals and staff officers, which he delivered on December 3, Frederick tried also to infuse his subordinates with the spirit of victory.

## FREDERICK'S SPEECH BEFORE LEUTHEN

Gentlemen: You are aware that Prince Charles of Lorraine has succeeded in becoming master of Schweidnitz, beating the Duke of Bevern, and taking possession of Breslau while I was of necessity absent, having been obliged to check the advances of the French and their allies. A part of Silesia, its capital,

**A.** Austrian Army, 80,000, under Prince Charles, with 210 guns—1st position.

**B.** Austrian advanced post, three regiments of Saxon Cavalry under Nostitz.

**C.** Prussian Army, 30,000 men, on the march.

**D.** Prussian advanced guard under the King destroys or captures nearly the whole of Nostitz's force; remainder fled in direction of Nypern and led Austrians to expect an attack there.

**E.** The Scheuberg, whence Frederic reconnoitred enemy's position.

**F.** Prussian Army in two lines marches under cover of low hills to attack Austrian left flank, wheels to the left, and attacks.

**G.** The advanced guard under Zeithen throws back Nadasti's left beyond the woods of Sagaschutz.

**H.** Prussian main body advancing in echelon to support Zeithen and attack Leuthen.

**K.** Austrian left flank thrown back on its center in confusion.

**L.** Count Lucchesi commanding on right tries to retrieve the day by charging Prussian battalions assaulting Leuthen.

**M.** Dreisen makes counter charge, taking Austrian Cavalry in flank.

**N.** Line of Austrian retreat.

Austrian losses—10,000 killed and wounded, 21,000 prisoners, 116 guns. Prussian losses—6250 killed and wounded.

# THE BATTLE OF LEUTHEN

*5th December 1757*

SCALE OF MILES

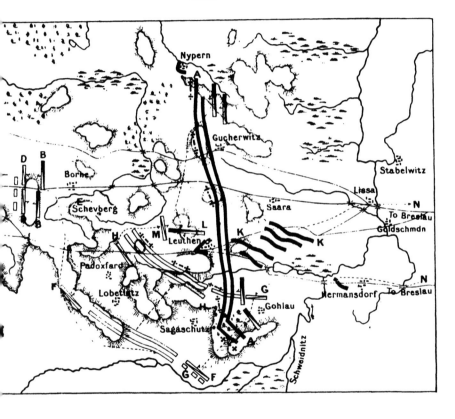

PLATE 23. Leuthen. (Major Gerald Gilbert, *The Evolution of Tactics*, London, 1907.)

and all of the munitions of war that were stored there have been lost; and my disasters would be regarded by me as being fully crowned and insurmountable were it not that I place the most unbounded confidence in your gallantry and courage, in that resolution and love of country which you have so nobly evinced on so many occasions. . . . There is not one amongst you who is not distinguished by some great, some chivalrous exploit. I can consequently flatter myself in the hope that, when the occasion offers, you will not fail to satisfy the demands that your country now makes upon your courage and devotion.

The decisive moment is approaching, and I should consider that I had accomplished nothing if I left the Austrians in possession of Silesia. Rely then on this, that contrary to every rule of art, I shall attack the army under the command of Prince Charles even though it may be three times my own strength, wherever and whenever I may meet it. The number of the foe, the strength of their position, are here matters of but secondary importance. All these must yield, I feel confident, before the unflinching bravery of my troops and the judicious execution of my orders. I must venture on this step, or all is lost. We must beat the foe or be buried beneath their batteries.

These are my feelings, and I shall act accordingly. Inform the different officers of the army of my purpose and resolves; prepare the private soldier for the events that are about to follow, impress upon his mind that I am justified in demanding the most implicit obedience from him. Finally, remember that you are Prussians and your actions will certainly be in accordance with that high distinction. If there be, however, any one amongst you who fears to share these dangers with me, he can this day demand his dismissal without being exposed to the slightest reproach from me. . . . Return to the camp and communicate to the regiments what you have now heard from me.

I shall immediately after the battle dismount and convert into a garrison regiment that cavalry regiment that does not immediately, on being ordered, burst impetuously on the foe.

The infantry battalion which, whatever the obstacles, halts for a moment, shall lose its standards and swords, and I shall cut the facings from its uniform. Fare you well, gentlemen, for the present. We shall soon beat the enemy and meet again.[28]

## THE PRUSSIANS ADVANCE

"The countenances of the men began already to be cheerful," Frederick later recalled, "and those who had beaten the French at Rossbach persuaded their comrades to take heart. A little repose restored the soldiers, and the army was disposed to wash out the stain received on the twenty-second whenever any occasion presented itself."

The next morning, December 4, Frederick's army broke camp and advanced in the direction of Neumarkt on the Breslau road. Frederick now had 35,000 men at his command—38½ battalions of infantry, 133 squadrons of cavalry, and 78 heavy guns, in addition to 98 battalion field pieces. The Austrians meanwhile had left Breslau on December 3, and were marching slowly along the Breslau road. Prince Charles and Daun had between them 85 battalions, 125 squadrons and 235 guns, better than 60,000 men in all. An advance guard of 1,000 Croats and two hussar regiments occupied Neumarkt.

As the Prussians approached this city Frederick rode with the vanguard of hussars. Here he learned that "the enemy had established a bakery in that town, that it was garrisoned with pandours, and that Daun's army was expected."[29]

## LEUTHEN: THE BATTLE. DECEMBER 5, 1757

The rising ground beyond Neumarkt gave the enemy a considerable advantage, if he was permitted to occupy it. The difficulty was to take the place, for the infantry had not yet arrived and could not join the vanguard until evening, there was no artillery present, and the only available troops were the hussars. It was decided to make a virtue of necessity. The King, unwilling to allow the Prince of Lorraine to encamp in the vicinity, had some hussar squadrons dismount. These crashed the town gate and a regiment following them on horseback entered at a full gallop. Another regiment made a circuit by the suburbs and gained the Breslau gate. The attack was so successful that eight hundred Croats were taken prisoner by the hussars,[30] who immediately occupied the site of the camp where they found pickets and the traces that the Austrian engineers had left to mark the positions of their troops. The Prince of Württemberg took command of the advance guard which, reinforced by ten battalions that night, encamped at Kammendorf. The same day the cavalry passed through the defile [of Neumarkt]; the main body of the infantry cantoned in the city of Neumarkt and the neighboring villages.

The King then received reliable intelligence that the Prince of Lorraine had left the camp of the Lohe [near Breslau] and had advanced beyond Lissa [see Plate 23–A]; that his right flank rested on the village of Nippern and his left at Gohlau, and the small rivulet of Schweidnitz covered his rear. The King rejoiced to find the enemy in such a position, which facilitated his enterprise, for he was obliged and determined to attack the Austrians wherever he could find them. . . .

The disposition of the march was immediately worked out and the army placed in motion before daybreak, December 5. It was preceded by an advance guard of sixty squadrons and ten battalions headed by the King in person. The four columns of the army followed at a slight distance, with the infantry forming the two middle columns and the cavalry, the wings [C]. On approaching the village of Borne, the advance guard discovered a large line of enemy cavalry [B], the right of which was drawn back toward Lissa and the left, which was more advanced, supported by a woods on the right of the Prussian army. Originally this was taken to be a wing of the Austrian army, the center of which could not be seen. Those who made a reconnaissance affirmed that it was the advance guard: it was even learned that it was commanded by General Nostitz and that the corps consisted of four regiments of Saxon dragoons and two of Imperial hussars.

To play it safe, the ten battalions were slipped into the woods covering Nostitz' left flank, upon which the Prussian cavalry, having formed, fell upon the Austrians with great spirit. Nostitz' regiments were dispersed in a moment [D] and pursued to the front of the Austrian army. Five officers and eight hundred men were taken and marched all along the columns to Neumarkt to animate the soldiers by this successful example. The King had difficulty restraining the fury of the hussars, which their ardor conveyed: they were on the verge of assaulting the center of the Austrian army when they were assembled between the villages of Heidau and Frobelwitz, within cannon range of the enemy.[31]

From there [E] the Imperial army was so clearly visible that it would have been possible to have counted it man by man. The Austrian right, known to be at Nippern, was hidden by the great wood of Lissa, but of the center as well as the left nothing was out of sight. Upon the first inspection of these troops it was judged by the terrain that the main attack must be delivered against the Austrian left wing, which was extended on a knoll encumbered with pine trees, but poorly supported. As soon as this post had been carried the advantage of terrain would be gained for the rest of the battle, because from that point the ground sloped off in one continual descent toward Nippern. If, instead, the attack were to be made against the Austrian center, the troops of the [enemy] right wing would have been able, by crossing the wood of Lissa, to fall on the flank of the attackers. In any case it eventually would have been necessary to attack this knoll since it commanded the whole plain. To have delayed would have been to postpone the greatest difficulty until the time when the troops would be harassed, fatigued, and incapable of great efforts; whereas by overcoming the greatest danger at the beginning, one could take advantage of the initial ardor of the soldier, and the rest of the task would become easy.

For these reasons the army was made ready to attack the Austrian left immediately. The columns that were in the order of deployment were reversed. They were placed in two lines, and the platoons by a quarter-wheel filed off by the right [F]. The King with his hussars kept pace with the march of his army along a chain of knolls that concealed from the enemy the movements that were being made behind. Being between the two armies the King could observe that of the Austrians and direct the march of his own. He sent some reliable officers to observe Daun's right and others toward Kanth to watch the steps of Draskowitz, who was encamped there. At the same time he reconnoitered the enemy along the rivulet of Schweidnitz to be sure that nobody reached the rear of the army when it was engaged with the enemy.

The plan that the King was preparing to execute was to bring his entire army on the Imperial left flank, to make his greatest efforts with his right, and to refuse his left with enough prudence that he would not have to fear the same mistakes that happened at the battle of Prague and later had caused the loss of Kolin.

Already Wedell,[32] who with his ten battalions of the advance guard was to form the first attack, had arrived at the head of the army; already the heads of the columns had gained the stream of Schweidnitz without being observed by the enemy. Marshal Daun mistook the Prussian movements as a retreat and commented to the Prince of Lorraine: "These people are going; let them go."

Wedell, however, had formed in front of the two lines of infantry on the right. His attack was supported by a battery of 20 twelve-pounders that the King had stripped from the ramparts of Glogau. The first line received the order to advance in echelons,[33] the battalions at a distance of fifty paces behind each other, so that the line being in movement, the extreme right was 1,000 paces in advance of the extreme left. This disposition made it impossible to engage without orders.[34]

Wedell now [one P.M.] attacked the wood where Nadasti

commanded [G], encountering no strong resistance and carrying it promptly. The Austrian generals, seeing themselves
turned and taken in flank, endeavored to change their position:
they attempted, but too late, to form a line parallel to the Prussian front. The whole art of the King's generals consisted in
not giving them the necessary time. Already the Prussians
had established themselves on a hill commanding the village
of Leuthen, and at the very instant when the enemy tried to
throw infantry into the village, a second battery of 20 twelve-
pounders fired upon them with such timely effect that they
gave up the attempt and retreated. On Wedell's side of the
attack the Austrians seized a knoll next to the stream to prevent him from sweeping their line from one end to the other.
Wedell did not allow them to stay there for long, and after a
longer and more obstinate fight than the one preceding he
forced them to give up the ground. At the same time Ziethen
charged the enemy cavalry and put it to rout. Some squadrons
of his right received a volley of case shot in the flank from
bushes that bordered the stream. This fire caught them unexpectedly and drove them back. They formed again beside the
infantry [G].

The officers who had been ordered to observe Daun's right
then came to inform the King that the Austrians were crossing
the woods of Lissa and would appear immediately on the plain,
upon which Driesen[35] received orders to advance with the left
wing of the Prussian cavalry. When the Austrian cuirassiers
[L] began to form near Leuthen [5 P.M.] the battery in the
center of the King's army saluted them with a volley at the
same time that Driesen attacked them [M]. The mêlée did not
last long. The Imperialists were dispersed and fled in disorder.
A line of infantry that had formed beside the cuirassiers behind Leuthen was taken in flank by the Bayreuth dragoons
and thrown back upon the volunteers [free battalion] of
Wunsch,[36] losing two entire regiments with officers and colors.

With the enemy cavalry being entirely dispersed, the King
had the center of his infantry advance upon Leuthen. The fire

was hot but short, because the Austrian infantry was only scattered among the houses and gardens. Upon leaving the village the Prussian generals noticed a new line of infantry that the Austrians had formed on an eminence near the Sagschütz windmill: the King's army had to endure their fire for some time, but the enemy failed to notice in this confusion that Wedell's corps was in their vicinity. They were suddenly taken in flank and rear by this brave and able general, and that beautiful maneuver, by determining the victory, ended this important battle.[87]

Collecting the first troops that presented themselves, the King went in pursuit of the enemy with the cuirassiers of Seydlitz and one battalion of Jung-Stutterheim, directing his march between the rivulet of Schweidnitz and the Lissa woods. The darkness became so great that he sent some cavalrymen forward to reconnoiter the forests and to bring intelligence. Occasionally he ordered artillery volleys fired toward Lissa, where the main part of the Austrian army had fled. Upon approaching this city the advance guard sustained a discharge from about two battalions, but not a man was wounded. It replied with several volleys from the artillery, still continuing its march. On the way Seydlitz's cuirassiers brought in prisoners in bands. Arriving at Lissa the King found all the houses full of fugitives and unattached men of the Imperial army. He at once seized the bridge, where he placed his artillery with orders to fire as long as any powder remained. On the road to Breslau, where the enemy had retired, he threw some infantry platoons into the houses nearest the stream of Schweidnitz to fire on the opposite bank throughout the night, as much to keep up the terror in the vanquished as to prevent them from sending troops . . . to dispute his passage the next day.

This battle had begun at one o'clock in the afternoon and it was eight o'clock when the King arrived with his advance guard at Lissa. His army was 30,000 strong when it went into action against the Imperialists, who were said to have 60,000 combatants. If night had not come on this battle would have been one of the most decisive of this century.[38]

# FROM LEUTHEN TO TORGAU

Leuthen was Frederick's Meisterstück—according to Napoleon "a masterpiece of movements, manoeuvres, and resolution" which in itself would suffice "to immortalize Frederick and rank him amongst the greatest generals. He attacks an army of superior strength to his own, in position and victorious, with an army composed in part of troops which had lately been defeated, and gains a complete victory without purchasing it by a loss disproportionate to the result. All his manoeuvres in this battle were in harmony with the principles of war."[39] The German General Staff history quietly noted that this was "the first and only time" that Frederick's famous oblique order was "completely carried out in the presence of the enemy,"[40] and the late eminent military historian and theorist, General J. F. C. Fuller, comparing Rossbach and Leuthen, writes: ". . . they represent the oblique order of attack at its worst and at its best. At Rossbach there was no generalship; the combined commanders had no plan, and . . . they were novices at manoeuvre . . . mere copyists of a system they did not understand. . . . At Leuthen, Frederick moved, concentrated, surprised and hit. Co-operation was perfect, and so were the dispositions of the three arms."[41]

The battle of Torgau, fought three years later, presents a startling contrast. In Napoleon's judgment, Frederick on this occasion "violated the principles of war, both in the conception and execution of his plans; of all his battles it was this in which he made the greatest number of mistakes, and the only one in which he displayed no talent."[42]

The events between Leuthen and Torgau may be summarized briefly. After his victory over the Austrians, Frederick swept them out of much of Silesia. Then both armies went into winter quarters. In 1758, outnumbered and pressed on all sides as before, Frederick opened the campaign by investing Olmütz, the most important fortress still held by the Austrians. When a much-needed convoy of 4,000 wagons was destroyed by the Austrians and Croat light infantry, Frederick raised the siege, marched to the north, and defeated the Russians at Zorndorf (August 25). Returning south to counter Austrian movements he was surprised and defeated by Daun at Hochkirch (October 10), after which the armies went into winter quarters.

The Austrians came back in full force in 1759, uniting with the Russians to defeat Frederick at Kunnersdorf (August 12). On this dreadful day Frederick came closer to using the poison pills that he always carried with him than at any other time during the war: he had lost nearly half of his army (19,000 out of 42,000), and for once it was the enemy cavalry that had made the difference. Yet Frederick soon regained his composure and by a skillful series of maneuvers he and Prince Henry managed to reoccupy all of Saxony except Dresden. On November 21, he suffered another blow when a detachment of 15,000 was cut off and captured at Maxen, but the end of the fourth year of war found Frederick where he had been at the beginning.

The allied strategy in 1760 called for Daun to stand firm (stand pat might be a better term) in Saxony while another Austrian army under Loudon cooperated with a Russian army in Silesia. The campaign began as the previous one had ended—with the annihilation of a Prussian detachment near Landshut. Frederick successfully repulsed an Austrian attack at Liegnitz (August 15) in a battle which again demonstrated the superior quality of the Prussian soldier despite the wastage of war, but which did not materially improve Frederick's strategical situation. The Austrians and Russians remained in Silesia; another Russian army and the Swedes ravaged Pomerania; the Austrians and Imperialists controlled Saxony; and for a short while in October even Berlin was in the hands of the Russians and Austrians. After forcing the allies to evacuate Berlin, Frederick set out once again for Saxony, where he encountered the Austrians in a strong defensive position near Torgau. Daun had 50,000 men and 360 guns on the Süptitzer hills between Torgau and the Dommitzsch heath, with his camp protected in front by a steep slope, streams, and marshes and impregnable on either flank. Despite the natural strength of the Austrian post and his own inferiority in numbers (40,000 troops and 280 guns), Frederick decided to attack by executing what in modern military parlance would be termed a pincers movement.

## TORGAU: THE BATTLE. NOVEMBER 3, 1760 [Plate 24]

Daun's right flank was supported behind the Grosswig ponds. His center covered the hill of Süptitz, and his left ended beyond Zinna, extending toward the ponds of Torgau. Besides this, Ried observed the Prussian army at the edge of the forest of Torgau[42] and Lacy, with a reserve of 20,000 men, covered the causeway and the ponds at the extremity of the place where the Imperialists had anchored their left. The ground on which the enemy stood, however, lacked depth, and their lines did not have intervals of 300 paces—a very favorable circumstance for the Prussians because, by attacking the center in front and rear, they would place the enemy between two fires where he could not avoid being beaten.

To produce this effect the King divided his army into two corps. One of these was intended to approach from the Elbe, after having passed through the forest of Torgau, and to attack the enemy in the rear on the Süptitzer heights while the other, by following the road from Eilenburg to Torgau, was to establish a battery on the hill of Grosswig and at the same time attack the village of Süptitz. These two corps, acting in concert, would necessarily cut the Austrian army in the center, after which it would have been easy to drive the debris toward the Elbe, where the terrain, one continued gentle slope, would have played into the hands of the Prussians and would have procured for them a complete victory.

The King began his march on November 3, at dawn: he was followed by thirty battalions and fifty squadrons of his left.[43] The troops crossed the forest of Torgau in three columns. The route of the first line of infantry led through Mockrehna,

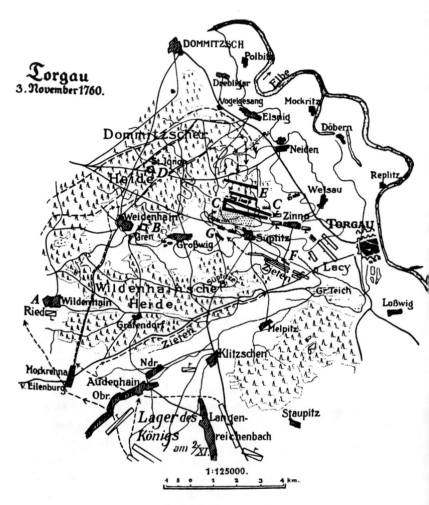

PLATE 24. Torgau. (*Die Werke Friedrichs des Grossen*, vol. IV.)

**A.** Frederick's column first encounters Austrian hussars, dragoons, and pandours, which are quickly dispersed.

**B.** He next finds his way blocked by Austrian infantry, which soon falls back upon the main Austrian army (*CC*).

**D.** St. Ignon's regiment of dragoons is caught between the two advancing Prussian columns and is destroyed.

**E.** Scene of Frederick's attacks against the main Austrian position.

**F.** Ziethen is drawn into demonstrations against Lacy, instead of moving directly against Daun's main position (*CC*) as Frederick had instructed.

**G.** Ziethen arrives in time to salvage the victory for Frederick.

Wildenhayn, Grosswig, and Neiden; that of the second, through Pechhütte, Jägerteich, Buchendorf[44] to Elsnig. The cavalry, comprising the third column, crossed the wood of Wildenhayn to go to Vogelgesang. Ziethen began his march at the same time with the right of the army, consisting of thirty battalions and seventy squadrons and filed off on the road that goes from Eilenburg to Torgau.[45]

The part of the army led by the King found Ried posted at the edge of the Torgau forest with two regiments each of hussars and dragoons and three battalions of pandours. A few volleys of artillery were fired at him, upon which he fell back toward the right of the Imperialists. Near Wildenhayn[46] there is a small clearing in the forest where ten grenadier battalions were seen, well posted, which gave the appearance of disputing the passage of the Prussians. They fired several cannon shots against the King's column, to which the Prussians responded. A line of infantry formed to charge them, but they fell back on their army. The hussars brought word at the same time that the regiment of St. Ignon was in the woods between the two infantry columns, and that it had even dismounted. It was attacked immediately, and since the dragoons found no escape, the entire regiment was destroyed. Both the grenadiers and St. Ignon's regiment were to have set out together to attempt a stroke against Düben,[47] and St. Ignon, who was captured, complained bitterly that Ried had not informed him of the approach of the Prussians.

This trifling affair cost the troops only a few moments: they proceeded on their way and the heads of the columns arrived at one o'clock, emerging from the forest onto the small plain of Neiden. Here some dragoons of Batthyani and four battalions were noticed coming from the village of Elsnig. They fired several cannon shots at random and discharged a volley with their small arms, doubtless a movement of surprise caused perhaps by having seen some Prussian hussars. These troops retired on a height behind the defile of Neiden. In this place there is a large marsh that begins at Grosswig and goes to the

Elbe, over which it is possible to cross only by two narrow causeways. Had this corps established itself on the advantageous terrain where it was, beyond any doubt there would have been no battle, for however determined the King might be to attack the Imperialists, such an attack would have become impossible: he would have had to renounce his entire plan and retrace his steps very quickly to regain Eilenburg. But things turned out otherwise.

These battalions hastened to rejoin their army, to which they were allured by a heavy cannonade which they heard from the side of Ziethen. The King believed, since there was every probability, that Ziethen's troops already were in action with the enemy. This induced him to cross the defile of Neiden with his hussars and infantry, for the cavalry, which ought to have preceded him, had not yet arrived. The King glided into a small wood and personally reconnoitered the enemy position. He judged that the only proper ground on which to form in front of the Austrians lay on the other side of the wood, which provided some measure of cover for his troops and from where it would be possible to gain a large enough ravine to shield the troops from enemy artillery while they were being formed. This ravine was in fact only eight hundred paces from the Austrian army, but the rest of the terrain, which descended like a glacis from Süptitz to the Elbe, was such that if the army had been formed in this part, half of it would have perished before it could have approached the enemy.

Marshal Daun had difficulty believing that the Prussians were marching against him, and it was only after repeated reports that he ordered his second line to face about and had most of the artillery of the first line brought to the second. No matter what precautions the King might take to cover the march of his troops, he could not prevent the enemy, who had four hundred pieces of artillery ready to fire, from killing many of his men. Eight hundred soldiers were killed and thirty cannon were destroyed along with their horses, train, and gunners, before the columns arrived at the place where they were to be deployed.

The King formed his infantry in three lines, each of which, consisting of ten battalions, made an attack.[48] If his cavalry had been on hand he would have thrown a couple of dragoon regiments into low-lying ground that was on the right of his infantry to cover its flank, but the Prince of Holstein, who never allowed anything to disturb his slackness, only arrived one hour after the action had begun. According to the original dispositions for the attacks, they must be made simultaneously; then the center of the enemy at Süptitz would have been pierced either by the King or by Ziethen. But instead of attacking, Ziethen busied himself for a considerable time with a body of pandours that he found on his way in the forest of Torgau; next, he engaged in an artillery duel with Lacy's corps which was, as we have said, posted behind the ponds of Torgau. In brief, the disposition was not carried out; the King attacked by himself without being supported by Ziethen and without his cavalry.

All this did not prevent him from following his plan. The first line of the King left the ravine and marched boldly against the enemy, but the prodigious fire of the Imperial artillery and this sloping terrain gave the enemy too much of an advantage. Most of the Prussian generals, battalion commanders, and soldiers were killed or wounded. The line folded and fell back with some confusion, pursued by the Austrian carabiniers who took advantage of the situation and let go their hold only after having received a few discharges from Frederick's second line. This second line was put in motion immediately, and after a fight more bloody and obstinate than the preceding one, it too was repulsed. Bülow,[40] who led it, fell into enemy hands.

At last the Prince of Holstein arrived with his long-awaited cavalry. The Prussian third line was already engaged. The Prince Henry regiment, attacking the enemy, was charged in turn by the Austrian cavalry. Hundt, Reitzenstein, and Prittwitz rushed to the support of this regiment with their hussars and in vain the Austrians endeavored to rout it. The terrible fire that the Imperialists had made with their artillery had consumed their ammunition too quickly. They had left their reserve artillery on the far side of the Elbe, and the contraction of their lines did not permit them to move their ammunition wagons between them for distribution to the batteries. The King took advantage of the moment that their fire slackened to attack their infantry with the Bayreuth dragoons. Bülow[50] led them with so much valor and impetuosity, that in less than three minutes they took prisoner the regiments of the Emperor, Neipperg, Gaisruck, and Imperial-Bayreuth. The cuirassiers of Spaen and Frederick at the same time assaulted that portion of the enemy infantry that was further on the right of the Prussians, routed it, and took many prisoners. As for the Prince of Holstein, he was placed to cover the left flank of the infantry. His right wing touched the infantry and his left was drawn back toward the Elbe. The enemy soon appeared opposite him with eighty squadrons, his right toward the Elbe and his left toward Zinna. If O'Donnell, who commanded this Imperial cavalry, had had the resolution to attack the Prince of Holstein the battle would have been irretrievably lost for the King, but he respected a ditch a foot and one-half wide that the skirmishers were forbidden to cross. The enemy took it for a considerable obstacle because the Prussians made a pretense of fearing to cross it, and they remained opposite the Prince of Holstein, gazing at them with arms folded.

In the meantime the Bayreuth dragoons had just cleared the height of Süptitz. The King sent the Maurice regiment, which had not been engaged, to the spot, and an old and worthy officer named Lestwitz[51] brought up a body of 1,000 men, which he had formed from regiments that had been repulsed in the previous attacks. With these troops the Prussians seized the Süptitz hill and established themselves there with all the cannon that they could assemble in a hurry.

Finally, Ziethen, having arrived at his destination, attacked from his side. It was already night, and to avoid Prussians fighting against Prussians, the infantry on Süptitz beat the march [with their drums]. Ziethen soon joined them, and scarcely had they begun to form with some order on this site before

Lacy came up with his corps to dislodge the King's troops. But he arrived too late and was twice repulsed. Rebuffed at being so poorly received, he withdrew at 9:30 in the evening in the direction of Torgau, and the battle was over.

The Imperialists and the Prussians were so near to one another in the vineyards of Süptitz that many officers and soldiers on both sides were taken prisoner by straying in the darkness after the battle, when all was in order and tranquil. The King himself, while trying to repair to the village of Neiden in order to expedite orders relative to the victory and to proclaim the success in Brandenburg and Silesia, heard the sound of a wagon nearby. He asked for the password and the man replied *Austrian*, whereupon the King's escort pounced on them and captured two field pieces and an entire battalion of pandours that had lost their way in the night. A hundred paces farther on he encountered a mounted troop that answered when challenged: *Austrian carabiniers*. The King's escort attacked and dispersed them in the forest. Those who were captured disclosed that they had lost their road with Ried in the woods and that they believed that the Imperialists were masters of the battlefield. The entire forest that the Prussians traversed before the battle and that the King was riding beside at the time was full of large fires. No one could understand what these might be, and some hussars were sent to obtain information. They reported that soldiers sat around the fires, some in blue uniforms and others in white. Since more accurate intelligence was necessary officers were sent, and a singular fact was brought to light, the likes of which I doubt is found in history. They were soldiers of both armies who had sought refuge in the woods. They had made a bargain between them that they would wait and remain neutral until fate decided in favor of the Prussians or Imperialists. Both sides had made up their minds to follow the side of fortune and to surrender to the victorious.

This battle cost the Prussians about 13,000 men, 3,000 of whom were killed and 3,000 of whom fell into enemy hands during the first attacks that the Austrians repulsed.[52] Bülow and Finck were among this number. The King's chest was grazed by a ball and the Margrave Charles received a contusion: several generals were wounded. The battle was stubbornly fought by both armies. This tenacity cost the Imperialists 20,000 men, of whom four generals and 8,000 men were taken prisoner. They lost twenty-seven colors and fifty cannon at Torgau. Marshal Daun was wounded during the first attack.

When the enemy saw the first line of the Prussians give way, they frivolously dispatched couriers to Vienna and Warsaw to announce their victory. That night they abandoned the field of battle and recrossed the Elbe at Torgau. The following morning Torgau surrendered to Hülsen. The Prince of Württemberg was sent over the Elbe to pursue the enemy, who fled in disorder, and he added to the number of prisoners taken in the battle. The Imperialists would have been totally defeated if Beck, who had not fought the previous day, had not covered their retreat by posting his corps between Arzberg and Triestewitz behind the Landgraben.

It rested only with Marshal Daun to avoid this battle. If, instead of placing Lacy behind the ponds of Torgau, which six battalions would have been sufficient to defend, he had posted him behind the defile of Neiden, his camp would have been impregnable. So great may be the consequences of the least oversight in this difficult profession of war.[53]

## POSITION WARFARE

Torgau was Frederick's last major battle. Henceforth, dwindling resources and the overpowering numbers against him forced him increasingly to resort to position warfare, where maneuver, fortifications and ground might compensate for other weaknesses. In Napoleon's judgment, "These last campaigns of Frederick no longer bear the same character. He becomes fearful, and does not venture to fight battles. Turenne was the only general whose boldness increased with his years and experience. It must, nevertheless, be remembered that the great advantage which the King had at the beginning of this war, the possession of an army of 120,000 men perfectly trained and inured to war . . . was daily diminishing, while on the other hand, that of the enemy was forming and acquiring experience. Even the French army, although so wretchedly commanded, was very different in 1761 from what it had been in the campaign of 1757."[54]

## THE POSITION AT BUNZELWITZ. 1761 [Plate 25]

The following is Frederick's description of his famous intrenched camp at Bunzelwitz, which for the time being saved Schweidnitz from being besieged by the combined armies of Russia and Austria in the late summer and early fall of 1761.

Nothing . . . could impede the junction of the Russians and Austrians. It was foreseen that these two armies would shortly assemble in the vicinity of Schweidnitz, in which case the King would have to provide for the security both of his camp and of the fortress of Schweidnitz. He could take a position at Pilzen, where nature seemed to bear all of the expense of fortifying a camp, but if the army would find safety there, one risked, on the other hand, that Loudon and Buturlin[55] would besiege Schweidnitz within sight of the King and the entire army, who would be powerless to prevent it. For this reason the position at Bunzelwitz was preferred because it covered the fortress and rendered a siege impracticable.

Still the fear remained that the army of the two empresses would send a detachment to Breslau which, compelling the King to leave the vicinity of Schweidnitz, would give his enemies the freedom to besiege the city and the means to do so. But it was impossible to counter all the enterprises that enemies so superior in number might attempt, and it was necessary to leave something to chance.

To secure the position of the Prussian army . . . the King

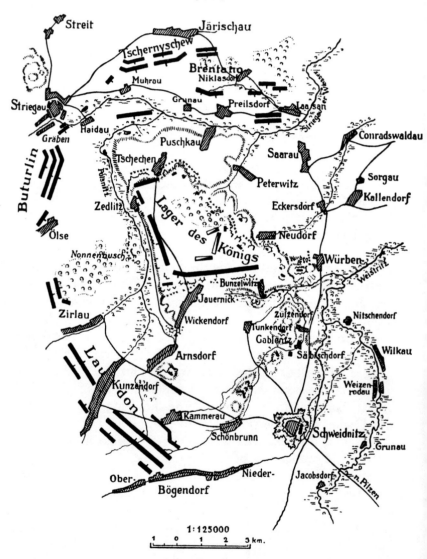

PLATE 25. The intrenched camp at Bunzelwitz. The wartime application of the principles of castrametation expounded in chapter VIII can be seen here. (*Die Werke Friedrichs des Grossen*, vol. IV.)

intrenched his camp on all sides, making it into a kind of fortress with the Würben mountain serving as the citadel. From this height as far as the village of Bunzelwitz the camp was covered by a marsh. The heads of the villages of Bunzelwitz and Jauernick were fortified and large batteries were erected there, placing under a crossfire the approach by which Loudon would have been able to attack the King, so that the Austrians first would have been forced to carry these two villages before they could come to grips with the main army. Between these two villages and slightly to the rear, the front of the infantry was covered by large redoubts that were provided with numerous artillery. Passages had been left between them to give scope to the cavalry, if this were found necessary.

Beyond Jauernick and behind the Nonnenbusch, four hills were intrenched. These dominated all the ground, and in front of them ran a muddy and impracticable ditch where the enemy could have been prevented from establishing bridges by the fire of small arms. Further to the right a large abatis intersected the Nonnenbusch, defended by chasseurs and free battalions. The muddy ditch mentioned above curved behind the woods and at the foot of the hills on which the army extended. At the extremity of the right, the flank commenced which, forming a parallel line to the stream of Striegau, ended at a woods covered by the defile that comes from Peterwitz. In these woods, located at the rear of the army, a masked battery had been established, which communicated behind an abatis with another battery placed at the extremity of the same woods, on the side of Neudorf. From this point an intrenchment resumed, joining, in the rear of the army, the works that had been constructed on the hill of Würben.

The intrenchments everywhere were 16 feet thick and the ditches 12 feet deep and 16 feet wide. The front was surrounded by strong palisades and the salient parts of the works were mined. In front of these, pitfalls were dug and beyond them the entire exterior was covered by one contiguous line of *chevaux de frise* embedded in the earth. The King's army, comprising 66 battalions, 143 squadrons and 460 pieces of artillery were dispersed among the different works; 182 loaded mines were ready to be sprung at the first signal.

¶ All the necessary dispositions were made for a vigorous defense. Little was to be feared during the day because of the infinite strength of the camp, but there was much to be apprehensive about at night because of the proximity of the armies. There was, besides, little likelihood that anything would endanger the Prussians unless, under cover of darkness, Loudon would surprise a part of the camp when the sleeping troops did not have time to rush to its defense. To prevent such a catastrophe the tents were struck every evening and the army, filling the intrenchments, spent the night in bivouac.

On the other side, Loudon stood so near to Schweidnitz by the posts of Kammerau, Schönbrunn, and Bögendorf, which he occupied, that the King was forced to make an intermediate detachment between Schweidnitz and the army in order to assist the former in case of need, and to . . . cover the convoys of the army, which drew all its bread, forage, and subsistence from that fortress. To this end, Gablenz moved with a detachment of several battalions beyond Tunkendorf, where his right flank was protected by the batteries of the camp and his left, by the artillery of Schweidnitz, and where he secured his position still further by good entrenchments with which he covered his front.

The same day the general officers received the disposition for the defense of the camp and the responsibilities for each in the sector he commanded. However extensive the Prussian-occupied terrain might be, means were found to reduce it to three points of attack. The first was between the villages of Bunzelwitz and Jauernick, which the King proposed to defend in person against Loudon, who had constructed his approach or intrenchment on that side. It was impossible for the Austrians to leave these fortified villages in their rear and to pierce the center, because they would have had to endure a heavy artillery fire on both flanks. It was therefore to be presumed that they would try before anything else to carry one of these two posts. The King decided to let them exert themselves there and to throw his cavalry against them only after they had sustained a considerable loss. Moreover, it was possible to strengthen the troops in these villages with fresh bodies of infantry for as long as it was judged appropriate. In addition, sixty cannon from lateral works defended the approach.

The second point of attack was between the village of Tschechen and the woods on our right flank. Here Ziethen commanded. The Russians who encamped opposite him were probably charged with this enterprise. To reach the Prussians they were forced to cross the stream of Streigau under the fire of musketry and cannon from our intrenchments. They would have lost their best infantry in making the attempt, and there were many other obstacles that still remained before they could approach the intrenchments; so that some opportune cavalry charges by General Ziethen would have sufficed to disperse the Russians.

The third point of attack was on the side of Peterwitz and the defile that covered this part of the Prussian camp. Ramin defended this sector, and the attack, by all appearances, would have evolved upon Czernichew and Brentano because their detachments were the nearest. It was decided to allow the enemy to advance peaceably as far as the Peterwitz defile, where he would have been taken in flank by a masked battery in the woods firing salvos of case shot. After this, Platon had orders to fall upon the enemy rear with forty squadrons debouching from a road through the woods especially constructed for this purpose.

The great strength of this camp consisted in the way in which it deprived the enemy of all three arms while saving them for the Prussians. The assailants could not employ artillery because all the terrain in front of the intrenchments was infinitely lower than that on which the Prussian works stood, and their guns would have fired without any effect. Nor could they make any better use of their cavalry, because as soon as it came within sight it would have been destroyed by the fire of the Prussian batteries. And how could the infantry have used small arms? Were they to fire musket shots against cannon? Could they tear up the *chevaux de frise* and batter down the palisades with their shots? Since all that was impossible, one could be assured of having profited in this position from every advantage that terrain added to fortification could give to one army over another. It was with these dispositions that the Prussians calmly awaited the enterprises of their enemies.[56]

## EPILOGUE

But Frederick was too much of a realist to credit his ultimate salvation at the end of the Seven Years' War to his own genius or to the demonstrated superiority of his troops. He was enough of a philosopher and historian to recognize the underlying reasons for the failure of the allies to defeat Prussia. These were as follows:

The lack of harmony among the powers of the grand alliance, and their opposite interests, which would not permit them to agree on certain operations.

The lack of unity between the Russian and Austrian generals, which made them circumspect when occasion required that they should act with vigor to overwhelm Prussia (which, in reality, they might have done).

The subtle, over-refined politics of the Viennese court, the principles of which led her to charge her allies with the most hazardous and difficult enterprises that she might, at the conclusion of the war, preserve her army in a better and more complete state than those of the other powers. Hence, it resulted at various times that the Austrian generals, by too much circumspection, neglected to give the death blow to the Prussians when their affairs were the most desperate.

The death of the Russian Empress with whom, in the same tomb, was buried the Austrian alliance.

¶ The summary of the events we have related . . . presents . . .

Prussia on the brink of ruin . . . past recovery, in the judgment of all politicians. Yet only one woman dies and the nation revives; nay, is sustained by that power which had been the most eager to seek her destruction. . . . What dependence may be placed on human affairs if the merest trifles can influence, can change the fate of empires? Such are the spoils of Fortune who, laughing at the vain prudence of mortals, excites the hopes of some, and pulls down the high-raised expectations of others.[57]

## NOTES: CHAPTER VII

1. Henri de Catt, *Frederick the Great: the Memoirs of his Reader Henri de Catt (1758-1760)*, Translated by F. S. Flint, with an Introduction by Lord Rosebery (Boston, 1917), I, 265; II, 84-85.

2. Grossen Generalstabe, Kriegsgeschichtliche Abtheilung, *Der Siebenjährige Krieg. 1756-1763*. III. *Kolin* (Berlin, 1901), pp. 65, 67 [*Kolin*].

3. Frederick's comments on the desirability of holding a council of war may be of interest here, although there is no indication that he solicited the advice of his generals in their meeting at the Golden Sun Inn. "Prince Eugene had the habit of saying that a general having no desire to do anything had only to hold a council of war—an assertion that gains credence from the fact that voices ordinarily are in the negative. Even secrecy, so necessary in war, is not observed. A general to whom the sovereign has entrusted his troops must act by himself, and the confidence that the king has placed in this general's capacity authorizes him to do everything according to his own insight. I am persuaded, however, that a general ought to take advantage of advice given to him even by a subaltern officer, since it is the duty of a good citizen to forget himself and look only at the positive aspect of the thing, without being concerned whether the course that he follows originates in his own mind or with somebody else, as long as he succeeds in his objectives." Frederick, *Instruction militaire du Roi de Prusse pour ses généraux* (Frankfort 1761), pp. 181-82.

4. Major General Johann Dietrich von Hülsen.

5. Frederick's memory is at fault here. According to the German General Staff history, which was compiled with elaborate detail, if not with inspiration, Hülsen commanded seven infantry battalions, five cavalry squadrons, and six pieces öf artillery, which were used to dislodge the Croats from the graveyard in front of Krzeczhofz. The first line consisted of fourteen battalions and thirty-one squadrons; the second comprised eight battalions and fifteen squadrons. The third column that

marched on the left as the Prussians approached the battlefield contained fifteen squadrons. Ziethen's advance guard consisted of fifty squadrons. Missing in Frederick's calculations are three flanking grenadier battalions from the first line, which were sent forward to reinforce Hülsen's attack. *Kolin*, pp. 72-73.

6. This claim is debatable Napoleon accused Frederick of being rash in making a flank march before an enemy strongly posted. "Some Prussian writers," he wrote, "have asserted that this maneuver would not have failed but for the impatience of a lieutenant-colonel who, annoyed by the fire of the Austrian fusiliers, gave the word to face to the right and form in line and thus engaged the whole column, but this is incorrect. The movement made by the Prussian army was prescribed by the first of interests, self preservation, and the instinct which teaches every man not to suffer himself to be killed without making any defence." Napoleon, *Memoirs of the History of France during the Reign of Napoleon, dictated by the Emperor at St. Helena to the generals who shared his Captivity and published from the original manuscripts corrected by himself. Historical Miscellanies* (London, 1823), III, 183. The Swiss theorist Jomini makes a similar criticism, and Count von Schlieffen, the architect of the German strategic plan in the years preceding the first World War, notes that Frederick failed to alter his initial orders to conform to a situation that basically had changed—a charge that could be laid at the feet of his own successors, as well. See *Generalfeldmarschall Graf Alfred v. Schlieffen Gesammelte Schriften* (Berlin, 1913), II, 77.

7. The General Staff history places Hülsen's attack at 2 o'clock, which would also correspond to the time of Ziethen's attack against Nadasti. Evidently Hülsen captured only seven guns in this affair—the others were taken by von Treschkow's nine battalions that had joined Hülsen when the assault was renewed. *Kolin*, pp. 73, 74.

8. Prince Maurice of Anhalt-Dessau (1712-60), promoted to the grade of Field Marshal on the battlefield of Leuthen.

9. Although Frederick understandably does not mention the incident, it was evidently at this stage of the battle that, probably seeking a hero's death, he collected forty soldiers and attempted to storm an Austrian battery. He was arrested by the cry of one of his officers: "Sire, do you want to take the battery alone?" *Kolin*, p. 85.

10. According to the statistics compiled by the German General Staff, Frederick lost 392 officers and 13,376 men at Kolin, of whom 9,702 are listed as killed or missing. The infantry suffered most, with 12,307 casualties; the cavalry lost 1,450 men and 1,907 horses. Statistics for the artillery are not given separately, but since this arm lost only 1 officer killed and 3 wounded in a battle that claimed 2 lieutenant generals and 5 major generals among the casualties, its losses may be presumed to have been

slight. Austrian casualties numbered 360 officers and 7,754 men. They captured 22 Prussian colors and 45 cannon. *Ibid.*, pp. 87-88; plan 6.

11. This is probably a reference to the counterattack of Lieutenant Colonel Ludwig Ernst von Benckendorff's Saxon Chevau-léger Regiment, which, together with two other regiments from the same command, succeeded in enveloping the Prussian cavalry on both flanks and driving it back. *Ibid.*, p. 82.

12. Frederick, *The History of the Seven Years War*, trans. Thomas Holcroft (London, 1789), I, 138-46. Holcroft's translation provides the basis for the selections in this chapter: minor changes have been made in spelling, punctuation, and choice of words to bring it into closer touch with modern practice. Portions have been freshly translated to keep touch with Frederick's intent.

13. Frederick to the Prince of Prussia, July 30, 1757, as quoted in Thomas Carlyle, *History of Friedrich II. of Prussia, called Frederick the Great* (London, 1886), V, 42.

14. The allies had 64,000 troops in the immediate vicinity, although of this number only 42,000 actually were in camp, three-fourths of whom were French. Max Hein, *Der Siebenjährige Krieg* (Berlin, n.d.), p. 35.

15. This is misleading. Frederick actually withdrew only a short distance and established a new camp between Bedra and Rossbach.

16. Comte Claude Louis de Saint-Germain (1707-1778), one of the few French officers to display any military ability during the Seven Years' War, left the army in disgust in 1760 after he had been denied an independent command. In 1775 Louis XVI appointed him Minister of War, in which capacity he carried out many of the reforms that later benefited the Revolutionary armies and the army of Napoleon.

17. I have had to take liberties with the translation here because the account as originally published is misleading. The allied army, composed of sixty-two battalions, eighty-two squadrons and forty-five heavy guns (114 cannon in all), left its camp at 11:30 A.M. and marched toward Frederick's left in three columns. The left column, or first line, consisted of sixteen German squadrons, sixteen French battalions, and twelve French squadrons: this was the only column that marched on the road. The others followed parallel routes across the fields, the second line, or column, comprising seventeen German squadrons and sixteen French battalions, and the third column, the French reserve corps and fourteen battalions of German infantry, followed by the German artillery reserve. The march consumed much time because the wide columns could not negotiate the hilly terrain in formàtion, and because the distance between the columns was small. Grossen Generalstabe, *Der Siebenjährige Krieg. 1756-1763. V. Hastenbeck und Rossbach* (Berlin, 1903), pp. 208-209, appendix 76 and 77 [*Rossbach*].

18. Prince Ferdinand of Brunswick, commanding the right flank.

19. Frederick is unfair to the French on this, as on so many occasions throughout his account of the battle. The two Austrian cuirassier regiments were the only allied cavalry to have time to deploy before the Prussians attacked. The rest of the Imperial cavalry could not maneuver: hit simultaneously on both flanks, it fell back in confusion upon the French cavalry. Broglie, with fourteen squadrons, then sought to outflank the Prussian left, supported by Mailly with ten squadrons. The Prussians reformed quickly to meet this new threat. The French mistook a regiment bearing down on their right for Imperial cavalry when in fact it was a regiment of Frederick's hussars, and, attacked in front and flank simultaneously, the French were thrown back, leaving their artillery in the hands of the Prussians. Seydlitz had thirty-eight squadrons in this cavalry combat; the allies had fifty-seven. *Ibid.,* pp. 215-16, 234.

20. Not indicated on this map. Reichartswerben seems to have been a continuation of Posendorf (Busendorf).

21. There were two Keith brothers in Frederick's service. The one mentioned here is James Francis Edward Keith (1698-1758), a Jacobite soldier who served first in the Spanish army and later with the Russians, where he was a general in the wars with Turkey in 1737 and Sweden in 1741-43. He entered Frederick's service in 1747 with the rank of Field Marshal and served with distinction until his death at the battle of Hochkirch in 1758. His brother George likewise became one of Frederick's favorites, serving as ambassador in Paris (1751) and Madrid (1758), and as Governor of Neuchâtel (1752).

22. Frederick himself rode with the Old Brunswick Regiment during the battle. *Rossbach,* p. 217.

23. This undoubtedly refers to the activities of the allied rear guard under Saint-Germain. As the Prussians pursued the allied infantry toward Pettstädt, Saint-Germain sent two cavalry regiments from his position north of Gröst to the high ground north of Obschütz, where they threatened the rear of Frederick's infantry.

24. According to the German General Staff statistics, the Prussian army lost 7 officers and 162 men killed, 23 officers and 356 men wounded, making a grand total of 548 officers and men. The Imperialists lost 2 officers and 38 men killed, 10 officers and 221 men wounded, 30 officers and 3,200 men missing and captured, making a total of 3,552. The French lost a total of 600 officers and 6,000 men. The Prussians captured many colors, 21 standards, and 72 cannon. *Ibid.,* p. 222.

25. Louis-Charles-César, Duc d'Estrées, Marshal of France.

26. Frederick, *The History of the Seven Years War,* I, 178-88.

27. Quoted in Reinhold Koser, *König Friedrich der Grosse* (Stuttgart und Berlin, 1903), II, 134-35.

28. Quoted in Francis Kugler, *Life of Frederick the Great, comprehending a complete History of the Silesian campaigns and the Seven Years' War* (New York, n.d.), pp. 254-56. Minor alterations of style have been made in this version of Frederick's speech to conform to modern usage. Although the exact wording undoubtedly has become blurred, since the speech was written down from memory, the following probably communicates the gist of what Frederick said on the eve of Leuthen. See Grossen Generalstabe, *Der Siebenjährige Krieg. 1756-1763.* VI. *Leuthen* (Berlin, 1904), pp. 138-39 [*Leuthen*].

29. *Ibid.*, pp. 9, 17.

30. The Austrian hussars fled at the approach of the Prussian advance guard, leaving their infantry in the lurch. Enough bread was found at Neumarkt for 80,000 rations. *Ibid.*, p. 16.

31. According to the General Staff history, Frederick used six battalions to cover his right while thirty squadrons of the first line assaulted the Austrians. Eleven officers and six hundred men were taken prisoner, and this quick victory was sweetened by the fact that the Austrian cavalry on this occasion included the same Saxons whose counterattack had broken Hülsen's battalions at Kolin. *Ibid.*, pp. 21-22.

32. Major General Karl Heinrich von Wedell.

33. A somewhat comparable arrangement is illustrated on Plate 12.

34. In the interest of historical accuracy, although Frederick's description of his dispositions at Leuthen is adequate for a general understanding of the battle, it should be pointed out that Wedell originally commanded twelve battalions in the advance guard. Six of these contained the Austrian left during the cavalry action at Borne; three battalions had been left behind to occupy that village when the army swung to the right flank march. This gave Wedell only nine battalions, six of which guarded the right flank of the cavalry wing, with the remaining three forming the head of the first infantry attack. *Ibid.*, pp. 21, 23, 25.

35. Lieutenant General Georg Wilhelm von Driesen.

36. Lieutenant Colonel von Wunsch, who had organized his own free battalion shortly before the battle.

37. According to the superb battle map in the General Staff history of Leuthen, the final Austrian line was formed not near the Sagschütz hill, but on rising ground a short distance north of Leuthen, where there were two windmills. This would more nearly correspond to the action that took place during this phase of the battle.

38. Frederick, *The History of the Seven Years War*, I, 197-206. Prussian casualties were 1,175 officers and men killed and 5,207 wounded, making a total of 6,382. The Austrians lost about 3,000 killed, 6,000 to 7,000 wounded, and over 12,000 prisoners, along with 46 colors and 131

guns. An additional 10,000 Austrians were captured during the pursuit. *Leuthen*, p. 41.

39. Napoleon, *Memoirs*, III, 202-203.

40. Grossen Generalstabe, *Leuthen*, p. 29.

41. Major General J. F. C. Fuller, *The Decisive Battles of the Western World and their Influence upon History* (London, 1955), II, 214.

42. Napoleon, *Memoirs*, III, 282-83.

43. Frederick's "half" of the army was composed of 42 battalions and 48 squadrons, or 21,000 infantry and 6,000 cavalry.

44. Probably Buchendorf.

45. Ziethen actually had under his command only 21 battalions and 54 squadrons—about 18,000 infantry and 7,000 cavalry, along with 48 heavy guns and the battalion artillery. Theodor von Bernhardi, *Friedrich der Grosse als Feldherr* (Berlin, 1881), II, 180-81.

46. From the maps it would appear that Frederick meant Weidenhain, which is about three miles north northeast of Wildenhain. If the grenadiers were encountered at the latter village, as stated in the original text, then it is impossible that St. Ignon's troops a considerable distance away would have been sandwiched between Frederick's columns "at the same time."

47. Düben is located about twenty miles east of Torgau as the crow flies.

48. In point of fact it would appear that Frederick's first attack involved ten battalions; his second contained thirteen battalions, later reinforced by three additional battalions; and eleven battalions formed the third line of assault. See Bernhardi, *Friedrich als Feldherr*, II, 190-92.

49. Lieutenant General Johann Albrecht von Bülow, not to be confused with the von Bülow of note 50.

50. Major General Christoph Karl von Bülow, Commander in chief of the Bayreuth Dragoons.

51. Johann Sigismund von Lestwitz, Major in the Old Brunswick infantry regiment.

52. According to Koser, Frederick actually lost a full third of his army at Torgau—almost 17,000 men, of whom 920 belonged to the cavalry and 15,900 to the infantry. So high a price did he pay for this victory, in fact, that he ordered his adjutants to keep the actual casualty figures secret. The Austrians lost roughly 16,000. Koser, *König Friedrich der Grosse*, II, 276.

53. Frederick, *The History of the Seven Years War*, II, 143-52.

54. Napoleon, *Memoirs*, III, 299.

55. Freiherr Gideon Ernst Loudon, the Austrian general, and Field Marshal Buturlin of the Russian Army.

56. Frederick, *The History of the Seven Years War*, II, 196-204.

57. *Ibid.*, pp. 268-69, 367-68.

# VIII

# *The New War of Positions*

In dramatizing the growth in the size and destructive power of armies since the days of Louis XIV, Frederick once invented a spirited dialogue between Prince Joseph Wenzel von Liechtenstein, the commander of the Austrian artillery since 1744, and the two generals most responsible for curbing French power during the war of the Spanish Succession, the Duke of Marlborough and Prince Eugene. "Then, with respect to the army," Prince Liechtenstein is quoted as saying, "we maintain 160,000 men, a number which never could be paid during your lifetime. For my part, I have labored for the perfection of the artillery and have spent 300,000 crowns of my own to make it respectable. The result is that an army no longer moves without a train of 400 pieces. You did not understand the use of cannon, with which our camps are converted into fortresses. You scarcely had thirty field pieces in your army."[1]

Frederick understood only too well the effect upon tactics of Liechtenstein's system of standardized guns, which improved both the accuracy and the mobility of the Austrian artillery, and the greater number of field guns. This and other developments in Austrian tactics during the first campaigns of the Seven Years' War provoked the following "Réflexions sur la tactique et . . . sur quelques changements dans la façon de faire la guerre," which Frederick wrote in the winter of 1758 and sent to Prince Ferdinand of Brunswick, the eminently successful commander of the Army of Operations in the west since the battle of Rossbach. The complete text of Frederick's "Reflections on Some Changes in the Method of Waging War" is given below.

## THE NEW AUSTRIAN TACTICS

*WAR HAS BECOME* refined since the days of Marlborough and Eugene. New and murderous practices have rendered it more difficult. It is appropriate to describe these changes in detail so that, having carefully examined the system of our enemies and the difficulties that they present to us, we might choose the proper means of surmounting them.

I am not talking to you about the plans of our enemies, based upon the number and might of their allies. United, their multitude and power are more than enough to crush not only Prussia but the forces of one of the greatest kings of Europe, who might wish to resist this torrent. Nor need I remind you of the maxim that they have adopted generally, namely to draw our forces from one side by a diversion in order to strike a major blow where they are sure to find no resistance, to maintain the defensive against a corps strong enough to cope with them, and to act vigorously against those whose weakness forces them to give way.

Neither do I remind you of the method I have used to sustain myself against this giant that threatens to squash me. Any method that has proved successful only because of the mistakes of my enemies, whose sluggishness has assisted my activity and whose indolence has kept them from taking advantage of the situation, should not be proposed as a model. The imperial law of necessity has forced me to leave much to chance. The behavior of a pilot more dependent upon the caprices of the wind than the direction of his compass ought never to serve as a guide.

The point here is to give a sound idea of the system that the Austrians are following in this war. I focus my attention on the Austrians, because of all our enemies it is they who have introduced the greatest art and perfection into this profession. I say nothing about the French, because although they are shrewd and skillful their inconsistency and indiscretion upsets whatever advantages their skill could bring them from one day to the next.

As for the Russians, as savage as they are inept, they are not worthy of mention.

The principal changes that I notice in the conduct of the Austrian generals during this war are manifested in their encampments and marches, and in this prodigious artillery which, acting alone without the support of troops, would be nearly enough to repulse, destroy, and overwhelm any attack. Do not think that I ignore the strong camps that skillful generals have selected and occupied in the past. . . . Prince Eugene chose one, not far from Mantua, which enabled him to check the progress of the French during the entire campaign [of 1702]; the Prince of Baden made the camp of Heilbronn famous [1694]; and in Flanders one can point to that of Sierck and others too numerous to mention.

What has particularly distinguished the Austrians of today is their constant choice of advantageous terrain for the site of their position and their ability to make better use than has been made before of natural obstacles in arranging the disposition of their troops. One questions when, if ever, generals have had the skill to form such powerful dispositions as those we have seen in the Austrian army. When has anyone seen four hundred guns arrayed on the heights in the form of an amphitheater and distributed in different batteries in such a way that, having the power of long range, they do not lose the principal and more murderous advantage of a sweeping fire.

But if an Austrian camp presents a formidable front, this is by no means the extent of its defenses. Its depth and multiple lines contain real snares, that is to say new tricks—places suitable for surprising troops disorganized by the charges they have had to make to reach their goals. These lines are prepared in advance and occupied by units designated for this use. It must be acknowledged that the great numerical superiority of their armies permits the commanding generals to place themselves in several lines without fear of being outflanked and that, having a superabundance of men, they can occupy all of the terrain that they judge proper to render their position more formidable.

If we descend, then, into greater detail, you will find that the principles upon which the Austrian generals make war are the result of long meditation, much tactical skill, extreme circumspection in the selection of camps, extensive knowledge of terrain, supported dispositions, and the wisdom to undertake only those measures that have as great a certainty of success as war permits. The first maxim of all generals is never to let yourself be forced to fight against your will, and the Austrian system is a continuation of this principle by which one seeks strong camps, heights, and mountains. The Austrians have nothing that is peculiar to them in the choice of positions, except that they are almost never found in a bad site and they always take special care to place themselves on unassailable terrain. Their flanks always rest on ravines, cliffs, swamps, rivers, or towns.

But where they differ most from their predecessors is in their dispositions. . . . They take extreme care to place each arm in the appropriate position. They combine ruse and skill, often presenting bodies of cavalry to lure the opposing general into making faulty dispositions. I myself have noticed, however, on more than one occasion, that when they array their cavalry in one continuous line they have no intention of fighting: if their cavalry is formed checker-wise, they really intend to use it. Observe further, if you please, that if you swallow the bait and charge the Austrian cavalry at the beginning of a battle, your cavalry—which assuredly will defeat theirs—will, if it makes the slightest pursuit, fall into an infantry ambush where it will be destroyed. From this it follows that when attacking this enemy in a post, you must hold back the cavalry at the outset so as not to let it be seduced by false appearances. Do not expose the mounted arm to the fire of either small arms or artillery, which robs it of its best ardor. Reserve the cavalry for the time when it can perform the greatest service—to save the battle or to pursue the enemy.

Throughout this war we have seen the Austrian army arrayed in three lines, surrounded and supported by this immense artillery. Its first line is formed at the base of hills, on terrain that is nearly level but with enough of a slope left to form a natural glacis on the side where the enemy can come. This is a wise method: it is the fruit of experience that shows sweeping fire to be more formidable than a plunging fire. Moreover, the soldier on the crest of the glacis has every advantage that a hill can offer without any of its disadvantages. The attacker, who is exposed and advances uphill, cannot damage him by his fire, whereas those posted on the ground above have the advantage of a sweeping and prepared fire. If he knows how to use his arms he will destroy the enemy who attacks before the latter can reach him. If he repels the attack he can pursue the enemy assisted by the terrain, which lends itself to his diverse movements. On the other hand, if the first line is posted on an eminence or too steep a hill, it dares not descend for fear of becoming disorganized, while the attacker, with a quick march, soon finds himself below the fire of the defenders and sheltered even from the cannon by dead ground.

The Austrians have carefully examined the advantages and the disadvantages of these different positions so that in their camps they save the heights, which rise in the form of an amphitheater, for their second line, which they strengthen and fortify with artillery as they do the first. This second line, which contains some cavalry units, is intended to support the first. If the attacker gives way, the cavalry is at hand to charge him. If the first line of the Austrians should yield, the advancing enemy finds, after a stiff fight with infantry, a formidable position that he must attack anew. He is broken by the preceding charges and forced to march against fresh troops, in good order and assisted by the strength of the terrain.

The third line, which serves at the same time as a reserve, is intended to reinforce the place in their position where the assailant proposes to make a breach. The flanks of the Austrians are furnished with artillery just like a citadel. They take advantage of every small salient in the terrain by placing there artillery that fires obliquely, in order to have as much cross fire as possible. The result is that to make an assault against a fortress, the defenses of which are unimpaired, or to attack an army thus prepared on its ground amount to one and the same thing.

Not content with all these precautions, the Austrians seek further to cover their front by swamps, deep and impassable sunken roads, streams—in a word, with defiles. Not trusting the supports that they have given to their flanks, they station large detachments in inaccessible camps 2,000 paces from each flank, or thereabouts. These detachments are intended to observe the enemy so that if he should be foolish enough to attack the main army, they are at hand to fall upon his rear. It is easy to visualize the effect that this diversion would have upon the troops engaged in attacking the Austrians, finding themselves suddenly taken in flank and rear. The beginning of the battle would at the same time be the end, and there would be nothing but confusion, disorder, and a rout.

How then, you ask, can one venture a battle with soldiers so well prepared? Can it be that these troops, so often defeated in the past, have become invincible? Certainly not! That I will never admit. But I would not advise anybody to make a hasty decision and to do anything to insult an army that has procured such great advantages.

Yet it is impossible in the long run for all terrain to be found equally advantageous, and for those who have the task of posting troops to commit no mistakes during the course of a campaign. I strongly urge you to take advantage of such occasions without worrying about the discrepancy in numbers, provided you have slightly more than half as many men as the enemy.

What kind of mistakes can be exploited? If the enemy leaves some hills in front of or beside his camp, if he places his cavalry in the first line, if his flank is found to be insufficiently supported, if he detaches one of those corps protecting the flank far from his main army, if the heights that he occupies are not very eminent, and especially if no defile prevents you from attacking him—I believe that a skillful general can profit from such mistakes.

The first thing you should do is secure the knolls or hills that would enable your artillery to dominate that of the enemy, to place as many guns there as space permits, and from there to blast the army that you intend to attack while forming your lines and column of attack. I have seen on several occasions how little courage the Austrian troops show under artillery fire: neither their infantry nor their cavalry can endure it. To make them experience all of the terrible effects of artillery you must have either several heights or completely level ground, for cannon and small arms have no effect, as I already have stated, firing uphill. To attack the enemy without first having procured the advantage of superior or at least of equal fire is the same as trying to fight against armed troops with men carrying only sticks, and that is impossible.

I return to the subject of the attack. Everything depends upon your judicious choice of the place where the enemy is weakest and where you anticipate less resistance than expected in those places where the enemy has taken better precautions. I believe that wisdom requires that you should take a fixed point of the enemy army, namely the right, the left, the flank, and so on, and that you should intend to make your most powerful effort at that point. Since it is probable that your first troops will be repulsed, you should form several lines to sustain each other. I advise against general attacks because they are too hazardous and also, in engaging only a wing or a section of the army, you save the main force to cover your retreat in case of misfortune and you can never be totally defeated. Consider, also, that in attacking only a portion of the enemy army you can never lose as many men as in an assault all along the line, and that if you succeed, you can destroy your enemy just as effectively, provided he does not find a defile too near the battlefield where some corps from his army can cover his retreat. [See Plate 26.]

It seems to me, moreover, that you can use that part of the troops that you refuse . . . by parading them and showing them constantly to the enemy opposite, on ground that he will not dare to leave in order to reinforce his troops opposite your main attack. In so doing you render useless a part of the enemy's army during the battle. If you have enough troops, it could happen, perhaps, that the enemy will weaken himself on one side to rush to the defense of the other, in which case you can profit further if you notice his movements in time.

Besides, you must unquestionably imitate what you find of value in the enemy's method. By appropriating the advantageous arms of the nations against which they had fought, the Romans

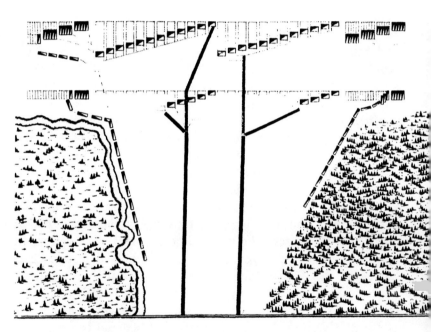

PLATE 26. The dangers of a defile. The army must form into columns before it can pass through the gap in the woods. At best, the subsequent deployment into line of battle involved delay; often, in the presence of an energetic enemy, it spelled defeat. Better than most Americans today, Frederick could have appreciated the dangers encountered by his contemporary, General Braddock, on his march to Fort Duquesne. (*Atlas* to the *Oeuvres de Frédéric le Grand*, Plan 10.)

made their troops invincible. Certainly the Austrian method of encampment should be adopted; in any event, be content with a narrower front in order to gain depth, and take good care to locate the flanks well and to secure them. And however cumbersome it may be, we must conform to the system of numerous artillery. I have had ours augmented considerably so that the artillery might compensate for the shortcomings of our infantry, the material for which can only deteriorate as the war drags on. . . .

So many difficulties in assailing the enemy in his posts have spawned the idea of attacking him on the march, of taking advantage of his decampments, and of engaging in rear-guard actions. . . . But the Austrians too have arrived at this conclusion by waging war only in rugged or forested country, by preparing roads through the forests or the marshy terrain in advance, and by following the valley routes behind the mountains, having taken care beforehand to provide these mountains or defiles with detachments. A number of light troops posted in the woods or on mountain summits covers their march, masks their movements, and provides complete security until the Austrians have reached another strong camp where you cannot attack them without taking leave of your senses. . . .

The detachments of the Austrian army are strong and numerous, with the weakest consisting of no fewer than 3,000 men. I have sometimes counted five or six of them in the field at the same time. They have so many Hungarian troops that, taken together, these would comprise a large *corps d'armée*, which means, in effect, that you have two armies to fight—the heavy and the light. The officers to whom they entrust these detachments are skillful, especially in their knowledge of terrain. Often they encamp near our armies, however, with the expedient caution of placing themselves on mountain peaks, in thick forests, or behind double or triple defiles. From this kind of den they send forth parties who act as the occasion demands. The detachment does not show itself unless there is the possibility of striking some important blow. The strength of these detachments permits them to approach near to our armies and even to encircle them, and it is very vexing to lack an equal number of this kind of troops. Our free battalions, formed of deserters, badly organized, and weak, dare not show themselves often before them. Our generals dare not send the free battalions forward for fear they will lose them, which enables the enemy to approach our camps and to disturb and alarm us day and night. In time our officers grow accustomed to these skirmishes and even come to scorn them, and unfortunately they acquire the feeling of security that became fatal to us at Hochkirch, where many mistook the Austrian attack against our right with their entire army for just another skirmish of light troops.

I do believe, however, not to conceal anything from you, that Daun could make better use of his Hungarian troops than he does. They do not cause us as much damage as they could. Why didn't these detached generals attempt anything against our foragers? Why didn't they try to surprise the wretched towns where we had our provision depots? Why haven't they on all occasions attempted to intercept our convoys? Why, instead of alarming our camps at night by weak detachments, haven't they tried to attack the camps in force and to take our second line in the rear, which would have led them to far more important and decisive results for the success of the war. No doubt they lacked, as we did, enterprising officers, men rare and sought after in all countries. Among the number of officers, many of whom are dedicated to the profession of arms without any calling or talent, these are the only ones who deserve the grade of general.

Here in a nutshell is the idea of the principles upon which the Austrians wage the present war. They have perfected them considerably, but even this need not prevent us from gaining the upper hand. The art which the Austrians employ so skillfully to defend themselves furnishes us with the means of attacking them.

I have ventured some ideas on the manner of engaging in combat with the Austrians. I ought to add here two things that I have omitted. First, take great care to give good protection to the flanks of the corps that you lead to attack the enemy, for fear that it should happen to be taken in flank itself while advancing, instead of striking the flanks of those whom it assaults. Second, impress upon the minds of the battalion commanders that when they lead their battalions into combat they should take special attention not to let them break ranks, especially when, in the fervor of success, they drive the enemy before them. For infantry has strength only when it is closed and in good order. When separated and nearly scattered, a weak body of cavalry that falls on it at this moment of disorder is enough to destroy it. Whatever precautions a general may take, there always remain plenty of risks in the attack of posts and in all battles.

The best infantry in the universe can be repulsed and put in disorder in places where it has to fight terrain, the enemy, and artillery. Our infantry, weakened and debased by its losses and even by its successes, must be led in difficult enterprises with caution. You must be guided by its intrinsic value, adjust your efforts to its abilities, and never expose it thoughtlessly to ordeals of courage that demand a patience and steady firmness in conspicuous perils.

The fate of states depends upon decisive actions: one emplacement well taken, a hill well defended, can maintain or overthrow a kingdom. A single false movement can lose everything. A general who misunderstands an order or who bungles it places your undertaking in the greatest jeopardy. Above all, those commanding the infantry wings must be carefully instructed to weigh maturely the best course of action, and as often as it is commendable to engage in battle if one finds advantages to capitalize upon, just as often battle must be avoided if the risk involved outweighs the possible benefit. There is more than one road to follow to the same goal. One must apply himself, it appears, to destroy the enemy in detail. What difference does it make which means are used, as long as one wins superiority?

The enemy makes numerous detachments. The generals

who command these are not equally prudent, nor are they discreet every day. You must seek to destroy these detachments one after the other. You must not treat these expeditions as trifles, but must march against these detachments in force, make a strenuous effort, and wage these small combats as seriously as you would fight decisive battles. The advantage that you will derive from them, if you succeed twice in crushing these separate corps, will be to reduce the enemy to the defensive. Caution will prompt him to hold his troops together, which possibly will give you the occasion to seize his convoys or even to move against his main army with success.

Still other possibilities come to mind. I hardly dare propose them in the present circumstances when, overburdened by the weight of all Europe and forced precipitately either to defend one frontier or to fly to the help of another province, we find ourselves forced to conform to the will of our enemies instead of dictating to them, and to govern our operations by those of our enemies. But since extraordinary situations do not last forever and a single event can produce a considerable change in affairs, I believe that you ought to be acquainted with my thinking on how to establish a theater of war.

As long as we do not entice the enemy onto the plains we cannot expect to obtain great victories over him; but from the moment that we deprive him of his mountains, his forests, and his intersected terrain, which he uses to such great advantage, his troops shall no longer resist ours.

But where, you will ask, are plains to be found? Will they be in Moravia, in Bohemia, or at Görlitz, Zittau, or Freiberg? Of course not. But such terrain is found in Lower Silesia, and sooner or later the insatiable fervor with which the Viennese court desires to reconquer this duchy will induce them to send troops there. That is the time when, forced to leave their posts, the strength of their dispositions and the imposing array of their artillery will be reduced to a mere trifle. If their army enters the plain at the beginning of a campaign, their temerity can bring them total ruin, and from that moment all the operations of Prussian armies in Bohemia or Moravia will succeed without difficulty. It is a vexatious expedient, you will tell me, to entice the enemy in one's own country. Granted, but because nature has endowed Bohemia and Moravia with mountains and forests rather than plains, it is the only way. No other course remains for us except to choose advantageous ground wherever it happens to be and not worry ourselves about anything else.

If the Austrians deserve praise for the skill they have demonstrated in their tactics, I can only censure them for their conduct of the higher aspects of war. These vastly superior forces, these people who rush upon us from the four corners of the earth: what have they accomplished? Is it allowed, with so many means, so many forces, so many arms, to accomplish so little? Is it not obvious that if all these armies had acted simultaneously by means of a well-arranged concert, they would have overwhelmed our corps one after the other, and that in shoving and pressing from the extremities toward the center they would have been able to force our troops to limit themselves to defending the capital alone. But their power has even been detrimental to them. They have relied upon each other—the Imperial general in the Austrian, the latter in the Russian, he in turn in the Swede, and at length the Swede in the French. This explains the indolence in their movements and the sluggishness in the execution of their plans. Lulled by the pleasing fancy of their hopes and the security of their future successes, they have treated time as their own. How many favorable moments have they let escape! On what favorable occasions have they not been negligent! In brief, what enormous mistakes have they not made, for which we owe them our salvation!

Behold the speculations that the recent campaign has afforded me—the only fruit that I have been able to reap from it. The living and recent impression of these images has become a matter for reflection. The subject is not exhausted: there remain many things to say, each of which merits special investigation. But unfortunate is the man who does not know when to stop writing. I would much prefer to stimulate meditation than to provide the last word, and to give those who read this occasion to think of things which, if they apply to them the faculties of their mind, would be better than these ideas I have sketched lightly and in haste.[2]

## THE EMERGENCE OF A SYSTEM

After the war Frederick enlarged upon and clarified his thoughts on the new war of positions. The following comes from one of his most important works on the subject of warfare, his "*Eléments de castramétrie et de tactique*." Frederick wrote this in 1770 and had it published simultaneously in French and German for the benefit of his generals. "I hope you will take every precaution to see that no one makes a copy of it," he urged in one of his covering letters, "and that no copy falls into foreign hands, because it is intended for our officers and not to enlighten our enemies."[3]

BEFORE THE LAST WAR I had given my general officers an *Instruction*[4] which at the time seemed to me sufficient, but the enemy, who was conscious of the disadvantage that he had labored under in fighting us during the first campaigns, has since perfected his castrametation, his tactics, and his artillery. Consequently war has become more refined, more difficult, and more hazardous, for we no longer have only men to fight, but rather the prudence that tactics teaches, the strong posts, and artillery, all together. That fact alone should compel us to study these aspects of war if we are to save our former reputation and to acquire new fame. The study of terrain and how its advantages and defects can be utilized constitutes one of the principal subjects to which a general officer should apply himself; for all his maneuvers in war depend upon the posts that he should occupy with advantage, those that he should attack with minimum losses, the terrain where he should fight, . . . and on this science which imparts a knowledge of using troops appropriately in each situation and according to the rules that experience has taught us.

Those who are persuaded that valor alone suffices for the

general officer, deceive themselves greatly. It is an essential quality, beyond doubt, but it must be supplemented with much other knowledge. A general who maintains order and discipline in his command is certainly praiseworthy, but that is not enough in war either. He must exercise judgment in everything, and how can he do this if he is deficient in knowledge? What kind of a general is he who does not know whether terrain is favorable or deficient and who fails to take advantage of the protection that terrain affords him? If he does not have a good grasp of tactics, his dispositions with the advance guard and the rear guard, his marches, attacks, and defense will be faulty because his ignorance will cause him to neglect arrangements that perhaps are essential. There are principles for everything. I point out the most necessary ones, but the general must take pains to meditate upon them and to practice them himself until they have become second nature.

We must study castrametation, tactics, artillery, and the way to use these to the greatest advantage. The infantry generals must apply themselves to the study of cavalry and *vice versa*, because when detached they will have some of the other arm under their command. I try to put the army in the best possible condition, but it must be kept well in mind that these are only instruments that one prepares. It is the generals who must use them, and these instruments, however good they might be, are serviceable only insofar as one knows how to make good use of them. To the degree that a clever general can be exonerated when he has poor troops who are incapable of carrying out his dispositions, so by the same token—I dare to say it impudently—our generals must forfeit every consideration if, with troops so well trained, they commit some folly through their ignorance.

It is therefore necessary to impress firmly on the mind that henceforth we shall have only a war of artillery to wage, and fortified positions to assault. This necessitates an extensive study of terrain and of the art of competently using it to every possible advantage both in the attack and in the defense.

High ground, especially the gentle slopes that form a kind

of natural glacis, is advantageous terrain for infantry and artillery: their fire is the most murderous. Often such gentle slopes are found in the plains and you must not neglect them. Woods fortified with good abatis are still very useful. As a general rule, whatever compels the enemy to break his front in order to approach you is to your advantage, and it makes no difference whether you are behind a stream or an abatis.

Hills, when they command the surrounding ground, offer the greatest advantage because they deprive the enemy of his artillery, which fires uphill without effect; of his small arms, which he cannot use if he attacks you; and of his cavalry, which he cannot use at all. And finally, hills compel the enemy to break his alignment during the ascent, and this is precisely the moment when your fire must overwhelm him and throw him into confusion and defeat.

The attacker, in turn, must pay attention to all knolls that could protect his troops who attack against the fire from the post. He must neglect no height capable of having artillery placed on it. He must try to bring that point of the enemy army that he attacks under a cross fire, insofar as the terrain and the enemy dispositions permit, in order to procure, if possible, fire superiority. He must strongly support his attacks by his army, which serves as their base, and if he possesses the means of directing one of his attacks against the enemy rear he must not neglect this advantage, which can be decisive for the victory.

Since this subject requires infinite detail, it will be best if, in exposing my system, I divide it by articles in order to treat the subject as methodically and at the same time as briefly as possible. I hope that my generals, being thoroughly imbued with these principles, will henceforth commit no major mistakes in war. This would be the most fitting reward for my work.

## CASTRAMETATION

A camp is a battlefield that you choose, because it becomes one as soon as the enemy attacks you. You must therefore apply every care to post yourself strongly there and to make good dispositions, so as not to expose yourself to a defeat through your mistake. The true principles, the rules for encamping, must be borrowed from the art of the defense of fortifications.

Let us examine these rules. One chooses an advantageous site, commanded on no side, to fortify. Ground that dominates, rather than low-lying ground, is taken. One side of this fortress is protected either by a river or an escarpment and, lacking some natural obstacle, it is strengthened with surrounding works. These outworks must provide mutual defense by flanking fire and they must, moreover, be supported by works behind them, as the covered way is supported by the counterguards,* the latter by ravelins,* and these in turn by bastions.* The works of the covered way must have fire that sweeps all the sunken roads around the fortress and all low ground, so that the enemy cannot slide furtively through these places to approach the works unexpectedly without being spotted.

A well-selected camp must therefore be occupied according to these rules. Your first line represents the covered way; your second, the works that defend it. Your defense line must have salient angles, and the terrain will indicate where these should be located. You will establish all your batteries in the first line to give you a cross or oblique fire, which doubles your strength. You will protect your flanks amply and try to render them unassailable by swamps, inundations, woods where you will make abatis five hundred paces in depth, rivers, or lacking any such natural obstacle, by strong redoubts connected by a good intrenchment.

In fortifying towns one tries as much as possible to limit the enemy to some point of attack: that is done by some salient angles that you project in front, for the enemy can never thrust himself into re-entrant angles. This method is so much the better if you compel the enemy by necessity to shatter the head of his attack at the place where you have prepared your greatest resistance, and where you can concentrate all of your attention. [See Plate 19.]

The best fortresses are those that impose the greatest limits upon the front of the attack, such as by marshes that the enemy can cross only on narrow embankments. Their advantage consists in the fire superiority automatically given to the defense. Similarly, the best camps are those where you include extensive terrain and where the enemy can assault you only by crossing unfordable rivers on bridges, traversing a causeway, or crossing a strip of land wide enough only to form a front of few battalions. That gives you an astonishing fire superiority, and if the enemy is bold enough to attack he is certain to be defeated and destroyed with everything that passes the defile. The second line is a good support for the first on every occasion, although in flat country it does not have the strength that the hills and mountains give it, when it is placed on terrain where it dominates the first line and thus forces the assailant to win two victories before becoming master of the ground.

## CAMPS ON HILLS AND HEIGHTS

Having established these general rules, we come to a more precise application of them. Should you desire to occupy hills sloping off onto the plains without being dominated by any high ground whatever within a distance of 3,000 paces, place your first line halfway up the hill, on the glacis of the hill, and the second on the crest. If the enemy can succeed in overthrowing this first line, he still finds the toughest part of his job ahead of him, namely to dislodge the second line. Using the analogy of the fortress, he has taken the covered way and must at once deliver an assault against the works.

You will carefully support your wings on large ravines by bending them back toward the rear and forming a strong flank. Be sure to place your first line in such a manner that each musket shot can carry to the foot of the glacis and so that no portion of the enemy can take shelter under a steep slope in attacking. Everything must be visible; the slightest hollow must be enfiladed by small-arms fire or cannon. You will array your troops to achieve this effect by posting them according to the configurations in the terrain, and you will forget about every straight line. Place your cavalry where it will be sheltered from artillery fire, behind the two lines, in such a way that it can advance and employ several squadrons in the event the enemy attack, thrown into disorder by the fire of infantry and of case shot, begins to wither. Then release several squadrons, according to my method, and they will destroy and take prisoner all of the corps attacking you.

The most advantageous moment for your defense is when the enemy climbs to assault you. This is the triumph of small arms and cannon loaded with scrap metal, especially if your infantry is arrayed so that its fire reaches the foot of the glacis. If your post has angles, this trebles the defense, and if your cannon can rake the ground with an oblique fire, you should be able to repel the enemy without difficulty. But your infantry should not pursue: it must remain firmly on its ground. If there is occasion to pursue, use the cavalry. Your advance guard can be placed on the right of the army to protect this flank, the rear guard, on the left for the same purpose, and your reserve must be carefully saved behind the post as a last resource. You must always have a reserve in each post proportionate to the size of the army, and in a small force, if you should only have one battalion in reserve, it is still necessary to have one. For fresh troops thrown into action have an incredible ascendancy over the fatigued soldiers who attack you.

## POSTS ON HIGH MOUNTAINS

Posts on high mountains have different rules from those on hills. High mountains have neighboring heights from which they are separated by valleys of 1,500 to 2,000 paces in width. Those where the enemy can place cannon do not permit you to occupy the middle of the slope, because his artillery will batter the troops that are placed there. Therefore you must limit yourself to occupying the mountain crest, as we did at the camps of Bärsdorf and Steinseifersdorf.[5] This type of position requires you to pay twice as much attention to the protection of the flanks and to watch the rear areas with as much vigilance as the front. You must have a good knowledge of all roads behind your height both to be able to evacuate the post without difficulty and especially to be sure that the enemy does not attempt to attack you by the rear. If there is some dangerous hill behind you commanding your position or contesting your line of retreat, you must occupy it at all costs, if only with a battalion with which you crown the summit. In addition, it is essential to have bodies of cavalry or infantry, depending upon the nature of the terrain, to scour all the routes that the enemy could use to approach you day and night.

As for the post itself, you must follow the general principle that I have laid down and constantly place the first line of infantry in such a way that its fire reaches into the valley. The batteries must be near to the edge of the precipice and, insofar as it is possible, they must be placed in such a way as to produce a cross fire. But since it is often impossible in the mountains for artillery to shell the valley below, I would want to form at different points along the front piles of ready loaded grenades which, placed on the glacis where the post is most accessible, could be ignited and rolled down on the assailant daring enough to risk such an undertaking. However rugged the mountain may be, you must place light troops at the bottom or midway up the slope, on the rear as well, to guard against any surprise.

A post such as I describe it is impregnable against an attack in force, and only surprises, especially night enterprises, need be feared. These light troops prevent any surprise, because the enemy could approach you only after dislodging them, and their fire will warn you of the attack and give you time to strike your tents and place your soldiers under arms. Then have fireballs* thrown to light up the ground, have your grenades rolled to the place where the attack is made, and order your infantry to fire into the valley. Your fire and the grenades will augment the confusion and the accompanying terror of all nocturnal enterprises.

Since you can never push foresight far enough in war, it would be a good idea to construct a *caponier*★ for each of your guards, or better still, a palisaded redoubt, which would frustrate completely any enemy undertaking.

## CAMPS ON THE PLAIN AND
## ON INTERSECTED GROUND

In selecting a camp your first consideration must be to choose ground that dominates, or, at least, is not dominated by other ground. Then you must think about the protection you must give to your flanks—woods, marshes, streams or rivers, precipices or hills. If you have woods on your flank, construct good abatis there, not by trees cut down and thrown at random, but with the trees ranged one after the other, the trunks lying toward you and the slashed tops facing the enemy. [See Plate 17.] Before this stanch abatis have still other trees felled for a depth of five hundred paces, so that everything is clear on your flank and the enemy is not free to hide in this forest and fire upon you from two hundred to three hundred paces. If there is a marsh on your other flank, explore it carefully to be sure that it is unapproachable. Then you can anchor your flank there. But never trust in appearances. If you rest your flank on a hill, fortify it with several redoubts linked together by an intrenchment, but well made with a large and deep ditch. Place strong batteries there, always directed to fire obliquely; and if the terrain permits, fortify this post with a redoubt that you will construct behind, which can defend it in case the enemy breaks through. Again comparing your post to a fortress, this redoubt serves as a ravelin which defends the covered way.

If you have a village in your front and your position makes it necessary for you to occupy it, have the front of the village intrenched some distance from the houses. But if there is no valid reason for holding it, be content to send some free battalions there to provide insurance against surprises. The enemy will be compelled to drive them from the village and to fire, which is a great advantage for you because any infantry who have fired have no desire to attack troops that are still fresh. Always keep an eye peeled for terrain that forms a gentle slope or glacis: this is the most advantageous for the fire of infantry, and a skillful general must take advantage of everything. Always observe the rules of fortification and see to it that all sunken roads near your post are covered by your fire.

When you have distributed your troops and arranged your camp, make a tour around the exterior and place yourself in the shoes of a general who has to attack it. In this way you will discover the vulnerable points and can make the necessary changes. . . .

In all situations pertaining to posts, the cavalry must be in the third line and, insofar as possible, sheltered from the fire of artillery. This does not prevent you from using it in case of need by having it pass through openings of infantry to the place where you want it to act. . . .

¶ But no matter what the terrain is like where you encamp, you must always observe the general rule and guard against leaving marshes and rivers close by in the rear, because if you are defeated . . . the fugitives crowd against one another to cross the bridge, or they hurl themselves into the river, or the enemy takes them all prisoner.

## CAMPS BEHIND STREAMS OR RIVERS

If you take up a post behind a stream or river, you must make a reconnaissance of all fordable places in order to take the most precautions at those points.

If it is a stream you have only to make a dike there and it will create a sort of flood. You will line this river bank with light infantry distributed in small groups. Your main body, several hundred paces to the rear, must occupy dominant ground higher than the opposite bank by which the enemy can come. Your batteries will defend the river and you will have several battalions advance under this protection to repel the enemy in the act of crossing. You will have, in addition to this, good redoubts closed and armed with artillery, which will render ineffectual the attempts of the enemy.

Such positions are rarely attacked in front; as a rule the enemy attempts to cross these rivers or streams beyond one of your flanks. It is thus to the two sides that you must devote your attention, either to attack the enemy where he crosses or else to have reconnoitered camps that you can take on your flanks and on that of the enemy. You must therefore always have patrols and scouts on the road to inform you of everything. A general must always be suspicious and foresee everything bad that can happen to him in order to take preventative measures and never be surprised.

## CAMPS WHERE THE AVENUE OF ATTACK IS NARROW

The best camps are those where the point of attack is narrow. Let us assume that you have a marsh or narrow valley that has only enough ground to hold two or three battalions abreast in front of you, and that your army is placed in a semicircle on an elevation that dominates this terrain. You understand that all your fire commands the enemy troops who emerge before you, and this fire superiority will certainly give you victory because the assailants must be ruined and destroyed before they are able to reach you. We had such a camp opposite the Russians at Neustädtel, in Silesia, in 1759. [See Plate 27.]

## INTRENCHMENTS

When redoubts are constructed they must be closed in the rear, because they can only be taken through the gorge.★

Your intrenchments must have ditches that are wide and ten feet deep. If palisades cannot be procured you can surround them with *chevaux de frise* driven into the ground; but if you have wood, palisades are preferable.

Good parapets are sixteen feet thick. They must have an

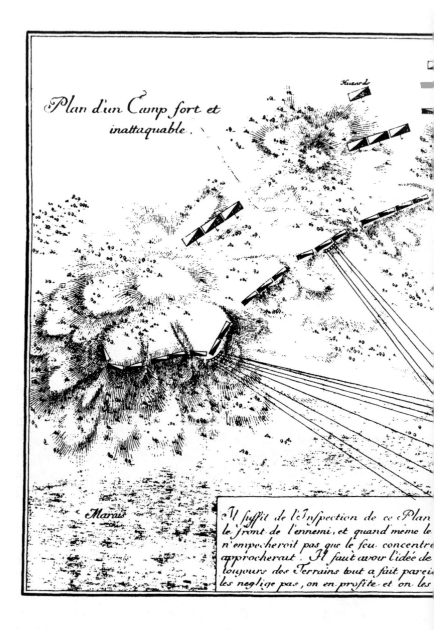

Plan d'un Camp fort et
inattaquable.

Hucard

Marais

Il suffit de l'Inspection de ce Plan
le front de l'ennemi, et quand même le
n'empecheroit pas que le feu concentré
approcherait. Il faut avoir l'idée de
toujours des Terrains tout a fait parei
les neglige pas, on en profite et on les

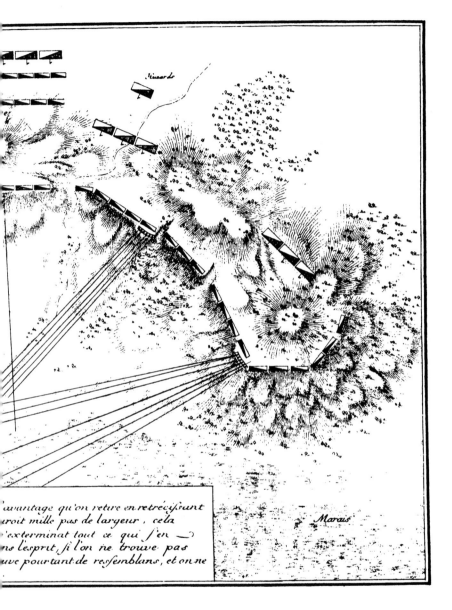

Hussards

avantage qu'on retire en retrécissant
roit mille pas de largeur, cela
exterminat tout ce qui s'en
ns l'esprit, si l'on ne trouve pas
uve pourtant de ressemblans, et on ne

Marais

PLATE 27. Defensive position in which the artillery, posted "in an amphitheater," commands the only possible approach. "You must always have the idea of this plan in your mind," Frederick advised his generals. (*Atlas* to the *Oeuvres de Frédéric le Grand*, Plan 7.)

escarpment so that the soldier in firing has only to lay his musket on it for his shot to carry to the point under attack. Fougasses* formed into a T like mines, in order to blow up the same place three times, can be added to the intrenchments. Their use is admirable: nothing fortifies a position so strongly nor does more to ward off attackers. [See Plate 1.]

## CAMPS COVERING TOO MUCH TERRAIN

¶ Defensive war often requires the selection of posts that cover a great deal of country. . . . Nothing leads more easily into temptation than posts that are overextended. To be sure, such posts by their nature are excellent, but they require 80,000 men to occupy and defend them and you only have 40,000. In such a case you must always remember that terrain in itself is nothing without men who defend it. The wisest course to take, whenever you can, is to seek to one side or the other, either in front or in the rear, positions more suitable for your forces and which you can hold. For the more you extend yourself the weaker you become in effect, and a single effort by the enemy makes him victorious. . . .

The best camps are those requiring as a garrison fewer troops than you have: then you have two lines with good reserves and can defend yourself like a madman.

Extensive terrain can be defended, however, principally in the mountains, where you occupy with a few battalions only the crest and some ridges and can stretch out your line, especially if the access to the mountains is rugged. . . . In 1759 I defended ten miles of terrain in Silesia with 30,000 men, from Köben to Herrnstadt; but I had the stream of Bartsch in my front, which cut between the marshes, and I had the passages occupied and defended by brigades intrenched and posted to such great advantage that 100,000 men could not have forced them. In 1758 the Austrians similarly defended the banks of the Elbe from Königgrätz to Arnau. These examples can in-

struct the officers of the need to judge carefully everything
that can be done, and to think before they act.

You must never, therefore, take up a position without having good knowledge of the locality and its advantages and
defects. In each camp that you take, moreover, you must make
the disposition for its defense and communicate your plan to
the officers responsible for executing it, for they cannot divine
what their general is thinking. But when they are so instructed,
then you can punish them severely if they do not carry out
your orders to the letter.

## THEORY AND PRACTICE

¶ The principles given above are without doubt sound: they
are the only ones to which you must adhere. But it would be
a serious mistake if one were persuaded that this theory alone
suffices to enable him to reach perfection in this art. The difficulties are perceived only when these principles are put into
practice.

Nature alone almost never provides terrain exactly the way
you want it. In order to obtain perfect posts you must always
improve upon nature, rectifying and attempting to strengthen
whatever is defective in the terrain. A stream is used, for example, to make an inundation. Redoubts and intrenchments are
built at weak points, and abatis . . . are thrown up in forests.
Skill is used to perfect nature. A position a mile or two in front
or behind is taken, one wing is refused and another is advanced,
the center is shoved forward. And finally, one hundred different steps are taken to squeeze all the advantages possible from
the terrain. But you must be active to observe everything and
a genius to take advantage of everything, which of necessity
requires an officer to be intelligent and industrious. . . .

Above all, it is necessary to have the roads leading into the
camp reconnoitered thoroughly, because it is here that the
enemy must advance upon you. . . . In camps on the plain you

must send a body of light troops forward, behind some defile, to observe the enemy. It is also prudent to have smaller detachments on the flanks to avoid being surprised. An army must be like a spider that spins its threads on all sides and from the vibrations is constantly informed of what goes on.

But—I repeat—theoretical knowledge is of no use if it is not supplemented by positive practice. You must train yourself to select terrain and make dispositions; you must reflect on this subject; and then theory, reduced to practice, makes all of these operations skillful and easy and teaches you how to judge at sight the number of troops that the site can contain.

## DIFFERENT ATTACKS

¶ We must draw up our dispositions for battles according to the rules of siegecraft. Since no one in our day any longer rashly attacks mined covered ways because such attacks are too hazardous and deadly, by the same token such attacks must also be renounced in general engagements because too many men are lost by the fire of case shot, and in the event of a defeat an army would be irretrievably ruined. Because the same objective can be accomplished at less danger, you must risk as little as possible and leave to fortune only that which lies beyond the province of skill.

The engineers recommend that you carefully surround the works you attack in order to have fire superiority over the fortress, that you establish your ricochet batteries in such a way that they infilade the lines of defense, that you have your first parallel overlap the others by a good margin to serve them as a base and a support, and that you move forward from your third parallel by zigzag trenches in order to establish yourself on the covered way.

Translated in terms of tactics, your two lines are your parallels. From the side where you wish to attack you will establish batteries to support the attacking troops, comparable to those saps* in a siege that are advanced to the salients of the glacis.

## ATTACKS ON LEVEL GROUND

It happens that one finds himself with an inferior army on flat terrain, such as that between Berlin and Frankfurt, between Magdeburg and Halberstadt, near Leipzig, or between Ratibor and Troppau. How does one support his flanks then? How does he take a position when there is none? I have often pondered the matter, because one does find himself in a situation where, without wishing to prejudice the successful outcome of the cause, it is necessary to stand firm on such terrain. Here, then, is the only practical idea that has occurred to me.

For my camp I choose somewhat low-lying ground where I am sheltered from the enemy. On the hill before my front I have redoubts erected so that the enemy believes this is the position I want to defend, and there must be some village there that must be fortified. If there is a wood on one of your wings this is an advantage, for the entire plan depends upon concealing your intended movement from the enemy. In this post, the generals who would come to reconnoiter me will base their disposition on my fortified village and my front filled with redoubts.

[Plate 28] illustrates the plan of my camp.[6] The enemy who sees the redoubts and fortified positions believes that I intend to maintain this post. He is tempted to attack me because I occupy low ground, and he makes his disposition on the basis of what I show him of my post.

[Plate 29] indicates the attack of my cavalry and the march of my army to strike the enemy's flank. . . . The moment the enemy deploys, my cavalry leaves and takes him in flank and in the tail. My infantry marches at the same time, and in [Plate 30] you see the enemy cavalry chased by the cavalry of my right wing and . . . the plan of my infantry attack after the enemy cavalry is defeated. Notice my infantry on the flank of the enemy infantry while my second line attacks the enemy in the rear. He can not change front to face my army because he

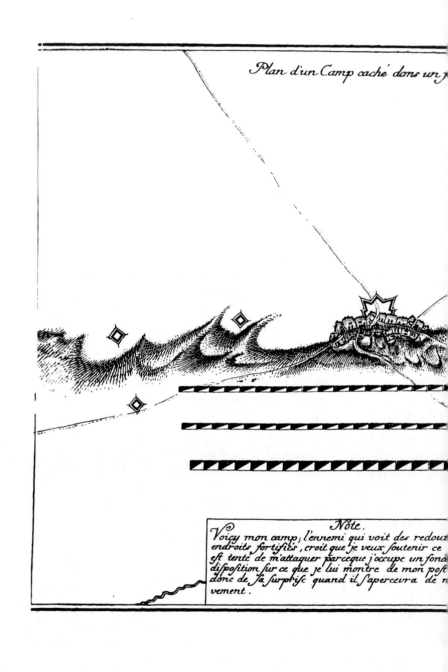

Plan d'un Camp caché dans un [...]

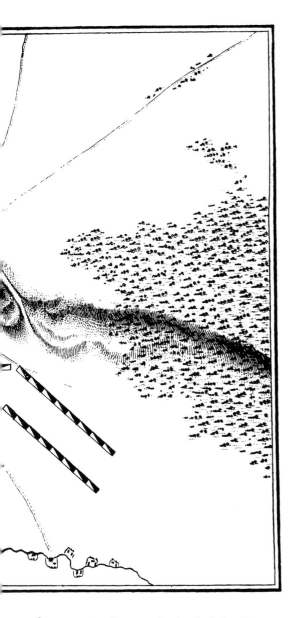

PLATE 28. One method of defending a post. The redoubts and the fortified village on the heights in front of the camp mislead the enemy as to the real position of Frederick's army, in formation below. (*Atlas* to the *Oeuvres de Frédéric le Grand*, Plan 19.)

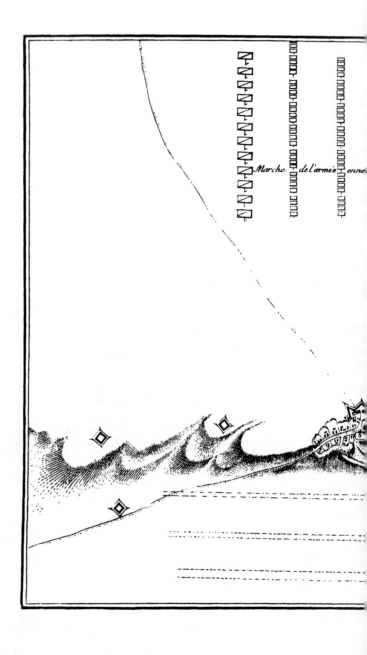

Marche de l'armée enne

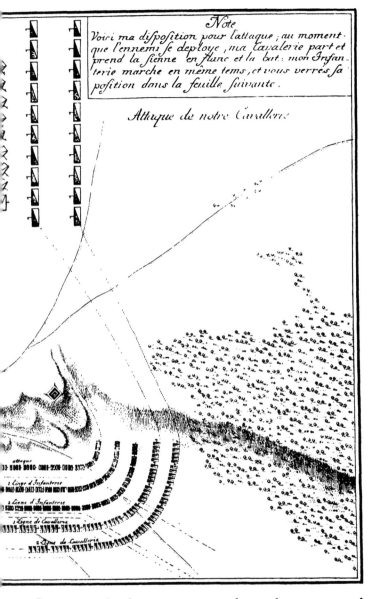

Note

Voici ma disposition pour l'attaque; au moment
que l'ennemi se deploye, ma Cavalerie part et
prend la sienne en flanc et la bat: mon Infan..
terie marche en même tems, et vous verrés sa
position dans la feuille suivante.

Attaque de notre Cavallerie

attaque
1 Linge d'Infanterie
2 Ligne d'Infanterie
1 Ligne de Cavallerie
2 Ligne de Cavallerie

PLATE 29. As the enemy approaches and prepares to deploy,
Frederick throws his cavalry against the enemy left flank.
(*Atlas* to the *Oeuvres de Frédéric le Grand*, Plan 20.)

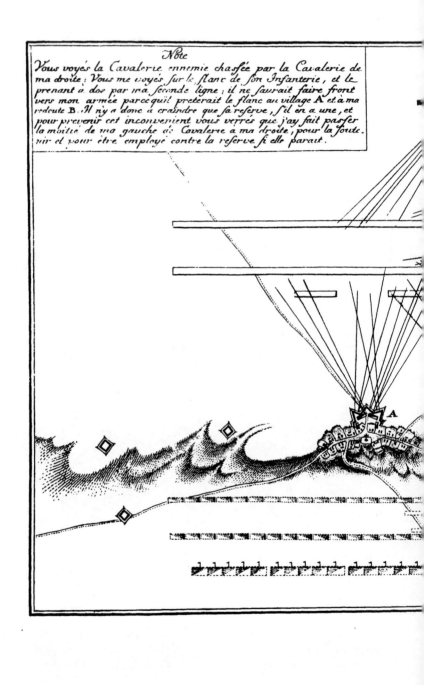

Note

Vous voyés la Cavalerie ennemie chasfée par la Cavalerie de
ma droite; Vous me voyés fur le flanc de fon Infanterie, et le
prenant à dos par ma feconde ligne; il ne faurait faire front
vers mon armée parce qu'il preterait le flanc au village A et à ma
redoute B. Il n'y a donc à craindre que fa referve, s'il en a une, et
pour prevenir cet inconvenient vous verrés que j'ay fait paffer
la moitié de ma gauche de Cavalerie a ma droite, pour la foute.
nir et pour être employé contre la referve fi elle parait.

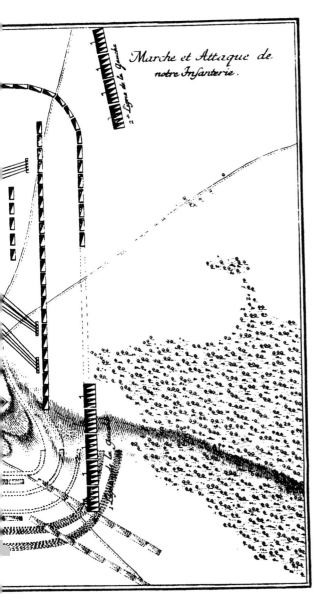

Marche et Attaque de notre Infanterie.

2.ᵈᵉ Ligne de la Gauche

PLATE 30. Unable to shift his forces to meet the threat on his left for fear of exposing his other flank to the fortifications in front, the enemy finds himself assaulted on his left and rear by Frederick's united army. (*Atlas* to the *Oeuvres de Frédéric le Grand*, Plan 21.)

would then expose his flank to the village [A] and my redoubt [B], therefore there is only his reserve to fear, if he has one, and to prevent this inconvenience you will observe that I have sent half the cavalry of my left wing to the support of my right wing to be employed against the enemy reserve, if it should appear.

Your cavalry must be put in motion only when the enemy wishes to deploy, so that he cannot change his dispositions.

You must supply the works of the village and the redoubt nearest to your right with cannon. If the enemy wishes to change his front, his flank will then be exposed to the fire from your village, and if he wants to attack the village, your entire army then takes him in flank. Everything, therefore, depends upon the shock of the cavalry: if this succeeds well, the enemy army is completely defeated. This is how, with a small number of troops, you nevertheless procure the victory.

## ATTACK ON A VILLAGE

I do not lose sight of the principles and methods of siege warfare. Therefore to attack a village in front of the enemy army, my two infantry lines will be the base of my attacks. I establish my batteries and form three or four columns, according to the need, to move against the village. These are formed at some distance from each other in order to allow the batteries to fire and to prevent their becoming intermingled, since they lead to a common objective. Each column is composed of three lines at intervals of 150 paces. The main battle line, which is found behind, must remain immobile at nine hundred paces from the village and advance only when the village is taken. The cavalry is still farther to the rear and always sheltered from the artillery as much as possible. Take a glance at [Plate 31].

## ATTACKS AGAINST HEIGHTS

The attacks of heights are the most difficult of all in war, because a skillful enemy occupies his terrain in such a way that it is impossible for his position to be turned, and you are

forced to attack him at points bristling with nearly insurmountable difficulties. But if there is a major force pressing
you to risk such an enterprise, what must you do?

1. Reconnoiter the enemy position carefully.
2. If possible, attack the enemy in the rear while demonstrat-
   ing with the army in his front.
3. If this is not possible, then attack the highest ground in his
   camp.
4. Place your batteries on all hills that can produce a cross
   fire, and form your attack according to that indicated on
   [Plate 32].

Take care especially to keep your army out of range of case
shot and to attack your hill vigorously. If your army is strong,
make a false attack against one side in order to distract the
enemy and divide his attention.

I have my reasons for insisting that you attack, preferably,
the highest point in the enemy position. . . . If you carry it,
and establish yourself there, everything is decided. Your superior fire must sweep away and scour the rest of the enemy
position without any trouble, whereas if you attack and carry
a lesser knoll instead, you will have won nothing and the obstacles will have increased in proportion as your tired troops
are repulsed.

The reader must remember that all my plans are contrived
and that it is impossible to sketch every kind of terrain where
one could fight. An intelligent man will apply my rules himself,
according to the circumstances surrounding the different posts
that he wishes to attack. I beseech him to remember that in
every attack against a post he must take care not to expose the
cavalry needlessly.

¶ Often a position is accessible only on one side, furnishing
then only a single point of attack. The entire army moves to
that point, but it can only support and reinforce the troops
that one leads to the charge. If the difficulties are too formidable, however, these attacks can be called off and the troops
recalled to the main army.

### Note.

Les regles de l'attaque des places veulent,
qu'on embrasse les ouvrages et les
poligones qu'on attaque le plus qu'il est
possible. J'ay choisi une position
désavantageuse pour moy dans ce village
dont vous voyes le Plan. Cependant
malgré l'armée ennemie qui le protege,
je l'entourre autant qu'il est possible. Voyés
la distribution des batteries A. Mon
Infanterie que je tiens à 900 pas et d'avantage du village et à l'abri du feu des Cartouches, et je n'engage que le corps qui doit
chasser l'ennemi, desorte que si mes attaques
etoient toutes les trois repoussées, elles
pourraient se replier sur l'Infanterie soute-
nüe de la Cavalerie pour lui couvrir le
flanc, sans compter que je me suis menagé
une reserve B soit pour rafraichir mes
attaques, si elles prosperent, soit pour la
porter en cas de retraite où le besoin l'exi-
gerait. Et en cas que vous emporties le village,
il y faut faire avancer la reserve avec du canon
attelé pour vous establir au plus vite dans le
village, sous la protection du quel vous pouves
attaquer et battre les lignes de l'ennemi.

A

Husards

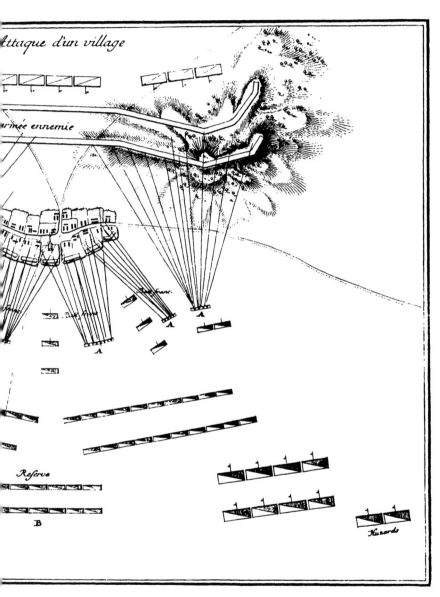

Attaque d'un village

Armée ennemie

Réserve

B

Husards

PLATE 31. Frederick's method of attacking a village in front of the enemy line of battle. (*Atlas* to the *Oeuvres de Frédéric le Grand*, Plan 22.)

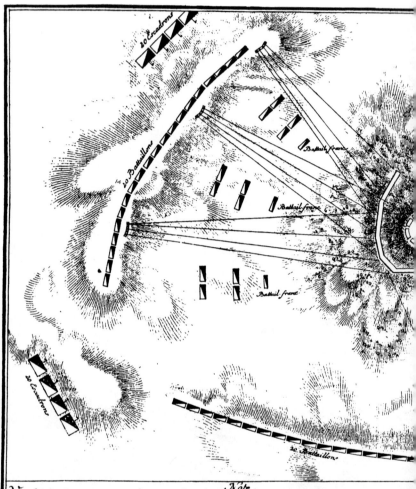

**Note**

Voici le plan d'une attaque ou l'on s'attache a la hauteur dominante du Poste ennemi A, et une
attaque B, pour faciliter la reussite de la veritable attaque. Observés que j'embrasse le plus qu'il m'e_
par mes batteries le point ou je dirige mes efforts ; mais pour peu que le terrain vous favorise,
rer encore d'avantage le point d'attaque. Observés aussitôt que vos Troupes seront maitresses de
d'avoir des batteries toutes attellées pour les y faire conduire, et pour vous y etablir, relevé
troupes de l'attaque par celles de vos lignes, car 12 Bataillons ne peuvent pas combattre contr
armée. Si l'ennemi voit son poste A. emporté, il vous voudra presenter encore un front en C. mais
possedés la hauteur dominante qui vous donne l'avantage du feu, vous le culbuterés facilement.

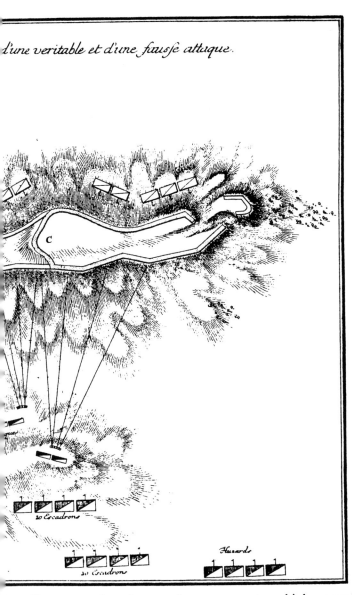

*l'une veritable et d'une fausse attaque.*

PLATE 32. Attack upon the enemy post on high ground. After making a false attack at *B* and effecting a crossfire with his artillery upon *A*, Frederick attacks with twelve infantry battalions preceded by the expendable free battalions. Point *A* is the key to the entire position: once it has been taken the enemy must yield the post. (*Atlas* to the *Oeuvres de Frédéric le Grand*, Plan 23.)

¶ Attacks on intrenchments must be based upon the same principles of siege warfare. Good batteries must be established, which bring the enemy intrenchments under enfilade fire. The attack must be preceded with heavy artillery fire, the troops that must attack should be distributed in nearly the same way as in the attack upon posts, and the army must be kept at a distance from these intrenchments so that it will not be exposed to the fire of case shot.

In the attack proper it is necessary to have designated soldiers fill up the trench with fascines.* Once master of the enemy's intrenchment you must establish yourself in it and not push forward with infantry. Instead, have your workers make openings through which the cavalry can pour and win the victory. For if you follow quickly it can happen that your infantry, in confusion through having crossed these intrenchments, is either defeated or repulsed suddenly by enemy cavalry awaiting it in good order.[7]

THIS INDUCES ME to observe that a general would be wrong should he be in haste to attack the enemy in hilly posts or on broken ground. I have sometimes been forced to this extremity, but when war is made with equal powers, more certain advantages may be procured by stratagem . . . and without exposing an army to as much danger. The sum of many small advantages will be great. The attack of a well-defended post is, moreover, a hard nut to crack, and the assailant is liable to be repulsed and beaten. It is only to be carried by the sacrifice of 15,000 to 20,000 men, which makes a grievous breach in the army. Recruits, assuming that you find them in abundance, restore the number but not the quality of the soldiers that you have lost. Your Kingdom becomes depopulated in reviving your army; your troops degenerate, and if it is a long war, you find yourself finally at the head of ill-disciplined peasants, with which you scarcely dare appear before the enemy. In a violent situation it is good when one discards rules: necessity alone can cause one to resort to desperate remedies, much as poison is given to the sick when there are no other means of cure. But except for such cases you must, in my opinion, proceed with more caution and act only with wisdom and circumspection, because the general who allows the least to chance is the most able.[8]

## NOTES: CHAPTER VIII

1. Frederick, "Dialogue between the Duke of Marlborough, Prince Eugene, and the Prince of Liechtenstein," *Posthumous Works of Frederick II, King of Prussia*, Trans. Thomas Holcroft (London, 1789), V, 37-57.

2. Frederick, "Réflexions sur la tactique et sur quelques parties de la guerre, ou, Réflexions sur quelques changements dans la façon de faire la guerre," *Oeuvres de Frédéric le Grand* (Berlin, 1846-56), XXVIII, 154-66.

3. *Ibid., editors note*, XXIX, x.

4. This appears to be a reference to Frederick's *Military Instructions to his Generals*, the major portions of which are contained in Chapters IV–VI.

5. Frederick occupied the camp of Bärsdorf in September, 1760, after the battle of Liegnitz. Steinseifersdorf, which is also near Schweidnitz, was occupied several times, the last occasion being during the siege of that fortress. *Die Werke Friedrichs Des Grossen* (Berlin, 1913), VI, 133 n.

6. Much of this and the following paragraph is taken from the description on the maps themselves, which evidently was intended to supplement the text.

7. Frederick, "Eléments de castramétrie et de tactique," *Oeuvres*, XXIX, 3-20, 22-25.

8. Frederick, *The History of the Seven Years War*, trans. Thomas Holcroft (London, 1789), I, xii-xiii. Several sentences from this passage were retranslated by me from the original.

# IX

# *Strategy*

Frederick never used the word *strategy*, for it was not a part of his vocabulary. Although the concept that later writers defined as strategy existed in the eighteenth century, the term used then by most military men was *campaign plans* (*projets de campagne*); indeed, the two terms were used well into the Victorian era. Initially strategy meant merely "the science of military movement beyond the visual circle of the enemy, or out of cannon shot." Born in the first decade of the nineteenth century, the word grew to maturity as war became increasingly complex and total. The airplane, industrial power, and nuclear weapons have given it new dimensions, until today strategy has come to mean the art of applying national power in the pursuit of national and even global objectives. From the selections in this chapter it appears evident that Frederick's concept of strategy as revealed in his writings on campaign plans is quite similar to the thought of the celebrated Swiss theorist, Baron Jomini (1779–1869), who defined the term as "the art of properly directing masses upon the theatre of war." Since modern translation deals with meaning rather than the mere words, the term *strategy* is substituted for *campaign plans* whenever it does not distort what Frederick was trying to communicate to his generals.[1]

*YOU WISH ME* to indicate the maxims that must serve as a basis for strategy. In order to satisfy this request I must limit myself to summarizing some general rules that are applicable. There must be different rules for offensive warfare, for war conducted between equal powers, and finally, for defensive warfare. Above all, you must pay attention to the nature of the country where you wage war—whether it is irrigated by rivers or filled with woods, whether it is intersected or offers you vast plains, whether it is defended by fortresses or destitute of strongholds, whether it is filled with crags and mountains, and what is its relative position to the sea. It is therefore necessary, first of all, that those wishing to formulate a campaign plan have an accurate knowledge of the enemy forces and of the assistance he can expect from his allies. He must compare the enemy forces with his own and with those his friends can furnish him, in order to judge what kind of a war he will want to undertake. There is open country where, with equal forces, you have the prospect of great success; but there is other terrain, full of defiles and posts, where a large superiority of forces is required if you are to wage offensive war. Take good care not to be satisfied with vague ideas in these matters, which require above all clear and precise thinking. If you have a poor knowledge of the chessboard, pawns, and pieces, there is every indication that you will not win the game. But war is vastly more important than chess. We will examine in general those rules that must constantly be followed in the three kinds of warfare—offensive, war between equals, and defensive.

We begin with the offensive. The first thing, as I have said, is to compare all the enemy forces, along with those of their allies, to your own and to the assistance that your allies will give you.[2] STRATEGY IS BASED' on the forces you have, on the strength of the enemy, on the situation of the country where you want to carry the war, and on the actual political condition of Europe. If you wish to wage war, you must know if you are superior to your enemy, either in numbers or in the intrinsic value of the troops, . . . whether you have rivers to facilitate the transport of your provisions or you must carry them in wagons, whether you have fortresses along the frontier or along what constitutes your lines of defense. In addition, you must know what kind of allies this prince has and the substance of the treaties he has made with them, the state of efficiency of their forces, and whether they will send auxiliaries or make diversions. All this knowledge is indispensable for making adequate preparations for war. Unfortunately these important matters are lightly treated by the ministers, who act for the most part according to their emotions, undertaking war by an impulse of vanity, the desire of blind lust, or even through hate and animosity. Whoever reads history—I do not speak of remote centuries, but only the most recent—will be convinced of the truth of my assertions. I believe that a rational man never deliberately begins a war where he is forced from the beginning to act on the defensive. . . . Any war that does not lead to conquest weakens the victorious and enervates the state. It is therefore necessary never to commence hostilities unless you have the most glowing prospects for making conquests, which at once determines the conditions of the war and makes it offensive.[3]

YOU MUST HAVE complete knowledge of the regions in which you are going to wage war in order to know the posts and the moves that you will be able to make there and to estimate beforehand the camps that the enemy will take to upset your plans. Above all, you must give thought to your subsistence, for an army is a body that travels on its stomach. No matter how good is the plan you have conceived, you cannot carry it out if your soldiers have nothing to eat. You must therefore provide for this in advance, form your magazines and arrange your depots . . . in such a manner that the magazines are within range of the places where you intend to act.[4]

THE FIRST RULE is always to establish the largest magazine

in the rear of your army and if possible in a fortified city. During the wars in Silesia and Bohemia[5] we had our main magazine at Breslau, because the Oder made it easy for us to replenish it. When magazines are established at the head of the army you run the risk of losing them at the first defeat and then being left without supplies. But if you establish these magazines one behind the other, you wage war prudently and a slight reverse can not lead to your entire ruin. . . .

There are two ways of forming magazines. Either you order the nobles and peasants to have their grain carted to the depot, in which case they are reimbursed according to the rate determined by the Chamber of Finance or their imposed taxes are decreased, or, if the country is lacking in fodder, agreements are made with entrepreneurs to provide a specified amount. It is the task of the commissariat to negotiate and sign these contracts. . . . Purveyors must never be employed except when absolutely necessary, because they are even more exorbitant than the Jews: they run up the price of provisions and sell them at an extravagant profit.

The magazines should always be established in plenty of time to be stocked with all the necessary provisions when the army leaves its quarters to take the field. If you wait too long the rivers will freeze over and prevent you from utilizing water transportation, or else the roads will become so bad and impracticable that you will be able to form the magazines only with the greatest difficulty.

¶ But if there are navigable rivers you must take advantage of them, for this is the only means of transportation by which an army can be abundantly supplied. . . . Special vessels are built expressly to transport flour and fodder through the rivers and canals. . . . In a war against Saxony the Elbe, and in Silesia the Oder must be used to facilitate the transport of provisions. In Prussia you have the sea, but in Bohemia and Moravia you can use only wagons.

Sometimes three and four provision depots are established on the same line. We did this in Bohemia in 1742, when we had magazines at Pardubitz, Nimburg, Podiebrad, and another at Brandeis, to be in a position to keep pace with the enemy and to follow him to Prague in the event he should think of going there. During the last campaign in Bohemia,[6] Breslau supplied Schweidnitz, the latter provisioned Jaromircz, and thence provisions were carried to the army.[7] Above all . . . the first consideration of the general must be for his provisions, and here it is not enough to plan ahead for fifteen days; the entire campaign must be considered.[8]

THE PRIMARY MAXIM for an offensive war is to formulate ambitious plans, so that if they succeed they will produce really significant results. Hit the enemy hard and do not be content merely to harass him on his frontiers. The only purpose of war is to force the enemy to consent to an advantageous peace as soon as possible, and you must never lose sight of this idea. When your strategy is decided and you have accumulated sufficient supplies to put it into effect, then you must devise every conceivable means of concealing your intentions from the enemy so that, when the campaign gets under way, your movements put him on the wrong scent and induce him to suspect intentions quite different from those you actually have.

¶ Before beginning operations you must, without any indulgence or self-deception, examine objectively every step that the enemy might undertake to thwart your plan, and consider in each conceivable case what means are open to you to fulfill your goal. The more you anticipate the difficulties in advance, the less surprised you will be should you encounter them during the campaign. Besides, you have already thought about these obstacles deliberately, and with composure you have perceived the means of avoiding them, so nothing can surprise you. Such was nearly the case with the expedition of Louis XIV against the Dutch in 1672. The enterprise would have ended gloriously had the French at first made themselves masters of the floodgates at Naarden and Muiden, which would have given them control over Amsterdam, and if the French army had not weakened itself by the number of garrisons that it left in even the smallest forts.[9] ANTICIPATE EVERYTHING, therefore, and in so doing you will have found remedies beforehand for all inconveniences. For what one thinks deliberately is a hundred times better than the decisions made in the field, since these are neither digested nor thought out. Improvisation can succeed, but it is always better when you have made plans in advance.

A distinction must also be drawn between strategy framed at the beginning of a war and that adopted after several campaigns. The former, provided it is well conceived, can determine the outcome of the entire war if you know well how to capitalize on all the advantages that your forces, time, or a post that you have been the first to control give you over the enemy. Plans adopted in the field are governed by so many circumstances that it is impossible to prescribe general rules except to guard your line of defense and avoid making deep penetrations into enemy territory. . . . To make good plans in the course of a war you must have spies in the cabinet of the enemy princes or in the war bureaus. As soon as you are informed of the enemy's intentions, it is easy to break up his measures and you can always undertake boldly that which he fears the most, for it is a cardinal rule that he must do the opposite from what he desires. The beauty of a war plan is that while risking little you place the enemy in danger of losing everything. . . .

¶ But since Europe is divided into two large factions in all our wars, the result is a certain balance of forces, which means that after many successes one is hardly ahead when general peace is made. Moreover, when one is compelled to divide his forces to face enemies on every front he scarcely has the power to bear the enormous cost required by three or more armies when all act on the offensive. In a little while efforts are made only on one front, while the other armies coast along in fruitless and idle campaigns.

If you wish to be assured of great benefits you must go after only one enemy and concentrate all your efforts against him. In so doing you are assured of the greatest possible success. But circumstances do not permit a person to do everything that he wishes, and often one is forced to take measures imposed by necessity.

The greatest errors in strategy are those which force you to make deep penetrations [*des pointes*], by which I mean sending a *corps d'armée* too far from its frontiers and beyond any support. This method is so faulty that all plans following it are, as a result, badly contrived. You must therefore begin by doing on a large scale what normally would be done on a smaller scale. To use the fortress analogy, anyone in a siege thinks of beginning not with the third parallel, but with the first. Provision depots are laid out and all the works that are pushed forward must be supported by those in the rear. Similarly, in battles, the only good dispositions are those that provide mutual support, where a corps of troops never is risked all alone but is constantly supported by the others.

Strategy must be treated in the same way. If you find a country where there are some mountains, make these your line of defense, occupy the principal gorges with detachments, and place your army on the side of the enemy to support this line; for you defend something not by taking up a position behind a river or mountain, but only by remaining on the far side.[10] If you find a country where there are numerous fortified strongholds, capture them all and leave none behind you. Then you can advance methodically and need have no concern for your rear. If you seize many fortresses, demolish the majority in order to save garrisoning them and spare only those that you need for your provisions and for security in case of a retreat.[11]

THE STRATEGY by which one proposes to attack the enemy with two, three, or more armies is more apt to fail than that involving a single army. Clearly it is more difficult to find three good generals than to discover only one, and if you propose, moreover, to make the major efforts in one province, the enemy who is free to act proposes to make his on another of his frontiers. Thus it often happens that you are forced to weaken your main army by sending help to one of the armies that has been defeated, and from that moment your offensive strategy is reduced to nothing. You find yourself on the defensive at a place where you should want to strike the greatest blows, and you must of necessity reinforce a defeated general in a province where your interests normally would not require you to make any effort. One has only to reread the plans of the court of Versailles, found at the head of each chapter in Quincy's *Military History of Louis XIV*, to be convinced of this truth. None of the campaigns fulfilled the plans that the ministers and generals had formulated. But how did that happen? For the mistakes of others must serve as a warning to us not to commit similar errors. The French were too confident of success, they did not give enough thought to the enemy's means, to the steps that demanded his interest, and, finally, to the most dangerous enterprises against French interests that the enemy could make. That is why I am so insistent that you not be superficial, but examine and imagine everything that the enemy could possibly do against you. Let your shrewdness and prudence remove everything possible from the realm of chance —luck still has too much influence in war. It happens that detachments are defeated either through the fault of the commanding officer, or by the greater strength of the enemy who attack. Forts can be surprised, battles lost, either because someone loses his head or because the only general officer acquainted with the intentions of the commander is killed or wounded and the other generals of this wing cannot execute the original battle plan. That is why you must never celebrate a victory before the enemy has been driven from the field of battle.

If you prefer examples to rules, I will outline a strategic plan incorporating the maxims established above.

## AN IMAGINARY WAR AGAINST FRANCE

Let us assume that Prussia, Austria, the Empire, England, and Holland have formed an offensive alliance against France.

This is how it would be necessary to proceed in devising a solid and carefully thought-out plan of campaign. I know that France can put 180,000 men into the field, that the French militia, 60,000 strong, can be used to garrison the triple ring of fortresses that line the frontiers, that of the French allies the King of Spain can supply 40,000 men, the King of Naples, 10,000, and the King of Sardinia, another 50,000, making a grand total of 270,000 men under arms, not counting those who guard the fortresses. I count only combatants.

Against this number the allies could raise: Prussia, 150,000; Austria, 160,000; the Empire, 40,000; England, 20,000, and a like number from Holland, together with their fleets, which must cooperate to facilitate the operations of the armies. The allies will therefore assemble 390,000 men, which would give them a superiority of 120,000 over France and her allies. I know further that French finances are entirely unstable and that France consequently would have trouble financing three campaigns. Spain, drained by its armaments against the Moroccans and the Algerians, could not support the war very long, and the Sardinian King is lost if some power does not send him considerable subsidies. It remains therefore to deliberate how France shall be attacked, and on which side the most telling blow will be dealt.

I believe that it will be through Flanders, as I will explain briefly. I therefore assign 100,000 men to attack the states of the Sardinian King through Lombardy: this army will find 90,000 Sardinians, Spaniards, and Neapolitans to fight. I assign a second army of 110,000 troops to attack France in Alsace: these will be opposed by 80,000 French. The largest army, composed of 180,000 soldiers, I reserve for Flanders—not to deliver a battle and take a couple of fortresses each year, which would entail seven or eight campaigns, but to penetrate into the heart of France, to advance along the Somme, and at the same time to threaten the capital.

Here is the objective of this strategy. The French, attacked in their home, will soon abandon Flanders in order to defend

Paris. The fortresses shall be garrisoned only with militia, who should be easy to overcome. Perhaps the French would weaken the army of Alsace considerably, the better to rescue Paris, which would give the allies on that front the means of obtaining great success, while in Flanders the principal fortresses that have been bypassed could be taken with a detachment of 40,000 troops.

In giving you the details of this plan I must inform you that, never having seen Flanders, I am guided by maps which perhaps are inaccurate. The principal magazines for the army must be formed at Brussels, Nieuport, and Veurne [Furnes]. The army will be assembled in the vicinity of Brussels and will move on Tournai in order to appear to threaten Lille and Valenciennes. You must seek to fight the enemy, win a decided superiority over him, and then to besiege Saint Vinox [Bergues] followed by Dunkirk, where you would be assisted by the English fleet. These are nearly all the operations that you will have time for during the entire campaign, although if possible you should further besiege and take Gravelines.

At present let us examine what measures the French could take to oppose this strategy. It would seem certain that they, seeing themselves about to be attacked in Flanders, will propose to forestall their enemies. They can besiege Tournai or Mons before the large allied forces are assembled. They can take up position at Oudenarde to force you to remain fairly close to Brussels for fear of losing your convoys. They could even encamp on the Escaut, between Condé and St. Ghislain. Who knows, they might even attempt to seize Brussels before the allies arrive there! In all these suppositions the allies must begin with a battle. There are few positions that could not be turned, and everything depends upon the outcome of the battle. If it is a decisive affair, even Brussels would be retaken in a short time. As for Mons and Tournai, you must leave them in French hands and not be swayed from the main objectives for mere trifles. While operating from the side of Vinox and Dunkirk with 120,000 men, you will still have

60,000 left who can cover Brussels and your rear, and the English fleet will supply you with provisions drawn from your magazines at Nieuport.

The second campaign will be more difficult than the first because you have tipped your hand, and the enemy, understanding your objectives, will want to oppose them. Doubtless he will select some fortified camp to block you on the way, in which case you devise means of dislodging and fighting him in order to besiege Gravelines and then Bourbourg, where the English fleet, arriving at the port of Gravelines, will supply you with provisions. From there you must move against Montreuil, where the English fleet, entering the mouth of the Canche, would bring your provisions. If the enemy still wishes to stop you further in front you must dislodge him, advance against Abbeville and have the English fleet sail to the mouth of the Somme, so that you do not lack magazines.

You will object, perhaps, that I leave too many fortified cities behind me, but I still have 60,000 men, one-third of whom will occupy convenient locations in my rear while the remaining 40,000 will besiege the fortresses defended by militia, such as Cassel, Aire, and St. Omer. Figure that the entire French army would quickly abandon Flanders after the beginning of the second campaign to cover Paris and that, by acting vigorously against this army, the French minister would hasten to conclude peace. Assuming that you capture Paris, it would be necessary to refrain from having your troops enter the city because they would grow soft and lose their discipline. You must be content instead with levying large contributions.

In order for this campaign plan to become sound, you should have the foresight to send good engineer officers and quartermasters who, disguised as peddlers, would survey all the places to correct whatever mistakes there might be in the plan both with regard to the terrain and the fortresses that you propose to take, and the ports, which are not accurately enough known to me.

# A FUTURE WAR WITH AUSTRIA

To avoid the mistakes into which ignorance of the country-side perhaps has led me, I will sketch for you the strategy of terrain where I am thoroughly at home. Let us assume that a war should break out between Prussia and the house of Austria. We know that Austria can put 180,000 men into the field. Assume further that Austria finds herself destitute of allies and foreign assistance. Prussia can form an army of 180,000 men, to which Russia must add 30,000 auxiliaries.[12] The garrison regiments are sufficient to garrison properly the most exposed fortresses.

From this sketch it is evident that the Prussians will enjoy a superiority of 30,000 men over their enemies. This raises the question: what will be the objective in this war, and since it is a matter of weakening the house of Austria, which Austrian province will it be to our greatest advantage to dismember? Clearly it cannot be Moravia, squeezed as it is between the principality of Teschen, Hungary, Austria, and Bohemia, and hence impossible to hold. Such is not the case with Bohemia which, once detached from Austria, could offer considerable defense against anyone wishing to invade it by making some strongholds in the mountains sloping off toward Austria, and on the Bavarian frontier.

My knowledge of this kingdom convinces me that it can never be conquered if we wage the war here, because Bohemia is surrounded by a mountain chain that must be crossed if you wish to stage an invasion. All that the enemy has to do, therefore, is to have the passes you have crossed occupied by a large detachment to sever your line of communications and supply. But even assuming that the enemy is not of a mind to take this course of action, you will find yourself involved in a country bristling with mountains and defiles where the enemy can block the way, mile after mile, and where it is virtually impossible to bring about a decisive battle because of the mountains and forests that shelter the vanquished. Even assuming that, favored by a series of victories, you should become master of Prague, you then face the unfortunate choice either of weakening yourself substantially by leaving behind a strong garrison or of taking your entire army with you and exposing your magazines to the mercy of the first enemy attempts to surprise this capital.

For these reasons it is necessary to resort to other means to facilitate the conquest of Bohemia. The surest strategy, although difficult to execute, is to wage the war along the Danube in order thereby to force the Viennese court to withdraw its principal forces from Bohemia, and thus to enable the invading army to execute their plan. It is from all these reflections that I establish my present plan of campaign.

The distribution of the army must be such that 110,000 Prussians and 30,000 Russians are assembled in Upper Silesia. Of this number, 10,000 will be destined to defend Silberberg, the principality of Glatz, or to move toward Landshut in case the enemy should attempt any move in that quarter. Thirty thousand men will be designated to penetrate into the principality of Teschen by detachments and especially to protect the convoys of the army. The magazine for these troops must be at Kosel. The main army will advance on Neustadt so that the enemy, deceived by this demonstration, makes preparations to defend the mountain routes leading into Moravia from Jägerndorf and Troppau, or to line the Mohra, whose steep banks are bordered with boulders. The army of Saxony, comprising 60,000 Prussians, will disarm the Saxons, if that is necessary, and establish its camp between Gieshübel, Peterswalde, and so on, in the mountains. It will wage a war of detachments in Bohemia and will remain content with frequent demonstrations to make the enemy uneasy, acting as though it intended to invade Bohemia at the first opportunity. Its detachments could go in the direction of Dux and Teplitz, reach into the Circle of Saatz, and perhaps penetrate as far as the Eger.

The big army of Silesia, when all measures are taken, will

take up position and encamp between the villages of Troppau and Jägerndorf: nothing can more effectively confirm the enemy in the opinion that the Prussians will cross the mountains to advance in the direction of Olmütz. Then it is necessary to move by Hultschin, Fulnek, and Mährisch-Weisskirchen, making this detour to avoid the mountain defiles and poor crossings of the Mohra and to enter Moravia by the plain. At that time the provision depots must be established either in Fulnek or Weisskirchen, whichever would be more expedient, and to safeguard the supplies you must erect field fortifications complete with fougasses. From there the army must march on Prerau or Kremsier.

Clearly the enemy, seeing himself turned by the Prussians, will abandon the mountains and the Mohra in haste. It is difficult to predict what place he will choose for his new position, but according to all appearances he will resolve to defend the March River, which he will leave in his front. This river is difficult to cross because of its marshy banks, and it is probable that this will be the first trick of the enemy when he disputes the passage. But there are ways to do everything in the long run, and in all probability the two armies will come to blows as soon as the Prussians will have crossed this river. If the Prussians should win, the victory must be exploited by pursuing the enemy vigorously until the first considerable defiles are encountered. That done, you must detach a corps to seize all the crops, cattle, and provisions within a radius of about twenty miles from the city of Olmütz and to have all the cooking stoves in the houses destroyed, both to deprive this fortress of supplies and to prevent the garrison during the next winter from making sorties on the troops . . . blockading the fortress.

Defeated, the Austrian army probably will seek asylum under the guns of Brünn. Do not leave him there in peace, but attempt to cut off the provisions that he will draw from Austria by way of Znaim. You could then send strong detachments to Thaya that could even penetrate as far as the neighborhood of the Danube. If the campaign begins in June, you could draw a tight blockade around Olmütz; by the following March it would have been deprived of all aid for ten months and famine might force the commandant to surrender, or capitulate after a token defense.

This defeat would force the court of Vienna to reinforce its army in Moravia, with large detachments being drawn from Bohemia. This moment would serve as a signal for our army of Saxony to spring into action. In the campaign that followed you would have to turn the enemies in their post, attempt to carry off their detachments or to defeat them, and carry the war forcefully toward the Thaya and the banks of the Danube. The army of Saxony should drive the enemy before them energetically and take Prague—where you could leave the 10,000 men that would be drawn from Silberberg. The united army of Bohemia could advance by Budweis and Wittgenau toward Linz on the Danube. This position would deprive the Austrian army of all the provisions that it draws from the upper Danube, and since not all of the 30,000 men from the main army would be needed to cover the rear, these could be detached by Skalitz on Pressburg if the campaign were going well. The embarrassment of the Austrians would become extreme, and I believe that, placed in a position where they risked losing Vienna, they would go along with any peace proposals.

Admittedly this strategy is studded with considerable difficulties, and you must have good fortune to carry it to a successful conclusion. But no man succeeds in his enterprises, be it in politics, war, or any human operations based upon future contingencies and on the calculation of probabilities, unless fortune extends a helping hand.

Perhaps these plans will strike you as being too vast and ambitious. Do not believe that I am the only general who formulates such strategy. I have only to call your attention to some of Prince Eugene's plans. Not content with small objects, this greatly talented man tried instead to strike blows that decided the fate of thrones and nations. You can read about his campaigns in the history books; I am content here merely to summarize them in a few words. This hero wanted to surprise Crémone, the French headquarters. He penetrated into the town but could not maintain his position there because the detachments which were to have contributed to this surprise arrived too late. The stroke failed, but this is beside the point. Let us examine what would have followed the capture of Crémone had Prince Eugene been able to hold the town.

First, he would have taken prisoner all the French generals, and there would have been nobody in a position to issue orders to the troops dispersed in cantonments. He then would have pounced upon this scattered army and destroyed it in detail, and the fleeing remnants would have been extremely fortunate to regain the Alps in bands and take refuge in France. Thus the capture of only one-fourth of the French army would have purged all Lombardy of French troops and restored Lombardy, together with Mantua and Parma, under the domination of the Austrians.

The man is not yet born whose plans all have succeeded, but if you conceive only small plans you always will be only a mediocre man; whereas if you succeed in only two out of ten enterprises in which you are involved, you will immortalize your name. Even if Prince Eugene failed in his coup against Crémone, it turned out that he made up for it handsomely by this masterly march that he made on Turin. He left detachments of the French army behind him to force La Feuillade from his intrenchments at Turin, and by this single blow rid Italy of the French, who, at the beginning of the war in 1701, were masters of it. A plan quite similar was that of attacking the French and Bavarians at Höchstädt, where they were defeated. The loss of this battle forced the French and Bavarians to abandon Bavaria and Swabia, and they considered themselves secure only after having recrossed the Rhine. . . .

Nor is it enough to have studied Prince Eugene as the model of the great generals. It will be no less useful to examine the mistakes that either the ministers of the court or the generals committed for lack of judgment and knowledge in devising their enterprises poorly. These examples are only too numerous: I will not probe into antiquity to point out the blunders of past eras, but will cite only the modern follies that . . . are more familiar to you.

Charles XII first comes to mind, the bravest and the least rational general that perhaps there has ever been. . . . It is a rule of war that deep penetrations should never be made and that wars waged near to the frontiers always produce more successful results than those where the army is ventured too far. . . . from its magazines . . . without protecting its rear and having provided for its security. But whoever made more clumsy abuses of deep penetrations than Charles XII. . . . The calamities that attended him he brought on himself by ignoring all the rules of war and by following his whims.[18]

The war that the Austrians undertook against the Turks in 1736 took such a bad turn for them only because of their false management. Prince Eugene considered the Danube as the wet nurse of the armies operating in Hungary, and he strayed from this river as little as possible. The court of Vienna, which did not even know Hungary, made plans that took his troops away from this river entirely, thus changing the strategy in the very midst of operations. The first comer with any brainstorm, in a manner of speaking, influenced the orders that the Emperor Charles VI gave to his armies, and that ruined all of his affairs. I shall not conceal the fact, however, that the poor conduct of his generals played its part in the disasters that this war brought to the Imperial house.

If we examine carefully the elements that ruined the French hopes to reduce the house of Austria in the year 1741, we will find most of them rooted in the false measures that the French took to carry out such a grand design. The French wanted to dismember the Austrian monarchy and to separate it from lower Austria, Bohemia, Moravia, and Silesia, which the Prussians had just seized. They figured on the help of 12,000 Bavarians and 25,000 Saxons, not counting the Prussian army, which was operating against the principal Austrian forces. The greater the plans, the greater must be the means to their execution. It would have suited the interests of France to have joined the Elector of Bavaria with an army of 80,000 men, to terminate this war in one campaign and also to have, with all of these troops, a preponderance over their allies. Far from adopting such a wise measure, the French merely sent 30,000 men to attack the Queen of Hungary in her states and to crush the powerful house of Austria. And even that would have succeeded if, after the capture of Linz, the French and Bavarians had marched directly against Vienna, for this capital was virtually defenseless and could not have resisted long. The King of Prussia himself would certainly have approached the Danube in haste, and all probabilities lead to the belief that France would have dictated the terms of peace. But either the French did not perceive these advantages or they miscalculated, which is quite possible in view of the fact that after the capture of Linz they turned without any valid reason toward Bohemia. This irreparable mistake ruined their great hopes and was the cause of all the misfortunes that they endured afterwards. May we learn from that how pernicious is false logic in this profession, and may we learn to reason accurately.

Let us note on this occasion that wars undertaken by a prince far from his frontiers rarely succeed, because the distance of his supply lines prevents recruits, remounts, munitions, and other needed supplies from arriving in time, and because the communications sometimes intercepted prevent him from passing on the necessary help. In offensive warfare you must either provide everything necessary for great enterprises or, lacking this, you must renounce your vast plans.

## WARS BETWEEN EQUAL FORCES

War waged between equal forces poses a different set of problems. You must limit your strategy to your forces and not risk undertaking that which you have not the means of executing. To be sure, the court can command a general to direct his efforts to gain this river or take that city, but it cannot prescribe his operations in any detail because, not having sufficient numbers of troops to force the enemy to follow his lead, the general must procure all the advantages over this enemy by himself, through his cunning and skill. It is in this kind of war that you reap greater benefit from the skin of a fox than from the hide of a lion.[14] CUNNING SUCCEEDS where force fails. It is therefore essential to use both, since force often is repulsed by force and on other occasions is obliged to yield to guile.

There are an infinite number of stratagems,* and I have no desire to cite the entire list here. They all have the same objective, which is to induce the enemy to make the unnecessary marches that we desire. We endeavor to conceal the real plan and to create an illusion for the benefit of the enemy by feigning views that we do not hold. When the troops are on the verge of assembling, we have them make several countermarches to alarm the enemy and conceal the point where we want to assemble the army and invade.

If you are in a country where there are fortresses, proceed to encamp in a spot menacing two or three places simultaneously. If the enemy throws troops in all these places he weakens himself, and you can take advantage of this to fall upon a portion of his army with your united forces. But if he has taken the precaution of reinforcing only one such fortress, then move against the city or stronghold where he has not sent help, and besiege it.

If it is your intention to make yourself master of an important post or to cross a river, you must withdraw your forces from the objective to entice the enemy after you, and when you have prepared everything and stolen a march, turn around at one swoop at the intended spot and seize it.

If you wish to fight the enemy and he appears to be avoiding a scrap, have the word spread that your army is diminished or give every indication that you fear the enemy. We played this role before the battle of Hohenfriedberg, when I had the roads repaired as though I intended, on the approach of Prince Charles, to march in four columns on Breslau. His vanity played into my hands by enticing him onto the plain, where he was defeated.

Sometimes we narrow the size of the camp to make it appear weaker and make small detachments that are announced to be considerable, so that the enemy scorns our weakness and gives up his advantage. If it had been my intention to take Königgrätz and Pardubitz in the campaign of 1745, I would only have had two marches to make by the county of Glatz in the direction of Moravia, and Prince Charles would not have failed to go there, because this demonstration would have aroused his fears for Moravia, the source of his provisions, so that he would have had to abandon Bohemia. For the enemy always takes fear whenever his communications with the capital and his lines of supply are threatened.

If you have no inclination to fight, let it be known that you are stronger than you actually are and put up a bold front. The Austrians are past masters in this art, and it is from them that one must learn. By virtue of your bearing you will give the impression of wanting to fight the enemy. Have the report spread that you have the most daring plans and often the enemy believes that his chances would be problematical if you should come, and he, too, holds himself on the defensive.[15]

OFTEN YOU MUST DECEIVE your own troops as well as the enemy, and this occurs when you are on the defensive. I call this waging a war of posture. . . . An army must always put up a good front, and when it is on the verge of withdrawing, it should give the enemy the impression that it intends to fight.

Always conceal your intentions from the enemy. Try to penetrate his plans. Reflect long and carefully, act quickly and promptly, never lack provisions, and in the long run you will be master of your enemy. But never be lulled into a false sense of security, and be especially alert after success. Good fortune can be dangerous in that it inspires a sense of security and a scorn for the enemy. That was the reason that so great a man as Prince Eugene lost his magazines at Marchienne after the battle of Denain [1712].[10]

ONE METHOD of outfoxing the enemy that cannot be recommended too highly is to be the first to enter on campaign, for in this way you win terrain and often either surprise the enemy or are presented with the opportunity to defeat a detachment in detail. A general must keep a firm resolution to assume the offensive as soon as the occasion presents itself. At the beginning of the campaign you must carefully conceal your intentions, put the enemy on the wrong scent, and know everything possible about the opposing general, his method, and his way of operating. The more you can penetrate the mind of your opponent, the better able you are to deceive him. You gain superiority over the enemy by striking a surprise blow at his camp, by overwhelming part of his army. . . . by winning decisive battles, by seizing the enemy's magazines, or finally, by placing yourself astride the enemy's communications and thereby forcing him to retreat and yield terrain. . . . But in menacing the enemy's magazines and communications, you must not forget to place your own in safety.

So as not to weary you with a succession of general rules, I will cite the example of a skillful general who, by his sagacity and genius, changed the form of the war that he waged. The general is Luxembourg, and you can read about his campaign of 1683 in the *Military History of Louis XIV*. The King had resolved to wage offensive war in Flanders; then he changed his plan and detached 40,000 men from the army which, under the command of the great Dauphin, was to march into Germany. The Prince of Orange, commanding the allied army, was encamped at Parc and appeared hard put simultaneously to support Liége and Louvain, both of which the French threatened to besiege. Immediately after the departure of these 40,-000 men, Luxembourg took the camp of Melder, and by this position he kept the Prince of Orange on edge. The latter immediately sent 12,000 men to occupy the intrenched camp at Liege.

Soon Luxembourg had a train of artillery prepared at Namur, which was then in the hands of the French. On hearing this news, the Prince of Orange sent additional reinforcements to the camp at Liege and arrived to encamp himself near Gete, between the villages of Landen and Neerwinden. This was not enough for Luxembourg, who wanted his enemy to weaken himself still more. Accordingly, Luxembourg sent a large detachment from his army under the pretext of marching toward the jurisdiction of Courtrai. But he had given the generals secret orders on how they must conduct their march. As soon as the Prince of Orange got wind of this detachment he sent the Duke of Württemberg with a large body of troops to oppose the French ventures, whereupon Luxembourg put his own army in motion and, joined en route by his detachment, he defeated the Prince of Orange at Neerwinden.

This victory, and the superiority that it gave him over the allies, was due to his genius alone. Weakened by the troops that the King had sent to Germany, he was even inferior in forces to the Prince of Orange. Yet his skill rendered him superior to his enemy and he finished the campaign with the siege of Charleroi, which he took. This example must always be present in the mind of a general who operates against an army of equal strength, not so that he can employ the same ruse but so that he can use similar ones. . . .

The reader should have no difficulty in understanding that the man who does not have a fertile imagination in resources and in expedients, who neither thinks about nor studies the profession of war, will never succeed in accomplishing similar achievements.

### DEFENSIVE WARFARE

I come now to defensive warfare, which requires still more skill than offensive warfare or a war between equals, if it is to be well conducted.

There are three times to wage defensive warfare; first,

when your troops are not numerous enough to act vigorously against the enemy; second, when your troops have been discouraged and weakened by some failure; and third, when you wait for help. It is a general rule of this kind of war never to limit yourself to a passive defense, and above all, not to lose sight of the idea of changing to the offensive at the first opportunity. Ignorant officers believe that they ·wage defensive war well when they retreat before their enemies to avoid every battle. So it was with the Duke of Cumberland who, having lost the battle of Hastenbeck by his own fault and because he conceded defeat, fled as far as Stade, on the seacoast, where he signed a disgraceful surrender with Marshal Richelieu. Had he been a general, this prince would not have abandoned 150 miles of territory so thoughtlessly, but would at least have contested the ground foot by foot and abandoned only what he could not hold. In this way he could have prolonged the war, and in consequence, he would without doubt have found occasions to place himself on an equal footing with the French.

Defensive strategy must be deeply thought out. Posts can be found that cover entire provinces and from which one can inspire fear even in enemy provinces. These posts must be occupied according to all the rules of the art, and since you must anticipate everything that a skillful general could plan against the interests of your state, you can assume that the enemy by his movements forces you to leave your place of defense. Therefore you must, in advance, have some other camp at one side or the other by which you can hold the enemy equally in check. Always think about the most dangerous plans that could be made against you, and seek always to have the means ready to counter them. Then if these plans materialize you will not be caught napping. . . .

Never base your defense on rivers unless they cut between rocks and have steep banks. You can defend a river that lies behind the army, but it has yet to be shown how a river in front of the armies can successfully be held.[17] AS MANY TIMES as you take up a position behind a river to keep the enemy from crossing it, that often you will be duped, because sooner or later the enemy, forced to display cunning, finds a suitable moment for stealing his crossing. Then you are often dependent upon the activity or the intelligence of an officer who makes patrols. If you divide your army to occupy the most likely places for a crossing, you risk being beaten in detail; if your forces are concentrated, the least that could happen to you is a withdrawal in confusion to select another post; in either case you have lost the stake because you have been unable to prevent the enemy from executing his plans.

I therefore reject this former method[18] of preventing a river crossing, which experience condemns, and I propose the simpler and surer method which, if executed by a skillful general, avoids the chance of being surprised by the enemy, of being informed too late, and, above all, of dividing the general's attention, which is the greatest difficulty of all, in my estimation. . . .

¶ Therefore this is what I propose: the only way to defend a river is to keep it behind you. You must have good communications established with the other side of the river, you must have at least two bridges, each of which is protected by intrenched bridgeheads, and you must take up your position two or three miles in front, in a camp so well adapted that the enemy would assuredly be defeated if he attacked you there, even assuming that his army was three times the size of yours. . . . With such a camp you prevent the enemy from crossing the river, because if he marches on either side to cross it he is compelled to abandon to you the provisions and magazines that he has behind him, which he certainly will not do.

What courses, therefore, remain open to him? No doubt he will attempt to make a river crossing with some detachment, but this detachment is forced to move along an arc in order to pass you and you will send a detachment on a direct line by your bridge which, moving to the side where the enemy wishes to cross, will be quite capable of defeating him in detail. If, however, the entire enemy army should desire to cross on one side of your army or the other by a simple movement, you have only to march against its rear and profit from the frightful confusion caused by your approach. This plan is simple, it frees you from uneasiness, and it concentrates all your ideas on the same point.[19]

A GENERAL CHARGED with a defensive war must be awake to the slightest fault of the enemy and must make him commit a mistake, if he can, in order to profit from the slightest negligences. As long as the enemy observes the rules of the art, remains vigilant, profits well from the terrain, encamps advantageously, does not easily risk his detachments, covers his marches and makes them in good order, assures his provisions, and forages with precaution, it is nearly impossible for the most gifted captain to attack him with any hope of success. But if the enemy is negligent, if he makes mistakes, you must profit either by attacking yourself—if the enemy's camp is poorly selected—by engaging in a rear guard action, if his poor leadership causes this, or by waging a war of attrition in seizing the enemy's convoys, defeating his foragers, and even by taking advantage of winter to fall upon his quarters, if they are not sufficiently secure. Multiplied, such small successes are the equivalent of a battle won, and in the long run, they decide the superiority.

I cannot cite a more perfect example of a defensive war well conducted on these principles than Prince Ferdinand's campaign in 1758 where, at the head of the same troops with which the Duke of Cumberland had been so cowardly, the Prince fell upon the French quarters, chased the enemy from the counties of Brunswick and Hanover and made them recross the Weser, the Lippe, and the Rhine in less than two months of operations. . . . The campaigns that he made afterwards, although less brilliant, are of the same style because the French had no fewer than 100,000 men in Germany, against which Prince Ferdinand could oppose only 60,000. This inferiority, which would have discouraged anyone else, did not prevent him from covering all lower Saxony and a part of Westphalia against the enterprises of the French, nor did it prevent him from defeating the latter twice in the course of one campaign. . . . He alone was worth 40,000 men to the allied army. . . .

If an army is reduced to the defensive by some reverse or lost battle, the rule and experience require that you retreat as little as possible after a defeat. It is rare indeed if a general does not find some position within a mile or two from the field of battle, and here he must stop for the following reasons. The farther you flee the more you augment your losses: the wounded who drag themselves along with difficulty for two miles cannot follow you three or four times that distance and as a result, are captured by the enemy. The more you shorten the road of your retreat the less your soldiers will leave the ranks. Observe further that in yielding little terrain to the enemy you diminish his victory considerably, because war is waged only to win territory. Above all, add to these reflections that an army is never less disposed to fight than immediately after a victory, when everyone shouts for joy, each exaggerates his great feats of arms, the multitude is delighted to have passed successfully out of great dangers, and nobody has any desire to face these dangers on the field. No general will lead his victorious troops into fire again on the next day. You can remain in your camp in complete safety and give your troops time to collect themselves. The soldiers will again get accustomed to the sight of the enemy, and in a short while their minds will recover their natural disposition.

If your enemy is 60,000 strong and you have only 45,000, you must not be in the least discouraged, because you have 100 ways to be avenged for your disgrace. Forty-five thousand men well led are worth more than 60,000 under a mediocre general. If you have only 30,000 men left against 60,000, which we assume is the strength of your enemy, your case becomes more perplexing and more dexterity undoubtedly is necessary if you are to avoid some unfortunate mishap. It is impossible that with 30,000 men you can re-establish a kind of equality between the two armies: if you should destroy even a detachment of 10,000 men, you will still remain inferior by too wide a margin to be able to dictate to the enemy, unless your opposite number is the most inept and the biggest imbecile of men.

The only course left for you, therefore, is to take impregnable posts wherever they are at hand, to maintain for yourself especially the free exits and areas to the rear, to wage war as a partisan rather than as an army commander, to shift posts if it is found necessary, and at the first sign that the enemy makes to attack you, to wage a war of posture rather than a real war, to procure all the small advantages that you can in order to command the respect and moderate the impetuosity of the enemy, and finally, to take advantage of everything that your industry, imagination, and mental resources provide by way of means and expedients for maintaining yourself.

The detachments that the enemy is in a position to make are those that are the most troublesome for small armies. If you oppose them with a detachment from your own small army, it cannot resist the larger enemy detachment, and at the same time you weaken your own army still further. If you have no troops to oppose enemy detachments, you run the risk of having your supplies or communication lines cut. If the enemy detachment is at a great distance from his main army, it would be better to fall upon it with your entire force in order to defeat it and thereby intimidate your adversary. Even so, it must be agreed that it is troublesome and unpleasant for the general who finds himself in this position, and he must redouble his activity, vigilance, presence of mind, and industry, if he can, in order to extricate himself with honor.

But in the case . . . where you have 45,000 troops against 60,000, the difficulties are not nearly so considerable, because if you are not strong enough to attack you have sufficient men at least to defend yourself. Often the enemy grows presumptuous after some recent advantages: believing himself sure of his fortune, he scorns the defeated and takes chances. He treats war as a trifle and no longer believes in the need to follow the rules of the art rigidly. He decides without reflection, acts without thinking, and gives you openings that you must seize, to regain the ascendancy over him that you lost as the result of a disastrous day. If you notice that security lulls the enemy, you must augment this feeling, because it is the forerunner of disasters that lie in wait.

And, finally, set traps of all kinds so that if the enemy does not fall into one he will not escape the others. Pretend to want to retreat before him, seek to cause him to make some false step, and take advantage of his slightest oversight without delay. If you are weaker than the enemy and await help, you commit an impardonable imprudence if you risk the least enterprise before help can reach you, because by your impatience you risk losing the advantages that these reinforcements surely would give you if you allowed them time to join you. It is therefore only in such cases where the general must restrict himself to the defensive in the strictest sense of the term.

## SUMMARY

The following is a résumé of the general maxims we have just established, which will provide abridged rules for strategy, according to the situation in which one finds himself.

1. Whoever wants to undertake a war must procure accurate knowledge of the strength of the enemy that he is about to fight and of the assistance that the enemy can draw from his allies, in order to compare the enemy's forces to his own and to judge which side is superior.

2. It is necessary to have an accurate knowledge of the nature of the country where one wants to wage war, in order to arrange the details of the intended expedition accordingly.

3. You must pay the greatest attention to the provisions you will need for this campaign, and must not limit your activities to collecting them, but must think beforehand of means to facilitate their transport. For nothing is executed with the most prosperous army if it lacks food.

These general rules are for every kind of war possible. Here are the particulars for offensive warfare.

1. Your strategy must pursue an important objective. Undertake only what is possible and reject whatever is chimerical. If you are not fortunate enough to follow a great plan through to its perfection, you will nevertheless go much farther than the generals who, acting without plan, make war from day to day. Give battle only when you have reason to hope that your success will be decisive, and fight not only to defeat the enemy, but to execute the course of your strategy that would fail but for this decision.

2. Never deceive yourself, but picture skillfully all the measures that the enemy will take to oppose your plans, in order never to be caught by surprise. Then, having foreseen everything in advance, you will already have remedies prepared for any eventuality.

3. Know the mind of the opposing generals in order better to divine their actions, to know how to force your actions upon them, and to know what traps to use against them.

4. The opening of your campaign must be an enigma for the enemy, preventing him from guessing the side on which your forces will move and the strategy you contemplate.

5. Always attempt the unexpected: this is the surest way to achieve success.

In a war between equals:

1. The more you employ stratagems and ruses, the more advantages you will enjoy over the enemy. You must deceive him and induce him to make mistakes in order to take advantage of his faults.

2. Always have as a goal to transform the war into an offensive on your part as soon as the occasion presents itself. All your maneuvers must lead toward this end.

3. Consider all the mischief that the enemy can do to you and prevent it by your prudence.

4. Do not attack the enemy when he adheres to the rules of war, but profit from his slightest mistakes without delay. Whoever lets the occasion escape is not worthy of seizing it.

5. Profit from the battles you win, follow the enemy to the utmost, and push your advantages as far as you can extend them, because such happy events are not common.

6. Leave as little to fortune as possible by your foresight—chance will still have too much influence in military operations. It is enough that your prudence shares the stage with chance.

7. To win advantages over the enemy you must procure them, both by a war of partisans and by defeating his escorts, seizing his provisions, surprising his magazines, often defeating his detachments . . . [and] his rear guard, attacking him on the march, and finally, by engaging in battle with him, if he is badly posted, and even by surprising his winter quarters and falling on his posts if he has not provided for the security of his cantonments during the winter.

Here are the general maxims you must observe for defensive warfare.

1. Intend to put all your resources to work to change the nature of this war.

2. Anticipate everything detrimental the enemy can plan against you, and study expedients to elude his designs.

3. Choose impregnable camps that can contain the enemy by threatening his rear in the event that he changes posts, and be sure to cover your own magazines.

4. Accumulate many small advantages which, taken together, are the equivalent of great advantages. Try to make the enemy respect you in order to contain him by the fear of your arms.

5. Calculate all your movements carefully and observe the maxims and rules of tactics and castrametation strictly.

6. If you have advantages, make the most of them, and punish the enemy for his slightest errors, as though you were a pedagogue.

If you are on the defensive after losing a battle:

1. Your retreat must be short. You must get your troops accustomed again to looking the enemy in the face. Encourage

them little by little, and wait for the proper moment to avenge your defeat.

2. Make use of ruses, stratagems, false information imparted to the enemy to lead to the happy moment when you can pay him back in his own coin—with interest—for the damage he did to you.

If you are less than half as strong as the enemy:

1. Wage partisan warfare: change the post whenever necessary.

2. Do not detach any unit from your troops because you will be beaten in detail. Act only with your entire army.

3. If you can throw your army against the enemy's communications without risking your own magazines, do so.

4. Activity and vigilance must be on the watch day and night at the door of your tent.

5. Give more thought to your rear than to your front, in order to avoid being enveloped.

6. Reflect incessantly on devising new ways and means of supporting yourself. Change your method to deceive the enemy. You will often be forced to wage a war of appearances.

7. Defeat and destroy the enemy in detail if it is at all possible, but do not commit yourself to a pitched battle, because your weakness will make you succumb. Win time—that is all that can be expected of the most skillful general.

8. Do not retreat toward places where you can be surrounded: remember [Charles XII at] Poltava without forgetting [the Duke of Cumberland at] Stade.

Of an army on the defensive awaiting reinforcements:

You risk everything by becoming involved in some undertaking before the juncture of your forces which, when united, would render you sure of whatever you would want to attempt. Thus you must confine yourself to the sphere of the strictest defensive during the period of concentration.

You can see by this presentation the extent to which the

knowledge of a real general must be varied. He must have an accurate idea of politics in order to be informed of the intention of princes and the forces of states and of their communications; to know the number of troops that the princes and their allies can put into the field; and to judge the condition of their finances. Knowledge of the country where he must wage war serves as the base for all strategy. He must be able to imagine himself in the enemy's shoes in order to anticipate all the obstacles that are likely to be placed in his way. Above all, he must train his mind to furnish him with a multitude of expedients, ways and means in case of need. All this requires study and exercise. For those who are destined for the military profession, peace must be a time of meditation, and war the period where one puts his ideas into practice.[20]

## NOTES: CHAPTER IX

1. Von Berenhorst (1733-1814), a natural son of Old Dessauer and sometime aide-de-camp or Adjutant of Frederick, defined *strategy* as the art of marching, *tactics* as the art of fighting. According to the Prussian theorist Freiherr Dietrich von Bülow (1757-1807), "(strategy) is the science of military movement beyond the visual circle of the enemy, or out of cannon shot." The word *strategy*, which is not to be confused with the eighteenth century term *stratagem*, or *ruses de guerre*, entered the English language toward the beginning of the nineteenth century, and periodically was redefined, as war and society became increasingly complex and intermingled. Some idea of the original confusion over the sense of the word is suggested in the English translation of the explanations on the maps in "Eléments de castramétrie et de tactique," which was published in 1811 under the title *The Strategical Instructions of Frederick the Second*.

2. Frederick, "Réflexions sur les projets de campagne," *Oeuvres de Frédéric le Grand* (Berlin, 1846-56), XXIX, 69-70 [*Projets de campagne*].

3. Frederick, "Pensées et règles générales pour la guerre," *ibid.*, XXVIII, 123-24 [*Règles générales*].

4. Frederick, *Projets de campagne*, p. 70.

5. The Silesian wars, 1740-42, 1744-45.

6. This would be the second Silesian war.

7. Frederick, *Instruction militaire du Roi de Prusse pour ses généraux*

(Frankfurt, 1761), pp. 9-15. The order of several passages has been changed to provide greater continuity of thought.

8. Frederick, *Règles générales*, pp. 125-26.

9. Frederick, *Projets de campagne*, pp. 70-71.

10. See below, pp. 328-30.

11. Frederick, *Règles générales*, pp. 124-26.

12. Writing in 1775, Frederick obviously was counting upon the Russians to live up to the treaty of mutual assistance signed in 1764 and renewed five years later.

13. For Frederick's analysis of the generalship of Charles XII, see Chapter X.

14. Frederick, *Projets de campagne*, pp. 71-83.

15. Frederick, *Instruction militaire*, pp. 70-73.

16. Frederick, *Règles générales*, pp. 131-32.

17. Frederick, *Projets de campagne*, pp. 83-86.

18. In his *Instructions* to his generals, Frederick originally recommended a concentration behind the river as the only means of defending a river line, and this only when the bank on the far side was commanded by higher ground on their own side of the river. Manifestly his experiences during the Seven Years' War altered his thinking, for in his later writings the course he recommends is just the opposite of that found in *Instruction militaire*, pp. 119-24.

19. Frederick, "Eléments de castramétrie et de tactique," *Oeuvres*, XXIX, 26-27.

20. Frederick, *Projets de campagne*, pp. 86-94.

# X

# *Generalship as an Art*

Frederick never ceased to ponder the lessons of his own past campaigns and those of his eminent predecessors. The following *Reflections on Charles XII*, written toward the end of 1759, represents in part Frederick's desire to find relief from the gout and other "distracting cares" by excursions into literature and history, but it also serves to summarize the wisdom and judgment of a Great Captain on the applied art of generalship.

Charles XII of Sweden (1682–1719) was one of the most spectacular practitioners in history. He was a king who succeeded ultimately in ruining the position and resources of his own country, a general who so often accomplished the impossible that even the rationalists began to suspect him of miracles. He was a man without peer for bravery and with few rivals—save for the early monks—in his willingness to set aside all earthly temptations. (The main difference between the personal lives of Charles and that of the early Christian martyrs is that the glory he cherished belonged to this world rather than the next.) This reincarnation of Alexander had already caught the eye of theorists like the Chevalier de Folard, who had once offered his services to the young king, and Voltaire, who detected in the person of Charles all the heroic virtues carried to excess and in his career, a sober warning to sovereigns (particularly his own) "to reject the madness of conquering." If Charles, for all his great skill and his magnificent soldiers, had failed, what, Voltaire wondered, "may other princes expect, who shall have as much ambition, with less talent and fewer resources."[1]

Frederick naturally saw other lessons to be learned from the campaigns of Charles. Having recently crossed the Oder at Köben, near the famous mill where the Count von Schulenberg's rear guard had held off the Swedes until the Saxon army could elude its pursuers in 1704, he conceived the idea of analyzing the military talents and character of Charles XII. "You will remember," he subsequently explained to his young literary crony, Henri de Catt, "that I have always said to you that the prevalent notions concerning this conqueror were neither clear enough nor precise enough. . . . I have not followed Voltaire, who sometimes praises and sometimes blames, according to the way the wind of circumstance and interest blows. . . . His contradictions . . . will be an eternal blot on the gentleman historiographer of the chamber. . . . I think that soldiers who read me will find that I have set down exactly what should be thought of so extraordinary a prince. . . . Never having read anything impartial or accurate about this prince, I desire that my work should have these two merits. . . ."[2]

Historians, moralists, philosophers, and poets have all been intrigued with the character of Charles XII. Here, then, is the considered and professional judgment by one national hero of another; by a general who preached (but did not always practice) obedience to the rules of the art, of another who for a time managed to dominate men and events alike by the force of his personality; and by a king well aware of his immense responsibilities of a brother monarch who galloped out of the pages of King Arthur—and into the limitless Russian forests.

## REFLECTIONS ON CHARLES XII

*I HAVE ENDEAVORED* for my own information to obtain a just idea of the character and military talents of Charles XII. I estimate his worth neither from the pictures drawn by his panegyrists nor from those drawn by his critics. Eyewitnesses and memoirs generally acknowledged to be authentic have been my guides. We ought to suspect all those particulars and minute relations which we too often find in history. Of a multitude of fictions and satirical remarks, few things are presented that are worthy of our notice.

Among those turbulent spirits who have been devoured by the passion to reign, those rulers who have fought to render nations happy or to subject them to servitude, none deserves to fix our attention except he whose genius was capable of embracing all things, and whose powers of mind created circumstances, as it were, from nothing, or profited by the most advantageous of those which presented themselves, to effect essential changes in the political relations between states.

Such was the genius of Caesar. The services he had rendered the republic, his great defects, his still greater virtues, and his fortunate victories all united to raise him to the empire of the world. Gustavus, Turenne, Eugene, and Marlborough, in a more confined sphere, were animated by the same spirit. Some of these great men made their operations conform to the plan they intended to pursue during one campaign; others united all their labors and several campaigns, to the chief object of the war they carried on, and their goal is discovered when we attentively pursue their enterprises, which were conducted with prudence and seconded by audacity, and which often were crowned with splendid success.

Such was the plan of Cromwell, that ambitious assassin of a king, and of Richelieu, that adroit priest who, in consequence of his perseverance, obtained the power by which he governed the grandees of the Kingdom with the iron sceptre of despotism, almost extirpated the Protestants, and humbled the Austrian monarchs, the irreconcilable enemies of France.

I do not intend to examine by what right Caesar overthrew the republic of which he was a member, nor is this the place to decide whether the Cardinal did good or harm to France during his administration, nor even to question how far Turenne deserved reproaches for having served the Spaniards against his country. We shall speak here only of the real value of great qualities and not of the proper or improper manner in which they have been employed.

The violent passions of Charles were, it is true, often obliged to cede to the estimates and sage measures of politics; but this king nevertheless is one of those unique apparitions that have excited the fear and astonishment of Europe. The grandeur and splendor of his actions surpass the expectation of the most ardent and determined warrior. King of a valiant nation and arbitrator of the north, he suffered excessive misfortunes. Forced to seek asylum among barbarians, by whom he was finally taken prisoner, he merits observation both during his good and his ill fortune, neither of which can be indifferent to warriors.

My intention is not to diminish the worth of this hero. I only mean to observe him with greater accuracy that I may exactly determine in what he ought to be imitated and proposed as an example.

To imagine a man who has attained perfect knowledge of any science whatever would be as ridiculous as to pretend that fire quenches thirst and that water satisfies hunger. To inform the hero that he has been guilty of error is but to make him remember he is a man. Kings, generals, ministers, authors, in brief, all you who must appear on the great world stage, are equally subjected to the decisions of your contemporaries and to the sentence of unpardoning posterity.

The tooth of criticism can make an impression only on excellence; bad writings are not worth the critic's trouble. It is the same with all the paths leading to the temple of fame. Common mortals are allowed to pass on without attracting attention, but the penetrating eye is fixed on those with uncommon talents who endeavor to open new roads for themselves.

Charles XII is, from many considerations, excusable in not having possessed all the perfections of the art of war. This difficult art is not innate with man. Though nature should have bestowed upon us superior genius, profound study and long experience are not the less necessary for the improvement of the most auspicious qualities. It is necessary for the warrior to begin his career under the guidance of a great captain or to be taught the principles of his trade at much expense and peril, and after having received many lessons. We cannot possibly deceive ourselves when we assume that all the capacity of a great general did not exist in a youth who was a king at sixteen.

Charles XII first saw the enemy when he first saw himself at the head of his forces. I shall here take occasion to remark that all those who have commanded armies in their early youth have imagined that only courage and rashness were necessary for victory. Pyrrhus, the great Condé, and our hero are examples of this.

But since the discovery of gunpowder has changed the art of war, the whole system has, in consequence, been changed. Strength of body, the first quality among the heroes of antiquity, is at present of no significance. Stratagem vanquishes strength, and art overcomes courage. The understanding of the general has more influence on the fortunate or unfortunate consequences of the campaign than the prowess of the combatants. Prudence prepares and traces the route that valor must pursue; boldness directs the execution, and ability, not good fortune, wins the applause of the well informed. Our young officers may learn the theory of this difficult science by studying some classical works, and train themselves by frequenting the society of men of experience.

These were the resources that the King of Sweden lacked. Whether it was to amuse him or to inspire him to love the Latin tongue, which he hated, he was obliged to translate the ingenious romance of Quintus Curtius; it is possible that this book awakened in him the desire to imitate Alexander. But it could not provide him with those rules that appertain to a more recent military art. Charles indeed, generally speaking, owed nothing to art but everything to nature. His genius was not resplendent with acquired knowledge, but his mind bore the stamp of audacity to excess and fortitude not to be shaken, so that it was capable of forming the greatest resolutions. Fame was the idol to which everything was sacrificed. His actions, by themselves, gain when they are examined more closely in proportion as his plans suffer loss. The firmness with which he opposed misfortune, his indefatigable activity in all his enterprises, and a heroic courage which was blind to danger were certainly the characteristic traits of this extraordinary monarch.

Destined by nature to be a hero, the young King followed the irresistible inclination that hurried him along at the moment that the cupidity of his neighbors provoked him to war. His character, which until then had been misunderstood, suddenly displayed itself. But it is time to follow the hero on his various expeditions. I mean to confine my remarks to his nine first campaigns, which open a vast field for observation.

The Danish King made war on the Duke of Holstein, who had married the sister of Charles. Instead of sending troops into Holstein, where they could only have aided in the ruin of the country he wished to protect, he ordered 8,000 men into Pomerania. He himself proceeded to Zealand with his fleet, repulsed the enemy troops guarding the coast, besieged Copenhagen, the capital of his foe, and in less than six weeks forced the King of Denmark to conclude a peace which was very advantageous to the Duke of Holstein.

The plan and its execution were equally admirable. By this first essay, Charles raised himself to the rank of Scipio, who carried the war into Africa that he might force Carthage to recall Hannibal from Italy.

From Zealand I shall accompany the young hero into Livonia, whither his troops marched with incredible speed; the *veni, vidi, vici* of Caesar were perfectly applicable to the entire campaign. The same enthusiasm that inspired the King in his enterprises animates our imagination at the recital of his memorable victory.

The conduct of Charles was sagely audacious, and by no means rash. It was necessary to relieve the town of Narva, which the Czar [Peter the Great] besieged in person, and for this purpose he was obliged to attack and to vanquish the Russians. Their army was numerous, but it was only a swarm of ill-armed barbarians, without discipline or commanders. The Swedes therefore might expect to gain the same advantages over the Muscovites as the Spaniards obtained over the savage tribes of America. Their success was perfectly correspondent to their hopes, and Europe heard with astonishment that 8,000 Swedes had beaten and dispersed 80,000 Russians [1700].

From this triumph I shall accompany the hero to another victory on the banks of the Duna, the only action in which he employed stratagem and by which he profited like a consummate general.

The Saxons were on the opposite shore, and Charles deceived them by an artifice he invented. He concealed his maneuvers by the thick smoke of wetted straw, under cover of which, together with an uninterrupted cannonade, he caused his troops to cross the river before old General Heinau, commanding the Saxons, had time to suspect such an action. Scarcely were the Swedes on the opposite side of the water before they were formed in order of battle to fall on the enemy. The cavalry made several attacks and the infantry, a few discharges, and the Saxons were dispersed and took to flight.

How splendid was such conduct! On passing the river how great was the presence of mind, the activity that Charles displayed, while he placed his troops in order of battle at the very moment that they landed, one unit following another! What valor did he demonstrate in gaining the victory so rapidly and with so much honor! Measures taken and executed after this manner merit the praise of all ages and of all nations.

But it is inconceivable to recollect that we are obliged to seek the master strokes of Charles in his first campaigns. Was it that he was spoiled by the uninterrupted favors of fortune? Or could he suppose that a man whom nothing resisted had no need of art? Or did his courage, as admirable as it was astonishing, so far mislead him as to entail on him the defeat of those warriors who possess no virtue but rashness?

Hitherto Charles had turned his arms only against foes whom he was forced to fight in his own defense. But after the battle of the Duna we lose sight of his objective. We perceive only a great number of enterprises without connection and without design, intermingled with brilliant actions, but which in no manner contributed to produce that great effect that he might reasonably have proposed to himself in making war.

The Czar, beyond any doubt, was Sweden's most powerful and dangerous enemy. Should not the hero have returned in search of him immediately after defeating the Saxons? The remains of the army beaten at Narva were not yet reunited.

Peter I had hastily assembled 30,000 or 40,000 newly raised men who were not of greater value than the 80,000 whom Charles had disarmed. He ought therefore to have attacked Peter again vigorously, to have driven him out of Ingria, and not to have given him time to re-collect himself. He should have profited by this situation and forced him to peace.[3] THE POLITICAL and military considerations required him to march into Estonia as soon as spring arrived, drive out the Czar, retake Petersburg, force Peter to make peace, and limit him to his former boundaries. It is evident that, after having conquered his most dangerous enemy, he would then have been master of Poland to dispose of it as he wished, because nobody could have resisted him.[4] AUGUSTUS THE STRONG, who had recently, but not unanimously, been elected King of Poland, beheld himself seated on a tottering throne. Were he deprived of Russian aid he would fall. Or Charles might have dethroned him whenever he pleased, supposing this to be a real advantage to Sweden.[5]

BUT WHAT DID HE DO? Far from following such a reasonable plan, he dared to make war against the Polish Palatine and to chase the handful of Saxons from one side to the other, thus giving the Czar time to drill his troops, attract skillful generals to his service, and introduce and carry out all the reforms that laid the groundwork for Charles's total defeat at Poltava.[6]

BUT INSTEAD of acting thus prudently, the King seems to have forgotten the Czar and the Russians who were at bay in order to give chase to I know not what Polish grandee of the opposite party. The pursuit of individual vengeance made him neglect real advantages and lose sight of the principal objective. After he had seized Lithuania, his army entered Poland like a torrent that overflowed and flooded the whole kingdom. The King was today at Warsaw, tomorrow at Cracow, and the next day at Lublin or Lemberg. His troops spread themselves through Polish Prussia, again appeared at Warsaw, dethroned King Augustus [1704] and pursued him into Saxony, where they peaceably took up winter quarters [1706].

We must bear in mind that these campaigns, which I skim over, gave Charles employment during several years. Here I shall stop a moment to examine his conduct. Let me remark, however, that during the interval of these marches and counter-marches the victory at Klissow was gained, for which he was indebted to an able maneuver that took the Saxons in flank.

The method Charles pursued in the Polish war was certainly very defective. The conquest of Poland, which is everywhere an open country without fortresses, is a thing of no difficulty; but to hold Poland, as Marshal Saxe well observes, is very precarious. The more easily conquered, the more difficult it is for a conqueror to fix and maintain himself. The method Saxe proposes no doubt appears slow, but it is the only one that can be followed by those who would act with safety.

The King of Sweden by nature was much too hasty to make profound reflections on the country in which he made war and on the dispositions suitable to his military efforts. Had he first established himself in Polish Prussia, had he progressively secured the Vistula and the Bug by throwing up intrenched strongholds at the confluence of the rivers or in other proper places, had he acted in the same manner on the other rivers that cross Poland, he would have obtained points at which to rally and he would have guarded the conquered districts. The places he occupied would have enabled him to raise contributions and form magazines for the army. By this conduct the war would have become more regular and he would have prescribed bounds to the inroads of the Russians and Saxons. The posts, well fortified, would have forced his enemies to undertake distant sieges, if they wanted to act effectively, and it would have been very difficult to transport the requisite artillery because of the poor roads in that country. His situation never could become desperate, in the event of a misfortune. His rear would have been open and by his posts he would have gained time to make good the loss and retard a victorious army.

By taking the opposite course, which Charles preferred, he was master only of the country that his troops occupied. His campaigns were continual marches, and the slightest reverse endangered his conquests. He was obliged to fight innumerable battles, and by the most glorious victory he gained only the uncertain possession of provinces from which he had long before expelled the enemy.

Gradually we approach the period when fortune began to declare against our hero. It is my intention to be still more circumspect than I have been in judging events whose termination was so unfortunate.

We ought not to pass judgment on the soundness of the plan by the outcome of an undertaking. Let us carefully guard against placing that reverse of fortune, which happens in execution, to the account of lack of precaution. It may be produced by invisible causes which the multitude call blind fate and which, notwithstanding their great influence over the destiny of men, from their obscurity and complication escape the most profound and philosophic spirit of inquiry.

We cannot in any manner accuse the King of Sweden of having himself been the cause of all his misfortunes. The success that had attended all his enterprises during the war in Poland did not permit him to observe that he often departed from rules of art; and, as he had not been punished for his errors, he was unacquainted with the danger to which he had been exposed. This constant good fortune rendered him too confident; he did not even suspect it was necessary to change his measures.

In what relates to his projects on the Duchy of Smolensko

and the Ukraine [1708], it appears he may be accused of not having taken the least precaution. Supposing he had dethroned the Czar at Moscow—the execution of his plan would not have done him any honor, since success would have been not the work of prudence, but the effect of chance.

The subsistence of his troops should be the first care of a general. An army has been compared to an edifice, the foundation of which is the belly. The King's negligence in this essential point was what contributed most to his misfortunes and most diminished his fame. What praise would the general merit who, in order to conquer, must have troops who have no need of nourishment, soldiers who are incapable of fatigue, and heroes who are immortal?

Charles XII is accused of having depended too inconsiderately on the promises of Mazeppa, but he was not betrayed by the Cossack.[7] Mazeppa, on the contrary, was himself betrayed by a fortuitous concourse of unfortunate circumstances which he could neither foresee nor avoid. Besides, minds as powerful as that of Charles are incapable of suspicions, and are never diffident until they have been taught by the wickedness and the ingratitude of men, by reiterated experience.

But I return to examine the plan and operation that Charles intended to execute during his campaign. It is true that I cannot say, with Correggio, "I also am a painter"—yet I will venture to present my ideas to the connoisseur.

That he might make good the error he had committed in having neglected the Czar for so long, it appears to me that the King should have penetrated into Russia by the easiest route, as the most certain way to overwhelm his powerful adversary. This route undoubtedly was neither Smolensko nor the Ukraine. In both there were impracticable marshes, immense deserts, and great rivers to cross before a half-cultivated country could be entered and the army could reach Moscow. By taking either of these routes Charles deprived himself of all the help he might have received from Poland or Sweden. The farther he advanced into Russia, the farther he found himself from his kingdom.

To complete such an enterprise required more than one campaign. Where was he to obtain provisions? By what road were his recruits to march? In what Moscovite or Cossack avenue could he obtain arms and clothing, which constantly have to be replaced in an army, along with numerous other things of less value but of equal necessity.

So many insurmountable difficulties should have taught him to foresee that the Swedes undoubtedly were doomed to perish by fatigue and famine, and that they must diminish and melt away even if victorious. If, therefore, the prospect of success was gloomy, how dreadful must be the picture of possible misfortune! A loss easy to repair in a different situation must become a decisive catastrophe to an army abandoned to chance, in a desert country, without strongholds and consequently without retreat.[8]

IF EVER A PLAN was conceived contrary to reason and common sense it was certainly Charles's march into the Ukraine and thence to Moscow. His intention was to dethrone the Czar, a plan that lay beyond the capability of his forces, for he had scarcely 30,000 men. He should therefore have renounced it, because in war, as in every action in life, the wise man can undertake difficult tasks but he must never become involved in impracticable projects. And this is not all. It is a rule of war that one must never make deep penetrations and that wars undertaken near to the frontiers always succeed more happily than those where the army is ventured too far . . . from its magazines into enemy territory, without protecting its rear and providing for its security. But who ever made greater abuses in the mania for penetrations than Charles XII? In the Ukraine he was completely cut off from Sweden, deprived of help from his country, without magazines and without the means of being able to collect any. From Poltava to Moscow it is about five hundred miles, a march that took him forty-five days. Even assuming that the enemy could not have stopped him on the road, it is known that the Czar had resolved to devastate everything along the way. To undertake such an expedition, therefore, the Swedes would have had to carry enough supplies with them to last at least for three months, along with sufficient amounts of cattle and vast supplies of munitions of war. It would have required at least 3,000 wagons which, each drawn by four horses, makes 12,000 horses to transport these provisions. How could this number have been found in the Ukraine? And even assuming that they could have been scraped together, would not the result of this have been that half of the Swedish army would have been required to serve as escorts for these provisions, the loss of which would have carried away the entire army.

If Charles XII had wanted to strike a telling blow against the Czar, it should have been by Estonia, where he could be aided with provisions and munitions by his fleet, and where he could even recruit for his army from the Finnish militia. The misfortunes that attended him he drew upon himself by deviating from all of the rules of war and following only his whim.[9] CHARLES SHOULD HAVE PROCEEDED immediately to Petersburg. . . . The Swedish fleet and the necessary transports, with a supply of provisions, might have followed by the Gulf of Finland. The recruits and other things necessary might have been sent on board this fleet, or marched through Finland. The King would thus have covered his best provinces without moving far from his frontiers. Success would have been more splendid and the utmost adversity would not have made his situation hopeless. Should he have seized Petersburg, he would have destroyed the new settlement of the Czar. Russia would have lost sight of Europe, and the only link connecting that empire with the quarter of the globe we inhabit would have been broken.

This major point gained, he would have been able to profit by success and proceed farther, though I do not perceive that it was at all essential that he sign the articles of peace at Moscow.

Permit me, for my own information, to compare the conduct of the King of Sweden during these two campaigns to the rules that the great masters of the military art have given.

These rules require that a general should never endanger his

army, nor advance with any corps that is not sufficiently supported. Charles buried himself in the Duchy of Smolensko,
without thinking of preserving his communications with Poland. Our instructors have established it as a law that we should
form a defensive line of communication and cover it by the
army, so that our rear may be open and our magazines safe.
The Swedes found themselves near the town of Smolensk with
provisions to last only a fortnight: they drove the enemy before them, defeated his rear guard, and pursued him at a venture
without exactly knowing where the fugitive was leading them.

We know of no precaution the King took for the subsistence of his army except that he commanded General Löwenhaupt to follow him with a considerable convoy. He therefore
ought not to have left this convoy, which the army could not
do without, so far in his rear. Nor should he have commenced
his march toward the Ukraine before its arrival; for the farther
he strayed from it, the more he exposed himself to defeat. He
should rather have chosen to return with his forces into Lithuania, but he continually pushed forward and thus accelerated
the loss of his army.

To this violation of all the rules of art, which alone was
sufficient to incur ruin, misfortunes were added which can only
be attributed to fate. The Czar attacked Löwenhaupt three times
and at length forced him to destroy a great part of his convoy.

The King of Sweden therefore was ignorant of the views
and movements of the Russians. If this were negligence on his
part he ought to have reproached himself bitterly, but if it were
occasioned by invincible obstacles, we must once again attribute this disaster to the account of destiny.

When war is made in a half-barbarous and almost desert
country, it is necessary to build fortresses in order to keep
possession. . . . The troops must aid in constructing roads,
mounds, and bridges, and in raising redoubts as each becomes
necessary. But a method so tedious was little to the taste of the
impetuous and restless spirit of the King. It has been rightly
remarked that in matters depending upon bravery and prompti-

tude, he was incomparable, but he was no longer the same man on occasions when regular plans or slow measures, which only time and patience could ripen, were to be observed.

These considerations prove how necessary it is that a warrior should be master of his passions, and how difficult it is to unite, in a single person, all the talents of a great general.

I shall pass over the battle of Holowczyn[10] as well as other combats of that campaign because they were as ineffectual, relative to the war, as they were fatal to those who fell, the sad victims. Charles in general was prodigal of the blood of men. There doubtless are occasions when it is necessary to fight, as for instance, when more may be gained than lost, when an enemy is negligent in camp or on the march, or when a decisive blow may force him to make peace. But many generals only fight so often because they do not know how otherwise to rid themselves of their troubles. Therefore such conduct is not attributed to their merit, but rather to their lack of genius.

At length we approach the decisive battle of Poltava [1709]. The errors of great men are exemplary lessons to those who possess fewer abilities, and there are few generals in Europe to whom the fate of Charles may not teach prudence, circumspection, and wisdom.

Marshal Keith, who afterward commanded in the Ukraine as a Russian general and who has seen and examined the battlefield, has assured me that the fortifications of Poltava were only of earth, surrounded by a bad ditch. He was persuaded that the Swedes on their arrival, without further preparation, might have carried it sword in hand, had not the King purposely prolonged the siege in order to attract, that he might vanquish, the Czar.

It is certain that the Swedes did not display there the ardor and impetuosity for which they were famous. It must also be allowed they did not make an attack until Menschikow had first thrown reinforcements into the town and had encamped near it, on the banks of the river Worskla. But the Czar had a considerable magazine at Poltava. Should not the Swedes, who were in want of everything, have seized this magazine with all possible dispatch in order to take it from the Russians at a blow and have abundantly supplied themselves? Charles XII undoubtedly had the most powerful reasons for pushing the siege with vigor, and he ought to have used every means to make himself master of this trifling place before help arrived.

Without including the rambling Cossacks of Mazeppa, who on the day of battle did more harm than good, the King had no more than 18,000 Swedes. How was it possible he should think of undertaking a siege and giving battle at the same time, with so small an army?

On the approach of the enemy it was necessary either to raise the siege or to leave a considerable corps in the trenches. The former course would have been disgraceful and the other would have much reduced the number of his combatants. This enterprise, which was totally contrary to the interest of the Swedes, was highly advantageous to the Czar and seems unworthy of our hero. It scarcely could have been expected even from a general who had never made war with reflection.

Without seeking to discover stratagems where there were none, without attributing views to the King which perhaps he never entertained, we ought rather to recollect that he very often was uninformed of his enemy's march. It is to be presumed that he had no intelligence of the march of Menschikow, nor of the approach of the Czar, and that consequently he did not think it necessary to hasten the siege because he imagined that Poltava had no alternative but to surrender. Let us further remember that Charles always made war in the open field, that he did not understand siege warfare, and that he had never had opportunities to acquire knowledge by experience. When we consider too that the Swedes lay three months before Thorn, the works of which were no better than those of Poltava, we may, without injustice, pronounce on their abilities for conducting sieges.

When Mons, Tournai, and the works of Coehorn and Vauban scarcely impeded the progress of the French for three weeks, and when, in contrast, Thorn and Poltava occupied the Swedes for several months, may we not safely conclude that the latter did not understand the art of taking towns? No place could resist them if it were possible to carry it by assault, sword in hand; but they were stopped by the most insignificant fortress before which it was necessary to open trenches.

If this proof is insufficient, I will ask, would not Charles, hot and impetuous as he was, have besieged and taken Danzig in order to make the city feel the whole weight of his wrath because of an offense he had received, or would he have been satisfied with a sum of money if he had not supposed the siege to be an undertaking above his strength?

But let us return to the principal object of this essay. Poltava was besieged, and the Czar approached it with his army. Charles still had it in his power to choose his post and there to wait for his rival. This post he might have taken on the banks of the Worskla, either to dispute the river passage or, the enemy having crossed it, immediately to have attacked the Czar. The situation of the Swedes demanded quick determination. Either they must fall on the Russians the moment they arrived, or else they must entirely abandon the plan of attack. To allow the Czar to choose his post and to give him time necessary to put himself in a state of defense was an irreparable mistake: the Czar already had the advantage of numbers, which was not small; and he was allowed to acquire the advantage of ground and of military art, which was too much.

A few days before the Czar's arrival the King was wounded while visiting his trenches. The greatest blame consequently fell upon his generals. It nevertheless appears that, as soon as he was resolved to give battle, he ought to have abandoned his trenches in order to be able to attack the enemy with more vigor. If he were victorious, Poltava would surrender as a consequence; if he were defeated, he would at the same time be forced to raise the siege.

So many mistakes united announced the issue of the unfortunate battle, the approach of which was daily perceived. It seemed as if fate previously had disposed of everything, to the disadvantage of the Swedes, and thus had prepared their downfall. The King's wound, which prevented him from personally heading his troops as usual; and the negligence of the generals, who by their erroneous dispositions showed sufficiently that they were unacquainted with the enemy's position, or at least that their knowledge was imperfect, greatly contributed to that remarkable catastrophe. The attack also was begun by the cavalry, whereas it was the business of the infantry and . . . artillery.

The Russian post was very advantageously situated and was made stronger with redoubts. Only a part of their front could be attacked, and the small plain on which it was possible to form for the assault was flanked by the crossfire from three rows of redoubts. One of the Russian wings was covered by an abatis, behind which there was an intrenchment, and the other was defended by an impracticable marsh.

Marshal Keith, who personally examined this famous ground, maintained that even with an army of 100,000 Charles could not have defeated the Czar thus posted, because the difficulties that had to be overcome successively would have cost an infinite number of men, and it is known that the bravest troops at length lose courage after a long and murderous attack, when they are opposed by new and unceasing obstacles.

I know not what the reasons were that induced the Swedes, in a situation as critical as theirs, to hazard an attempt so dangerous. If their necessity was absolute, the error of forcing themselves to risk a battle . . . under the most disadvantageous circumstances was great.

All that might well have been predicted happened. A considerable army, diminished by labor, necessity, and even victory was led to the slaughter. General Creutz, who by a circuitous route was to have taken the Russians in flank, lost himself in the woods and never appeared on the field.

Thus 12,000 Swedes attacked a post defended by 80,000 Muscovites, who no longer were that multitude of barbarians Charles had dispersed at Narva. They were transformed into well-armed and well-posted soldiers, commanded by able foreign generals, well intrenched and defended by the fire of a formidable artillery train.

The Swedes led their cavalry against these batteries and, as might have been expected, were forced to retreat despite their valor. The infantry advanced, and although it was received by the most dreadful fire from the redoubts, it seized the first two of them. But the Russians attacked the Swedish battalions at once in front, flank, and rear, repulsed them several times, and forced them to relinquish the field of battle. Disorder then spread through the army: the King, being wounded, was unable to rally his troops, and there was no person who could collect the fugitives soon enough because the best generals had been taken prisoner at the beginning of the battle. It was their fault that these troops, who fled as far as the banks of the Dnieper, were forced to surrender at discretion to the conqueror, for the Swedes had no place that covered the rear of their army.

An author of considerable wit but one who probably studied the military art in Homer and Virgil[11] imagines that the King of Sweden ought to have put himself at the head of the fugitives whom General Löwenhaupt had gathered on the banks of the Dnieper, and pretends that the fever which his wound occasioned and which, as he truly observes, was little calculated to inspire courage, was the reason that he neglected the only means which, in his opinion, remained for repairing his loss.

Such a determination might have been proper in ages when men fought with the sword and the club, but after a battle the infantry is always in want of powder. The ammunition of the Swedes formed a part of the baggage that the enemy had already captured; therefore, if Charles had been unwise enough to have headed these troops, destitute as they were of powder and bread—two things that force even fortresses to surrender— the Czar soon would have had the pleasure of giving audience to his brother Charles, for whom he waited with great impatience. Consequently, in a situation so desperate, the King could do nothing better than take refuge among the Turks, even had he been in perfect health.

Monarchs no doubt ought not to fear danger, but their dignity equally induces them carefully to avoid being made prisoners, less from personal considerations than from the dreadful consequences that result to their states.[12] French authors should recollect the considerable injury that their nation suffered by the captivity of Francis I. The wounds France received then still bleed, and the venality of state dignitaries, which was inevitable in order to raise the sum for the royal ransom, is a durable monument of that disgraceful epoch.[13]

Even in flight our hero is worthy of admiration. Any other man would have fallen under a blow so severe, but he formed new plans, found resources even in misfortune, and, a fugitive in Turkey, he meditated to arm the Porte against Russia.

It is with pain that I behold Charles degrading himself to the rank of a courtier of the Sultan, begging a thousand purses, and that I perceive with what headlong, what inconceivable obstinacy he persevered in wishing to remain in the states of a monarch who would not allow him to stay. I would have wished that the strange battle of Bender might be erased from his history.[14] I regret the precious time he lost in a barbarous country, feeding on vain hope, deaf to the plaintive voice of Sweden, and insensible of the duty by which he was so loudly summoned to defend his kingdom, which he seemed voluntarily to renounce while absent.

The plans that are attributed to him after his return into Pomerania [1715], and that certain persons have made originate with Count von Goertz, have always appeared to me so indeterminate, so monstrous, and so little consistent with the situation and exhausted state of his kingdom that my reader will permit me, on behalf of Charles's reputation, to leave them in silence. That war, so fruitful in fortunate and unfortunate events, was begun by the enemies of Sweden, and Charles, obliged to resist their plan of aggrandizement, was only in a state of defense. His enemies attacked him because they misunderstood and despised his youth. While he was successful and appeared to be a dangerous enemy, he was envied by Europe; but when fortune turned her back, the allied powers shook the throne of Charles and parceled out his kingdom.

Had this hero possessed moderation equal to his courage, had he set limits to his triumphs, had he reconciled himself to the Czar when an opportunity of honorable peace presented itself, he would have stifled the evil designs of the envious; but as soon as they recovered from their panic, they thought only of the means of enriching themselves by the ruins of his monarchy. Unfortunately the passions of that man were subject to no modification. He wished to carry everything by force and haughtiness, and despotically to triumph even over despots. To make war and to dethrone kings was to him but one and the same act.

In all the books about Charles XII, I find high-sounding praises bestowed on his frugality and continence; but twenty French cooks in his kitchen, 1,000 courtesans in his train, and ten companies of players in his army would not have caused his kingdom the hundredth part of the evils brought on it by his ardent thirst for glory and desire for vengeance. Insults made such a strong and vivid impression on his soul that the most recent mortification always erased all traces of those that preceded it. It may be said that we see arise the different passions that agitated the irreconcilable mind of this prince with so much violence, when we observe and attend him at the head of his armies.

He began by making war on the king of Denmark; he next persecuted the king of Poland without measure or limit; presently the whole weight of his anger fell on the Czar; and at length his vengeance selected the king of England as its only object, so that he forgot himself so far as to lose sight of the natural enemy of his kingdom, that he might encounter a shadow and seek an enemy who had become his foe from accident, or rather from chance.

If we collect the various traits that characterize this extraordinary man, we shall find him less intelligent than courageous, less sage than active, less attentive to real advantage than enslaved by his passions; as enterprising but not as artful as Hannibal, rather resembling Pyrrhus than Alexander, and as splendid as Condé at Rocroi, Freiburg, and Nordlingen. But he could not at any time be compared to Turenne, if we observe the latter at the battles of the Downs and of Colmar, and especially during his two last campaigns.

Though the actions of our hero shine with great brilliancy, they must not be imitated, except with peculiar caution. The more resplendent they are, the more easily may they seduce the youthful, headlong, and angry warrior, to whom we cannot often enough repeat that valor without wisdom is insufficient, and that the adversary with a cool head, who can combine and calculate, will finally be victorious over the rash individual.

To form a perfect general, the courage, fortitude and activity of Charles XII, the penetrating glance and policy of Marlborough, the vast plains and art of Eugene, the stratagems of Luxembourg, the wisdom, order, and foresight of Montecuccoli, and the grand art, which Turenne possessed, of seizing the critical moment, should be united. Such a phoenix will with difficulty be engendered. Some pretend that Alexander was the model on which Charles XII patterned himself. If that be true, it is no less true that the successor of Charles is Prince Edward, and if unfortunately the latter should serve as an example to anyone, the copy at best can only be a Don Quixote.

But what right have I to judge the most celebrated and the greatest generals? Have I myself observed the precepts I have just prescribed? I can only reply that the faults of others come into view with the slightest effort of memory, and that we glide lightly over our own.[15]

## NOTES: CHAPTER X

1. Voltaire, *The History of Charles the Twelfth, King of Sweden* (Hartford, 1833), pp. 13, 259, 272-73.

2. Henri de Catt, *Frederick the Great: the Memoirs of his Reader Henri de Catt* (1758-1760), Trans. F. S. Flint, with an Introduction by Lord Rosebery (Boston, 1917), II, 165-66.

3. Frederick, "Reflections on Charles XII," *Posthumous Works of Frederick II, King of Prussia*, trans. Thomas Holcroft (London, 1789),

V, 113-23. Minor changes have been made in the Holcroft translation to help it conform to modern usage [*Charles XII*].

4. Frederick, "Réflections sur les projets de campagne," *Oeuvres de Frédéric le Grand* (Berlin, 1846-56), XXIX, 80 [*Projets de Campagne*].

5. Frederick, *Charles XII*, p. 123.

6. Frederick, *Projets de campagne*, p. 80.

7. Ivan Stephanovitch Mazeppa, the Cossack Hetman or Headman entrusted with the defense of the Ukraine, had promised to furnish Charles 30,000 Cossacks if the Swedes would take the Ukraine under their protection. When he finally joined Charles deep in the Ukraine, slipping fortunes enabled him to bring only a small fraction of the force he had promised.

8. Frederick, *Charles XII*, pp. 123-29.

9. Frederick, *Projets de campagne*, pp. 80-81.

10. Holowczyn was the last great victory of Charles XII (July 13, 1708).

11. This unquestionably is a dig at Voltaire.

12. No doubt it was this sense of responsibility, together with his depressions that accompanied military reverses or frustrations, that prompted Frederick to carry with him throughout the Seven Years' War a small box of opium pills, "more than enough," he confided, "to transfer me to that dark shore from which there is no return." Quoted in Ludwig Reiners, *Frederick the Great* (New York, 1960), p. 198.

13. Francis I, King of France, was defeated by the Emperor Charles V and taken prisoner at Pavia in 1525. He purchased his liberty the following year by ceding Burgundy to Charles and surrendering his sons as hostages.

14. When the Pasha of Bender, acting on orders from the Sultan, tried to force Charles, by a display of military might, to leave his stone house near Varnitza, Charles defied an entire Turkish army, said to be 30,000 strong, with his 300 Swedes. In this wild melee, "which makes the deeds of Achilles and King Arthur seem adult and unromantic," Charles and his devout band of followers were captured. See William Bolitho, *Twelve Against the Gods* (New York, 1941), p. 227.

15. Frederick, *Charles XII*, pp. 129-46.

# APPENDIX I

# Glossary of Some Eighteenth-Century Military Terms

In compiling this glossary I have adhered to the practice universally followed during the eighteenth century and have copied whatever I needed from some previous work, without the proper acknowledgments. My only excuse for this unorthodox bit of scholarship is that I did not wish to depart any more than was necessary from the original wording for fear of distortion or misrepresentation. The principal works to which I am indebted are Thomas Simes, *The Military Guide for Young Officers: A large and valuable Compilation from the most celebrated Military Writers, Marshal Saxe–General Gland–King of Prussia–Prince Ferdinand, etc. including an excellent Military, Historical, and Explanatory Dictionary* (2 vols., Philadelphia, 1776); William Duane, *A Military Dictionary, or, Explanation of the Several Systems of Discipline of Different Kinds of Troops, Infantry, Artillery, and Cavalry; the Principles of Fortification, and all the modern improvements in the science of tactics* (Philadelphia, 1810); and *The Gentlemen's Dictionary. In Three Parts. II. The Military Art* (London, 1705). I have also consulted the very useful glossary of military and naval terms in the *Atlas to Alison's History of Europe . . .* by Alex. Keith Johnson (London, 1852).

ABATIS—Trees felled and so placed as to form a parapet to protect infantry. Usually the branches are sharpened and face the enemy, forming an obstruction somewhat comparable to the barbed wire of our own day.

ARQUEBUSS—An ancient firearm, no longer in use, that carried a ball weighing about three and one-half ounces.

ATTACK—To assault; *also* the disposition or formation employed by an army in the assault.

BANDOLEER—A small wooden case, covered with leather, that holds cartridges of powder for firearms.

BASTION—A part of the inner enclosure of a fortification consisting of two faces, two flanks, and an opening toward the center of the fortification called the *gorge*.

BOMB—A large cast-iron shell, weighing anywhere from fifty to five hundred pounds, filled with powder. A fuse made of hollow wood and filled with a composition of meal powder, sulfur, and saltpeter, is ignited by the flash of powder in the gun chamber, burns while the bomb is in the air, and, when the fuse is spent, fires the powder in the bomb.

BOMBARDIER—An artillery soldier employed in mortar and howitzer duty. He loads the shells, fixes the fuses, and fires the guns.

CADET—A young gentleman who, in order to attain some knowledge in the art of war, carries arms as a private individual.

CANISTER—*See* CARTOUCH.

CANTON—A military district in Prussia, assigned to a specific regiment as a recruiting district for replacements whenever quotas are not filled by voluntary enlistment.

CANTONMENTS—Troops are said to be in cantonments when they are quartered in neighboring towns and villages in the same manner as they encamp in the field.

CAPONIER—A covered passage or trench constructed on the glacis or in the ditch to obtain a flanking fire.

CARTOUCH—A combination of small shot contained in a cylinder of wood or canvas, for use as an artillery projectile against infantry or cavalry at fairly close range. Indiscriminately called grape shot, case shot, or canister, this was the most effective antipersonnel weapon before the invention of shrapnel in the nineteenth century.

CARTRIDGE—A case of pasteboard or parchment holding the exact charge of a firearm; cartridges for muskets, carbines, or pistols hold both the powder and ball for the charge.

CASE SHOT—*See* CARTOUCH.

CASTRAMETATION—The art of measuring or tracing out the form of a camp on the ground. Sometimes the term had a broader meaning, when it included all of the views and plans of a general. "The one requires a mathematician, the other an experienced officer." (Simes)

CHEVAUX DE FRISE—A large joist or piece of timber five or six inches in diameter and ten to twelve feet in length, with rows of wooden stakes, each of which was about six feet in length and one to two inches in diameter, driven into the main timber at right angles. First used at the siege of Groningen in 1658, *chevaux de frise* were especially effective in protecting infantry from cavalry and in filling breaches in fortifications.

CIRCUMVALLATION—See *Lines*.

CLOSE ORDER—The arrangement of any given number of men where the ranks are separated by one pace.

COLUMN—A formation of troops, usually with a narrow front and deep from front to rear. In Frederick's day, the army marched in long, deep files of troops and baggage and approached the battlefield in four, six, or eight columns. The column did not gain acceptance as a tactical formation until the wars of the French Revolution and Napoleon near the end of the century.

CONVOY—A supply of men, money, ammunition, or provisions conveyed into a town or to an army in the field. Sometimes the body of troops that guarded the wagons likewise was called the convoy.

CORPS, CORPS D'ARMÉE—In the eighteenth century, a corps was any body of forces destined to act together under one commander. The corps as a permanent administrative organization did not emerge until the Napoleonic wars.

CORPS DE BATAILLE—The main body of an army that marches between the advance and the rear guard.

CORPS DE GARDE—Soldiers entrusted with the guard of a post.

COUNTERGUARD—A narrow detached rampart located in front of an important work to protect it against being breached.

COUP D'OEIL—The gift or instinct of a general that allows him to distinguish at a glance the strong and weak points of the terrain. This was indispensable in an age when weapons and tactical formations were more or less uniform throughout Europe.

COVERED WAY, COVERT WAY—A space of ground 18 to 24 feet wide that crowns the outer edge of the ditch or moat surrounding a fortress and is protected from enemy fire by a parapet. The greatest effort in a typical siege is to make a lodgment on the covered way.

CUIRASSIERS—Heavy cavalry wearing metal breast, back, and head pieces.

CURTAIN—That portion of the rampart of a fortification that lies between the flanks of two bastions. Rarely was it more than 240 yards in length, which was the ordinary range of firearms of that day.

DECAMP—To break camp, to depart from a place where the army has been encamped.

DEFILE—A narrow pass that forces an army to form in columns. It is one of the greatest obstacles that can occur in the march of an army, especially if it is bordered by woods or marshes. A retreating army always tries to secure its retreat by taking shelter behind a defile. *To defile:* to reduce an army to a small front in order to march through such a narrow passage.

DEPLOY—Although this term, for want of a better, appears frequently in this translation, it was not a part of the soldier's vocabulary until the end of the eighteenth century. It means to spread out troops to form a more extended line of shallow depth, to deploy from column into line.

DETACHMENT—A picked number of men, sometimes drawn from several companies or regiments, sometimes comprising entire squadrons and battalions, placed under the temporary command of an officer entrusted with a specific mission. A detachment of 2,000 to 3,000 men usually is commanded by a general; a detachment of 800 or fewer is under a colonel.

DIVISION—In the eighteenth century this word normally referred to the union of two companies or platoons in tactical formations. It should not be confused with the term that later was used to designate a permanent administrative and tactical organization comprising several regiments or brigades.

EVOLUTION—The movements made by a body of troops when they are forced to change their form and disposition in order to fight at better advantage.

EXERCISE—Synonymous with drill; the practice of all those motions connected with the management of arms and the actions the soldier is apt to be required to perform in battle.

FASCINE—The eighteenth-century counterpart of the sandbag; a cylindrical faggot made of brushwood and used to strengthen the interior of batteries and trenches.

FILE—The line of soldiers standing behind one another. *To file off:* to defile from a large front to form a column.

FIRE—*Feu de joi:* running fire, occurs when a rank or ranks of soldiers fire one after another; *Grazing fire:* is the discharge of ordnance or musketry so directed that the shot skims the ground within three or four feet of the surface; *Enfilade fire:* occurs when a gun fires parallel to a line of soldiers or the parapet of a fortress, sweeping the target from one end to the other; *Plunging fire:* occurs when the shot is fired from a location considerably higher than the target;

*Ricochet fire:* occurs when guns are fired at a slight elevation (ten to twelve degrees) and with small charges, so that the shot are pitched over the parapet and roll along the opposite rampart; *Vertical fire:* occurs when a shot follows a lofty curve in the air before it falls, such as the fire from a mortar or howitzer; *Feu de haie:* In military terminology *haie* or "hedge" refers to a lane formed by two ranks of soldiers facing each other (presumably this would be a ceremonial exercise).

FIREBALL—A composition of meal powder, sulfur, saltpeter, and pitch about the size of a hand grenade. Coated with flax and primed with a slow composition of a fuse, the fireball is thrown into enemy works during the night to discover where troops are located.

FLANK—The troops encamped or in formation on the right or the left of an army.

FLAT FACES—A bastion comprises two faces, two flanks, and two demigorges. When the two foremost sides form only a slight angle, these flat faces constitute a weak point in the defense.

FLÈCHE—In field fortification, an arrow-shaped work designed to cover a gate or advanced post of a camp.

FOUGASSE—A small mine under a post, which is intended to blow up the position to keep it from falling into enemy hands.

FUSIL—A kind of small musket.

GENDARMES, GENS-D'ARMES—A body of horse, formed originally by Henry IV of France when he became king, which served as men at arms under the immediate orders of the king. By the eighteenth century the word had come to denote mounted trooper. Today it refers to a policeman, particularly in France.

GLACIS—That part of a fortification outside of the covered way; a gentle slope that extends from the parapet of the covered way to the natural surface of the surrounding ground.

GORGE—The rear, whether open or closed, of any bastion or outwork.

GRENADE—A spherical iron case, about three inches in diameter, filled with powder.

GRENADIER—A foot soldier, generally among the tallest and strongest men in the battalion, formed into special companies and especially equipped to throw grenades.

INTRENCHED—An army is intrenched when it has raised works, generally a parapet in front of which is a dry ditch, to fortify a post against the enemy.

LANDSKNECHT, LANSQUENETS—In the fifteenth century, a German foot soldier armed and trained to fight like the celebrated Swiss pikeman. Charles VII of France introduced these German mercenaries to the French service.

LINE—*Line of battle:* the disposition of an army for battle, with its front extended in a straight line as far as the ground and the numbers will permit. Each line is divided into a right and left wing. Ideally the flanks at each end should be anchored on a natural obstacle, such as a river, swamp, wood, or rough ground, to prevent the enemy from attacking the position from either flank or from the rear. *Line of circumvallation:* a kind of fortification, consisting of a parapet or breastwork, and a ditch, to cover the rear of an army besieging a fortification. *Lines:* a connected series of field fortifications, sometimes continuous, but often with intervals between the works.

OUTWORKS—Any advanced, detached, or exterior work of a fortress or fortified city that covers the main fortifications and at the same time serves to keep a besieging army at a distance.

PALISADES—Stakes made of strong, split wood, about nine feet in length. Generally these stakes were driven three feet deep into the ground in rows, six inches apart, either in the covered way or at the foot of bastions or the main glacis.

PANDOURS—Irregular light infantry, Hungarian in origin, raised initially by Baron Trenck to rid the country near the Turkish frontier of robbers. Carlyle describes the typical pandour as a "tall, raw-boned, ill-washed biped, in copious Turk breeches, rather barish in the top parts of him; carries a very long musket, and has several pistols and butcher's knives stuck in his girdle." (Carlyle, *Frederick The Great,* III, 164n.) Subsequently incorporated into Austrian service during the Silesian wars, these skilled marksmen proved exceedingly troublesome to the orthodox infantry of Frederick, especially during the Bohemian campaign of 1744.

PARALLELS (at a siege)—The trenches made parallel to the defenses of the place besieged. These deep trenches, fifteen to eighteen feet wide, linked the two approaches to the place under attack and contained sufficient guards to support the workmen if attacked. The first parallel generally was constructed about six hundred yards from the covered way, and the third often reached to the glacis.

PARAPET—An embankment of earth constructed to protect the soldiers from enemy artillery. Usually eighteen to twenty feet thick and six feet high on the inside, the parapet sloped to the outside to enable defenders to rest their muskets on the top and at the same time fire into the ditch.

PLACE—In fortification, a fortified town or city.

POINT D'APPUI—Support, prop, or fulcrum.

POST—A position fortified or strengthened to enable a body of troops to resist an enemy.

RAMPART—An earthen embankment, usually ten to fifteen feet high, that surrounds a fortified place. The parapet is on the exterior edge.

RAVELIN—The most common kind of outwork. Usually constructed in the form of a triangle, it is located in the ditch in front of the curtain.

REDANS—Lines or faces that form sallying and re-entering angles flanking each other.

REDOUBT—A square work of stone or earth, raised outside the glacis of a place, containing loopholes for the infantry to fire through, and usually surrounded by a ditch. In Frederick's day redoubts were often constructed to help protect a village or to guard any position of tactical importance.

SAP—A zigzag approach trench excavated by a besieging army in order to move troops and artillery closer to the enemy's works in relative safety. Usually an investing army digs a number of saps in order to bring its main siege lines, called parallels, close enough to the point under attack to bring it under effective artillery range.

SIEGE—The process of deliberate and regular attack on a fortified place by surrounding and blockading it, then by approaching the defensive works through the use of parallels and saps.

STRATAGEM—A trick or artifice by which an enemy is deceived.

STRATEGY—A nineteenth-century term; Frederick and his contemporaries spoke instead of plans of campaign.

SUTLER—An individual who followed the army and sold provisions to the troops.

TACTICS—The art of disciplining armies and placing them into the proper formations for fighting and maneuvering.

WINGS (of an army)—The right and left sections of an army drawn up in line of battle.

# *Pertinent Dates in the Life of Frederick the Great*

1712 January 24: birth of Frederick.

1730 August 5: Frederick is caught trying to escape the harsh rule of his father, Frederick William I. He is forced to witness the execution of his closest friend and then remain imprisoned until 1732.

1732 February 26: Frederick is freed to begin his apprenticeship as Crown Prince.
March 10: Frederick betrothed to Elizabeth of Brunswick-Bevern.

1734 July-October: Frederick accompanies Prince Eugene in his campaign against the French.

1736 August 8: First correspondence with Voltaire.

1739 *Anti-Machiavel.*

1740 May 31: Frederick becomes King of Prussia.

1740-42 First Silesian War.

1740 December: Prussians occupy Silesia.

1741 April 10: Battle of Mollwitz.
June 5: Alliance with France.
October: Convention of Klein-Schnellendorf.
December: Frederick resumes active campaigning.

1742 Invasion of Moravia, retreat into Bohemia.
May 17: Battle of Chotusitz.
July 28: Peace of Breslau.

1744-45 Second Silesian War.

1744 July 25: *Disposition, wie sich die Officiere von der Cavallerie in einem Treffen gegen den Feind zu verhalten haben.*
August: Invasion of Bohemia.
November: Retreat into Silesia.

1745    June 4: Battle of Hohenfriedberg.
        September 30: Battle of Sohr.
        December 15: Battle of Kesselsdorf.
        December 24: Peace of Dresden.

1747    *Instruction pour les généraux qui auront à commander des détachements, des ailes, des secondes lignes et des armées prussiennes* (revised in 1748 and again, in German translation, in 1753; English translation, 1940).

1748    *Aus der Instruction für die Generalmajors von der Cavallerie.*

1752    *Das politische Testament.*

1753    *Instruction militaire du Roi de Prusse pour ses généraux* (translated in 1761 from the German edition; English translation, 1762).

1755    *Pensées et règles générales pour la guerre.*

1756-63   Seven Years' War.

1756    August 29: Frederick invades Saxony.
        October 1: Battle of Lobositz.
        October 16: Surrender of Saxon army at Pirna.

1757    April 18-22: Prussians invade Bohemia in four columns.
        May 6: Battle of Prague.
        June 18: Battle of Kolin.
        November 5: Battle of Rossbach.
        December 5: Battle of Leuthen.

1758    May-June: Campaign in Moravia.
        July 1: Siege of Olmütz raised.
        August 25: Battle of Zorndorf.
        October 14: Battle of Hochkirch.
        December 27: *Réflexions sur la tactique et sur quelques parties de la guerre, ou Réflexions sur quelques changements dans la façon de faire la guerre.*

1759    March: *Instruction pour les généraux-majors de cavalerie.*
        August 12: Battle of Kunersdorf.
        October: *Reflections on Charles XII* (English translation, 1789).
        November 20: Capitulation of Maxen.

1760    June 23: Defeat of Fouqué's detachment at Landshut.
        August 15: Battle of Liegnitz.
        October: Russians and Austrians occupy Berlin.
        November 3: Battle of Torgau.

1761    August-September: Intrenched camp at Bunzelwitz.
        October 1: Fall of Schweidnitz.

1762    January 5: Death of the Empress Elizabeth of Russia.
        July 21: Battle of Burkersdorf.
        October 9: Recapture of Schweidnitz.
        October 29: Prince Henry's victory at Freiberg.
1763    February 15: Peace of Hubertusburg.
        *History of the Seven Years War* (English translation, 1789).
1768    *Das militärische Testament.*
1770    *Eléments de castramétrie et de tactique.*
1771    *Avant-propos* (de l'extrait tiré de la Marquis de Quincy, *Histoire militaire du règne de Louis XIV*).
1772    First partition of Poland.
1773    *Règles de ce qu'on exige d'un bon commandeur de bataillon en temps de guerre.*
1775    July: *History of my Time* (English translation, 1789).
        December: *Réflexions sur les projets de campagne.*
1777    July: *An Essay on Forms of Government and on the Duties of Sovereigns* (English translation, 1789).
        October: *Des marches d'armée, et de ce qu'il faut observer à cet égard.*
1778    July-October: Frederick's campaign in Bohemia during the War of the Bavarian Succession.
1779    May 13: Peace of Teschen.
        June: *Memoirs after the Peace: Chapter III: Of the Military* (English translation, 1789).
        September: *Réflexions sur les mesures à prendre au cas d'une guerre nouvelle avec les Autrichiens.*
1782    *Instruction für meine Artillerie.*
1786    August 17: Death of Frederick.

# Selected Bibliography

## FREDERICK'S WRITINGS

*Instruction militaire du roi de Prusse pour ses généraux.* Frankfort and
Leipzig, 1761.
   Originally dictated in German by Frederick in 1753, this work
fell into the hands of the Austrians in 1760 and was translated into
French by a Saxon Lieutenant Colonel named Faesch. It was pub-
lished also in London in 1761 under the title, *Essai sur la Grande
Guerre, de main de maitre: ou instruction militaire du roi de Prusse
pour ses généraux, Avec de courtes maximes pour la petite guerre.*
There is an English translation of the 1753 *Instruction militaire* en-
titled, *Military Instruction from the Late King of Prussia to his
Generals to which is added, by the same Author, Particular Instruc-
tion to the Officers of his Army, and especially those of the cavalry.*
(Translated from the French by Lieutenant Colonel Foster. London,
5th edition, 1818.) *The Instruction of Frederick the Great for his
Generals, 1747* has been translated more recently and is found in
Major Thomas R. Phillips, *Roots of Strategy.* Harrisburg, Pennsyl-
vania, 1941.
*Oeuvres de Frédéric le Grand.* Berlin, 1846-56. 30 volumes.
*Posthumous Works of Frederick II, King of Prussia.* Translated by
Thomas Holcroft. London, 1789. 13 volumes. Contains translations
of the *Anti-Machiavel, An Essay on Forms of Government and on
the Duties of Sovereigns, The History of My Own Times,* and *The
History of the Seven Years War.*
*Die Werke Friedrichs des Grossen.* Berlin, 1913. 10 volumes. Frederick's
writings, which for the most part were in French, are here available
in German translation.

## FREDERICK AND HIS CAMPAIGNS

BERNHARDI, THEODOR VON. *Friedrich der Grosse als Feldherr*. Berlin, 1881. 2 volumes.

*Das Bildnis Friedrichs des Grossen. Zeitgenössische Darstellungen*. Berlin, 1942.

BOETTICHER, COLONEL FRIEDRICH VON. "Friedrich der Grosse," in Major General von Cochenhausen, *Führertum: 25 Lebensbilder von Feldherren aller Zeiten*. Berlin, 1930.

CARLYLE, THOMAS. *History of Friedrich II of Prussia, called Frederick the Great*. London, 1886. 6 volumes.

―――. *Journey to Germany: Autumn 1858*. Edited by Richard Albert Edward Brooks, with an introduction, notes and commentaries. New Haven, 1940.

CARRIAS, COLONEL EUGENE. *La Pensée militaire allemande*. Paris, 1948.

COLIN, COMMANDANT. *L'Infanterie au XVIIIè siècle*. Paris, 1907.

CRAIG, GORDON. "Delbrück: the Military Historian," in Edward Mead Earle, ed., *Makers of Modern Strategy: Military Thought from Machiavelli to Hitler*. Princeton, 1942.

DE CATT. *Frederick the Great: The Memoirs of his Reader Henri De Catt* (1758-60). Translated by F. S. Flint with an introduction by Lord Rosebery. Boston, 1917.

DELBRÜCK, HANS. *Friedrich, Napoleon, Moltke*. Berlin, 1892.

―――. *Geschichte der Kriegskunst im Rahmen der politischen Geschichte*. Berlin, 1920. 4 volumes.

DETTE, ERWIN. *Friedrich der Grosse und sein Heer*. Göttingen, 1914.

EASUM, CHESTER V. *Prince Henry of Prussia, Brother of Frederick the Great*. Madison, Wisconsin, 1942.

ERGANG, ROBERT. *The Potsdam Führer: Frederick William I, Father of Prussian Militarism*. New York, 1941.

GAXOTTE, PIERRE. *Frederick the Great*. Translated by R. A. Bell. London, 1941.

GERMANY. Militärgeschichtliche Forschungsamt. *Beiträge zur militär- und Kriegsgeschichte*. I. *Rückzug und Verfolgung. Zwei Kampfarten 1757-1944*. Stuttgart, 1960.

GERMANY. Grossen Generalstabe. Abtheilung für Kriegsgeschichte.

―――. "Friedrich des Grossen Anschauungen vom Kriege in ihrer Entwickelung von 1745 bis 1756," *Kriegsgeschichtliche Einzelschriften*. XXVIII. Berlin, 1899.

―――. *Die Kriege Friedrichs des Grossen*. Part 3. *Der siebenjährige Krieg, 1756-1763*. Berlin, 1890-1910. 9 volumes.

————. *Die Kriege Friedrichs des Grossen.* Part 3. *Der siebenjährige Friedrich den Grossen wahrend der Friedenzeit 1745 bis 1756," Kriegsgeschichtliche Einzelschriften.* XXVIII-XXX. Berlin, 1900-1902.

GOLTZ, FREIHERR VON DER. *Von Rossbach bis Jena und Auerstadt: Ein Beitrag zur Geschichte des preussischen Heeres.* Berlin, 1906.

GOOCH, G. P. *Frederick the Great: the Ruler, the Writer, the Man.* London, 1947.

GREENLY, MAJOR W. H. "The Cavalry of Frederick the Great: Its training, leading and employment in War," *Journal of the Royal United Service Institution,* LIII (1909).

HAMLEY, COLONEL E. B. "Carlyle's Frederick the Great," *Blackwood's Edinburgh Magazine,* XCVIII (1865).

KOSER, REINHOLD. *König Friedrich der Grosse.* Stuttgart, 1903. 2 volumes.

KUGLER, FRANCIS. *Life of Frederick the Great, comprehending a complete History of the Silesian campaigns and the Seven Years' War.* New York, n.d.

LLOYD, E. M. *A Review of the History of Infantry.* London, 1908.

LLOYD, MAJOR GENERAL HENRY. *History of the Late War in Germany.* London, 1766-81. 2 volumes.

MITCHELL, MAJOR GENERAL JOHN. *Biographies of Eminent Soldiers of the last Four Centuries.* Edinburgh, 1865.

NAPOLEON. *Memoirs of the History of France during the Reign of Napoleon, dictated by the Emperor at Saint Helena to the Generals who shared his Captivity and published from the original manuscripts corrected by himself.* London, 1823. 7 volumes. Volume VII contains Napoleon's "Review of the wars of Frederic II."

PALMER, R. R. "Frederick the Great, Guibert, Bülow: From Dynastic to National War," in Edward Mead Earl, ed., *Makers of Modern Strategy: Military Thought from Machiavelli to Hitler.* Princeton, 1943.

PETERSDORFF, HERMAN VON. *Fridericus Rex: Ein Heldenleben.* Berlin, 1925.

QUIMBY, ROBERT S. *The Background of Napoleonic Warfare: The Theory of Military Tactics in Eighteenth Century France.* New York, 1957.

REINERS, LUDWIG. *Frederick the Great: A Biography.* Translated and adapted from the German by Lawrence P. R. Wilson. New York, 1960.

RIEDWEG, FRANZ. *Friedrich der Grosse: Soldat, Staatsmann, Denker.* Berlin, 1942.

RITTER, GERHARD. *Friedrich der Grosse: Ein Historisches Profil.* Heidelberg, 1954.

SIMES, THOMAS. *The Military Guide for Young Officers.* London, 1774. 2 volumes.

SPAULDING, OLIVER LYMAN, HOFFMAN NICKERSON AND JOHN WOMACK WRIGHT. *Warfare: A Study of Military Methods from the Earliest Times.* Washington, 1937.

VALENTIN, VEIT. *Friedrich der Grosse.* Berlin, 1927.

WERTHER, ERNST LUDWIG. *Der Eherne Herz: Friedrich der Grosse im Siebenjährigen Krieg. Briefe, Berichte, Aufzeichnungen.* Munich, 1939.

WILKINSON, SPENSER. "Recent German Military Literature," *United Service Magazine,* V (1891).

# *Index*

# INDEX

*On Guard.* Hussar vedettes sent forward "to reconnoiter the march and provide information of places where the enemy could be lying in ambush." (A. Menzel, *Illustrationen zu die Werke Friedrichs des Grossen*, Berlin, 1886.)

*A walking battery.* Prussian grenadiers firing, reloading and replenishing ammunition from the cartridge boxes of the fallen. "The Prince of Anhalt, who had studied war as a profession . . . invented some iron ramrods and found the way to instruct soldiers to load with incredible speed." (A. Menzel, *Illustrationen zu die Werke Friedrichs des Grossen*, Berlin, 1886.)